The Inter-Galactic
Playground

CRITICAL EXPLORATIONS IN SCIENCE FICTION AND FANTASY
(a series edited by Donald E. Palumbo and C.W. Sullivan III)

The Inter-Galactic Playground

A Critical Study of Children's and Teens' Science Fiction

FARAH MENDLESOHN

CRITICAL EXPLORATIONS IN
SCIENCE FICTION AND FANTASY, 14
Donald E. Palumbo *and* C.W. Sullivan III, *series editors*

McFarland & Company, Inc., Publishers
Jefferson, North Carolina, and London

Portions of this book, in different form, have been published previously. They are:

"With Meccano to the Stars" was published in *Time Everlasting: Representations of Past, Present and Future in Children's Literature*, edited by Pat Pinsent. Lichfield, Pied Piper Publishing, 2007, 215–235.

"Cognitive Development, Science Fiction and Science Fiction for Children, or 'Does Ontogeny Recapitulate Phylogeny?'" *New York Review of Science Fiction* 191, vol. 16, no. 11, July 2004, 1–11.

Is There Any Such Thing as Children's SF: A Position Piece" in *The Lion and the Unicorn, A Critical Journal of Children's Literature*. Vol. 28, no 2, April 2004, 284–313.

LIBRARY OF CONGRESS CATALOGUING-IN-PUBLICATION DATA

Mendlesohn, Farah.
      The inter-galactic playground : a critical study of children's and teens' science fiction / Farah Mendlesohn.
            p.   cm.   (Critical explorations in science fiction and fantasy ; 14)
      Includes bibliographical references and index.

      ISBN 978-0-7864-3503-6
      softcover : 50# alkaline paper ∞

      1. Science fiction — History and criticism.   2. Children's literature — History and criticism.   3. Children — Books and reading.   I. Title.
      PN3433.8.M46   2009
      809.3'876 — dc22   2009014728

British Library cataloguing data are available

Cover art ©2009 Wood River Gallery

Manufactured in the United States of America

McFarland & Company, Inc., Publishers
   Box 611, Jefferson, North Carolina 28640
   www.mcfarlandpub.com

To Gordon Leek (1934–2008),
who once gave me a suitcase full of books,
and changed my world.
Without him, this book would not exist.

Acknowledgments

I must begin by thanking the librarians in the Children's Department of Birmingham Central Library whose choice of book stock led me seamlessly from Amabel Mably Owens to Robert A. Heinlein; and my parents, Ralph Mendlesohn and Carole Underwood who both in their different ways believed in and nurtured an ideal of *competence*.

I also want to thank Jan Bogstad and Mike Levy for suggesting that I write for their special issue of *The Lion and the Unicorn* on children's science fiction, the Eileen Wallace Collection for the grant to use their resources at the University of New Brunswick; Alice Bell for permission to read and cite from her Ph.D. thesis, "Science as Pantomime: Explorations in Contemporary Children's Non-fiction Books" and Noga Applebaum from her book in progress, *Representations of Technology in Science Fiction for Young People: Control Shift* (Routledge, 2008). Jessica Yates, whose interest and constant flow of material kept me informed (and particularly for showing me *Henry's Quest*). Neil Gaiman, Cory Doctorow, Karen Traviss and Ken MacLeod for blogging the survey; people who filled in the survey and members of LiveJournal who willingly answered daft question after daft question. Meredith Snyder who made me feel my work wasn't silly. Paul Bowers Isaacson of the Nuffield Curriculum Centre. Karen Traviss and Jon Courtenay Grimwood for consistent interest and support. Ben Little who introduced me to graphic art criticism. Edward James who won't let me get rid of any books. Philip Reeve for writing *Mortal Engines*. The members of Child_lit, who provided many further reading links and lots of argument. All quotations from LiveJournal and internet mailing lists are printed here with the permission of the author. Also Judy Collins and Feòrag NicBhrìde for assistance in the final stages. And finally a thank you to my head of department, Maggie Butt, who has been an unending source of support and encouragement.

The index to *Out of this World*, edited by Amabel Williams-Ellis & Mably Owen, 1960–1972 was provided by William G. Contento, and can be found at http://www.philsp.com/homeville/ISFAC/k11.htm.

And I want to thank once again Karen Traviss who shredded my ideas of where writers come from and where good science fiction for teens might be found.

This book has required compiling lists of over five hundred books and analyzing over nine hundred survey forms and I have relied heavily on the assistance of friends and colleagues. A full list of the books can be found at: http://young-sf-list.blogspot.com/2008/04/full-list.html.

Finally, thanks to the following for all of their help:

Research Assistant: Zara Baxter who is co-author of Appendix C.

Editorial Assistants: Tanya Brown (particularly work on Appendix C), Jess Nash, Maureen Kincaid Speller and Shana Worthen.

Index: Leigh Kennedy, whose personal knowledge of the field was an invaluable help in indexing both this book, and my previous book, *Rhetorics of Fantasy*, from whose acknowledgment page she was unaccountably left out.

Proof reading: Maureen Kincaid Speller.

Fitness support: Mike Harwood and James Bloom.

Emergency beta reading: Edward James, Tanya Brown, Penny Hill, Kari Maund, Una McCormack, Sam Kelly, Dan'l Danehy-Oakes, Helen Spicer.

The students in Writing for Children, 2007–08.

Table of Contents

The child who is learning to speak a more mature form of language gets a lot of help. Every step of his way, in the home and outside it, he will find adults ... who understand "baby talk" but also already know mature language. These are people with whom the learner can constantly interact as the old language is being replaced by the new one. This is not the case for the changeover from the primitive to the new scientific world picture. Here the child's source of help and interaction is almost always limited to the parsimonious fare of the American school-room.... And the adults around the learner of science, including the parents and many of the teachers, are themselves usually still stranded at the level of the baby-talk scientific world picture.— Gerald Holton, 1984: 7

Introduction

This project came out of a dissatisfaction with the children's and "young adult" science fiction I was reading in the 1980s and 1990s. It built on my own experiences as a child and teen reader, and my vague awareness that from anecdotal evidence the route into science fiction was *not* through the material produced for children and teens, but directly through the adult genre. On the surface this seemed an anomaly: I had read teen romance as a child and gone on to read adult romance (although not for long). I had fond memories of the "detective" or treasure-hunt novels of Geoffrey Trease and Enid Blyton and had gone on to read adult crime novels. My reading of children's historical fiction was one of my routes to three degrees in history, and furthermore, a route common to many historians of my generation and previous ones. Yet discussions at science fiction conventions about early reading always centered on the writers for adults whom we had read as teens. There were two notable exceptions to whom I will return in chapter one, Robert A. Heinlein and Andre Norton, but these of course proved the rule in that both writers had a strong line of books aimed at what was then termed the Juvenile market.

One of the issues that arose at discussions I participated in or listened to at science fiction conventions in 2001 was that we could not remember the names of many of the people we had read as children. Jessica Yates, in her contribution to the *International Encyclopedia of Children's Literature* (1996), was able to list over fifty authors, but our awareness of them was nostalgic; unlike their contemporaries in children's fantasy such as E. Nesbit, C. S. Lewis, Edward Eager, Lloyd Alexander, Susan Cooper, and Alan Garner, these writers had not secured a long-lasting reputation. Even writers such as John Christopher, Monica Hughes and H. M. Hoover, who dominated the field for teen science fiction in the 1970s, did not seem to have the same ongoing readership that allows adult readers to take children's fantasy with them all their lives. Alongside this was the awareness that Hughes and Hoover were specialists: by the 1970s there were very few contemporary science fiction writers for adults of the same stature as Heinlein and Norton also writing for teens or children. Ben Bova and Pamela Sargent continued to write sf for children, but by the mid–1980s Sargent could no longer get contracts for these books. Gwyneth Jones has continued into the present period, but publishes her children's and YA fiction under the name of Ann Halam.

The discussion panels were held in 2001 and we were on the edge of a renaissance in children's science fiction — something which this book reflects— but we did not yet know this, although several of the panelists, themselves editors, were hoping to promote one and had been working on publishing science fiction written particularly for the market by authors writing for the adult market, such as Simon and Schuster's *Web* series (authors such as Ken MacLeod, Stephen Baxter and Graham Joyce contributed but the series flopped) or the more recent launch of a Tor YA imprint which has repackaged a number of sf novels for the YA market. In the event, the renaissance did not begin with the "mainstream" editors, but with small non-genre presses in Britain, Ireland and Canada (for which you will not find any explanation here). Finally, however, these panel discussions revealed that too many of the titles we considered did not feel wholly satisfactory.

Of the titles that were initially suggested to these panels, many when scrutinized turned out to be fantasy (Eleanor Cameron's Mushroom Planet stories, for example), or to focus on issues other than science, or social science, or in some other way to *somehow* not feel quite like science fiction. These panels were not the first to make this point. In 1985, Perry Nodelman may have been the first to stand up and say "there is a problem here." In his article "Out There in Children's Science Fiction: Forward into the Past" in *Science Fiction Studies,* Nodelman argued that children's science fiction deployed a relatively small palette of sf problems and trajectories in which children break from enclosed, decaying societies (usually cities or community settlements) into the reinvigorated wild. Nodelman referred to Norton, Hoover, Suzanne Martel and Anne Schlee, but the same theme and trajectory is evident in the works of twenty-first century writers such as Scott Westerfeld (with his Uglies sequence), David Stahler, Jr., and Jeanne DuPrau.

For Nodelman, the ubiquity of the theme was noticeable, but so too was the degree to which these books were pushing metaphor — a problem in itself as I will discuss in chapter six. These societies were not closed in order to explore what might actually happen in a closed society (for which see Gregory Maguire's *I Feel Like the Morning Star,* 1997), but "they treat the enclosed societies they describe as metaphors for closed minds" (287). And yet, as Nodelman goes on to describe, these novels are themselves frequently closed-minded. As Noga Applebaum observes in her book and as corroborated by the wide range of texts I have read, the books written for the young frequently promote an "anti-technological and even anti-evolutionary bias" (Nodelman, 1985, 288). The "natural" world is given primacy, with little question as to what this means (Westerfeld's *Specials* [2006] is a rare exception and Westerfeld writes for the adult market also). The notion of changelessness is promoted: humans in these books are rarely the kind of humans we might recognize as creative and resistant.

Furthermore, many of the books Nodelman read, and many of the books which I have read, do not posit a future as somewhere more exciting than our own present, but as a degraded and tarnished version of our ideological (if not manifest) ideal. Nodelman concludes by pointing out that "instead of leaving home, going somewhere exotic, and then returning home again, these characters happily leave an exotic but deficient place which *is* their home for an ordinary place which they find exotic and delightful but which is more like *our* home" (293). In this Nodelman concludes, sf for teens and children is very like general fiction for teens and children. What it is *not* like is science fiction for adults. It is worth noting that in 1989, Thomas J. Morrisey published a rebuttal to Nodelman's paper, also in *Science Fiction Studies.* As will frequently prove the case in this book however, Morrisey was forced to "fall back" on an author, Pamela Sargent, who is best known for her work for adults.

When I first offered these structural and ideological arguments, while writing the 2003 essay for *The Lion and the Unicorn,* Michael M. Levy argued that everything I have outlined above was an imposition:

> ... a tendency to privilege what you call "full science fiction" over coming-of-age stories ... for adults the sf story that actively engages with the society or science and its problems is more interesting, but the novel in which a child or young adult simply finds his place in society is a standard form of YA fiction ... the writer who does this kind of book is not so much failing to write a better kind of book as s/he is simply working within standard YA genre conventions. You can criticise books for not doing more, but should you more clearly acknowledge the fact that the writer wasn't trying to do what you'd prefer him/her to be doing? [email, 10/22/02]

Levy's points are sensible. I am, in Lesnik-Oberstein's terms, attempting to discern and define the quality of a book in terms of those values which I believe children should assimilate from a particular genre (39), or, as John Stephens would argue, imposing a top-down reading which draws on a set of codes established by adult readers (30). But then it is a commonplace that fiction written for children is the ultimate "outsider" text, one which is written by and with different intentions and desires than that embraced by the adult reader community. Books for children are not written by children (Hollindale, 1997). Given this, the implied community for a children's sf book might be those who are directing the reading of children towards securing a readership for adult science fiction. If the "hidden curriculum" of children's books is to keep children reading, then it seems not unreasonable for a reader or critic of adult sf to argue that the best science fiction for children has, as its hidden curriculum, the desire to persuade children to move into the adult genre .

The failure to privilege the universe of adult sf does not necessarily make the book a bad book (I have enjoyed many of the same books which have frustrated me), but it does make one suspect that the book is less likely to appeal to those who are already reading in the genre or who are likely to be attracted to adult sf. These books can then be tested against what Raymond Williams argues is an idea of quality through "tradition," a way of judging books by the extent to which they promote the values of the communities in which they are marketed (Wood, 122). If we accept sf as a community — and this book will proceed on that assumption — then it *is* valid to consider these texts in terms of whether they support the beliefs and ideological structures of the genre. This is why John Rowe Townsend was wrong to argue that genre-critics are ignorant when they enter the field of children's literature (1974). So that while Levy may well be correct that what I am engaged in is an exercise in prejudice, his own rebuttal, which argues for a different genre category, confirms rather than denies the thesis. If the writer is trying to "do something else," then it is a reasonable project to say so. This is reinforced by a recognition that the problem is not unique to YA sf. Gary K. Wolfe argues that this problem infects the sf/thriller crossover in which "the very intellectual challenges that traditionally define an effective technological science fiction story seem to mitigate against the largely anti-intellectual (or at least anti-scientist), technologically ambivalent tone of the paranoid thriller." Differing ideologies of power, Wolfe contends, makes it hard for an sf writer to produce effective thrillers, or vice versa (Wolfe, 2002).

All of the above, however, assumes that the fuzzy sense that "this is not science fiction" is based on some common understanding of what science fiction is. Such is rarely the case. The debate about what science fiction is has been raging since the 1920s: frequently you can tell most about a critic's understanding of the field by which progenitor figure they cite: if they choose Mary Shelley they may be focusing on technology, or on enlightenment attitudes; if they move further back, fabulous adventure stories grant the exploratory mode primacy. A critic who moves forward to the 1920s (as under other circumstances I would do) is almost certainly adhering to a communitarian definition of the genre in which the conversation in the American magazines of the period is what generates "science fiction" and all else is "science-fiction*al*." But for this project, which is dealing with a large number of variables and working across categories, some kind of parameters were needed. For once a science fiction critic is going to resort neither to Damon Knight's famous *Science fiction is what I point to when I say "science fiction"* approach, nor rely wholly on Darko Suvin's arguments about cognitive estrangement. Instead, this book will, in chapter one, suggest a structural understanding of the genre in which it is the trajectory of the narrative that tells us we are in a science fiction book. This will not stand alone, however. Just as vital to the question I am proposing: *Is there any such thing as children's science fiction?* and my final response, *Yes, but nowhere near enough*, are issues of the attitudinal position of science fiction. This picks up from Nodelman's expressed concerns, that children's science fiction does not seem to share the worldview of the adult genre, and leads us into another matter entirely which I have come to regard as central to the whole debate, and that is to assert that we cannot conflate the terms "juvenile," used to describe fiction for teens before the 1960s, with "young adult," used to describe fiction for teens after that point.

This book will argue very strongly that while "Juvenile" and YA" may be thought of by many (including publishers today) simply as marketing labels, they are in reality clear descriptions of ideological positions. "Juvenile" science fiction of the 1950s and early 1960s seems to have shared most of the values of the adult form. "YA" science fiction of the late 1980s and the 1990s mostly does not. In the shift that took place in the 1960s, the YA label serves as a clear marker of a huge change in the lives of people in the thirteen- to eighteen-year-old age bracket. The change in terminology at the time was ideological and reflected a changing idea of what teenagers were like, changing expectations of teenagers (particularly as the school leaving age rose) and a changing idea of what fiction for this group should be like. The book market changed dramatically to accommodate this, and fictions which did not address what were conceived of as "Young Adult" concerns were marginalized. Such concerns, which I will discuss in greater detail later, can be delineated loosely as "teen angst" over drugs, dating, pregnancy, and family. Gone was the world of work, so central to many of the Juveniles.

Many of the ideas of this book rest heavily on the belief that there are genuine differences between the two modes of publishing — Juvenile and Young Adult — so a generic term which encompasses both of these groups of books and the readers of these books is useful. Throughout this book I will be using the terms "teenagers" and "teens" to describe readers between thirteen and eighteen years of age, and "books for teens" as a generic term to describe the books marketed at this age group. In various chapters I will be distinguishing between "YA fiction" as a genre, and "Juvenile fiction." "Juveniles" was the term used prior to the 1970s. This is not because I wish to supplant current terminology in which this entire category is described by the ALA as "YA fiction," but because I wish to keep the term "YA fiction" to describe that historically specific marketing category or genre which begins with the works of S.E. Hinton, and which espouses specific (if malleable) values.

Does any of this matter? The fundamental contention of this book is that children who are likely to want to read science fiction as adults should have access at all ages to science fiction that matches values with the genre as it is produced for adults. It is not enough to tell me that a certain book is popular with children and therefore *must* be good. If that book does not resemble the adult market, then the children it is popular with may well be the ones who are repelled by adult science fiction when they encounter it with its whole new set of values and structural expectations. Worse, if that book does not resemble the provision of the adult market, then the children who might like science fiction may very well avoid it hereafter, because their first experience looked like science fiction, was packaged like science fiction, but adhered to a set of values quite other from science fiction.

Four years ago I set out to write a 75,000-word book on some of the problems I perceived with the science fiction marketed to children and teens. During that period, several things happened: first, I found far more authors than I and those I had consulted had anticipated. This book has drawn on the resources of the collections of the University of New Brunswick and of Toronto Public Library, every new and second-hand bookshop I could find, and many gifts from friends. It includes every book I have looked at, which number far more than are cited in the text. Of the 700 I have catalogued, I read approximately 450. There are others for which I currently have only dust-jacket notes. These notes can be found at *The Inter-Galactic Playground* (http://farah-sf. blogspot.com), a blog which accompanied this research. It is a random selection which sometimes glosses over other people's old favorites, and which by no means exhausts the titles of the most prolific authors such as John Christopher and Monica Hughes.

It is ironic that the one collection of books I never really had time to consult in depth is that sitting in the British Library, twenty minutes from my home. It really didn't help that at about the same time I started working on the book, writers started to turn in the kinds of books I wanted to see. In the end also, I think I have written about a relatively narrow cluster of books, no more than a fifth perhaps of the whole, because so many of the texts in my collection were utterly unmemorable even with the help of a database.

Other problems appeared alongside the sense that I was running the Red Queen's race. The more I read about cognitive development the more I became baffled by the educational material I was reading; there seemed to be a mismatch. The more I read in the newspapers about the behavior and treatment of children and teens the more I, a childless woman who teaches students mostly in their twenties, became uncomfortable with the expectations being imposed on them, alongside a range of restrictions which seemed to be having a depressing effect on the "ambition" that was represented in fiction. As the much older sister of a brother in his early twenties and a sister who has just turned nineteen, I also became aware of the huge gulf not of technological change precisely, but of the visibility of the bones of the world I had inhabited versus the plastic, locked "don't tamper with this seal" world in which they had grown up. All of this influenced the book I have finally written.

This book is, to quote the current definition of a UK Ph.D., an original work which can reasonably be expected to be completed in the time given: four years in the case of a Ph.D. and, as it turns out, more or less four years in the case of this book. In the end I had to abandon some of the statistical research into the background of authors (what proportion in each period wrote for adults) both because of time constraints and because my collection is so arbitrary, bought when and wherever I saw a book. I never did have the time to interview editors, although it is obvious to me, looking at the clusters of books at certain publishing houses at certain times, that some children's book editors were clearly hospitable to science fiction while others were not. I did not have the time to talk to the authors I wanted to interview, and although those who are personal friends were very generous with their time, I have no formal record of these talks. I did not have the time to contact the librarians and bibliographers whose work I've discussed in chapter two. I wish very much I could have gone ahead with my original plans and conducted interviews with children, but again time and also ethical constraints intervened. Perhaps most absurd, the original issue, the literary merits of many of these books, disappeared from the radar almost completely. The book is, however, as complete now as my skills and four years of research can make it. I hope that the issues I raise will prove interesting enough for others to explore further.

The first chapter of this book tackles what we mean when we say "science fiction" and offers the parameters for this book, concluding with a discussion of what was considered "best practice" in the heyday of the Juveniles.

Chapter two is essentially contextual, and addresses what I have come to think of as some of the elephants in the living room of children's literature criticism which make it very difficult to approach science fiction for children, and considers how many of them are actually red herrings grounded in very specific and unproven arguments about the nature of childhood. This chapter will challenge the argument common among sf fans and critics that one learns to read science fiction as one approaches the age of abstract thought.

Chapter three begins to move towards our target by looking at the cultural context of science in a child's world, and the ways in which science and the doing of science are depicted in film, in the classroom, in popular nonfiction and eventually in science fiction.

From here, chapter four leads the reader through what seems to be a rough periodization of sf for children and teenagers in which quite clear ideological understandings of who and what children and teens are, and what their attitude to the world should be, undergo significant changes.

Chapter five deals with a concern common to children's fiction criticism, the socialization of the child, but seeks not to ask whether it is happening, but rather in what direction sf writers for children and teens seek to socialize children, on the basis of the kinds of societies they have built and the kinds of ambitions they propose.

Chapter six looks at the tension between theme and plot in sf for children and teens, and the ways in which adult anxieties have created a peculiarly technophobic future for children.

Finally, the book proper concludes with my own sense of Best Practice Now.

The book has four appendices. Appendix A lists all the stories in the Amabel Williams-Ellis collections, *Out of This World*, which are used extensively in chapter one. Appendices B and C consist of the questions that went out in the reader survey which accompanied this book, and the analysis of that survey by Zara Baxter. I draw on this survey at various points in the text.

Throughout, this book draws on fiction written for all age groups, from one year old to the point at which YA peters out. However, because it was not possible to give the small number of picture books fair consideration in the book as a whole, there is an additional discussion of these texts included as Appendix D: "The Golden Age of Science Fiction is *Three*." Although included as an appendix, in some ways this might be the most important section of the book, because it challenges the idea that we grow into science fiction, and asserts rather that we are born into a science-fictional world and only slowly are allowed or encouraged to grow out of it. The reading of science fiction is not learned, it is unlearned.

CHAPTER ONE

What Do We Mean When We Say "Science Fiction"?

Because the underlying argument of this book is that there is a problem with what is offered as science fiction to children and teens—that it does not resemble the adult form — and that this problem is not usually found in science fiction's sister genre fantasy, a working definition of science fiction is a necessity. It cannot simply be glossed over, nor is it acceptable to opt for "it is science fiction if I say it is," both because I am, after all, the person who is saying "this is not really science fiction" and because by the very nature of this book it would be cheating. I would have offered nothing for you, the reader, to test my arguments against. This first chapter then, attempts to set out what I believe science fiction to *be* and the way in which the science fiction offered to teens in the 1950s and 1960s worked with this definition.

The Tropes and Icons of Science Fiction

To an extent, science fiction is defined by its tropes. Rocket ships and super-weapons are science fiction. Dragons and curses are not — unless, of course, your dragon is constructed through a genetic engineering program and your curse is a carefully written computer virus. This is probably enough to clarify that while the use of certain icons and tropes are the first selection criteria used in this book, they are not the final arbiters. The mode of production of certain icons can either rule in a text or rule it out: Eleanor Cameron's Mushroom Planet stories have not been included here because their facilitating devices are always presented as somehow magical; many books were excluded because spiritual or fantastical solutions pre-empted the technological. This set of criteria was enforced far more rigidly than I would prefer in other contexts, but I was anxious to reduce at least one variable. All the books actually discussed here are firmly in the center of this criteria for science fiction: excluded, for example, is a children's picture book called *Rosie's Zoo* (2001), not because

9

the rocket Rosie rides on is imaginary, but because she rides *on* it. In other tales of imagination, if the conceptualization of the icon is within the mechanical, it has been included. Apart from the above, some of the stories are set in the future, some in the past, some in the present. The representation of science fiction for children as "futuristic fiction" which I found in some of the bibliographies is misleading. Beyond these very superficial brushstrokes however, I prefer to work with a more structuralist and attitudinal approach about what science fiction is, and the following sections outline what it is I expect of a science fiction text.

The Structure of Science Fiction

Science fiction is less a genre than it is a mode. It is a *way* of writing about things, events and people, rather than a description of which things, events and people should be written about. This *way* of science fiction is essentially ideological, as has been argued by critics such as John Clute (1997), Darko Suvin (1979) and Gary K. Wolfe (2002), the contributors to *The Cambridge Companion to Science Fiction* (2003) and Paul Kincaid (2008). I am able only to skate the surface of some of the arguments here, but the two most important approaches to sf for my purposes are the "grammar" of science fiction, and the ideological intentions of science fiction.

The grammar of sf is essentially a structuralist's argument. In *The Encyclopaedia of Fantasy* John Clute argues for the concept of the "full fantasy," defined as a process of identifying WRONGNESS, THINNING, RECOGNITION of the moment of turn (what we might call an epiphany), and the process of HEALING.[2] If we borrow the term and the ideas behind it, we can reach for the concept of the "full sf story." The full sf novel might be summarized, to use Clute's style, as DISSONANCE, RUPTURE, RESOLUTION, CONSEQUENCE. Applying this formulation to science fiction written specifically for children and teens is informative.

What I have termed DISSONANCE is constructed by the novum and the element of cognitive estrangement. The novum is the idea or object that creates the rupture within the world as we understand it. This may be a robot, a new vaccine or disease, or a change in the social structure. The role of the novum is to be "tackled," either defeated or encompassed within the world order. One apparent marker of sf for small children is that it is oriented towards the novum, or its most rudimentary form, the icon. In children's sf, the novum's role may be limited to its novelty value rather than what its function is. In Babette Cole's *The Trouble with Dad* (1985), Dad's robots are the cause of much hilarity and chaos, but the changes they cause are resolved when a rich man buys them for his desert. Their qualities as robots are only marginal to the narrative; they could just as easily be out-of-control pets. Ricky Ricotta's robot in *Ricky Ricotta's*

Mighty Robot vs. The Mecha Monkeys from Mars (Pilkey, 2002), could be any large, clumsy best friend. In older stories, such as the *Tom Swift* books (Appleton II), the robot or other invention is a tool, but it is a tool like a car is a tool: it does a job, and it is at best an extension of human reach. In neither case is the robot-ness of the robot significant. Although there is DISSONANCE, that dissonance does not actually lead to RUPTURE of the expectations of the world or its narrative.

What I have here termed RUPTURE, in order to mimic Clute's grammar, is more commonly known as cognitive estrangement. Cognitive estrangement is intrinsic to science fiction, but it is generated not simply by the presence of the dissonant, but by the cohesion of the dissonant world, and the relationship of the protagonist or point-of-view character to that dissonance. Early science fiction frequently posited only one point of dissonance — the appearance of a miraculous invention or an invader, or one thing changed in the world which is recognizably ours. Children's sf (less so that for teens) repeats this early pattern. Sylvia Waugh's *Space Race* (2000), Lesley Howarth's *Maphead* (1994) and Nicholas Fisk's *Trillions* (1971) take place within our world, but aliens arrive. The cognitive dissonance is minimized because in most of these books (*Maphead* is the exception) we begin from a point of more or less normality and the dissonance is introduced to us: the sf is reduced to its base level of the meeting of the unknown. The rupture is marginal.

Where a world is made fully dissonant, that is, it is not our world and we must begin to know it, science fiction has developed ways to exaggerate rather than play down the cognitive dissonance. Specifically, sf has developed what Clute has termed the competent character: the point-of-view character who understands his or her own world and feels no need to explain its strangenesses to us. Children's and teen sf has often been weak in this. John Christopher in *The Lotus Caves* (1969) evades the issue by taking his protagonists out of the space habitat with which they, but not we, are familiar, and sending them on a journey into an unknown world. Sylvia Engdahl in *Heritage of the Stars* (UK, 1972) does something very similar as her hero leaves his village to enter the wider world. Neil Arksey in *Playing on the Edge* (2000) and Rodman Philbrick in *The Last Book in the Universe* (2000) both take their heroes from protected childhood into political adulthood and into a world that is not quite what they think. Each chooses to minimize cognitive estrangement by sending the protagonist away from what s/he knows and creating a level playing field between author and character. There is plenty of science fiction for adults that does the same, but it is usually mitigated by much fuller world building which allows the characters to take the dissonance of their point of origin with them.

There are books for children and teens which achieve full estrangement: Nicholas Fisk's *A Rag, a Bone, a Hank of Hair* (1980), in which a child of a future city is asked to take "revived" children of the past around, is one of the best.

No explanation is ever provided for much of what we see, and Brin, rather than acting as guide, takes us through his own familiarity with the city. Diana Wynne Jones's *A Tale of Time City* (1987), which I have not used elsewhere in this book because I could not decide whether it is sf or fantasy, uses the trick of seeing her city through the eyes of native children who are very bad guides, because their own interests are very different. Philip Reeve's *Mortal Engines* (2001), set in a city on wheels, sometimes manages this full estrangement, but Reeve often opts for a guided tour through a section of his city, ignoring the actual knowledge of his characters.

In the end, to achieve this full rupture or cognitive dissonance, the author must be willing to demand that the reader identify with a complete other reality in which nothing is questioned or explained. David Lewis argues that "absorption into the fiction world would be impossible without the reader's knowledge of the rule and code and convention that go into the construction of different kinds of texts" (135). Yet despite the ubiquity of this in fairy tale, and, as I shall point out more than once, the fact that children spend their lives learning strange environments, many modern sf children's authors seem to balk, accepting Lewis's superficial statement, while apparently rejecting its implicit insight that *all* texts are constructed and must be decoded by the reader. It is hard to be sure why, but one possibility is that the assumption that books for children should be educational is confused with the concept that books for children should be challenging. Hugo Gernsback, the founder of the first sf magazine, *Amazing Stories* (1926), himself conflated these two: his understanding of science fiction was that it should teach children real scientific knowledge, and we can see this reflected in the contemporary didacticism of the *Andrew Lost* (Greenburg, 2002) books and William Sleator's *Strange Attractors* (1990). This understanding of sf cannot risk that anything be left uncomprehended. What this leads to is a refusal of sf (within these texts) as a literature of extrapolation and reason, an element of sf which I will discuss further when we consider sf's ideological structures.

After DISSOLUTION and RUPTURE we have RESOLUTION. This is perhaps the least contentious element of the "grammar" I have outlined. All fiction requires some form of resolution, but, in a point to which I will return, it should be borne in mind that the resolutions in science fiction may well not be personal, but leave an individual stranded in a resolved future that does not suit them. But more important, in the "full sf story," the resolution is not the end of the story, it is the beginning, for sf resolutions are about *change* and *consequence*. Not infrequently, the resolution of a problem is merely the beginning of an sf story. Frederik Pohl's "The Midas Plague" (1954) begins in a world which has solved all its energy problems. But far from being a utopia, this is a world in which the poor are forced to consume, and the rich flaunt their wealth through ostentatious austerity. The "story" is merely beginning.

Without CONSEQUENCE any sf tale is incomplete. It is crucial to the sf universe that consequences be more than individual wish fulfilment: this is not fairy tale in which the invention/magic trick can raise the pauper to prince without some kind of change in the social structure. In very old sf it is the absence of *consequence* that can be most frustrating for the modern reader: an invention appears, causes chaos, and is blown up at the end. The world returns to the status quo. John Clute has argued that this is about the profound fear of the future, but as a historian I tend to think it is about an inability to speculate about the future and the chaotic effect of new modes of production or new scientific theories. "History" only really emerges around the 1850s, and you need to have a sense of historical change before you can start thinking about change in the future. The development of sf has gone hand in glove with the emergence of new historiographical theories.

Consequence in science fiction is the rippling out of effect, the quantum butterfly that flaps its wings and triggers economic panic on the far side of the world. Robert A. Heinlein was the first formally to identify this, and its significance for science fiction, and it was also Heinlein, one of the most important author-critics in the field, who defined adulthood as the age at which one was able to do higher math. The two are not unrelated: children's grasp of consequence evolves relatively slowly not helped by adults' often inconsistent application of the idea (Byrnes, 173). We can see this cognitive marker reflected in a sub-genre of the YA publication market, the game books of the 1980s, in which children chose the routes they would take through the books. Children become interested in this kind of gaming around the age of ten and are absorbed into it around the early teens, a trajectory which the survey indicates matches the pattern of entry into science fiction reading (see Appendix C). Identification of novum and cognitive dissonance usually leads to the idea of causality and consequence; that "what if?" needs to be followed by the concept of "if, then."

Yet in many of the novels aimed at children and young adults produced between 1970 and 2000 which I will discuss in this book, maturity (the growth into adulthood) substitutes for the political and social consequences of the rupture. In Fisk's *Trillions*, Monica Hughes's *The Keeper of the Isis Light* (1980), and Dan Guttman's *Virtually Perfect* (1999) there are no consequences. Even Jan Mark's *The Ennead*, published in 1978, one of the most political texts of the period, ends with Isaac, the protagonist, securing his place in the family at the expense of rejecting the political consequences of the social structure he has accepted. The rupture is ended, its manifestations destroyed, and the world restored to the status quo: the structure is closer to horror than it is to science fiction (Leffler, 97–136). It is in the absence of an opening out — and the frequent substitution of family settlement for this trajectory — that we can start to see the ideological differences between the YA and Juvenile books and it is this that I want to address next.

The Ideology of Science Fiction and the Juvenile/YA Turn

Robert Heinlein's "Juveniles" are almost all open-ended, and the resolution of the immediate problem opens out challenges for the future. The hero of *Tunnel in the Sky* (1955) becomes a pioneer; that of *Between Planets* (1951) is left engaged in an interplanetary war but with his future significance reduced. In *Space Cadet* (1948) one achievement simply points the way to new challenges. Similarly, Troy, in Andre Norton's *Catseye* (1961) is denied the possibility of return — he is a refugee — and all his problems are externalized in a changing world in which there cannot be any end point, and the stasis of the prevailing social structure is not consolatory, but life threatening.

Underlying this entire book is an argument that Juvenile and YA science fiction are not quite the same things, that the term cannot be used interchangeably. In chapter four I will address this in much greater detail, focusing on the values that emerge to shape the YA label, but here I want to focus on what it was that *Juvenile* science fiction did, the sensibility and values it espoused, and alongside it, what we know from this period about what was considered "suitable reading" for the teen age group. I want to introduce you to the highly successful practices of Juvenile science fiction, that created a body of readers who became readers of the adult form. For those reading from the perspective of a knowledge of science fiction, this will be familiar material. For those coming from children's literature, one of the things that may stand out is the degree to which some of these fictions cut across ideas that one should not preach to children, that fiction for children should not be didactic. It is an issue that will be dealt with in greater detail in chapters two and three, but it is worth being aware of as we go into the next section of the discussion. Science fiction for *adults* has carried with it a pedagogic load at least since Hugo Gernsback set out his mission statement for the field in the 1920s. This position can be traced back further, to the monster listening outside a house and learning to be human, in the classic sf novel, *Frankenstein*. This is a fiction in which what one learns from each text, as many of the respondents to the survey indicated, is central to the genre.

Juvenile sf, like its adult progenitor, points outward, with a reverse mirror image that says, "if something happens in the macro-world, how will it affect my own life?" As we will see in chapter four, the trajectory is for the young person to join that macro-world, to become involved in the wider consequence of *what happens if...*? This is true even in the series juveniles such as the *Tom Swift* books (see Osten, 2004). These books accept the idea that change is permanent and chaotic; the universe cannot be returned to its starting place and our role is to ride the wave. Successful sf may console, but it is rarely consolatory. Furthermore, successful sf frequently demands of the reader dissatisfaction with the world as it is. As Nodelman pointed out in 1985, YA science fiction frequently asks the reader to be dissatisfied with the promised future and regard the present as the better option. Juvenile science fiction was certain that the future, while not necessarily better, was definitely more interesting.

One way to understand this is as competing models of childhood, something I will be discussing more than once in this book. J. Piaget accused the adolescent of "egocentricity ... as though the world would submit itself to idealistic schemes rather than to systems of reality" (cited in Wood, 191). David Wood tries to ameliorate this: "The Task of the adolescent is to recognize that a view of the world that might be true 'ideally' may turn out, on further reflection, observation and experiment, to be unrealistic and unworkable. "To give up idealism" (Wood, 191). But sf writers and readers would, I think, tend to recognize themselves in Piaget's and Wood's descriptions and *take pleasure in them.*

Science fiction has a sensibility and an ideology. It is curious, it wants to know how the world works, and it assumes that *out there* is where the interest lies (although *out there* may be the inner workings of the brain, or the blood corpuscles). What science fiction is rarely interested in is the "you-me" dynamic of relationships, unless it is trying to figure out how, for example, a new and interesting sexual disease might affect them. It is not that human relationships and angsts don't matter, but as a general rule I would suggest this summary: if Hollywood would advertise a film with the tag-line, *In the chaos of war, they fell in love!* science fiction would pronounce, *In the chaos of love, they fought a war!* A good example of this is Lois McMaster Bujold's classic novel, *Shards of Honor* (1986), which begins by posing against the Hollywood tag-line, but ends firmly in the science fiction camp. Juvenile science fiction held quite firmly to this construction and used it to shape an ideology which, like its YA descendant, had quite clear ideas about where a young person could be understood to be going and what skills they needed to get there. Repeatedly, there was an emphasis on practical skills, and on curiosity, and always a sense that there was more out there to know about.

The Juveniles and Texts Marketed to Juveniles

Although a wide range of authors were listed by the individuals who participated in the reader survey (see Appendix C) the two names most frequently cited were Robert A. Heinlein and Andre Norton. For those coming to this book from children's literature my next sentence may be contentious; for those coming to this book from the science fiction field it will arouse nothing more than an awareness that I am stating the obvious. Heinlein and Norton between them set the gold standard for what science fiction for teens could be. For most readers of science fiction between the ages of 40 and 70 years old Heinlein served as the gateway into science fiction. Norton, writing a decade later, had a later impact, but when she died in 2006 it was uncontentious for the Science Fiction Writers of America (an organization of professional authors) to establish a prize in children's sf and fantasy in her name.

Heinlein and Norton did not come to Juvenile sf from the same direction. Heinlein was already an established writer of short fiction for the magazines, with several novels published, when Scribner commissioned a series of Juveniles. Andre Norton began writing boys' adventure stories (for which she adopted the pseudonym) and then drifted into science fiction for the Juvenile market. Both however were enormously prolific which presents a problem for the limited space in this chapter. There is no easy way to select texts in this situation so I will be honest and say that these are simply four of my favorites from each author. The texts to which I will be referring are, from Heinlein, *Space Cadet* (1954), *Starman Jones* (1954), *Citizen of the Galaxy* (1957) and *Have Space Suit — Will Travel* (1958); and from Norton, *Star Man's Son* (1952), *The Stars Are Ours* (1954), *Cat's Eye* (1961), and *Plague Ship* (1956).

The issues I want to discuss are the language, the tone/rhetoric, the educational values, the social values, the ambitions of the protagonists and the relationship to "the parent" or other authority figures. Each of these aspects, and the treatment of them which Heinlein and Norton deliver, argues for a particular relationship between the child and the world and it is this relationship that I still believe forms "best practice," and which later I will be arguing is absent from much material produced in the later part of the twentieth century and marketed under the label YA.

The plots of the books vary considerably: *Starman Jones* tells of a lost space ship and the difficulties of astronavigation in unexplored space; *Space Cadet* is the most overtly "career" book (a term I will explain later) with its dual tale of learning how to be a man, and also how to negotiate with aliens; in *Citizen of the Galaxy* the plot hinges on industrial espionage and a move to undermine the inter-galactic slave trade. In *Have Space Suit — Will Travel*, a child and a teen save the world in a law court. Norton's *Star Man's Son* is a tale of lost civilizations and post-nuclear worlds (a very common theme in sf of the early 1950s), both a digging for the past and a reconstruction of the future; *The Stars Are Ours* follows a small group of resisters as they build a rocket to leave a United States in the grip of religious mania up to the point where there is an implication that they have met aliens; *Cat's Eye* tells of a refugee who rescues psionic animals and makes a new life in the wilderness; *Plague Ship* is the career book in the selection, but its plot is about trading competition and dealing with aliens.

To summarize, these eight novels manage to discuss (in rough order) navigation, diplomacy, economics, law, history and archaeology, constitution-making and governance, migration and migration conflicts, religion, scientific thinking, planetary exploration, the politics of colonization, the politics of a refugee crisis, and arguments about the ethics of big business. As we move through this book, it will be hard to avoid the realization that these eight books contain a wider span of plots and themes than the majority of the rest of my collection (around seven hundred books) put together, and this despite the fact that not one of them contains any of the modern staples: cloning/genetic engineering, time-travel or invasion. Furthermore, all of these topics are *adult* topics: there is no sense that they have been selected for their presumed interest to the teen, although this may be a shift in the adult sense of what teens are interested in.

All of the plots I have just described are outwardly directed. With the exception of *Have Space Suit— Will Travel*, getting on with the family is never an element of the story: the people one wants to get on with are always the Other. More important, they are about *aspects* of the world, rather than the world as a whole. This may make more sense after later chapters, but in much of the fiction which I will be discussing teens have far too much influence: they uncover the secret of the world, they unseat the alien power, they overturn the government, they change all of society's attitudes. In Heinlein's and Norton's worlds, teens change their own lives, and they sometimes change the lives of those immediately around them, but part of the lesson they learn is that they are a cog in the universe. This is not to imply that Heinlein and Norton diminish teens; it is that their understanding is that we are all cogs, and as such, are simultaneously vitally important, and a very small part of the whole. The plots they generate are plots of socialization, but the target is to encourage both ambition and personal context (I am deliberately avoiding the term teamwork; sometimes that's a factor, sometimes not).

These books, however different, are all concerned with one person's development: they are all in one way or another, *bildungsroman*, but they are *bildungsroman* whose definition of "the man" lies outward with society, rather than at home with family.[2] They pose the question: *given these circumstances, how will the boy grow up?*[3] So that in *Starman Jones* a belligerent boy whose mother's selfishness has driven him — in opposition — to hold the same values learns to work with a ship and crew, to become part of a team and to see himself as responsible for his own choices. In *Citizen of the Galaxy*, Heinlein demonstrates how a boy brought up as a slave can still carry the pain of that with him many years after he has achieved freedom so that every decision taken is one which seeks to deflect rejection and injury. In Norton's *The Stars Are Ours* Dard Nordis, living with his sister and brother in poverty to escape the eyes of those who would kill scientists, is so focused on survival that he no longer sees himself as worth anything, which nicely complements Fors in *Star Man's Son*, a young man protected by his father's position who must now negotiate his own role of outsider to change the society he had hoped to join as its leader. Fors, unlike Dard, has a strong sense of self so that the trajectory to adulthood is a remaking. Perhaps the most interesting of these books (in these specific terms) is Norton's *Catseye*. Troy is a refugee, just old enough to remember what his life was like on Norden's ranges, when he was the son of a Herder. Stuck in the Dipple, a refugee ghetto, on a planet that does not give citizenship to refugees, Troy is in a constant state of tension between his own pride and the need to humble himself for what little work is available. He makes friends with telepathic animals which have been used as spies, and is also offered a way out: to betray his friends to the Rangers in return either for a place on his own planet, or to join the Rangers who patrol the wilderness. Troy, in an unusual subversion, opts to remain an outlaw.

Each and every one of these books is, in some way, structured as a career book, a category which no longer exists but which was very popular in the 1950s, when many teens could expect to be in full-time work by the age of seventeen. In each, the young protagonist is in search both of a mentor and, by way of the mentor, a career. Andre Norton's *Plague Ship* and Robert Heinlein's *Space Cadet* are the two which wear this most visibly. Norton's Dane Thornton is a Cargo-master apprentice on a free trade merchant space ship. He fails to gain a place with one of the corporations, and this and the previous book in the series, *Solar Queen*, are in part about coming to terms with this failure. In *Plague Ship*, Dane is learning his role within the company and learning adulthood from the men around him. Heinlein's *Space Cadet* is an even clearer example. Matt progresses through his training, looking up first to older cadets who shape even the ways he addresses people and the questions he asks (eat your pie with a fork and don't ask someone where they come from), and then to the men with whom he serves. The primary lesson he learns in this book (there is no sequel but the sequel is imaginable within the hints given at the end) is that respect for duly constituted authority is part of what adulthood is about. When his ship crashes on Venus, it is respect for the authority structure which allows Matt and his friends to negotiate with the Venusians and to get his injured captain to safety. At the end this is underlined when Matt is given not a commission, but his next training place. All education is *continuous*, and without end. Matt goes on to Hayworth Hall for Higher Level cadets. Max in *Starman Jones*, who has served as a ship's captain in an emergency, is bumped down to apprentice, but is delighted to be given the chance to learn; in *Citizen of the Galaxy* the scene closes on Thorby's perusal of documents as he attempts to come to terms with the trading empire he has inherited. Similarly, Fors in Norton's *Starman's Son* sets out in search of complete knowledge and at the end is provided with an entire new world-archive. In a more mundane fashion, Dane in *Plague Ship* is shown hitting the books at every opportunity, while Dard Nordis eventually wins his place on the space ship by demonstrating his willingness to learn. This pro-continuing education strategy is at its most explicit in *Have Space Suit — Will Travel*. When Kip responds to a signal he overhears in his second-hand space suit he is launched into an adventure that will take him through the universe ultimately to the defense of humans in a court of law. But Kip's tale begins with a conversation with his father about his school education and its relative merits and ends with an overhaul of his curriculum as he begins to see the value of his father's idea that education should be information-dense. As Fred Erisman has argued, Heinlein understands the path to adulthood as proceeding through the acquisition of cultural literacy in its widest sense (1991: 47).

The first and second aspects of the trajectory however, are essentially about direction and about leaving behind: adulthood is *out there*. There is some hint of romance in *Citizen of the Galaxy* and in *Starman Jones* but in the first it is couched in terms of finding someone who will help one in the work *out there* (the idea is reiterated in *Star Beast*, 1954) and in *Starman Jones* it comes to nothing because Max is, in the end, too young and too committed to his career. Love happens, but it is never of interest to the story or to the protagonist: it is never the outcome. Some of this is about the values of teen fiction in the 1950s, but it is also about the values of science fiction, which rarely valorizes romance-as-center-of-the-story (although there are some notable exceptions). While we can argue that this serves to infantilize the heroes, I would suggest that it is also extends the appeal of these books beyond the intended age range in two ways, first by emulating the values of the adult genre, and second by recognizing that teen romance is more embarrassing to an aging reader than is teen adventure.

If Heinlein and Norton offer a particular relationship between the child and the world, it is one that is both continuous—children move seamlessly into the adult world — and argued, in the sense that *what* that adult world should be is frequently an issue. It is ironic therefore that their fiction should be labelled "Juvenile" since its success is argued through its contiguity with the adult form.

Heinlein and Norton wrote very specifically for the Juvenile market. I have been valorizing their works for the degree to which they operated as gateway texts, sharing the values of the adult market. For this argument to be sustainable, however, I need some evidence that these values did indeed appeal to contemporary teens. Some evidence can be culled from the letters pages of the science fiction magazines of the period, which suggest an entry age between thirteen and fifteen years old for both boys and girls (this is almost certainly indicative not of when individuals started reading — the survey suggests nine for boys and ten or eleven for girls — but the age at which teens had the money to purchase their own copies). However, this evidence is diffuse — we cannot see easily what stories the teens liked, and there is no sense of them as a discrete market.

The twelve-year production of an anthology series of adult science fiction stories marketed to teens is something else. From 1960 to 1973 Amabel Williams-Ellis and Mably Owen (replaced by Michael Pearson for the final volume) produced ten volumes of an anthology called *Out of This World: An Anthology of Science Fiction*. While again the existence of a teen market is shadowy, the success of this series can be read as an understanding on the part of the publisher (Blackie, a Scottish publisher specializing in teen fiction) that teens could perfectly well cope with the values of the adult genre. Similarly, the widespread presence of this anthology series in libraries suggests that they were both deemed suitable by librarians and were actually borrowed.[4] The introduction to the series by Bertrand Russell presumably aided their respectability although homegrown UK sf has always had a higher respectability quotient than have the contents of the U.S. pulps, and the inclusion of stories by Italo Calvino, Howard Fast and Graham Greene may have further assured librarians of the eminent suitability of the collections. For the teen reader, what they offered was a glimpse at the writing of some of the best-known writers in the field: Aldiss, Asimov, Heinlein, Wyndham, Leinster, Clarke, Clement and others are all included in these volumes. Williams-Ellis and Owens were very clearly focused on constructing a gateway into the field. For a full listing of the stories turn to Appendix A.[5]

What strikes the reader is how many of the stories are problem-solving stories. Whether concerned with evolution, with the physics of alternate worlds, or with politics, well over half the stories are structured in such a way that the tag is a solution to be discovered, or a link which clarifies a situation is to be unravelled (this last is most common with alien encounter tales), picking up on the idea of continuous education that was so near the surface in the Heinlein and Norton Juveniles. These stories are astonishingly information-dense. In chapter three, this will be a crucial issue in my argument about the configuration of modern sf for children and teens. In each of these stories the emphasis is on working things out and applying fairly straightforward solutions: they are tales not of invention, but of ingenuity. There are all sorts of political issues here, worked into a simple enough story of psi powers: collaboration versus individuality, identity politics, the importance of community and friendship, the nature of the cold war. What all the stories have in common in fact is complexity and challenge; they can be read on the level, but none of them make their readings obvious. What is also noticeable is the absence of a trope which runs through Juvenile and YA sf in which "getting to know the alien will resolve our problems" is the dominant (and frequently allegorical) narrative. Of the eighty-one stories, only Murray Leinster's "The Aliens"—in which humans and aliens turn out to be interested in different planets—embraces this approach with any enthusiasm.

The *Out of This World* anthologies contain a far wider range of sf staples—time travel, invention, invasion, subversion, chemical and physical experiments, ideas about evolution, ethical dilemmas etc.—than does the collection of Juvenile and YA sf I have assembled for this book. What they don't contain is any sex, and there is little emphasis on interpersonal relations unless, as in Robert Presslie's "Another Word for Man" (2), the relationship has a philosophical or ethical concern at its root (an alien convinces a priest of its humanity when it gives up its life to save his). The key values encapsulated in these stories are that humans can fix anything, but that if they don't, there is little chance of rescue. There are few incidents of *deus ex machina*. Curiosity is the most valued of qualities. The stories draw on basic engineering, a knowledge of psychology, economics, math, chemistry, biology and physics and a very great deal of ethics and philosophical argument. They demand of the reader an open mind and a willingness to engage in information density. A full discussion of these stories is impossible within the space of this book, but I have posted a detailed commentary at http://www.farahsf.com/outofthis.htm. The remainder of this book will consider the presence and absence of these qualities in sf written for children and teens, in the increasingly discrete market, from the 1950s onwards.

CHAPTER TWO

Red Herrings and Living-Room Elephants: How We Understand Children and Children's Reading

Beginning this book was one of the most difficult things I have ever done. *Starting* this book was easy: it began with an idea, an idea that there simply wasn't very much science fiction for children and teens, and that this had a great deal to do with what children were capable of understanding. My original contention fell in with the standard truism that science fiction had to be *learned*, and that this process precluded the young from the field. But as the research proceeded this original notion came under pressure from many directions. To begin with, the results of the survey suggested that awareness of science fiction begins around the age of eight or nine years, considerably younger than is commonly held to be the case; and the more I read of research on children's cognitive development the more confused I became about what exactly is so difficult about science fiction for children. As this confusion deepened, so too did my confusion over science pedagogy which, the more I considered it, far from being shaped by current ideas of "the child" and "the child's capacities," seemed to be ignoring not all the research, but inconvenient sections. All too frequently it seemed to be imposing adult fears on to children (particularly the fear of "hard facts" which will be taken up in greater detail in the next chapter). At the same time, other ideas that came to the fore in the early research grew stronger — that what children's science fiction can do is conditioned by two key factors: the values of those who are writing it, and what their expectations of a child's relationship to the world is. Overwhelmingly, what became most obvious to me is that much of the critical understanding of children's fiction valorizes qualities that run at variance with the qualities that are valorized by science fiction readers. This coalesced into a set of challenges to what I have come to regard as the truisms of the criticism of children's fiction. At one point I considered organizing this book as short chapters, each introduced with one of these truisms:

1. Children are not a market.
2. Boys don't read.
3. Didactic fiction is poor fiction.
4. Children don't want to be lectured/preached to.
5. Children cannot handle narrative complexity.
6. Children want books about people like them.
7. Teen fiction should be about personal and interpersonal growth.
8. Fiction should be about character.
9. Children want relevance.

Now, I know that very few sane, sensible people would accept all of the above without question, but they have become the paradigm in which the study of children's literature as a multidisciplinary field, operates. In case you think I'm exaggerating (because I have to assume that some of you who are reading this are coming to the book from the study of science fiction rather than the study of children's fiction), let us take a single paragraph from an author, Patrick Brown, writing in Sheila B. Anderson's *Serving Older Teens* (2004), an author and book who and which otherwise impressed me immensely and from whom I will be citing extensively later on. On the whole this is a book deeply sympathetic to the demands and needs of teenage readers, but for reasons that passeth all understanding, when faced with a choice of fiction that he did not comprehend, rather than actually asking teens why they made the choices they did, Patrick Brown wrote:

> Genre readers move quickly into books written for adults, in particular the areas of horror, science fiction and fantasy. These books usually have nothing to do with adolescent concerns, and they may not even appeal to teen readers apart from the desire for teens to act, and therefore read, like adults [106].

When I posted this paragraph on my LiveJournal (a source of reaction and comment I have found very useful in this project) outraged comments included: "I read genre books as a teen because 90% of teen books either annoyed me or bored me (and a good portion of them made me think the world was a dreadful place that just hurt people)"; "And the books addressed *my* teenage concerns, such as ... is this all there is to life?"; "When people say you should 'write what you know' and thereby try to exclude genre, I always say that the one thing everyone knows is what it is like to be thirteen years old and surrounded by aliens"; "Oh dear. We're only supposed to read fiction that addresses our real-life concerns? Obviously I've been doing it all wrong" (http://fjm.LiveJournal.com/333457.html).

I want to tease out some of the assumptions in Brown's statement because his paradigm is one that I will be challenging throughout this book (and which, to give him credit, Brown also tackles elsewhere). The first is the peculiar sense Brown gives that teens do not know what they actually want, that they are the victims of what the Marxists called "false consciousness," lured into the cheap thrills of "fashionable" reading for status. This in turn ignores the point that, as he demonstrates in his unexpectedly sneering tone, genre fiction does *not* garner adult approval — most sf readers remember reading illicitly — and as the survey in Appendix C demonstrates, the engine of genre reading is overwhelmingly peer recommendation.

Central to this book is Brown's assumption that he knows what "adolescent concerns" are, and in his eyes they are the concerns *of* and *about* adolescence. Presumably he also thinks that children's concerns are the concerns *of* and *about* childhood. What this says of the critic's, author's and just generally adult's interaction with children's literature I will come back to in a moment, but my interest here is simply how patronizing an assumption this is, and one which is immediately obvious if one applies the substitution test as, for example: these books usually have nothing to do with *women's* concerns, and they may not even appeal to *female* readers apart from the desire for *women* to act, and therefore read, like adults.

The wince is instant, and it occurs on two grounds, first that we are assuming a limited horizon of a given group, and second that we are assuming that all members of the group will share the same set of interests or, at best, will share the same conditions of interest. Not all women are the same, and to state the utterly obvious, not all children and teens share either the same notion of what being at that age is about, or whether they are even interested in reading about representations of themselves. Many critics do recognize this issue, but most representation of this understanding — that not all readers want representation of themselves tackling "adolescent" personal concerns — is to be found in the discussions about the reading of teen boys.

In the work of Alison Follos (2006), I find recognition that for a segment of the potential male teen readership most of Patrick Brown's assumptions about relevance are misguided. Holly Virginia Blackford (2004) working on girls' reading habits, also comes to the same conclusion, but unlike Follos, Blackford's acceptance is riddled with resistance. In actuality, in both of these studies, the young readers are not interested in what Brown and so many commentators on YA literature think of as "adolescent issues," issues which are often about relationships and internal angst. Too often the investigators are blinkered in that they ignore some of the things teens do care about: exploring the world out there through mountain climbing, motorcycles, economics and astronomy. And that list is deliberately weird. Brown's statement (which I have appropriated to stand for the many that I came across) seems blind to the complexity of the market. And this is the rub. Much of the criticism in the field seems to deny the operation of the market, even as it talks (particularly at the picture-book level) of books that appeal to children. Because it is crucial to this book that I believe there is a sub-set of the children's market whose values are very different to the majority, I want to begin this book by tackling these two contentious issues: the existence of a children's market, and the clash between the values of mainstream criticism and that of the child who might want to read science fiction.

The Child Reader and the Reading Child

In the conclusion to a previous book, *Diana Wynne Jones and the Children's Fantastic Tradition* (2005) I suggested that the apparent conflict between the demands that authors such as William Mayne, Alan Garner and Diana Wynne Jones placed on the child, and the concept of the child reader as someone who had to be tempted and coerced into reading, could be explained very simply if one took out of that category "the Child Reader" that sub-set of children who, in contrast, have to have books forcibly removed from their hands in order to gain any nourishment, see where they are going, and otherwise interact with their surroundings. Despite all the interest in getting children to read, this child, whom I dubbed "the Reading Child," is rare in the literature of childhood studies, education or children's literature (see Clarke, 1976). This is an odd absence because, ironically, the Reading Child is the goal of many teachers and librarians: it is what is hoped for when children learn to read. Yet, when such children do emerge, they are invisible in the literature, which focuses overwhelmingly on the reluctant reader.

The absence of the Reading Child from the literature seems to be related to the insistence that children are not a market. This idea has a number of origins: it descends from the days when books were expensive and most people's access to reading was through the local public or private lending libraries, and furthermore when the librarian's control over child readers extended to control of tickets and of book choice — although I will be challenging even this later in the chapter. As an idea it has also been supported by Jacqueline Rose's hugely influential work, *Peter Pan and the Impossibility of Children's Literature* (1984). Jacqueline Rose's primary argument was that because fiction for children is not written by children, then children are unusual in having the impressions and understandings of their condition shaped and imposed upon them by others not from their own community. Up to a point, I agree with this statement but what I do not agree with is the corollary, that appears to have turned into a ubiquitous mantra, that "children are not a market." I want to unpick this mantra as a step towards my discussion of what science fiction for children has done, and is doing, where its catchment area is, and why it may not even have one.

I will start with Rose's idea, because I think it has reinforced what was essentially a social and economic situation that even by 1930 was riddled throughout with holes. Rose's idea that children have no literature because children do not write literature can be challenged from two directions. The first is simply that the exceptionalist model does not hold water. Writers are a tiny minority of the reading public — and many writers do not in fact read very much. If we consider who writes, then male writers are disproportionately represented in the sense that there is a higher proportion of male writers of fiction than there are male readers of fiction (the non-fiction numbers look different). The class make-up of writers is substantially middle-class, but the make-up of readers is not so easy to discern, and is confused by what people will and won't admit to doing with their leisure time. Many working-class women did not used to admit to reading because it implied neglect of household duties. Then, if they did, it would be couched as "well, I like a romance" or "just Catherine Cookson." Research on women's working lives in the 1960s, and many autobiographies, revealed that far more women held paid jobs than anyone had realized, because women were under-reporting either from guilt or a feeling that part-time work was not real work. In the field of reading studies there are indications that several groups may be under-reporting their reading patterns, of which I would suggest young males and older women are the most likely categories. William Blintz found one 11th grader, labeled a resistant reader, who said she loved reading at home, and would sometimes feign sickness to do so. What she did not like was reading assignments (1993: 610). This young reader was not an isolated case. Blintz found that many of them read widely: "Their out of school reading was meaningful, functional and purposeful ... including high interest magazines. Specific reading interests included race cars, aviation, hunting, romance novels, science fiction, historical fiction, nonfiction, U.S. Civil War, weapons, sports, mechanics and religion" (611). Yet their teachers, when interviewed, labeled these pupils as non-readers and believed that "tightening classroom control" (612) was the solution. Alison Follos makes similar points. When it comes to provision for a market there are also issues that challenge Rose's exceptionalist model: as the number of books on the market by black writers remains relatively small, one must assume that most black readers are reading books by white people as well. Similarly, gay and lesbian readers have long taken their reading pleasures where they could. To turn around and suggest that literature written by an outsider yet marketed to this group somehow excludes the notion of the literature belonging to the reading group is problematic because it excludes two notions: one, that readers are quite capable of putting a book down if it does not appeal, and that this is true also of children, and also that readers are quite capable of subverting a text to their own needs (see Sheenagh Pugh, 2006, on the range of slash fiction available, and Janice Radway's seminal book *Reading the Romance*, 1984) and that this too is quite within the reach of the child reader (see Crago and Crago's work with their own child, Anna). As it happens, there is increasing evidence of what children do want to read in their own writings, as the study of "writing by children" is expanding, and as publishers have decided that very young writers are a saleable commodity. The results are complex in that some children hate reading other children's writing, while Christopher Paolini's *Eragon* (2002) became a best-seller. But when we study the printed writings of child authors, what we find in terms of content is not very different from what is on the market. Both Paolini's *Eragon* (2002) and Austen's *Love and Freindship* [*sic*] (1790) reiterate the content and tropes of the genre they chose.

Rose's exceptionalist model is fundamentally tied to Patrick Brown's assumptions about the reader's "proper" interests. To understand what's wrong with this we need to get a grip on the idea that reading has always been a minority passion. A recent New York Times survey of children's reading habits led to a degree of discussion on the children's literature discussion list Child_Lit about what was a "heavy" reader, and it was a shock to realize that there is a huge gap between the child who reads one or two books a week, and is considered by non-readers to be a heavy reader, and the reading practices of those who identify themselves as heavy readers, whose total between the ages of 12 and 18 was closer to sixteen a week (a number of books which also has consequences for the idea of a children's market). This revelation should persuade us to separate the functional requirements of literacy from the pleasure activity of reading.

Living in an economy that requires a functional level of literacy to survive, imbued as we are in our own culture of reading, surrounded as we often are by other readers, it is really difficult sometimes to grasp that being A Reader is as much an active hobby as being a fencer or a stamp collector. Reading for pleasure, so often communicated as a natural thing to want for our children, should be reconstituted as the equivalent to learning a sport. Some of us, many of whom are engaged in education, are "extreme sport" readers, and we tend to have the same approach to reading as our physical education teachers had to hockey: "if only you try hard enough you'll just *love* it!" This seriously distorts the way "we" understand the culture in which children read but ironically, it seems to be the urge to tempt that leads extreme readers to avoid the reasons why *they* read — which I would suggest often has to do with the simple pleasure of words in the head, as physical exercise provides pleasurable feelings in the muscles for those who practice[1] — and look instead towards things that tempt the non-reader: we offer not what we enjoy, but justifications for why we enjoy it. These tend to focus on functionality in a range of different ways from societal literacy, to the power of story-telling and metaphor (although as we will see later, some functions are valued less than others). Francis Spufford, the popular critic, draws attention to the degree which it was the *sound* of words which attracted him to fantasy, to the delight in discovery, "I could say these words over, and shape my mouth around their big sounds. I could enjoy their heft in the sentences" (2002: 72), but the academic literature I have read concentrates on the content of the books/comics/magazines being offered to children. Within my own reading, only Philip Nel's *Dr. Seuss: An American Icon*

(2004) discusses children's understanding of the aesthetics of sound, while the idea that one might enjoy reading for the sheer pleasure of getting better at it, just as one enjoys playing the violin *for the sheer pleasure of getting better at it*, is utterly absent from the criticism of the process of reading. Seen that way, the notion of reading as a natural interest starts to disappear, and with it, the notion that there is a natural interest in certain types of reading begins to disappear.

This leads me in two directions, both of which will be important for this book: the issue of narrative complexity, or what children can cope with, and the issue of whether the values that readers ascribe to the texts they choose are valid or not.

Narrative Complexity

Narrative complexity and the Reading Child is remarkably understudied. There is some work on the development of complex storytelling technique (Lewis, 2001) and Crago and Crago (1983) very carefully tracked the development of complex narrative understanding in their daughter, Anna. But most of the work on what children can and cannot absorb is to be found in the study of picture books, where it is very heavily value-laden. The tension that exists is between those who see children's lack of pre-conceived narrative structures as a state of ignorance and a distraction, and those who see the same lack of pre-conceptions as potential to be exploited and stretched.

Although it is a little unfair to cite as his current opinion a text written in 1988, Perry Nodelman's *Words Without Pictures: The Narrative Art of Children's Picture Books* is an exemplar of the idea that the purpose of picture books is to teach children to focus on a particular understanding of narrative in which the "significant" is central to the frame. Nodelman cites McLuhan's idea that non-literate people do not sift out the irrelevant but scan each image as if they were pixels; "Anyone who has watched young, preliterate children with little experience of books scan pictures in just this way, and consequently focus their attention on what are meant to be insignificant details, will appreciate the extent to which pictorial perception depends on this learned competence"(7).[2] For Nodelman, the focus on the center of the frame is a gain in competence. In contrast, Helen Bromley sees the diffuse focus of young children both as a positive asset, and as something to be exploited by the clever author. In "Spying on Picture Books: Exploring Intertextuality with Young Children" (1996) Bromley asked children to identify the stories and rhymes that they recognized in *The Jolly Postman* (Ahlberg and Ahlberg, 1986). Bromley described the children's acknowledgement of their own pleasure in recognition, and their awareness that these inter-textual elements worked alongside the main narrative, as, "theorizing their practice as readers" (103). Another text, *Not Now, Bernard* (McKee, 1984), was rewarding for what was found in the corner of the page. "One group of children discovered that Elmer (the patchwork elephant) was to be found on the toy shelves of the badly behaved Bernard" (105). Similarly Morag Styles in *Children Reading Pictures: Interpreting Visual Texts* (Arizpe and Styles, 2003) pointed out that however detailed her own analysis, small children regularly spotted things she had not (x). Styles also cited B. Kiefer's 1993 observations: "Noticing details seems to come first ... sharing 'secrets with the illustrator may in turn help children become more sensitive to the artistic qualities in picture books..." (Arizpe and Styles, 48).

Styles, observing that older children no longer seem to disparage picture books, wonders if "times may be changing and that increasingly older children are more responsive to visual texts than they were, and that this might be because children had grown up in a much more visual world" (xi). David Lewis concurs: picture books inculcate, "double-orientation, the ability to look in two directions at once," either text and picture at variance, or picture and picture (68). Lewis, Styles, Kiefer and Bromley all argue for a mode of reading that appears to be lost with age, an ability to see a wider concept of narrative in which the central tale may be enhanced by what is seen in corners or, with some texts, the central narrative or counternarrative may actually be constructed *by* the "text" buried in the corners. While picture-book artists and authors seem comfortable with the idea that children's openness allows greater narrative complexity, many writers and editors working with the older market seem to assume that the ability to handle narrative complexity is acquired only with maturity, and that "narrative complexity" is inherent in Nodelman's idea that there is a central narrative which should be focused on. Some authors have challenged this: authors such as Daniel Pinkwater, Aidan Chambers, Anne Fine, Alan Garner, Diana Wynne Jones and Tim Wynne-Jones (no relation) have all discussed the willingness of child and teen readers to cheerfully accept and "read" complex narratives which baffle adult readers.

The issue of what complexity children can handle matters here because when we discuss whether writing sf for children is possible, one of the limiting factors frequently offered is the issue of whether the reader can handle the world-building, cognitive estrangement and narrative complexity of modern science fiction. As with the picture-book scholars, the cognitive and developmental scientists suggest that small children can cope with far more complexity than is sometimes recognized in the literature on reading. A smart author can, as Bromley observed, take advantage of this. Two sf picture books which succeed admirably, and which in doing so rupture the notion that sf is a learned reading strategy, are *Dr. Xargle's Book of Earthlets* (2002), by Tony Ross and Jeanne Willis, and *Maybe One Day* (2001), by Frances Thomas and Ross Collins.

It is rarely put this way, but science fiction can be metaphorized as the small child saying "Da ... ad ...?" while working out which "why" to ask next.[3] *Maybe One Day* makes this sf *bildungsroman* "storyable." On the surface this is a little boy's imaginary journey through fantastical space, and the fact that the little boy is a monster gives it a science-fictional appearance but does not make it sf. But Little Monster is engaged in narrating the universe, asking questions of it and working out his own answers in the face of his father's (fantasy) distractions. The tale begins with Little Monster declaring that he has a problem: he wants to be an explorer and this will mean leaving his parents behind. "Maybe we could come with you" (2) his father says. "Don't be silly," says Little Monster. "Explorers don't take their mummies and daddies"(3). This sets the tone. Daddy will propose something preposterous and Little Monster will correct him. Little Monster explains that on the moon one can jump as high as a house; Daddy says "You might bounce all the way back into space"(6), but Little Monster says that cannot be done. When Daddy warns him about Martians, Little Monster denies their existence. Daddy warns him not to slide off the rings of Saturn, but Little Monster focuses on the dangers of the meteorites. As Katherine Nelson has observed, young children frequently recast the story "told" into something they prefer, but here the power is handed over to the child. It is Daddy who tries to retell the "story of the universe" at variance to the evidence (Nelson, 207–209).[4]

Throughout, Daddy keeps trying to impose a fantasy narrative onto the adventure, while Little Monster is resolutely in favor of science fiction and experimentation. Ross and Willis's *Dr. Xargle's Book of Earthlets* functions in a not dissimilar way. The alien Dr. Xargle is instructing his young charges before they begin a visit to Earth. Most of the book is dedicated to describing human babies, and the misinterpretations are glorious. "To stop them leaking, Earthlets must be pulled up by the back tentacles and folded in half. Then they must be wrapped quickly in a fluffy triangle or sealed with paper and glue." The accompanying picture shows a very disconcerted child covered in brown paper and tape. "After soaking, Earthlets must be dried carefully to stop them shrinking. Then they are sprinkled with dust to stop them sticking to things," accompanied by a picture of a child apparently drowning in talcum powder. But Dr. Xargle absolutely relies on dissonance and cognitive estrangement. The book is hilarious to adults because it relies on sarcasm. Recent research, however, suggests that children "could start to understand the concept of sarcasm by the age of five, but did not start laughing until they reach the age of ten" ("Findings: A Higher Form of Humour," THES, 14 March 2003). So how and why might children find these two books, with their emphasis on challenging a received truth, funny?

In their reports on their own daughter's reading development, the Cragos noticed that around the age of two years and ten months, Anna would accept departures from reality, but was noticing if the text contradicted the pictures, and by two years and eleven months noticed if color schemes were inconsistent across the book, although this became a pleasure rather than an objection (154).

Children live with an idea of estrangement, that begins in a fully immersive mode: everything they meet is accepted as *real*, and only later do they begin to distinguish. In effect, they begin as participants in a science fiction world. *Maybe One Day* works because it relies on the child insisting on the "reality" of the world against an adult's attempt to divide the world into the mimetic and the fantastical. Small children are also enormously competent at extrapolating meaning from context and syntax. Consider this comment on how a three year old learns language and can decode the sentence "The duck is gorping the bunny":

> Even though you have never heard the word "gorping" before you could infer various things about its likely meaning. Its placement between "is" and "ing" strongly suggests that it is a verb. These same cues suggest as well that it refers to some on-going action — to something that is happening in the present. Finally the three-part A-B-C construction suggests that it is a transitive verb and that the duck is the one doing the gorping and the bunny is the one being gorped [Flavell et al., 2002, 304–5].

Flavell and co. call this "syntactic bootstrapping" and argue that it is possible because children are born with the innate drive to sort and regularize. This drive is "proved" by children's attempt to regularize the words they meet at the expense of accuracy (sheeps instead of sheep). In addition, children are able to "fast map," that is they can deduce meaning without full comprehension. Asked to bring in "the chromium tray, not the blue one, the chromium one" children will presume that chromium is a color (Flavell, 302). As David Lewis argues, children "take the illusion of the story world pretty much for granted" (Lewis, 134).

Adult linguistic "talents" and scientific curiosity are both leftovers to be maintained as long as possible, rather than understood as "progression." These baby talents are the fundamental *key* to science fiction, that ability to accept new words as both indicative and real, and this is a retention of childlike behavior, rather than a function of maturity (Gopnik et al., 105, 110).

Dr. Xargle also uses children's bootstrapping ability to equate what they know with what they don't know. In order for this book to work a child must be aware of what is actually happening in the pictures, how it would be described, the literal meaning of Dr. Xargle's description, and the concept of metaphor. It works because of what it asks children to do, it asks them to adopt the classic sf reading strategy which relies on the literal truth of metaphor. *Dr. Xargle* relies on the classic Wimmer and Permer test of 1983.

> The child watches a boy (Maxi) place chocolate in a cupboard, then leave the room. Someone moves the chocolate.
> The child observer is asked to guess where Maxi will look for the chocolate first.
> 3-year-olds predict Maxi will look where the chocolate has now been placed.
> 4-year-olds predict that Maxi will look where he himself put the chocolate [Nelson, 255].

Dr. Xargle absolutely relies on the boundary between the age groups. One might expect a four-year-old to laugh at the three-year-old comprehension of

Dr. Xargle. It, and to a lesser extent *Maybe One Day*, represent an important leap forward in what is expected of the child reader. The world of the imagination and the world out there are to be challenged and defined, made knowable, subject to understanding through evidence and experiment, one of the central conceits of sf.

Yet the odd thing is that the extrapolative competence expected of the small child in these two books—commonly known as *cognitive* bootstrapping—and the understanding that the world is made up of strangenesses and therefore all strangenesses are equal, disappears in the chapter books offered to pre-teens, and is very slow to re-emerge in the fiction written for teens. A book such as *Andrew Lost* (2002) is oddly catechistic: Andrew asks questions and is lectured to by his robot. Andrew never challenges received wisdom the way the small children in the two picture books do. This is true also of Malorie Blackman's *Whizziwig* (1995), Jeanette Bresnihan's *The Alphabet Network* (2000), and Alan Durant's *Gameboy Reloaded* (2005). In all of these examples of pre-teen reading, children are not expected to be able to negotiate the strange. The "immersion" in a strange world which Willis and Ross took for granted that a small child could handle, is almost entirely missing from fiction written for teens from the 1980s until the turn in 2001. Although some authors, such as Margaret Haddix and John Christopher, felt able to set their protagonists down in futures very different to ours, very many authors, including writers such as Nicholas Fisk, Ben Bova, Monica Hughes, Rodman Philbrick, Neil Arksey, Louise Lawrence, Lois Lowry and others seemed unable to construct fully immersed worlds, insisting on explanations from the outside, as if the teen reader could not possibly make the move into another world without a map. The struggle to write within the demands of sf but for children seems to demand compromises or negotiations. This can manifest in a variety of ways: Lesley Howarth seems to feel obliged to structure her work around the familiar, and when faced with a real possibility of science, balks at its possibilities. For Philip Reeve it is in the language which veers from the politically sophisticated and demanding to the romantic or comforting at moments of stress. William Sleator explains chaos theory, but in the end bases his plots on much more linear understandings of time. Yet these compromises may not be necessary: Ken MacLeod's *Cydonia* (1998) and Robert Westall's *Futuretrack 5* (1983) refuse to make compromises and are, ironically, more stable texts but are also indistinguishable from much sf marketed for adults. *Cydonia*, indeed, is indistinguishable in either language or political demands from MacLeod's adult novella, *The Human Front* (2001): both books require the reader to doubt the wisdom of the actions of the young protagonist, rather than accepting a sealed world, and both require immersion in the world of the protagonist with little contextual explanation. Stephen Baxter's *The H-Bomb Girl* (2007) begins in familiarity but as the world gets stranger, the protagonist does not blink, because it is *her* world, logically proceeding from where she is. We the readers have to cope with it, knowing that as the pages pass, this is less and less our world. If a reader is capable of handling this, then s/he is capable of reading adult science fiction. That sf written for teens has generally had lower expectations of what teens can cope with is clearly evident when we consider that most teens move straight on to modern adult science fiction in which immersion in a strange world has been the default "norm" since the 1950s—even planetary exploration stories or first-contact stories usually begin in a future not like ours and take that future with them when they step outside. Sf for adults has long been committed to syntactic and cognitive bootstrapping.

Values

Valorizing children's values should be a natural outcome of Jacqueline Rose's arguments, but there remains—and will probably always remain—a tension between the critic/child development theorist/librarian/teacher's belief that children's values should be cherished, and the desire to shape those values into those we believe are more "critical."[5] This tension is inherent in Patrick Brown's statement, but, as the statement also reveals, the tension is stronger when the child chooses a genre not esteemed by the adult. At its most basic, it is very noticeable that the reading of *fiction* for pleasure is given primacy by every critic in childhood reading habits I have studied, with the admirable exception of Alison Follos, even though library lending figures suggest that many people enjoy non-fiction more than novels. The issue of guiding children's reading is even more problematic when s/he chooses a genre whose values are unclear to the guiding adult. J. A. Appleyard (1990), again an author from whom I have otherwise found very valuable material, falls right into this trap.

Appleyard is very interested in cognitive theories of reading comprehension—what children can and cannot process, and the stages at which their interests should "develop." What struck me most forcefully reading Appleyard's commentary was the similarity to Freudian thoughts on women's sexuality, which ascribed immaturity to certain desires and behavior on the basis of their value to the authority figure in the relationship. First, Appleyard claims that young teens (13 and upwards) turn against series books. He does not actually provide evidence for this, and I find the statement dubious given the ubiquity of series books in the adult market (Patrick O'Brian, Lindsey Davies, Alexander McCall Smith, just to name a few), but even more problematic is the argument he offers for this process:

> It is not simply that romance [adventure] pictures the world imperfectly; the child's view of the world enlarges, and what was an adequate way of making sense out of the world no longer is ... character becomes more important than action. A boy or girl age 10 to 13 is interested in and can imagine the thoughts and feelings of others in ways that are beyond the capacity of children ages 7 to 10. Their growing

self-consciousness about their own inner states, their contradictory and unresolved feelings, and their confused thoughts find no mirror in the underdeveloped characters of adventure stories, certainly not in the eternal juveniles of the series books [87].

The issue of what character *is* and how genre-specific it is I will tackle in a later chapter, but for now it is worth noting that Appleyard uses *The Wizard of Oz* (1900) as a text which explores character, although Dorothy remains a self-possessed child who exhibits little internal reflection throughout the book. What is more important here is that Appleyard ascribes value to this transition. He takes a sample child: a boy called Stephen, aged 15, "is beginning to shed the need to read about heroes, but has not entirely found a new way of reading yet" (90–1). "The need to read about heroes" is, it is implied, immature. So too, and not surprisingly, is Stephen's reading of science fiction:

> He retells with enthusiasm the plot of a five-volume series called The Chronicles of Amber by Roger Zelazny....
>
> In one sense Stephen seems to be looking backward, at the magical world of childhood, at heroes and villains involved in struggles between good and evil, where power settles everything. There's not much ambiguity in this world and no overt sex: "The biggest things I stay away from are romantic stuff and things that have to do with humanism ... [character development] just slows down the story." But in another sense Stephen uses literature as a source for rethinking the world in ideal terms. His stories are exuberantly if somewhat conventionally inventive and draw on a supply of literature ranging from James Bond to J.R.R. Tolkien. His intelligence makes special demands on a book. Magic in science fiction, for example, has to be consistent....
>
> School does not challenge Stephen the way this stuff does ... Steinbeck bores him.... Difficulty to Stephen at this point seems to be entirely a matter of plot complexity; the emotional intricacies of the Steinbeck characters' lives or the moral issues they face do not count [89–90].

The boy has coped with the Odyssey but the implication is that because he read it for plot, it didn't count. I am aware that many, if not most, of my readers will be sf fans, but some may not so to be clear, the choice of Roger Zelazny's Amber sequence is *not* the choice of an immature reader or of one who avoids ethical issues. What Appleyard seems to be doing is valorizing the ethics of intimacy — note that he draws attention to the lack of sex — over the ethics of involvement in the wider world. A short study of students in her care by Alaine Martaus, Head Librarian at the Arkansas School for Math, Science and the Arts suggested that these attitudes are endemic and that they are particularly strong when teachers and librarians interact with "bright" students and students on a humanities track. Her students, mostly with a math and science orientation were, like "Stephen," attracted to fantasy and sf for its complex narratives, the sheer depth of the world often exhibited in the presence of the fleeting characters derided by external critics, and the intertextuality of the material. A crucial issue many identified (and here I summarize in my own words) is that fantasy and sf valorized intellectual qualities they felt that they shared, rather than the social abilities many felt that they lacked. There was no division in the tastes of boys and girls, but all had experienced the accelerated reading program which focused on "classic" literature of the kind Appleyard approves, and had been put off reading. Worst affected was a student on the small arts program: "She is particularly fascinated by fantasy literature, particularly fairy stories and dystopian feminist literature. But she is constantly encouraged to start reading 'real' literature" (unpublished *ICFA* paper, 2007). This discrepancy in value structures will, as I will discuss in later chapters, be a major source of tension in terms of the sf that is written for the child and teen market under the YA label.

The way in which science fiction is seen by many bibliographers similarly reveals preconditioned ideas not just about what children should read, but *why* we think children should read. A good example can be found in Lucy Schall's *Teen Genre Connections: From Booktalking to Booklearning* (2005). Schall sets out to pick excellent and interesting books, and then give teachers and librarians ideas about how to discuss these books with teens. Although there is very little science fiction listed — it forms one fifth of section 5, Fantasy/Science Fiction/Paranormal, and is restricted to "Futuristic" fiction, which is a mere sliver of what sf is — the choices are solid: *Feed* (2002) by M.T. Anderson, the *Fire-us* trilogy (2002–2005) by Jennifer Armstrong and Nancy Butcher, *The House of the Scorpion* (2002) by Nancy Farmer and *The Crux* sequence (2001–2002) by Mark Waid.

My concern is with the orientation of the "Learning opportunities" notes in each section. There is a *prima facie* assumption that children read for character, with character defined as interpersonal relationships. For the *Fire-us* sequence, for example, we are asked to think about naming; about how the shopping-mall setting influences the book, to focus on the character of Anchorman/Angerman and his name, the dynamic of each new character, the role of the Apocalypse, and whether a main character should have died. For the *Crux* series, we are asked to consider issues of ritual; how principles of the every day as well as the ideal "apply to character in this [Han Nolan's *When We Were Saints*] setting" as well as the mythology of science fiction/adventure; discuss the dualities each character represents. "Be sure to consider their physical appearance as well as their mental and emotional qualities; match these qualities with people you know"(213). Where Schall has attempted to reach outside of this orientation towards the external issues of politics, economics and science, she demonstrates a discomfort with extrapolation, a need to pin it down to "relevance," as in "*The House of the Scorpion* is a science fiction thriller with insights for our modern world. List the messages or themes that you find in the story" (209), or in a discussion of *Feed*, to consider the role of advertising in the modern world. It is interesting however that when Aidan Chambers tackled a similar issue in his 1973 book, *Introducing Books to Children* his complaint, about very similar questions, was that they were too fact-oriented. The issue may be less the questions themselves, than what Chambers terms "parade-ground drills" and "grab bag" project or thematic approaches insensitive to the actual interests of the authors (23).

John Gillespie and Corinne Naden in *Teenplots: A Booktalk Guide to Use with Readers Ages 12–18* (2003) are even less comfortable with science fiction on its own terms: although — laudably — they select adult titles to recommend to teens, of the seventeen sf/fantasy titles only four are actually science fiction. But it is the way in which they write about the texts that is revealing. Each book receives a "Suitability and Critical Comment" note, followed by "Themes and Subjects" and "Passages for Booktalking." For *Ender's Shadow* (1999) we get "This adult novel is best suited for the good reader who is a fan of science fiction and interplanetary warfare. It is filled with so-called war games on a futuristic level in a battle school that molds children of super-intelligence into a superior force that will save the world" (38).

You can just feel the dislike leaking through. The themes identified are "Courage, discipline, gene altering, intelligence, interplanetary, science fiction, travel, war games"; all this is true but also very superficial. The rigorous (if problematic) ethical dimension of the book is entirely ignored: this is a book whose keywords could include population control, genocide, and human nature. Yet all of the passages selected for suggested Booktalking are (with the exception of the last one) family- or identity-oriented. One glancing comment made about Michael Crichton's *Timeline* (1999) is revealing. *Timeline* (1999) is described thus: "This adult novel is probably best attempted by good readers with some understanding of and a good interest in science of the future, such as the field of quantum technology" (148). To which my irritated husband, both a medievalist and science fiction fan responded, "What crap: it is about the Middle Ages!"[6] When identifying *themes*, the themes chosen begin with interpersonal themes, only then followed by any sense of "the other," as valorized in those early LiveJournal responses discussed at the beginning of the chapter, or the notion of knowledge acquisition. Although Susan Hall's book, *Using Picture Storybooks to Teach Character Education* (2000) is a slight deviation here, it demonstrates precisely what I mean. This is the list she provides.

Cooperation	Generosity	Perseverance
Courage	Helpfulness	Prudence
Courtesy	Honesty	Resourcefulness
Diligence	Hope	Respect
Discernment	Justice	Responsibility
Empathy	Kindness	Self-discipline
Forgiveness	Loyalty	Tolerance
Fortitude	Patience	

With the possible exception of Perseverance and Diligence, these are almost all "in relation to people" qualities.

I do not want to give the impression that all reading guides approach the field of sf for the young as outsiders. D.T. Herald's *Teen Genreflecting* (2003) and Herald and Kunzel's *Strictly Science Fiction* (2003) are excellent guides which don't assume that young readers are either misguided or mistaken in what they say they want.

By this time, it may be becoming obvious that a lurking tension — and one that is frequently acknowledged by professionals in the field — is gender. The "children" cited as sf readers are almost always boys. This takes me right back to some of the truisms at the beginning of this chapter, and also to the validity of the choices of readers. If "boys don't read," why is science fiction a predominantly boys' field? And if "someone to identify with" and "just like me" are the driving attractions in reading, why do some girls resolutely reject literature directed towards their real lives, and head straight for space ships, aliens, and (particularly in older texts) male characters? An extensive discussion of the gendering of YA science fiction will form part of chapter five, but here I am most interested in the way in which the selection of values considered important to reading for teens is defined in gendered terms, or *not* defined in gendered terms.

Despite the sense many people have that girls enjoy the shelves of series romance, but are in fact willing to read anything — hence the idea that you need to cater to the boys' interests— there is very little research on what girls want to read. As with the relative absence of studies of successful readers to see how they do it, there is relatively little exploration of what it is Reading Girls actually want, because Reading Girls seem to be *willing* to read anything proposed to them. While there may be far more material out there that I have missed only two pieces seemed to directly address this issue, an article from 1954 by L. Fenwick, and a recent monograph by Holly Virginia Blackford, *Out of This World: Why Literature Matters to Girls.*

Fenwick's article, "Periodicals and Adolescent Girls" deals with teen girls in the era of the Juveniles. In 1954 the school leaving age in the UK had only recently been lifted to 15. The girls interviewed saw themselves as neo-adults, preparing for work, and for bringing money into the home. Fenwick was fighting a battle familiar to many, for the right of young people to choose their own reading without being patronized, and specifically for school libraries to include the material that girls *said* they wanted to read as well as books that would "uplift" them. In this case Fenwick was arguing for the provision of periodicals. Fenwick's study was of Secondary Modern pupils. There is no U.S. equivalent of this kind of school, but girls experiencing the Secondary Modern education in the 1950s would have been expected to aim either for a technical role in hairdressing or shop work, or at the highest a secretary. The teaching profession was reserved for Grammar School girls (perhaps the equivalent of a modern "Honors" class).

Fenwick outlined seventeen categories of periodical reading, which included comics for young children, boys comics, and weekly papers aimed at teenagers. The girls' weeklies came second on the list of "average" reading, and amongst both the fourteen- and fifteen-year-olds they were listed as the fourth most popular reading material. The weeklies produced specifically for this market tended to be a common reading experience, but not the most popular. Because of this Fenwick distinguished between reading, acquisition and a sense of ownership, which is where things get interesting, because although Fenwick presents the process as relatively passive — "girls read what is lying around" — the behavior can be construed as essentially active, a process of *foraging* for reading rather than being fed. Most of the publications the girls read were listed as household rather than personal expenses. "Although the girls read everything in their homes so avidly, the only periodicals they seem to regard as their personal property are *School Friend*, *Girl* and *Girl's Crystal*" (31). Of the appropriation of boys' and adults' reading matter Fenwick has two things to say: "Choosing a book from a library some distance away is much more difficult than reading everything which is delivered to the home" (30–31), and "Probably more of the boys' comics in Group ii are read than the girls' weeklies because the girls do not pay for the boys' comics themselves [Fenwick does not seem to have asked]. While some girls stop reading the boys' comics as their taste matures, other adolescent girls continue to read them because they are provided at home, even though the girls may regard them as childish"(34), a value-laden comment but still useful. Although Fenwick does mention a Mr. Jenkinson in relationship to a similar study of the reading of Grammar School girls, Fenwick does not support Jenkinson's assumption that appropriation of boys' reading material "suggests a strong, if subsidiary desire to be boys" (35). Rather. Fenwick seems to position the more voracious choices as an indication of maturity, noting with amusement, "One intelligent girl who read no comics said they were still bought regularly at the home. Her father brushed aside all suggestions that the comics should be discontinued for economy because he himself read them"(34).

For girls, personal purchase of reading material may drop as other demands on their purse, associated with socialized femininity, escalate. Fenwick makes the point that girls' magazines before the war did not carry advertisements because the readership was assumed not to have money of its own, in sharp contrast to boys' weekly papers. Justine Larbalastier's work on women and the science fiction community suggests that women were reading a far wider range of material than they felt in a position to buy (2002). But what really interests me here is that even the most "conservative" of teenage girls in Fenwick's survey were, if they were active readers, going outside the "recommendations" of both teachers and publishers. They were not passively confined to the texts thought suitable for them.

This notion of foraging for reading, taking on the reading of those around you, can be seen in Holly Virginia Blackford's *Out of This World*, a fascinating study of a group of girls' reading habits, and their reading desires. The value of Blackford's study is almost entirely in her willingness to suspend her original thesis and go with what the girls were actually telling her. Although Blackford did no work on where the girls were getting their books from, the range of fiction the girls tell her they read opens up the idea of girls' books. These girls rejected Blackford's agenda that they read in order to discover the kind of girls and women they wanted to be (2). They rejected entirely the notion that they should wish to identify with the protagonist. Consequently, they rejected much social realism and a great deal of the "YA" literature on the market. Many of them owned classics such as *Little Women* (1868) and many had read the classic YA literature, but these books were discussed only when specifically raised by Blackford. Instead, the girls were reading science fiction and fantasy (although Blackford calls both of these fantasy), adventure, horror, mystery, and were well into what we are taught are conventionally "boys" books. What Blackford discovered is that the very process of reading for female children and teenagers challenges the notion of gender-divided reading to a far greater degree than the standard truism "Girls will read books about boys." What Blackford was moving towards was an idea that girls were dutiful enough to read the books given to them as "appropriate" and "relevant," but in private and with a free choice were reading the same books that boys were, but where boys — reluctant to read the recommended — may declare themselves as non-readers, girls are more likely appease authority by reading one book for themselves, and one for authority (a construction Homer Hickam Jr. mentions in his memoir, *Rocket Boys* [1998] and which I remember vividly myself). Furthermore, when girls do read "the classics," Angela E. Hubler discovered that they were perfectly capable of editing out of their memories the conclusions to these books in which the heroine's parent or culture "folds her back into the cult of domesticity" (1998: 267).

One thing the survey in Appendix C revealed was that men's memories of what they read as children were far more oriented to writers who also wrote for adults. It was the women who remembered the specialist children's authors. What I would tentatively suggest is that this may match with the higher use of school libraries by girls that teachers frequently report, a usage pattern which will inevitably steer female readers towards books marketed directly at them. In contrast, boys may well be much more tied into peer-to-peer book swaps; this was cited by the majority of cohorts 4 and 5, which are the generations to have aroused serious concern about boys' reading (the younger generation report buying new books), and we do have a comparable situation with the growth of peer-to-peer music swapping which, at least according to anecdotal evidence, is predominantly a male activity. The end result, however, is that boys' reading may be almost invisible to many teachers. When we look at Alison Follos's experiments later, it is worth considering that what she achieved was to create a visible peer-to-peer structure within the school in which she worked.

The issue of what books are for, and the models they provide for children, has always been gendered. The history of boys' books is tied in with the history of genre development itself and with a nineteenth century sentimentalization of motherhood and other female roles, and a model of manhood which emphasized gentlemanliness and courtliness (see *Tom Brown's Schooldays*, 1857; which is a novel about taming masculine brutality). As Segal noted in 1993, prior to the emergence of the boy's adventure story towards the end of the nineteenth century, fiction for children was domestic in setting and emphasized a range of godly virtues:

> The liberation of nineteenth-century boys into the book worlds of sailors, pirates, forests and battles, left their sisters behind in the world of childhood — that is, the world of home and family. When publishers and writers saw the commercial possibilities of books for girls, it is interesting that they did not provide comparable escape reading for them (that came later, with the pulp series books), but instead developed books designed to persuade the young reader to accept the confinement and self-sacrifice inherent in the doctrine of feminine influence. This was accomplished by depicting the rewards of submission [172].

Segal notes the growing sense of books as both promoting the domestic and being themselves an accoutrement of the domestic.[7] This brings us to one of the great tensions in all adventure literatures — and one which Alison Follos is the only critic to tackle directly, as we shall see — which is the assumption that adventure literature still requires a quiet, domestic space in which to be consumed. Whereas fiction traditionally intended for girls has the home either present or in the background (a place to move out from, and — willingly — return to), fiction traditionally intended for boys assumes that a boy's primary interest will be in leaving the home ... at the same time as he sits on the couch and consumes it. This is one of those comments that here may seem like a red herring, but when I discuss the changes in "the idea of the child" over the past sixty years of science fiction for the younger market, this mismatch is central to many of the problems that haunts the genre.

When discussing the way in which boys read, there are real issues both with gender expectations and value expectations of the written text. Boys are expected not to want to read. Both W. G. Brozo (*To Be a Boy, to Be a Reader*, 2002) and Alison Follos discuss the way in which the problematization of boys reading results in (to exaggerate a little) ritual defiance in which "not reading" becomes a badge of boyish or manly value. But Brozo and Follos also point to other issues that are more about the issue of value found in books, and the way in which value is found in reading. Brozo is the most straightforward, pointing out that reading is frequently framed as the reading of fiction, yet:

> Adolescent boys are also known to be especially enthusiastic for nonfiction and informational books (Herz & Gallo, 1996). For most boys, however, reading nonfiction in school consists almost exclusively of reading textbooks, which has been found to be a principal culprit in creating disaffection with reading for both

boys and girls (Clary, 1991). I am always amazed at how turned-on junior and senior high students become when I pass around non-fiction and informational books. I watch adolescents shift their postures from complacency and disengagement to involvement and curiosity [17].

Although I do not feel that in this context the books on literacy I have read necessarily represent classroom practice, non-fiction was rare in the material on literacy. Anne Simpson's 1996 study is one of the very few to include it. Observing classroom practice in a suburban Australian school, she noted that a quarter of the boys' fiction reading could be ascribed to just two boys; thirteen girls between them recorded reading only three non-fiction books. Yet, "non-fiction texts were rarely focal points in the curriculum" (272). Where non-fiction did appear it was almost always linked to project work, when the boys displayed a much wider range of interests than the girls who, where books were available, chose animal-related topics. "Three of the seventeen [boys] chose reptiles, three mechanical topics, four countries, and the remainder elected to research spiders, sharks, otters, sport, UFOs, volcanoes, and pirates" (272). When Simpson tested this by bringing in a range of books, she again found a wide ranges of interest among the boys, but a limited range among the girls. However, what Simpson argued was that this was not being fostered, and nor were girls being encouraged to expand their interests:

> The traditional dominance of narrative fiction in primary classrooms is perpetuated through teacher training courses on literature for children.... Though many English teachers express concern about boys' reluctance to read, the boys in this classroom at least were reading a broad range of texts including expository and information texts. What they were *not* reading as much of were the novels which were so highly valued in the teacher's reading program. The majority of the texts they were reading came from outside of the classroom and were read alongside the main program [Simpson, 276].

In summary, the boys were being stretched outside their chosen reading practices, yet at the same time, the types of reading they were interested in (and there were two girls in the class who fell into the same category) were being continuously devalued or linked to "work" rather than pleasure.

Literacy, it seems to be presumed, is intimately linked to storytelling. Non-fiction as both Simpson and Brozo point out, is seen as work, as functional. The idea of reading non-fiction for pleasure is absent from most literacy texts. That many children do read non-fiction for pleasure however, is going to be an important element in chapter three. That this is not recognized by many guiding adults is, I think, both a gender issue as Brozo suggests and as Simpson observed — library borrowing surveys suggest that women mostly do not read non-fiction for pleasure and Follos points out that over 80 percent of the library profession in the U.S. is female (134) — and a divide between the adult world and the child world. I want to offer a specific thought that will be at the heart of chapter three: curiosity, and a thirst for knowledge, is the very definition of childhood. Its loss is one of the ways we formally define maturity in animals, and informally ascribe it to humans. When we assume children won't like factual books, we are imposing on them a very adult state of mind.

Related to the issue of whether we value non-fiction as *reading* may be the value we ascribe to the non-fiction elements of a fiction text: looking back at the Booktalk recommendations about how to approach reading, and to the work of Appleyard, it is overwhelmingly the fictionalization of *relationships*— and relationships of a certain kind, based on family and pair bonding — that is valued. Questions such as "what do you learn about the city in which the tale is set"; or "make a bow and arrow from the directions given in this book" are completely missing.[8] If we follow the line of argument, boys are being told first that they don't read or that reading is primarily for girls and that they should emulate girls, and then that what many boys choose to read — non-fiction, and much genre fiction such as horror, adventure, thriller, informational, sf, crime and detective, monster/ghost, sports, war, biography, fantasy, historical material — *does not count* (see Brozo, 80.) This may explain the interesting and unexplored anomaly that "boys don't read" while slightly over half of genre readers are male (see Appendix C). Children learn socially acceptable truths very young: a television program which put a group of eight-year-olds on a World War II diet found that all of them, when asked, declared the contents of their lunch packs as "a sandwich, a drink, a piece of fruit." When unpacked the lunch packs contained extra fizzy drinks, chocolate, biscuits, potato chips, and so on. At eight, the children knew what the correct answer was.[9] In an example closer to my own material, David Buckingham (2000) reported that while working-class students of both sexes, and middle-class female students chatted happily about their televisual experiences, middle-class students showed a propensity to wish to deliver the approved answer, and among

> middle-class boys (aged eleven to twelve), for whom sneering at the shortcomings of popular television appears to confer considerable peer group status.... Admitting to enjoying anything, with the possible exception of documentaries and "adult" films, is much more difficult. In many cases, these boys would only admit to watching programmes "to see how stupid they are" — although their knowledge of them is at least equal to the self-confessed fan [114].

I suspect that exactly the same process is occurring when boys are asked about reading: there is both surreptitious, secret reading going on, and there are large swathes of reading occurring that boys have been taught "don't count" or which, they are told, "will do" until they get on to something better.[10] So comics, graphic novels, non-fiction are seen as mere way-stations, literary teddy bears. If they are validated, other types of material may be invalidated. The 1995 University of Nottingham report for example, while it does mention that 2.8 percent of the children interviewed read solely non-fiction, does not explore any of the non-fiction reading of any of the children interviewed. 78 percent of that 2.8 percent of children were boys. We have no indication which of the 97.2 percent of children read non-fiction in addition to fiction, or what that non-fiction was (Hall et al., 7). Similarly Jonathan Wicks in his 1996 essay for *New Library World* opens the analysis of the non-fiction the boys read with the statement: "Non-fiction use was largely utilitarian. One quarter was for school use, 35% hobby related, and a further 28% sport-related. Just 10% appeared to be for general interest"(15). Apparently reading non-fiction on subjects that interest one, or in order to pursue a hobby, is "utilitarian." Furthermore, there is none of the genre breakdown that Wicks provides in the fiction section, yet as we saw earlier from William Blintz, this not only gives a skewed idea of what is being written, but of who is actually reading it. Emily Bazelon, in a short article for *Slate* in 2006, wrote about how this writing out of a particular set of interests can distort how we understand children's pleasure: "The real appeal of *Little House* [*on the Prairie*] for many boys probably is not the narrative, but rather the precise and detailed descriptions of how to tap a maple tree for syrup or load a musket."

However much they are otherwise encouraged, children will pick up the message that they should not be reading this material (populist fiction or non-fiction) if that is what the questions they are asked about their reading imply. At this point however, I should remind us all, that as Holly Blackford discovered, there are a lot of boy readers out there who look like girls. The kind of division I've been using so far is actually quite limited. There is a whole mindset out there which we could call "boyish" but I am going to call the "science-fictional child" and whose values sit apart from the values of much of the literacy culture as it exists in our schools. But before I leave this issue I want to turn to a project which set out to meet male readers on their own grounds, to adjust the understanding of what kind of activity reading is, and who does it, and where.

Alison Follos began a project to get her school to read, which had a two-pronged attack. First of all, she turned it into a challenge named after a local mountain climbing challenge — 46 peaks in one summer, or the 46 mountain trek. She called it Booktrekkers and set 46 books each summer (*Reviving Reading: School Library Programming, Author Visits and Books That Rock!* 2006). Second, she decided that she wanted to engage people in YA literature as a concept, as she had noted that while adults knew a lot about literature for younger children (to whom they often read) they were ignorant of the material available in the YA category. One of the most refreshing aspects was that she was comfortable with all genres and saw YA literature as immensely powerful. Crucially, Follos could see that while "themes" are important, theme is not always the point.

To return to some of my earlier points, Follos established a model that we might call "structured foraging." Readers were offered a wide path of texts (one for each of the local hills that climbers liked to tick off). A crucial element of her strategy was to get all teachers involved, not seeing it as just something to tack on to English teachers' roles: "Get the science and history teachers engaged, and let the buzz spread down the halls and wash out into the community ... what reluctant reader is not apt to try a book recommended by their basketball coach before trying one recommended by the librarian?" (119).

The emphasis on fiction was retained, but the sense of who read fiction and why was placed under pressure. Follos persuaded staff to check out books, got them to journal over the summer and to lead booktalks. One of her big concerns was to get male staff involved. Brozo makes the point that "U.S. culture portrays reading as a *female* activity" (146), and I have found no argument against this. Follos suggests that this needs to be challenged. "If the male faculty are visibly reading, you're taking steps to dispel the myth that men don't read" (134). Follos's point, however, was not simply that if men read, boys would think reading cool; it was that men frequently understood reading differently, placed it in a different context or simply talked about books differently. I'm going to quote the description of one such re-contextualization of reading in full.

> Men make a literature program exciting. Let them share the program, and help them to realise that creative energy will provide the shot in the arm to get kids reading. Collaborating with male staff has wondrous results. For instance, whereas I chose to promote reading during the doldrums of winter through a cozy tea-time after-school book club, a male staffer chose a more assertive approach. He challenged students to a grueling combo readathon/ironman event. This was *his* idea of a good time.
>
> The weekend before our Thanksgiving book fair he launched a Triple Trek weekend activity. I noticed only boys signed up. The point is that they did sign up. Students trekked a mountain, read a Title Trek, wrote about it in their journals, and then watched an episode of *Star Trek*. Prior to the event the teacher commented, "If we have the time, maybe we'll also ride a Trek bike — so it could be a quadruple trek!" They rode the bike, took it apart, carried it to the top of the mountain, and reassembled it. Boys being boys, they took a picture of it for proof and posterity. Here was male ingenuity at its peak, literally and figuratively.
>
> The Triple Trek began at 6:00 A.M. and concluded at 8:30 P.M.—fourteen-and-a-half hours later! On Monday morning journals were on my desk and the students were proudly complaining about how hard it had been and how tired they were. Males are into grit, brawn, and competition. Everything about the Triple Trek — meshing reading with activity — psyched up our male students....
>
> In preparation for the event, we collected books with "trek" in the title or books about outdoor adventures, climbing, biking, sailing, athletic pursuits, and exploring — and there are lots....
>
> The Triple Trek was completely successful due to the energy from this male teacher. He had invested in the reading program over the summer, having written journal entries on twenty-nine YA and children's titles. He promoted the reading program within his classroom, using several of the titles that he had read the previous summer. Then he organised a stimulating weekend activity pivoting around the Title Trekking. Does collaboration get any better? [125–6].

In this book I will be talking about a group of readers who, while not necessarily wishing to associate reading with physical exercise (there are legions of jokes about the sedentary native of the average sf fan, although this may be changing — fitness seems to be becoming the new geekery), do tend to be *doers*.[11] Books are frequently chosen for the things sf fans want to know more about, the unknown, not the familiar, a trek through knowledge, to steal Follos's ideas. This, mild statement though it might be, cuts right across the whole "find them something to identify with" approach to many *tempt 'em to read* programs.

Children as Market

By this time it must be obvious that there is an elephant in the living room: if there is a tension between what adults want, and what children want (even if that is to be left alone to *not* read) then the truism that children are not a market is problematic. What I have been working up to is to assert, very loudly, that children are active and informed "purchasers" in their market and that this begins very young. My survey material, and the work of Blackford, suggests this happens from around the age of eight, but we can go right back to what we see in children's approach to picture books. The assertion that children are not a market rests on a set of truisms and, ironically, a belief that adults control children far more than is the case. Ironic because the argument comes precisely from those critics who argue that we cannot fully understand children or write for them because we aren't children, and I don't necessarily disagree; I just do not believe that the two arguments are linked in the way they so often are.

The resistance to recognizing this is rooted in the collectivization of all children as somehow holding the same relationship to the book world, one in which they read only because adults encourage them to do so. The idea that adults control the reading of the child reader may be true; but that an adult can control the reading activity of the Reading Child, the extreme sport reader, is simply wrong, if only (and here I ask you to think back to your own experience if you were one of these children) because the Reading Child reads too much for an adult to track.

From the very beginning, children are (to use a phrase Peter Hunt once coined), deviant readers: as Nodelman protested and Bromley celebrated, we can place a picture book in front of a small child but we cannot tell them how to read it, we cannot control that process of reading. Once a child gets to the stage of library and bookshop then we are very quickly into matters of active choice as to what is read: no adult can force a child to read a book for pleasure if they don't take pleasure out of it. In the footnote I am attaching here you will find a link to an observation I asked one of my students to undertake for me. Rhys Morgan was working in one of the major UK chains and I asked him simply to watch for interactions between adult and child and to record them for me.[12] In only one of the five cases did a parent enforce a choice on a child, and I am amused to note that the book bought was *The War of the Worlds* (1898).

That children have "pester power" is known and accepted in other retail industries but does not appear in the literature on reading. Alongside this is that as critics we are in danger of exaggerating the power of librarians and other adults in charge of book selection simply because we assume that children, as children, have a different relationship to these marketplaces than do adults.

The standard argument is that children are not a market because their "purchasing" is interfered with by adult intermediaries. To pick up on my opening statement this is every bit as true for adult readers: for library users of all ages their choice is restricted by stock, and for purchasers their choice is restricted by the selections of the book buyers, often for major chains. For more "literate" purchasers their choices may be guided by reviewers. What there is not is any kind of free will in which an audience can demand "x kind of book" and see it produced. The market intervenes at all levels.

But, and this is the assumption that is frequently made: only children have their reading *actively* decided for them. The problem is that for all this statement is made, there is simply no evidence to support it. Gretchen Galbraith, in her 1997 book, *Reading Lives: Reconstructing Childhood, Books, and Schools in Britain, 1870–1920*, discovered an active process of foraging in the reading memoirs of her subjects, and it is from Galbraith I have borrowed the term when I used it earlier. While shortage of money in working-class families meant that fathers made the primary choice of book or newspaper purchase:

> Working-class children's search for books and magazines spiraled outward from their homes. Most began with the few books on their families' shelves, reading them repeatedly. A few writers had memories of a glorious windfall of books sent by a wealthy friend or a parent's old employer, but most had to work harder to find their next cache. Hannah Mitchell's uncle supplied her with exercise books; she did her brothers' chores in exchange for books they brought home from the schoolmaster. As word of her love of books spread, neighbours offered her the use of their small libraries.
> Like their parents, children would pass magazines round among themselves. The ability to buy and swap magazines depended upon pocket money that usually came with a job, but all children had one source of free books: Sunday schools and elementary schools used prize books to reward good behaviour and achievement. Whether retrospectively treasured or overly pious, these books were remembered as hard-won markers of achievement [31].
> ...
> Young readers too far from a library or too intimidated to enter one, could usually browse in a local bookstore. Too poor to buy books, J.M. Severn was lent old papers and magazines by the local newsagent. Some autobiographers read entire books in "snatches" at a local bookstall and depended on the stall owner's advice on the rare occasions when they came to buy a book [32].

Reading children (as opposed to the reluctant readers of the literature) were and are, active pursuers of literature. Margaret Clark, in one of the rare studies of fluent readers noted that the children she spoke with were actively in search of books. "Few obtained sufficiently exciting or stimulating reading material through the school or in great enough quantities" (50). But the problem with libraries was the age-based reading restrictions, which were frequently subverted by parents. "The restrictive policies were particularly limiting on some of the boys who wanted access to encyclopedias and other non-fiction books" (50). For the Reading Child the need to read may well form an outward pressure in which *any* book satisfies the craving for the reading experience. In this context, content is rather irrelevant. I suspect many a Reading Child's career was decided by a text encountered first because it was the only book available.[13] The survey of science fiction readers supported these contentions: even the oldest correspondents, those who could most expect to be affected by lack of pocket money, and rigid librarians' attitudes, were perfectly capable from a very young age of subverting the agendas of those who wished to guide their reading. Follos, Brown, Blackford, Appleyard, and many of the bibliographers I've used understand this (although do not always favor it). Young readers subvert and explore the market in a number of ways—first by simply reading too many books for any adult to be able to guide or restrict their choice (the peak in reading seems to be in the mid-teens); second through peer recommendation; third through second-hand purchasing which frequently provides access to books which might be less attractive or available new; and finally simply through demand. This project led me to watch many a bookshop interaction, which could be summarized thusly:

> PARENT: Wouldn't you like this one? It is highly recommended by....
> CHILD: No! My friend says this [insert name here] is really, really good.

Children now have far more access to money than they once had. In the UK, pocket money runs to around £5 per week, the price of a paperback. There are many demands on that money, and children's social pressures to spend it on certain things, but a child who wished to buy books, could.

Why then the insistence that children are not a market? Some of this is, I think, a desire to think we as adults are important in the reading process—the work done on adult roles suggests we are, but only as examples, not really as guides. But some of it is about the way the world of children's literature reviewing works. Galbraith noted that at the end of the nineteenth century, "For most part, reviewers concentrated on books that, judging from their prices, were destined for middle-class nursery shelves, discussing working-class children's reading practices briefly, if at all" (47). The editor of *Little Folks* magazine, "was both acknowledging that few children could buy their own magazines and urging readers to participate in defining children as recipients of gifts from adult relatives" (55). At one point in this research, deluged with books, I offered to review for the *Horn Book Magazine*. The magazine showed a great deal of interest until it became clear that most sf for children is in paperback (email, 31 March 2006). The *Horn Book Magazine*, the most esteemed reviewing platform in the field, does not review the printing format that children can afford, or would be likely to persuade parents to buy on a generic Saturday afternoon.[14] In essence, it has a huge stake in declaring that the real market for children's books is adults. Until relatively recently, when paperback purchase became the preferred option for cash-strapped libraries in a booming market, the situation was similar for many librarians and teachers. As the market shifts this perception may change, but for now the idea that children are not a market is, I feel, entirely the expression of a vested interest. In this book this will be shown to have consequences for the ways in which science fiction has been written for children. Only by accepting that children and young people *are* a market (even when I hate what they choose) can there be a real engagement with what they might actually want to read.

Chapter Three

Science, Information Density and the SF Reader

Should Schoolchildren Learn to Be Inventors?*

Malcolm Kay, superintendent head of school, Greater London:
We value Trevor Baylis's message — innovation is important in education. The value lies in embedding his ideas into the education that already takes place. In 2006, two of our student groups went to Namibia and they raised funds to take clockwork radios and wind-up torches with them, so they are familiar with the benefits. The international baccalaureate requires every student to take a science subject. These all involve taking a hypothesis, testing it and re-evaluating it — basically, invention. The IB learner profile wants pupils to be enquirers, thinkers and risk-takers. This is about approaching unfamiliar situations with forethought and having the independence to explore ideas.

Ann Morphew, parent, Dorset:
Inventing as part of the national curriculum is an interesting thought. I can see that Trevor Baylis would have benefited from some information on how to market his invention, but surely his wind-up radio was the product of his own fertile mind? Can such inventiveness be taught? There should be room for developing a child's inventiveness, but not at the expense of other, routine methods of learning. Perhaps there's a place for courses based on the work of Edward de Bono or similar. If such teaching were available to children from an early age, the benefits could be enormous.

Charlie Ridey, aged eight, from Surrey:
Yes, they should! I think it's very important, like literacy and numeracy. When you invent, you do what you want, but you need to go with it and see if it works, so you'd be combining science and numeracy. I think it would be easy enough to teach, if the children behaved — the teachers at my school are very good. We're designing mini Minotaur mazes in DT, and me and my friends have created a video game we want to post off to Nintendo. It's called Skello, and we got the idea from a little Lego skeleton. Usually skeletons are bad guys, but in this game they're good, they save everyone from danger. They can't die because they're already dead, but if you lose all four of your hearts, you go down into this place we've called Boney Bits until your hearts load up again. We have a bad guy called Fire Beast. He has wings and can breathe fire and he can have children without getting married as we don't want any romance in it. I want to be an inventor when I grow up and I bet I'm not the only one.
　　Interviews by Hester Lacy. "Multiple Choice" series. *The Guardian*, 1 April 2008.

*Copyright Guardian News and Media Ltd., 2008.

The disjunct shown above between the responses of Malcolm Kay, a head teacher, Ann Morphew, a parent, and finally, the eight-year-old Charlie Ridey to technology, information, and *learning* will be the primary subject of this chapter.

In the general chat about the nature of children's reading, in mailing lists and at conventions, and in the academic conversation of the children's literary journals, lurks an insistence that children are uncomfortable with the idea that a book might teach them something, or that reading may be an educative experience. While this ties in with the predominance of the reluctant reader in the discussion, although interestingly not with the widespread concern for boys' reading, it also has much more deep-seated roots in the current anti-intellectual and anti-knowledge based cultures of America and the United Kingdom (I am in no position to comment on other countries) and specifically the two nations' divide between science and the arts, with its suspicion of the scientifically literate and societally approved evasion of mathematics and science (see the introduction to Natalie Angier's *The Canon*, 2007). This situation has clearly intensified since the 1950s, the heyday of Juvenile science fiction. In the United States and the United Kingdom, home-grown Ph.D. students in the sciences are short on the ground. In both nations, children drop science as fast as they can. Science careers are now rarely seen in children's and teens' books: "success" is usually framed within sports or the arts. This extends into science fiction: of the books published between 1985 and today, collected during this project, only Ann Halam and Janet McNaughton envisage a scientific or technical career for one of their protagonists (in *Siberia* and *The Secret Under My Skin*, respectively, both 2005) and none envisages the kinds of careers in economics, finance and computer work which have replaced science careers in adult sf. Furthermore, interest in the sciences and the values of science, which still shape the adult genre (even when its readers frequently bemoan the absence of scientific ingenuity), are missing from much modern sf directed at children and teens. Why?

My answer is a response to Natalie Angier's argument in *The Canon* and to the ideological position displayed in that clipping from *The Guardian*: adult ideas of what children are interested in, and more importantly what they are *not* interested in, are too often an imposition. Specifically, where many adults see science as difficult and needing to be framed "accessibly," most children — at least until they are socialized into the same mind-set in their teens — regard science and information about science as very exciting indeed. The kind of didacticism that repels adults is exactly where a ten-year-old's mind is at.

This chapter deals with two issues: the place and presence of scientific reasoning in sf for children and teens, and the role of information density. To get there however, I need to take you on a few by-ways, beginning with a discussion of what I think we can understand as the "sf-ready" child, moving on to a discussion of modern science pedagogy, and from there onto the popular science books available for children. Only then will I move onto the science fiction that has been produced for children and teens over the past thirty years and explore the degree to which it has responded to the current climate and/or to the demands of the genre which I outlined in chapter one. The role of this chapter is to support my argument that it is not enough to say "but children like this book which has been labeled science fiction or uses science fiction tropes" if the children who like and read science fiction probably would not.

The SF–Ready Child

In chapters eleven and twelve of Mary Shelley's *Frankenstein*, the monster lurks outside a house and — in true Romantic fashion — acquires an education. It is these chapters, and not those of the animated corpse, which truly place *Frankenstein* as the progenitor of sf. In these chapters Shelley argues for nurture not nature, and heralds the obsession of science fiction with the scientific and rationalized education. Shelley also, in these two short chapters, defines and creates what I have come to think of as the sf child, the child hungry for *knowledge*. To listen to some discussions of children's fiction, one would think that this kind of child cannot exist: *children do not read fiction to learn, they read to be entertained*. This is a stance that denies the kind of pleasure taken by many children in their fiction, and may help to explain the very strange orientation of the descriptions of sf books in the teen bibliographies I discussed earlier, so that Orson Scott Card's *Ender's Game* becomes a book about space battles rather than about philosophy (despite the endless pages of discussion of philosophy and politics by Ender's elder siblings). This attitude, not only misses the point of some books (and can serve to deny their quality by demanding they meet a rubric they did not set out to meet — the very accusation I have faced with this book), it denies the existence of some *children*. That is a very strong comment to make, so here is an example, which indicated to me for the first time how very strong is this attitude.

In 2006 there was a panel at the Medieval Studies conference at Kalamazoo on children's historical fiction. One of the panelists, the only man, talked about how children's historical fiction should teach history and if successful should inspire children to want to read more history. There appears—from later accounts— to have been some misunderstanding, with some members of the audience assuming that the panelist was arguing that books should teach moral lessons. This was not the case, but as it happens I am not sure that he would necessarily have objected to this, given that the man in question rather enjoyed the work of Charlotte M. Yonge as a child. A well-delivered moral lesson is a discussion of philosophy, not brainwashing. A bright child is as happy to question this as anything else, and many modern "issues" books—some of them wrapped in sf tropes—are just as moralizing, but with a rhetoric more acceptable to current rhetorical norms.[1]

When the account of the Kalamazoo panel arrived on the Child_Lit mailing list, contributors to the list fell over themselves to condemn it. Now, I am not the most attentive of wives, and it took a few exchanges before it occurred to me that my partner, the noted science fiction critic and medieval historian Edward James, had mentioned to me that he was on a panel about children's historical novels. Consequently, I knew that not only was he *not* discussing moral lessons, but that what was happening in the discussion was precisely the process I have been trying to describe in these pages. In the desire to insist that the reason that Edward James could argue for didactic, information-dense novels for children was because he "did not know anything about children's literature," the experts in the field were invalidating the reading experience of an entire set of children, children like Edward James and myself, and many people I know who went on to study history, or to read science fiction, who read Arthur Ransome's *Pigeon Post* (1932) for the gold-mining, Cynthia Harnett's *The Woolpack* (1951) for details of the wool trade, and D.S. Halacy's *Rocket Rescue* (1968) for career advice; the experience of children who read for informational, not emotional satisfaction, and might have been hard put to it to remember either the plot or the characters, but for whom that *information* was a source of desire and empowerment.

It is not enough to just state the above; we have to have some evidence about how typical the above response is. Does it exist at all? Does it exist among the adult sf reading community? The survey I undertook was not designed to answer this, because the question had not yet come up, but I was always interested in the degree to which the sf community was distinctive by its curiosity: anecdotal evidence from sf conventions suggested that this was a hallmark of the breed. I have frequently joked that there is no subject for which I could not only find a discussion panel, but also an audience. Science fiction fans seem to find *the world* intrinsically interesting. This did show up in the survey. Although to our surprise the non-fiction component of people's childhood reading was small, with only 4 percent reading more than 50 percent non-fiction, while 54 percent of the survey reported reading less than 20 percent non-fiction, this suggested that 42 percent were reading between 20 percent and 50 percent in the non-fiction field. It is not unreasonable to see this as perhaps one book in three. This cuts across both sexes, and is significantly different from the surveys of school-age children discussed in chapter two. Non-fiction clustered in biography, history and science. The second of these is interesting as although there are few sf historians, there are rather a lot of historians involved in sf and fantasy fandom (the Medieval Congress at Kalamazoo frequently has panels on sf and fantasy authors) and more than a handful of sf and fantasy authors with history degrees. Within these broad categories however the sheer range of topics covered would fill a library: handicrafts were as likely to turn up as sailing ships. The overall picture was of precisely the kind of eclecticism and curiosity that the anecdotal evidence suggested. These readers were, and saw themselves as, information gatherers.

The second element of the survey that seemed relevant were the indicators of what the readers claimed to be looking for. When aged 13 and under, what readers remembered looking for was setting, tropes, modes of engagement and qualities of narrative. Politics, ethics and worldview entered the picture after the age of 13. Of interest is that inventors and scientists as characters only really register for the under–13 age group. That is, they *do* register here; the activities of this group of people are not uninteresting. This is important because when we look at the most popular of the popular science books, the Horrible Science series, there is an underlying assumption running through the books that children are uninterested in science and invention and have to be tempted.

Running alongside this was that although a stated desire for information density was a small category, it was cited at low levels by *all* age groups, with a slightly higher score for the under–13s. Although there was a dip with regard to memories of teen desires (which coincided for a *male* desire for more sex in the books) the adult scores rose, and what seemed to change was the desire for a more sophisticated delivery. The actual direct interest in science was lower than we expected for adults in their current reading (only 5 percent) but 45 percent recall a strong interest from when they were under 13 and into their teens. As a supporting element it is worth noting that learning about other places and discovering the exotic was one of the highest scoring elements.

Before moving on I want to introduce one last piece of "evidence." The quotation marks are because this survey was even more unscientific than the reader survey; even the test I used is highly contested. The Myers-Briggs personality test is based on Jungian archetypes. The test is not in use within the psychology profession where it is regarded as tainted by the Foyer affect (people are too willing to agree with very general statements), but is very popular in business and anywhere where team-building is required, and appears regularly as a meme in LiveJournal communities. It tends to be well regarded by people who have experienced a number of personality tests, in part because it is amenable to change over time (life experience is recognized) and in part because it appears to explain both affinity groups, and team experiences. Furthermore it partially accounts for the Foyer affect by positing that what it shows is not necessarily who or what we are, but how we feel about who and what we are. I want to introduce you to one group within the test (which can be taken at http://www.humanmetrics.com/cgi-win/JTypes1.htm, should you be curious). The Myers-Briggs groups people into one of 16 types, each codified by four letters: I/E; N/S; T/F; J/P. Introversion or Extroversion;

Intuitor or Sensor; Thinker or Feeler; Judger or Perceiver. Each of these is much more about how one feels one should do things, and the introvert/extrovert category is about where one feels energized (so that a very outgoing person can be an introvert if they are exhausted by large groups, while an extrovert may be very quiet). Unsurprisingly, readers generally tend to score as introverts, but not always. I intend to ignore the I/E split and focus on the remaining three letters.

In the wider world, the NTJ grouping is the minority. It stands for intuitor (better translated as a synthesizer, a pattern maker), a thinker (who prefers to respond to "logic" rather than feelings), and a judger (someone who likes to make decisions). INTJ, which adds introversion, makes up 3 percent of the tested general population in the U.S. This is about values. Someone who scores as a Thinker is someone who believes that thinking is the way to approach life: it does not necessarily mean they are good at it.

As there has been no mass testing of science fiction fans, I ran a quick and dirty poll by asking LiveJournal "friends"[2] to take the test at humanometrics. com over a 24-hour period. A self-selecting affinity group with myself — a well-known sf fan — as the node, all but five identified as science fiction fans (and those five are readers of science fiction) of the 123 respondents, 29 percent were INTJ, another 16 percent were INFJ while ENFJ and ENTJ (the extrovert expression) took 12 percent.[3] This is an almost direct reversal of the U.S. national trend.[4]

The INTJ personality, as outlined by the Myers-Briggs categories, places emphasis on the desire for information density. "INTJs' ... self-confidence, sometimes mistaken for simple arrogance by the less decisive, is actually of a very specific rather than a general nature; its source lies in the specialized knowledge systems that most INTJs start building at an early age."[5] Perhaps pure coincidence but in 1984 the science fiction editor David Hartwell wrote, "Science fiction people tend not to be well rounded but rather multiple specialists."[6] INTJs are pragmatists ("does this work?") and system builders, and want the emotional world (and other people) to *make sense*.[7] Joe Butt's analysis of the type is "Others may see what is and wonder why; INTJs see what might be and say 'Why not?!' Paradoxes, antinomies, and other contradictory phenomena aptly express these intuitors' amusement at those whom they feel may be taking a particular view of reality too seriously. INTJs enjoy developing unique solutions to complex problems."[8] Taken as a whole the INTJ personality type is one that revels in *information gathering*. Bill Watterson's *Calvin and Hobbes* captures this beautifully, with Calvin's refusal to learn anything in school, but his in-depth grasp of the latest taxonomical systems for dinosaurs. A perfect example of the kind of fiction that fits this "type" is Kim Stanley Robinson's much admired *Years of Rice and Salt* (2002). Apart from history and geography, the author is happy to take several pages to instruct the reader how to separate gold from other metals. This level of information density is less evident in science fiction for children of any age, or written in any period. Yet cognitive development scientists and educationalists increasingly point to the avidity with which many young children approach information acquisition.

Modern Pedagogy and Information Acquisition in the Child

Science pedagogy is another area which hosts elephants in its living room. Perhaps the largest of these elephants is simply the degree to which science pedagogy has proved recursive. If one were to conjure a popular history of science pedagogy it would look like this: "In the beginning was the fact, and rote learning, and the teaching of science to an elite, and science was boring and children hated it and no one wanted to be scientists. Then, on that golden day, science discovered the child, science became oriented to the child, exploration was on the agenda, children's imaginations were captured, all children took science and a new age of learning and scientific achievement was born."

I am being sarcastic, but there are reasons for this sarcasm. When I began reading in this area, I expected a relatively linear development towards modern science education and pedagogy. What I found instead were endless loops, spirals and *a priori* assumptions. Just to give an example, the notion of the child as investigator, what comes to be known as the "constructivist" method, appears to have been reinvented — or at least pronounced as new — several times. The first mention of it, for example, is sponsored by the British Association and particularly in the writings of a Professor H.E. Armstrong in the 1920s (Brown, 1930, 30).

The main areas of contention are: what scientific thinking is, who science is for, what is it for, how to inspire students, and finally, and most contentiously, how do children learn and what are they capable of learning? As we shall see, the same ideas were reinvented, and presented as new, continuously.

Definitions of scientific thinking have overwhelmingly focused on the "scientific method," usually understood as *observation, recording* and *analysis*. Criticisms of this focused on the problem that science is not always susceptible to "logical" explanation, and second on the tendency of children to report the results that they knew were "correct" rather than what they saw. Both of these turn up as criticism of too much "experiment" in class (Wellington, 2002: 62). What no textbook that I saw included — no matter what age or ability range it was aimed at — was that the idea behind the scientific method was to construct hypotheses for a general explanation of (aspects of) the world which are *susceptible* to disproof. This idea does begin to emerge in the early Schools Council work in the 1960s, but it took until the *Beyond 2000* report of 1998 to become embedded as a crucial concept in the curriculum (Millar and Osbourne: 58). Ironically, it is the development of independent curricula in science and public understanding which seems to have supported this trend, not science curricula themselves.

The importance of the "method" notion of science is that it connected to the evident need on the part of many science educators to defend the notion of science. To the ears of an outsider, this may seem a little odd, but for science educators in the 1930s, science was still earning its place in the classroom. As late as the 1950s science was what the less able children in British grammar schools were encouraged to study; the brightest took classical languages. Entry to the upper echelons of the British Civil Service was almost entirely secured by a classical education.[9] Prior to the pressures exerted by two world wars and a cold war, science in both the UK and in America was slightly infra-dig. In the UK, classics led the field, followed perhaps by law. In the U.S., it was classics, law, and later business studies. Science was technical. It was for boys (and some girls) who were *practical*. Class and gender prejudices overwhelmingly determined which subjects children studied. Ormerod and Duckworth's summary of research from the 1960s and 1970s suggested that while boys from professional and skilled homes were equally represented in science, in arts the boys from professional homes predominated. For girls the situation was reversed; girls from higher-class homes were the more likely to study science at university (Ormerod: 101).

In the 1960s science was resituated as a subject for the very bright. Shortly after, a complex argument emerged about "extending" the science curriculum to the less able, without ever actually pausing to consider that science had once been understood as for the *less* intelligent because it was practical. No one in the UK, for example, ever thought to teach the grammar school curriculum to children in a secondary modern (the working-class technical schools) and assess the results. The assumption made — on no evidence whatsoever — was that the curriculum as it stood was too hard. The emphasis was entirely on reducing the complexity of ideas to be taught.[10] Hubert Dyasi, in a 2006 report for the New York City Board of Education, is still complaining of these assumptions, but repeats them himself with the statement, "For science for all children to be successfully implemented, however, inclusive quality pedagogical approaches are essential, approaches that are authentic not just to the nature and content of science, but also to children's diverse cultural and personal strengths" (89). The *only* exception I have found is a book by Gordon Nunn, published in 1951. This book is remarkable for two things: it does not assume students will be either disinterested or incapable; it does not replace "rote learning" with "experimentalism" (an issue I will tackle later), but instead makes the equation between "abstract" and "vocational." Nunn argued that the technical colleges should be providing vocationally-oriented science, for students in building. "The science which they do in school should be based on statics and hydrostatics, the chemistry of building materials, and the study of chemical reactions involved in such processes as cement manufacture, the drying of plaster of

Paris and paint and the corrosion of materials" (18). For textiles, "the simple study of fibers with the study of the physics and chemistry of fibers. Mechanics would also be useful since those who work in textile factories have to deal with machines. An introduction to the knowledge of color and dying would be helpful" (19). The emphasis is on motivation and relevance. There are many reasons to disapprove of this, but it generates a very different kind of teaching in which interest and specialization allows depth without a simplification of the curriculum *per se.*

Nunn's book leads us in the direction of the next issue: how science was and is taught, both in terms of method and content. A constant thread running through science education literature can be summarized as: *in the bad old days science was taught by rote, and was teacher rather than discussion centered.* There are several issues here; the first is that I can find no evidence that teaching "by rote" (if we are to interpret as "rote" the chanting aloud of scientific "facts") was ever in favor in twentieth-century science pedagogy. Rather, there is a constant emphasis on the need for experiment and demonstration. The debate actually centers on when children should be given factual information, and how much they should receive. And here we must turn to Constructivism and to the work of Piaget.

There are two "extremes" in this debate, although I will try also to explain the middle ground, and quite quickly one realizes that science fiction is traditionally quite firmly on one side in terms of world-building and the building of knowledge base, but firmly on the other side when it comes to narrative strategy.

On the one side is the behaviorist strategy: "children must be taught." On the other are the "constructivists": "children must experiment and find out for themselves." The first approach tends to be thought of as conservative, the second is associated with liberals. Both approaches are allied to Piaget.

Piaget argued two things: children are natural observers, they look, they analyze, they come to conclusions. Children are, however, limited by their cognitive development; they do not achieve concrete reasoning skills until they are around six or seven, they do not achieve abstract reasoning until around puberty (although later commentators point out that many adults seem to lack this ability, see Bliss, 159). Most current researchers in child development are comfortable with these general observations but argue that the cut-off points are not absolute and that a child may develop abstract reasoning skills in one area but not another. Both the behaviorists and the constructivists accept these points and regard themselves as heirs of Piaget. The differences are in the weight they give these points and the order in which teaching takes place.

Although this is simplifying greatly, behaviorists—or advocates of "directed learning"—are more likely to present a theory and then demonstrate, through experiment and exploration, how we can see this theory in action. Constructivists are more likely to present an experiment, encourage exploration, and then explain the theory. The difference seems minor, but they contain quite profound differences about the nature of children and of science, and the irony is that the confidence in children does not lie where one might expect.

Constructivism argues that children are naturally curious, and naturally capable of problem solving, *but* and this is crucial, there is an underlying argument amongst constructivists that children are put off if information is delivered from above. The 1997 Nuffield Guide to Primary Science (under–11s) for example contains this comment: "We are not suggesting that teachers need understanding so that scientific ideas can be taught didactically. That could only lead to rote learning and would be severely damaging to children's confidence in their own ability to make sense of their experiences. One thing we know is that the only way children develop ideas they fully understand is through their own thinking. Teachers cannot do the thinking for them, neither can they short-circuit the learning process by presenting the key ideas for children to learn" (4). The delivery of information is *explicitly* conflated with rote-learning.

Constructivists seem to ignore the extent to which children adore the acquisition of "facts," whether through endless visits to dinosaur exhibits or the collection of baseball cards or Top Trumps trading cards.[11] Constructivists, for all their professed faith in the abilities of children, actually demonstrate very little when it comes to estimating children's powers of comprehension. Here is an example of the extreme constructivist position.

Lazer Goldberg's *Teaching Science to Children* (1970) begins with an anecdote: an eight-year-old child, observing acoustic tiles being put up and being told by the fitter what they are for, asks the author if he could use these tiles to build a box and he further asks, if he placed in it a ringing bell, would it hold the sound. Receiving an affirmative, his follow-up question is: when the bell stopped ringing, if the box was opened, would the sound come out having been "saved up." Here is the answer Goldberg provides:

> It was a stunning question. All that sound cannot just disappear. It must register its presence somewhere. I was tempted to give an impromptu lecture on energy conversions and the conservation laws, but I resisted the temptation.
> "When children practice on their instruments in the music room, can you hear them all over the school?" I asked.
> "No." He shook his head.
> "Why not?"
> "I guess the music gets used up," he replied, raising his shoulders.
> "I guess the ringing of the bell also gets used up," I said.
> The boy clearly was not satisfied. I showed him a little booklet on sound. He thumbed through it and took it with him. If the puzzle he had discovered proved to be sufficiently compelling, he would find something to do about it. Perhaps he might even build the box and check the results for himself. I knew he would pursue the problem, to the extent of his interest and ability. The school would provide encouragement, time and materials [4].

The complacency of this response—and Goldberg's subsequent query; "What are the conditions of learning that will encourage children to observe the events in their common experience and to note the uncommon, puzzling qualities about them? What can adults do, or refrain from doing, to cultivate children's devotion to questions...?"—is just astonishing. Goldberg does not recognize that he lied to the child, that he prevented the child from receiving the information that might have led to other thoughts, and that crucially, he withheld "the giants' shoulders" that most scientists understand supports their own work. Science proceeds by *not* requiring each generation to recapitulate the discoveries of their predecessors but instead to accept that they are (mostly) true until proven otherwise.

The constructivists seem to be operating from Rousseau's notion of the "natural" child. They also seem to be operating in a pre–Newtonian world in which all science is "transparent," the world easily observable, easily decoded, and this despite constructivists' awareness that children come to school with myth-narratives about the world already in place, that they have, in fact, observed and got it wrong. A common "example" cited for constructivist education is that a child introduced to a skeleton of a dog should not be told what it is, but should instead be allowed to work it out, and specifically should be allowed to reach the wrong answer.[12] The theory behind this is that as a child acquires more knowledge, they will revisit and rework their ideas (Chaille, 41). There is no evidence in the research I have read to suggest that this is the case. Rather, the evidence suggests that children have a great deal of trouble rejecting old ideas and (as in matters of appropriate behavior or language choice) are much more likely to run ideas in parallel, one for school, one for internal use.[13]

The dog skeleton is a useful experiment to consider when discussing the behaviorist or directed learning approach to science education. Derided as "top down" this might more properly be described as "leg up." Where the constructivist might say "look at this skeleton, how do you work out what it is?," the behaviorist is more likely to say, "these are the features of the dog skeleton, compare it to these others, what are the differences? Can you work out what that might indicate?" On a wider scale, the behaviorist is likely to offer the general theory first, and then an experiment. The difference is significant: the constructivist is quite likely to teach the child an experiment-specific idea. The experiment is the center of focus; there is no reason at all for children to generalize outwards. The behaviorist approach valorizes the total theory, the experiment is a demonstration of a wider generalization. In the behaviorist approach (which is much less theorized) three arguments are in play: the first is that science *cannot* begin from first principles each time anew, and scientific progress is only possible because we accept (until proved otherwise) the validity of the experiments performed by others; the second is that we are not all Newton and that to expect children to make the leap that he made after twenty years of mathematics is unreasonable; and the third is that, as with reading and reading comprehension, there is a certain "backwards bootstrapping." It matters not that the child might not have understood the theory or the explanation, s/he would have left knowing what it was s/he needed to learn about. One day, returning to the issue with greater knowledge, it would all seem transparent. To the behaviorist partially comprehended information is not off-putting, it is tantalizing.

Despite the arguments of both sides it is unclear whether children as a group respond better to one or another mode of teaching.[14] Education experiments are notoriously biased by enthusiasm for the new and increased resources. Typically (although there are exceptions), the enhanced results of any new method peter out after about three years, both as enthusiasm wanes, and as the constituency of "deliverers" extends beyond the enthusiastic and motivated.[15] The second problem is that this may be a case of different children responding to different methods, and while this may have something to do with those nebulous concepts of interest and aptitude, other factors shape the results. In a summary of science education research Omerod and Duckworth cited Jensen's 1973 report. Jensen argued that while there was little to choose in the results of memory or associative learning skills between middle-class and working-class students, because Discovery (constructivist) Learning requires the command of an investigative vocabulary and practice in discussing the abstract, or making deductions from data and the deriving of explanatory theories: "No conceivable method of teaching could be better calculated to favor the middle-class child."[16] Crucially, discovery learning may require children knowing how to ask questions (even being willing to ask questions), a facility which is highly cultural.

The third problem is the degree to which ideology influences the research. Ronald G. Good's otherwise exemplary *How Children Learn Science: Conceptual Development and Implications for Teaching* (1977) resorts to assertion when he outlines his conditions for the teaching of science and his definition of the role of the teacher, arguing for example that the Lecturer and Question and Answer approach cannot deal with wide variations in children's development. Good argues that the role of Activity Facilitator is the most compatible with the development of theoretical models, but does not consider how this might leave the most able children in a large classroom unstretched (220).[17] Neither models are illustrated with classroom practice.

Although Good is an extreme example, too much of the research on science teaching does not actually prove what the researcher claim it proves, a point made forcefully by Michael R. Vitale and Nancy R. Romance in their 2006 examination of education research (47). Specifically, while there is plenty of evidence that there are issues with long-term recall, when children experience directed or "top down" teaching (Burnett, 93–96), there is little evidence that constructivism has better results (as the assessment is also frequently changed to accommodate the method, it is hard to compare the assertions that have been made)[18] and the better results it does have aren't always in the area of recall, which remains an important asset in cumulative science education (Carin, 36); second, many other subjects also know that their subject will be forgotten the moment the classroom is left behind. For some reason, this causes far more concern in science and math than elsewhere.

There is a desperate anxiety among science educationalists to target their subject towards people who will not become specialists in science. We can see the concern in the degree to which so many texts begin with a discussion of what science education is for. A not untypical example (paraphrased) runs:

- a basis for understanding and coping with their lives, and for understanding "the applications and effects of science in society"
- learning about science, the concepts and methods of scientific enquiry and what science is like as an activity
- contribute to their intellectual development
- the curriculum should address the needs of future specialists [Amos, 4]

Missing is any indication that science should provoke, and cater to, curiosity. Millar and Osborne write:

Society, as we have noted above, does need a steady flow of people wishing to become science specialists. But this is a route which only a minority of the 5–16 population will follow, and it should not therefore be allowed to influence unduly the form and content of the science curriculum offered to the majority....

...

school science should aim to produce a populace who are comfortable, competent and confident with scientific and technical matters and artifacts. The science curriculum should provide sufficient scientific knowledge and understanding to enable students to read simple newspaper articles on science, and to follow TV programmes on new advances in science with interest. Such an education should enable them to express an opinion on important social and ethical issues with which they will increasingly be confronted. It will also form a viable basis, should the need arise, for retraining in work related to science or technology in their later careers [9].

Only at key stage 4 (14-year-olds) do they argue that there should be a clear split between science for scientific literacy and science for training. There is no clear indication as to how children interested in the latter, and the evidence is that interest in science stabilizes between 11 and 13 (Ormerod, 40–41), will be kept interested within a "public understanding of science" curriculum.

Furthermore, science educationalists seem to have lost sight of the fact that while education is about opening doorways, not all children have to go through every door. As with my argument about sf for children in the introduction there seems to be a genre mismatch, with an attempt to reshape a junior genre for children who would not want to read the adult genre anyway. However, the situation is not that simple. Attempts to increase the levels of directed learning and the information density of the English and Welsh curriculum in the 1990s,[19] and to concentrate on the "likely scientists" proved disastrous: enrollment in upper-level science classes continued to decline, if anything, at a more rapid rate.

Challenges to the success of science in the classroom may have very little to do with the curricula: educators run up against the difficulty that the science curriculum accumulates. Whereas in other subjects, topics may be dropped, in physics the basics remain the same, but complexity extends into future research with the result that school science looks ever more archaic. Mike Coles reported, "During the definition of a core for A level physics syllabuses in 1992, a commentator speaking for the Institute of Physics felt moved to remark that it was a pity a core for advanced physics education in the late twentieth century contained no twentieth-century physics" (Coles, 89). For many children, science seems unconnected to the world of work opportunities that they see around them. Few of today's children in either the UK or the USA have contact with raw materials industries. In the creative and service industries that now form the cultural backbone of the USA and UK, science is less visible. As Millar and Ormerod point out, "Increasing technological sophistication is reducing, rather than increasing, the need for people to understand the principles on which devices and artifacts are based ... fewer and fewer repair jobs can be carried out by non-experts" (Millar and Osborne, 11). Even were we to decide that the purpose of a science curriculum was to produce computer-game designers, the current state of technology is such that most pupils could pull "design your own game" kits from the internet, and proceed without any scientific knowledge. The disappearance of the "make your own" culture may make it ever more difficult to sustain interest in entry-level science.

There is also the difficulty of where to find science teachers. As fewer people continue with science, there are fewer to teach it. But it is also a function of changes in society. There are now far more opportunities available for working-class students: teacher training looks less attractive when a science degree is welcomed by many non-science related businesses. Furthermore, the huge expansion of education in the late nineteenth and early twentieth century may have been possible only because of the concurrent existence of the early feminist movement, the great loss of men during the First World War and few other opportunities for women (see Nicholson, *Singled Out*, 2007). The result is that the potential pool of enthusiastic science teachers has shrunk enormously, and whatever the merits of constructivist and directed learning, one of the very few correlations regularly validated in research is the enthusiasm and knowledge of the teacher. Oddly, this is very rarely mentioned directly. Only the Nuffield Council insists on its curricula being accompanied by in-service training.

Constructivism is popular, I think, because it appeases the anxiety of the tutor by turning science into entertainment and reduces the perception of coercion. Challenges to this notion of coerced interest are unusual. Richard E.

Mayer's forceful advocacy of guided discovery learning, "Should There Be a Three-Strikes Rule Against Pure Discovery Learning?," is relatively rare in the pedagogic material, although reports on practice in the classroom suggest that guided discovery has dominated for more than seventy years. When challenges do arise, they don't usually come from the classroom. A U.S. television program, *Mr. Wizard*, started in 1951 and produced tie-in books and a Mr. Wizard's Science Club, with around 50,000 members who received mimeographed experiments. Mr. Wizard (Don Herbert) wrote, "My experience is that most children aren't really uncomfortable with science — at least, not the kind of science I do on my programs— because they are used to learning things. But it is different with adults. It is as though adults don't know how to learn any more; they assume anything that's even the least bit "instructional" must be for children.... I think it is when children reach their teens that they start to pick up the adult prejudice against learning" (Hays, 39).

Similarly, Elaine Levenson, a scientist who made a practice of visiting primary schools, wrote in the preface to an activity book of her experience at one school, where the first round of questions— about career prospects and other non-science matters— was clearly devised by the teacher:

> I finally said, "Are there any questions you always wanted to ask a scientist? I cannot promise to answer all of them — maybe there are no answers yet. We keep learning new things every day. What I cannot answer I will try to find out by asking other scientists."
> They sat for a moment in silence. Then the first hand went up and a small boy said, "Why is it that every time just before I start a fight, I sweat?" I answered that, and the next question was, "I watch preying mantises eat some leaves and he looks like it is good. But when I try chewing those leaves I get sick. Why is that?" Another asked, "Are we sort of a sack of blood? It seems like any place you get cut blood pours out. What good is that?" And so the questions came —for nearly two hours [52].

Levenson believes in children's ability to absorb complexity until they are ready to revisit it. So do the behaviorists and so do many writers of fiction for children. Diana Wynne Jones has said: "I never worry about putting in things that are not within children's capacities, because I don't think this matters. I think it is very good for children to notice that there's something going on that they don't understand.... Children are used to not knowing, and therefore they make sure that they *do* know and remember" (Jones, 162). This attitude — rightly or wrongly — is entirely absent from science pedagogy. But it does exist in the world of popular science.

The Idea of the Child in Popular Science Books

While science as it is taught in schools focuses on the experimental or constructivist method, for children interested in science (or encouraged to be interested in science) there is a thriving market in popular science which appears to have far more in common with the behaviorists.[20] As literacy rates rose in the 1920s and night school, correspondence courses and mechanics institutes became common ways for working people to extend their education, a number of commercial firms took on the task of providing scientific education to those who (as we saw in the previous section) were regarded as scientifically ineducable by the education establishment. This might range from part-works published in magazines such as *Popular Mechanics*, which published at least one collection of its articles (from the same plates) as *Radio for the Millions*, to the *Observer* guides of the 1970s and 1980s. For the young there were the Ladybird books, with exciting titles such as *British Wild Flowers, The Weather, Butterflies, Moths and Other Insects* and *The Story of Our Rocks and Minerals*.

What strikes the reader is how information-dense these texts are and how demanding. *Radio for the Millions* (1945) takes no quarter: it explains what each component does, and the theory of resistance, in tiny print on cramped pages, full of product codes and hand-drawn circuit diagrams. The *Observer* guides were small, pocket-sized books, ideal for children's hands and crammed full of statistics on everything from trees and insects to shipping and weather forecasting.[21] There is no analysis, no attempt to make the material user-friendly. The *Ladybird* books, aimed at around the 7-year age group, were structured around double-page spreads of a page of text, and a page of illustration, on topics such as sedimentary rocks or asbestos, or on the habitat and lifestyle of the wildlife in question.[22] The emphasis is very firmly on the accumulation of knowledge.

As the surveys suggested that popular science books were an important element in the grooming of sf readers, I want to take a brief look at modern popular science books. In order to avoid prejudgment through selection, I'm going to discuss the shortlist and winners of the Junior section of the Aventis prize for popular science writing for the years 2001, 2002 and 2005.[23] The shortlist for this prize is selected by a jury of adults. The winner is selected by a jury of children and tends to be biased towards the titles for younger readers.

Certain patterns stood out. The first was how information-dense these books were. David Burnie's *The Kingfisher Illustrated Dinosaur Encyclopedia* (2001), Chris Maynard's *Bugs: A Close Up View of the Insect World* (2001), and Robin Kerrod and Sharon Holgate's *The Way Science Works* (2002), presented closely packed pages of *facts*. Even the books for younger readers, such as Mike Goldsmith's *Dead Famous: Inventors and Their Bright Ideas* (2002), and Nick Arnold's *Horrible Science: Suffering Scientists* (2002*)* are packed full of information. Nicola Morgan's *Blame My Brain: The Amazing Teenage Brain* (2005) managed to combine social advice with neuroscience.[24] Richard Platt's *Forensics* (2005) was rather out of date, but summarized the basics of forensic science. Nicki Greenberg's *It's True, Squids Suck!* (2005), covers everything from the anatomy to the neuroscience of the squid family. Johnny Ball's *Think of a*

Number (2005) gives the history of mathematics, presents mathematical lems and demonstrates how math is useful. Only two books resist information density: Kate Petty's and Jennie Maisels' *Global Garden* (2005), with its pop-up format, which assumes either that adults will be able to explain everything, or is not too worried if children don't recognize the various things that appear,[25] and Georgina Andrews' and Kate Knighton's *100 Science Experiments* (2005), to which I will return.

The majority of these popular science books defy the idea common to the pedagogy that children resist factual information, that they need hands-on experience to engage them. Across these books there were different ideas about what a "fact-filled" book should achieve, and sometimes there appeared to be an internal conflict as to what the author thought was interesting and their *a priori* assumptions about their audience. Nick Arnold's *Suffering Scientists*, for example, uses the appalling things scientists went through — both physical harm and political persecution — to explore the development of the scientific method, but one aspect of his jokiness is constantly to say, "You wouldn't want to do that, would you?" The book ends: "And even when it is horrible, it is horribly fascinating, amazing and even exciting. And although science lessons can be boring — real science is never boring" (224). While it is clear this is meant to be ironic, to encourage children into science by making it seem cool and something adults wouldn't want them to do, there remains a note of disparagement.

The most common strategy was to assume that huge numbers of facts, assembled together with excellent pictures, would in themselves arouse curiosity. David Burnie's *Dinosaur Encyclopedia* offers incredible detail and clearly linked ideas and information, showing how the latter led to the former, not the other way around. Each double page spread covers a topic. Each page contains glossy painted illustrations, continuous prose and small "enhancement" boxes with additional material. Process is described to explain why "factual material" is evidence for the claims being made. Each page works to demonstrate how information is a jigsaw puzzle that is consequently in the process of throwing up *new* questions. So, for example, in "A Question of Size" (84–85), Burnie explains gigantism as driven partly by predation (larger animals survive, but larger predators are also more successful) and the way in which the larger dinosaurs' digestive system worked, which put a premium on the generation of heat from larger and larger stomachs. However, gigantism is stalled by "increasing difficulties mating and laying eggs" and the strain put on the heart by the *geometric* increase in mass.

> To visualise how this happened, imagine three "dinosaurs" shaped like cubes, with sides 1cm, 5cm and 10cm long. The second dinosaur is only five times as long as the first, but is weight is 125 times as great (the result of multiplying 5x5x5). The third dinosaur is 10 times as long, which means that it weighs a thousand times as much as the first. Once sauropods reached lengths of about 20m, each additional metre meant a jump in weight of over a tonne — a tremendous burden that still had to be supported by just four legs.

The strength of a leg depends on its cross-sectional area, rather than its volume. This means that if an animal gets larger while keeping the same overall shape, its weight outstrips its strength, so its legs are put under greater and greater stress. Sauropods coped with this by modifying their leg bones, and by keeping bending to a minimum, but in the end it would have been weight, rather than anything else, that brought their growth to a halt.

Burnie succeeds in demonstrating the openness of science and the degree to which one element of knowledge rests on many others, that knowledge is an expanding jigsaw, not independent particles. Burnie recreates the process of following the information trail, into "experimental thought." Instead of "do this, then do that," it is "think of this, then think of that." The irony is that this is missing from one of the books that claims to be precisely to be about getting children to think scientifically or to think as scientists.

Georgina Andrews' and Kate Knighton's *100 Experiments* is a great book to occupy children. It is full of games. What it is not full of is experiments, and woe betide the parent of a "why?" child who does not themselves have a scientific education. Each double-page spread contains an "experiment," which consists of a list of instructions, followed by an explanation. The problem is that the explanations never go far enough, so that what a child is doing is practical mechanics rather than science. Here is a typical example.

> 1. Soaking blotting paper in red cabbage, then using the strips to test vinegar, bicarbonate of soda and water, and just water. Here is the explanation.
> *What's Going On?*
> The indicator papers change colour when you mix them with an acid or an alkali. Acids always turn the paper red as an acid and alkali detector. Vinegar is an acid and bicarbonate of soda is an alkali. Water is neutral — it is neither acid nor alkali — and so does not make the paper change colour. Try testing other things such as fizzy drinks, tea or milk.

There is no explanation at all of why any of the above happens. What exactly *is* the role of that cabbage? That is not an explanation. It is a description and it says the same thing at least two, if not three times. It is a brilliant example of pre–Newtonian science in which each observation is discrete to that set of ingredients. There are examples of more thoroughgoing explanations: one that does work, and rather shows up the others, is an explanation of meringue which at least mentions that albumen is made of chains and has a diagram to show the way that, after whisking, the chains uncurl and trap bubbles. But for the most part, Andrews and Knighton seem to be with Lazer Goldberg in their assumption that telling children partial or "friendly" stories will aid their understanding of the world.

Only two of the shortlisted titles manage to combine both information density and experimentalism successfully. Robin Kerrod and Dr. Sharon Ann Holgate's *The Way Science Works* is a superb example of science as process. With each topic we are given the history of the "discovery," have it explained in terms of the theory, are given a practical example, and provided with an experiment to do. Each experiment is explained in clear terms which match the theory that has been offered; the experiment is not presented as "specific" in its results but as an illustration to the theory. Johnny Ball's *Think of a Number* is a very delayed tie-in to his 1980s television show, and the layout of the pages and the language of the text match the exuberance of that broadcast. Each page is dense with information and diagrams, each topic is followed by examples, and the examples are followed by numbers. I'm not sure I can do justice to Ball's book, but to give one example, Ball entraps the child's imagination about numbers in one double-page spread which asks the reader to imagine a world without numbers by using news headlines: a lottery of colored balls, a game with "lots and lots of goals," a high-jump record "a bit higher than the last record." But the book itself is astonishingly information-dense: there are sections on the history of numbers and math, there is instruction on geometry, and excellent pages on patterns in numbers such as the Fibonacci sequence and Pascal's triangle. It expects children to get excited and it deliberately provides more than they could possibly manage (excepting the odd genius) on each page. Ball, like Kerrod and Holgate, has reversed the processes advocated by the constructivists: all three present theory and information, followed by exploration — a guided tour, not a magical mystery tour. What is unnerving about so much of the pedagogy is that alongside celebrating the child's capacity to explore, there is a continual thread of pessimism: science is difficult, most children won't be able to cope. In contrast, Ball, Kerrod, Holgate, and Burnie demonstrate enormous faith in children's capacity.

I want to leave this section with one last thought: almost all of the books discussed here are for children and young teens. Only Nicola Morgan's book can be considered for the older age group. It is as if, as Natalie Angier observed, general interest in science is seen as an occupation for children: teens are expected either to be interested in science and hence studying science and reading popular science books intended for adults, or to be a lost cause. It is a pattern strikingly like the one found in science fiction for children and teens.

Information Density in Science Fiction for Children and Teens

One book which captures a sense both of information density and systematization is Graham Oakley's *Henry's Quest* (1986). A picture book, *Henry's Quest* has to be read on twin tracks: words and pictures do not reinforce each other. Instead, the words relate a fairytale quest narrative, in a quiet, demotic voice, while the pictures reveal a science fiction story. Information density is a necessary part of the interpretation of the future; it teaches the value of accumulated knowledge and its application to analysis through the required reading strategy.

In a small village kingdom surrounded by trees, the King declares a quest for petrol. The one who finds it will marry his eldest daughter. Henry, a shepherd, takes up the quest with his donkey and travels many miles. He helps merchants fight off bandits, meets people and arrives in a fabulous city where the Emperor fetes him, and a minstrel tries to embroil him in a coup. Henry is the innocent, clueless as to the politics which go on all around him. When the Emperor accidentally sets light to the petrol store Henry is lauded as a hero by the minstrel who deposes the Emperor and takes his place. The minstrel sends Henry home with more petrol. In the written story, Henry gradually catches onto the corruption of the Emperor, and realizes that the usurper is as bad. This is done subtly. We aren't told every step in Henry's reasoning, but instead are asked to work out what he has worked out. The reader is an active participant in the story. This element of reasoning is optional to the written narrative but vital to the pictorial narrative.

Oakely's pictures are astonishingly dense. Lurking in almost every picture is a hint: in the first illustration there is junk in the woods. In the second, a jousting match takes place among chicken coops made from cars and televisions, and one of the jousters wears a motorcycle helmet. The symbols on the shields of knights allude to mundane jobs such as pie-making or shepherding. Over the page, a sign for Boots the Chemist has been overwritten to read "Tom Boots and Son" and then overwritten again with the word "herbalist." When we first see Henry, he sits in a wood, but one of the trees is a vegetation-covered electricity pylon. Oakley demonstrates a rare sense of the way the historical landscape accumulates. To a historian, all television historical dramas look slightly wrong, because they "dress" the people and places absolutely of the moment. But of course culture is not like that. Look around your own home: note that plywood door which replaced the old panel doors sometime in the 1960s, which you have been regretting ever since. The 1930s fireplace surrounding the 1990s gas coal-effect fire in the 1880s house. Reality is made up of this kind of density. Oakley's science-fiction world is constructed from the lingering past: one of the most beautiful pictures is of a grounded British Airways airplane turned into an Anglo-Saxon style long-house. On the facing page a woman milks a cow in an overgrown petrol station. Oakley presents all sorts of ideas about change, scarce resources, and a culture of re-use and ingenuity. It is this informational density which typifies science fiction.

At one time, information density, and the expectation that children should learn from the fictive worlds they perused was the norm. Girls' stories from the 1920s and 1930s seem determined to teach girls everything from herbalism and laundry to basic French and German. Historical novels, as I pointed out at the beginning of the chapter, expected children to take an interest in the structures of guilds, the creation of pigment for medieval manuscripts and the wool trade. Later examples of both of these genres (from the 1960s onwards) are much more concerned with social interaction. The same expectations, and the same change can be seen in science fiction.

Alan Chapman's 1922 book, *The Radio Boys' First Wireless,* is not, strictly speaking, science fiction. It is about the present, the technology is recognizable, and the speculation extends bare months into the future. But the early history of science fiction is very bound up with the early history of radio (through the sf editor and radio amateur, Hugo Gernsback), and this book offers both the sense of wonder (at the idea of a music concert heard from many miles away) and precisely the kind of information density ("science through scientification") which Gernsback advocated.

The story is set in a learning culture. *The Radio Boys* valorizes the reader who might be expecting to read it. Intellectual interest is never presented as a social handicap. On the contrary, it is the jocks who are disparaged: Buck teases the boys for believing in the possibilities of radio. "The whole thing is bunk, if you ask me," replied Buck with the confidence that so often goes with ignorance" (12). To which Joe retorts, "Anyone has a right to have a club foot or a hunched back or cross eyes, but he does not usually go round boasting of them" (15). There is a *two-page* explanation —from an adult— about how to build a crystal radio set. The reader is expected to read through this as avidly as the boys are depicted listening to it (59–61). Supporting this is the fact that the technology is fundamentally visible: you can follow every word with only a basic grasp of physics, and all things can be built with the contents of the shed. The ability of the boys to affect the materiality of their world is much greater: there is the ubiquity of useable material and the willingness of their parents to let them use the machinery and sharp tools. The boys make the radio in their basement and the families happily hand over paraffin wax, they drill holes and use saws. I am not at all convinced that this kind of scenario is plausible in modern science fiction unless it were to be thrown into a survivalist future which reconstructed a make-do-and-mend society: of the modern sf books for the market only Philip Reeve and Julie Bertagna construct this kind of world, and mostly this kind of development mechanics is left to adults. In *City of Ember* (2003), Jeanne DuPrau is unable even to conceive of a world of re-use, her underground community is running out of manufactured goods, and there is no sense of the kind of ingenuity we see in *Radio Boys.*

During the 1950s you can see an extension of these forms of density (information; transparent and replicable technology; cultural expectation of both curiosity and competence) replicated in the "career book" genre. These lightly fictionalized tales had as their purpose to socialize young people into the workplace and were heavy on the details of the job concerned.[26] The effect of this on plot and trajectory is discussed in another chapter. Here I want to take a brief look at some of the career book novels of science fiction.

Charles Coomb's 1957 *The Mystery of Satellite 7* is an almost textbook example of the genre. Coombs, like many of the sf writers for this market, also wrote for adults and was the author of *Celestial Space Inc., The Case of the Purple Mark* and *Treasure Under Coyote Hill.* The story is straightforward enough:

Steve and his friend Karl live in Florida where their fathers work on private satellite launch projects—the satellites are for television communication. Seven of the eight satellites have gone wrong and there is a suspicion of sabotage. Mostly the boys sit around, listen and watch. They stumble across the saboteurs, are tied up, and are rescued by a journalist. Relations between the two boys and the girl are jovial rather than romantic. She is a "pal," bossed and teased and treated like a second-class boy. The emotional trajectory of the book, such as it is, is towards assimilation in the work place.

The boys are allowed a surprising amount of involvement—Karl helps check equipment and is generally treated as if he were an apprentice although he has no formal involvement at the base and is still in school. Accompanying this is a very great amount of scientific discussion. However, even as early as 1957 there is a growing problem with transparency, which in an engineering novel based in near-future mechanics cannot be waved away. Scientific explanations turn out to be mere description. "Until the firing switch was thrown closed, there was no way of anticipating what numerous unsuspected opponents lay in wait to reach out and ambush the project. It could be a slight cloud in one of the fuel lines. It might be a microscopic crack in a turbopump blade. Vibration might sever the filament of a critical subminiature vacuum tube" (20).

Donald Wollheim's *Mike Around Mars* (1964) is a more effective version of the same kind of story. Part of a long-running series, this is a very methodical look at what space flight might really be like. The side plot of competition with the Russians, leading to Russian spies, a kidnapping, and the laying of mines in space, is pretty weak and has no tension. There is also a possible message from outer space, but nothing comes of it. The tone is very solid, everything is explained. Everything follows the procedure of the period; two groups of three compete to be the crew—Wollheim avoids any unpleasant emotional fall out by having the other team put out of the race by the Russians. The tension in the book is the beauty of space travel and the possibilities, while the sense of wonder is tied to human achievement directly tied to the informational density of the text: the aim is threefold, to awe, to educate and to recruit. The result is that many descriptions in the text go beneath the surface of the object described:

> ...while they inspected the space conqueror, Van Ness reviewed their lessons about the C-5 Advanced Saturn.
>
> Its first stage, which stood 140 feet high by itself, consisted of a cluster of five gigantic F-1 engines, each greater in power than any single Atlas booster. Thirty-three feet in diameter, its tanks were planned for a fuel load of over 200 tons of liquid oxygen and kerosene, and its thrust capacity was over seven and a half million pounds.
>
> Atop that, the second stage, seventy feet long and also thirty-three feet in diameter, utilised five J-2 engines with a thrust of a million pounds. This second stage was a liquid hydrogen-fueled job, the largest of its kind ever attempted [53].

This is not mere info-dump: the trajectory of socialization here is not just to the career, but to a particular view of the world as a machine in which each element, each person, plays a part, an information-dense world, and a world where information is power: "Goddard keeps track of satellites. It charts their orbits, keeps the records of their messages, listens to their calls and complains. Let a satellite get into trouble out there in the dark, empty void, Goddard hears it and heeds its call" (93). All the emotional exuberance is reserved for moments in which knowledge and skill combine: the book concludes "Space is an enemy that must be conquered by concentration, ability, training, vigilance."

Career books have become increasingly rare, and with the loss of that trajectory has come a loss of interest in the construction of the world, although whether this is a necessary correlation is unclear. One trend in science fiction novels for the young has been for careers to be assigned by either heredity or by lottery. The latter, seen in *The Wind Singer*, by William Nicholson (2000),[27] and Jeane DuPrau's *City of Ember* simply makes no sense in science fiction because it does not seem "fit for purpose." The former is possibly linked to the theme of youth rebellion (discussed in chapter four). Certainly, in Bev Spencer's 1993 *Guardian of the Dark*, Gen trains to replace his father as leader of an underground world, only to break with him and lead some of his people towards the light. Although the arguments against lotteries and hereditary careers in all these books are laudable, the effect in each case is to represent formal education as dull and stultifying, and the trajectory the protagonists follow is to break away from a career rather than work towards one. Even where careers are chosen, formal training is frequently abandoned. In H. M. Hoover's *The Lost Star*, Lian Webster's ostensible career as an astrophysicist is abandoned in favor of amateur archeology. Only in Janet McNaughton's *The Secret Under My Skin* is science education and a formal career path presented as interesting. Elsewhere, informal education is everywhere celebrated and schooling dismissed: the Orion series for younger readers, *The Web 2027* (1997 and 1998) and *The Web 2028* (1998, 1999) written by a number of well-known sf authors including Stephen Baxter, Graham Joyce, Pat Cadigan and Ken MacLeod, while generally being pro-skill acquisition, continually downgrade formal schooling, although several of the books *do* value a model of apprenticeship which we saw in the earlier texts.

Recently, Charles Sheffield attempted to revive the career book and its emphasis on information density, with a particular emphasis on Heinleinian notions of competence, and an intensely ideological approach to pedagogy which similarly dismisses formal education, but this time because the curriculum is considered anachronistic, not because formal education itself is passé. *Higher Education* (with Jerry Pournelle, 1996) *Putting Up Roots* (1997) and *The Cyborg from Earth* (1998) all proceed in a similar fashion, featuring children who are failing at school/are unwanted/who are victims of hereditary wealth, are somehow stranded and/or forced into school. In each case, the telling of the story is essentially a light framework for teaching: a great deal of science and math are explained, complete with diagrams and formal education (even if delivered through computers) is a must.

Higher Education is a classic of the kind: Rick Luban gets kicked out of school and is recruited by Vanguard Mining Corps who teach him what school is really like. At the end of the book he is taught some real skills and sent on up into the company. What the protagonist learns in terms of science and engineering, the reader learns too. There is no hand-waving, no vague descriptions of classes having taken place. As we move on to texts written by modern authors, one question which arises is to what extent sf novelists for children have abdicated this duty to teach knowledge as well as critical faculties. Gary K. Wolfe, in a review of *Higher Education,* disparaged this and by implication the later books with the following comment: "The idea that a bad educational system was one that failed to prepare kids for careers in industry might have made sense then.... As far as today's kids are concerned, those of them likely to get past the first chapter of this novel probably don't need homilies about math and reading" (2005: 345).

Wolfe is correct but misses several points: first, there is actually a desperate shortage of home-grown graduates entering industry in the western world — physics and chemistry departments are full of immigrant students. Second, the children in the second category Wolfe identifies need as much validation as other children, and there are few other places for them to get it in a culture that regards scientists as necessary but odd. Third, the book's information density, which focused on math and engineering, is not replaced in modern sf for children by a similar informational density of knowledge for modern careers, and finally Wolfe misses the point that a text that valorizes a mode or subject of learning can be reassuring for the reader who shares that enthusiasm — that the reader already exists does not negate the need for the text.

Modern books such as L.J. Adlington's *The Diary of Pelly D* (2005) are far more interested in the way in which the future shapes the emotional lives of the protagonists than the way in which the future itself develops. Pelly D, for example, is a young girl on an alien planet. When the politicians begin to use genetic markers to divide the population, the book focuses less on what is happening and the issues of whether genetics matter than what Pelly D feels about it, how it affects her friendships, and her love life. Even the "future beyond the war" section is more interested in the internal personal dynamic of the boy who digs up her diary than it is in the world he lives in. This is not a criticism of the book — the world-building is exemplary; Adlington conjures the future in hints and sidelong glances, and in the context of Pelly D's experiences — but there is no science on offer here, no knowledge to add to the reader's store cupboard. Similarly, Alison Goodman's *Singing the Dogstar Blues* (1998) in which an alien child is shown around school as an exchange student, offers little in the way of xeno-anthropology; far more important is the heroine's relationship with her mother, and her efforts to work out who she is. The time travel section of the narrative is motivated by Joss's search for personal identity and contains no physics. The students remain as users of the technology; they never become makers. Yet sf representing children as users simply emulates the degree to which children today live in a user-interface, not a maker-interface. Two texts worth comparing in this light are Terry Pratchett's *Only You Can Save Mankind* (1992) and Sandy Landsman's *The Gadget Factor* (1984).

The Gadget Factor is one of only two books I have found that is interested in computer programming (the other is Cory Doctorow's *Little Brother* [2008], which will be discussed later). Michael Goldman is a thirteen-year-old Freshman at Franklin college. Roomed with older, but still precocious, Worm, he is introduced by Worm to computer gaming. With Michael's math skills and Worm's interest in computers they realize they can build their own game and they become fascinated with producing a total universe simulation. Worm becomes entropy, while Michael is the creator-god; Worm injects technology; Michael injects morals and philosophy; and the beings still keep blowing each other up. In a desperate attempt to help them out, Michael uses some suggestions he has seen in a science magazine to invent time travel, and then realizes that if his universe parallels the real one, he may have solved the time travel problem for real.

Michael finds the author of the original equations, Dr. Terry Miller, in Ohio, and is gratified that he is being treated as an equal, but when they model the full set of equations on his game program, they see life die: the beings are dumping their toxic waste in the future and mining the past for resources.

Michael wants to withhold publication, but Terry announces he is going to present the research in Chicago. Michael (with Worm now in tow) races after him. Worm manages to change some of the equations in the paper but Terry manages to work through the changes. In desperation, Michael turns to Worm and asks for possible challenges. Worm runs through a list and hits on anti-matter. Michael packs him off to the library to get an article on it and prepares to ask his question. Worm arrives just in time and Michael challenges Terry to add anti-matter into the equation. Terry does and the model falls. Michael explains later that he originally had three equations in his model. On the way to Ohio he had reduced them for two "for elegance," forgetting why he had three in the first place, and Terry Miller had only seen the two.

There are several issues of "information density" here. Within the book, the math, physics and the computer programming are "visible"; they are explained in enough detail that I left the book feeling I'd learned something. There is also a clear sense that the game is a composite construction, one which Michael and Worm work on together, and that it is the process rather than the finished product that is the centre of the plot. Finally, the book has a sense of consequence, it reaches forward into a future in which Michael will develop his mathematical modeling, and someone else will take up the challenge of the time travel equations. And one final point, in *The Gadget Factor* the nerds are valorized, positioned at the centre of the plot. Elsewhere, modern sf for children and teens marginalizes them, rendering them sidekicks at best, on the sidelines at worst. Malorie Blackman's *Hacker* (1992), in which a girl rescues her uncle from an unfair charge of embezzlement by hacking a bank computer, and Cory Doctorow's *Little Brother*, in which seventeen-year-old Marcus brings down the Department of Homeland Security, are rare exceptions. We can see this in my second sample.

All of the changes that take place in sf for children are visible in Terry Pratchett's excellent and hard-hitting *Only You Can Save Mankind*. Johnny Maxwell plays computer games, but he does not understand programming, and generally changes homework with one of his friends. The technology of the plot will remain invisible to the protagonist. This sidelining of the techno-logical child is emphasized by the homework swap: Wobbler does Johnny's computer homework, Johnny writes Wobbler's history homework, which is frequently of the "empathize with a person in a castle" kind.[28] The story itself is about the ethics of technology, with the emphasis on the divorce of ethical understanding from the use of weapons, and it is precisely the empathy exer-cise that will prove most relevant to the dilemmas Johnny will face. However, it is a one-way street: ethics is brought into the debate, but the technology itself—both in the virtual world and on the newscasts of the Gulf War which Johnny watches intermittently — remains impermeable to those who make the ethical decisions. Wobbler remains as sidekick, making jokes. His position as nerd mutates almost into the "mad scientist" as he sits in a room doing incom-prehensible things. Wobbler sits on the sideline, and the technology is reduced (for the reader) to something that comes with a joystick attached.

In D.J. MacHale's *Pendragon* sequence (ongoing from 2003), the nerd is reduced to a passive spectator. Bobby Pendragon—high-school jock, good grades, the girls all love him — is kidnapped by his Uncle Press and taken down a tunnel which transports them to another world which Bobby is supposed to help. As the books go on the importance of what Bobby is doing grows, and by book three we know the villain (Saint Dane) is out to destroy the universe. Bobby, "an ordinary boy," is expected to stop him. Bobby, like his Uncle Press and some of the other people he meets, is a Traveler. In each of the books, there is a problem to be solved, on planets which appear alien and which are ori-ented to technology rather than magic, or he occasionally travels in time; but the emphasis is on emotional growth not technical knowledge. Bobby is per-fect. He is good at sports, bright (although MacHale later backs up a bit and makes him bad at history), and everyone likes him. He is *popular* in the con-ventional American high school sense.

There is something odd going on here. Who is the target audience? The old assumption that science fiction is targeted at the "nerd" and intended in part to validate that reader is problematic, because Bobby is the antithesis of the typical sf reader. However, Bobby's adventures are related through journals that Bobby sends via a magic/technological ring to his old friends Courtney and Mark. Mark is the nerd. If this were an sf novel, it is Mark who would be having the interesting adventures—frankly, he is the one who has the brains for it. Instead, we get to read the novel with Courtney and Mark and *admire* Bobby. The effect, and I don't know if MacHale meant to do this, is that we identify with them, not with Bobby. This has mixed results, by reminding us every so often that we are actually sitting with Mark and Courtney, and are relegated to a cheering audience. This is compounded by the fact that Mark and Courtney's adventures hiding the manuscript, discovering that Mark's family seems never to have existed (even their house is gone), are so much more interesting than the universe-crashing quests of the perfect (and rather arrogant) Bobby. Compounding my sense of confusion over whom these novels are for, all of this is written with painful attention to emotion, self-analysis and group hugs. These are very American teens in that they know the emotions they are supposed to feel, and how they are supposed to deal with them. This therapy-speak takes the place of any kind of information density, and relegates the technological brilliance of Mark to the margins. Presentation, not knowledge, is at the head of the value structure here. I have been told by both parents and librarians on the Child_Lit list that the Pendragon books are extremely popular with boys and I don't intend to challenge this, but they are books which valorize the boy who does not read rather than the Reading Boy, and they consistently under-play the role of intellect, and as a consequence also underplay the role of factual knowledge. Bobby does not need factual knowledge because his emotional responses and his natural talent will win out every time. The worlds he enters can be described superficially because his interactions with them will be superficial. The mechanism of travel can be ignored, because he is the prize passenger, not the pilot.

In the absence of an actual interest in science, informational density is increasingly restricted to the construction of the future or sometimes the past, rather than to the delivery of scientific understanding. Frequently it is in the development of the politics of the world that the density is focused. Susan Price's *The Sterkarm Handshake* (2000) is one of the best of the time-travel novels in my collection, but like so many of the time-travel books for younger readers, the nature of time, or the physics or philosophy of time travel, is not at issue. The effort, the density, is concentrated on constructing the past, as it is in Stephen Baxter's faux time-travel story, *Webcrash* (1998), set as it is in a virtual Viking community. The issue at hand in Price's novel is colonial and corporate exploitation, and the element of reason which is demanded of the reader is similarly directed here and away from the implausible and unexplained science of the *other-dimensional* sixteenth century. Elsewhere, Zizou Corder (a mother and daughter team) has produced three books about a boy who can speak to cats. Of the three, the first, *Lionboy* (2004) is the most interesting as science fiction. The world Corder constructs is carefully detailed and you can feel the changed economy all around, but the actual *issue*, the genetic engineering of cats to trigger human allergies, is never really explored in any of the three books and the tale remains at the level of a futuristic adventure. Oisín McGann's *The Harvest Tide Project* (2004) is one of the very few sf novels set fully on an alien world. His main characters are shapeshifters and one of the elements that make this novel so good is that this is not wish-fulfillment: flesh has to be modeled like clay, it does not just move, and it is not all that comfortable. This is partly what I mean by density of world-building, a sense that the mechanics of the process have been thought through. The tale itself is built around the politics of tyranny and oppression, but these are divided, each of the characters who comes to join the two children have their own motivations. McGann uses these motivations to increase the complexity of his world. However, although the plot spins around the liberation of a scientist, and his growing awareness of the political realities of his world, again the actual science of his work remains opaque.

Of recent novels the two books which most effectively use politics to build density are Conor Kostick's *Epic* (2004), and Cory Doctorow's *Little Brother*. *Epic* (improbably, perhaps) is based on computer gaming but there is no programming here. The lesson instead is on how to be a creative user, to exploit the potentials of technology to the full. On an unnamed planet a group of colonizers play the interface game of Epic. Once a mere pastime for bored star-travelers, over the centuries Epic has come to be the arena of the economy and of law. Victory in the graduation tournaments can bring a university place. Armor bought with the pennies stolen from kobolds become tractor allocations or books for a school. Presiding as a referee over the system is Central Allocations. Made up of the most prestigious and victorious players this Committee ensures fairness in everything from hip replacement operations to luxury goods.

The difficulty is that over the years, the colony seems to be doing worse, although CA is forever talking about improvements in the future. Equipment is degrading, people's lives getting harder, and the gap between the rich and poor in the game seems to be growing. The protagonists find a new way to play the game, one that undermines the precepts behind the distribution of goods on their planet. The book offers a number of different critiques of the system, which I will discuss in the chapter on politics. The combination of these critiques deepens the world and offers to the reader a great deal of political philosophy, and extensive information on economics. Kostick is an economic historian by training, and matches the engineer-writers of the 1950s for the enthusiastic communication of disciplinary information. While supporting the user role, Kostick's argument is that simply accepting the configuration of the world as one has been given it is problematic. At the very least one should be reading the manual and looking for the loopholes.

Cory Doctorow is very keen on loopholes, and is also very keen that his readers can take apart a computer at both the hardware and software levels. Of all the books discussed in this section, his is the one that comes closest in terms of delivery of *knowledge* to the older juveniles which, given its complete lack of the respect for adults characteristic of the older form, is rather amusing. In *Little Brother*, Marcus, aka "w1n5t0n," is a high-schooler. Like many others of his generation he is in an ongoing skirmish with encroaching school and parental surveillance. For Marcus "competency" skills have less to do with what he is taught in class than his ability to hack and subvert the computers that track his every move and control his access to the virtual (and real) worlds. Then San Francisco is caught in a major terrorist attack and Marcus and his friends — out where they shouldn't be — are apprehended by the Department of Homeland Security. One of them disappears, seemingly forever, and the remaining three are released only on condition they lie about their whereabouts. Terrified and sick, they collude in their own oppression.

As the DHS moves into San Francisco however, Marcus realizes that the initial collusion has made him vulnerable to more repression. Furious, he resolves to take down first the school and then the DHS. I won't go into details, as I'm less interested in what Marcus does than how Doctorow shows it: *Little Brother* is the answer to the conundrum Gary K. Wolfe posed. If the problem with Charles Sheffield's *Higher Education* and its sequels is that it advocates the study of math for careers young people are no longer interested in (engineering), then the success of *Little Brother* is that it advocates studying math (and reading) precisely to support the acquisition of super-cool skills such as computer-hacking and generally staying one step ahead of the adults. This is one of the very few recent sf books for teens that champions intellectualism and also explains how to break beyond the status of simple user, how to challenge the invisibility of the technological world.

Before leaving this section I want to discuss *Jumpman: Rule One* (2002) by James Valentine. Valentine offers a genuine time-travel dilemma and also a serious look at the problem of relaxing onto the surface of the world. In *Jumpman: Rule One* Theo Pine wins a new edition Jumpman in a competition, but instead of taking him to a hot new time-spot, he finds himself in "Mil 3," the worst of times, and to top it off, he's in phase, absolutely Present. Jules and Gen, two teens, are in the room in which Theo materializes, and need to keep him occupied at the same time as they sort out their own problems. While Theo works out how to get the coordinates to go home, they jump with him to different times, including the First Fish, and the Last Whale. Eventually, when Theo falls sick, Jules jumps forward to bring back his parents. The text offers density in several ways. Theo's reaction to "the Present" is constructed through misapprehension. He becomes (in effect) an archeologist guessing at the use of objects. Through Theo's lack of understanding of his own society's technology, Valentine draws the reader's attention to how much s/he is a surface user of the world. Finally, although not as sophisticated as William Sleator, Valentine is keen that readers leave with a grasp of the philosophy of time travel, and this is represented as a cognitive leap; Jules gets to figure out the philosophy of time travel. It is complex, not all readers will get it, and the author is clear that this is just fine, but the emphasis at all times is that learning how to manipulate your world reduces the degree to which the world (and adults) can threaten you.

Science and Reasoning

Although information density was highly prized in sf for children before the 1960s, evidence of scientific reasoning is scarcer and less frequently delivered. Karen Sands and Marietta Frank, in their study of science fiction series for children, argue that there is no correlation between the level of scientific knowledge and scientific reasoning in these books and the intended age of the child (76). The only real correlation is with the author's own comfort with science and their own comfort with science fiction for adults, so that the most technically and scientifically ambitious books they consider are the *Danny Dunn* series by Jay Williams and Raymond Abrashkin, and Jane Yolen's *Commander Toad* sequence, both produced by writers comfortable with the adult genre, but aimed at younger children. I would go further and suggest that, if anything, sf for pre-teens is often less distracted by other issues and more likely to foreground the science than is the work for teens written post–1985. There is also no real "periodicity" visible. One difficulty may be that structural narrative inclines authors to the *discovery learning*, constructivist model, but the desire to communicate *information* or a sense of wonder, encourages more directed information delivery. The two exist in tension and may be responsible for the phenomenon known colloquially as "infodump" or, at its most didactic, "As you know, Bob..."

The sf narrative most naturally friendly to discovery learning is probably the tale of exploration: going out into the unknown leaves an authority gap which can be filled with poking, prodding and generally asking questions. Some contexts, however, are freer of educational authority than others. Kenneth Oppel's rip-roaring air adventure, *Airborn* (2004), contains two major "stories": the first is the story of Matt Cruse's rise in the hierarchy of the zeppelin guilds— and this is a tale structured by information density of the "how do I fly this zeppelin, how do I navigate hierarchies," kind — and the second is that of Kate, a neo–Victorian miss with a passion for natural history. Kate's interest in what is *out there*, combined with her knowledge of what has already been discovered, shapes an explore-discovery narrative that is essentially grown-up naturetable: Victorian discovery and classification.

More satisfying is Jill Paton Walsh's *The Green Book* (1981), which is a classic tale of colonization. The colonization narrative in children's fiction is predominantly used to explore dynamics of settlement and family. Frequently they are nothing more than futuristic versions of *Little House on the Prairie*; even Heinlein's *Farmer in the Sky* (1950) is essentially a career book and War of Independence parable. *The Green Book*, however, is precisely about the kinds of reasoning needed to cope in a new place, and Walsh makes use of the different adaptabilities of different ages of children to structure the tension.

The Green Book is structured around two issues: the books a group of colonists choose to take with them, and the struggle to survive on a hostile planet. The book narrative is also the political narrative of the tale, as the colonists come to realize they may have made poor choices, and the father of the central family bargains his position in the colony both with his own labor and knowledge, and the text he carried with him, *Intermediate Technology*. The tale of survival however, is one of discovery learning. The children, who are part of the labor force of the colony, have their own concerns, and as they explore, come to understand the planet better than the adults. Frequently, it is the increased leisure time of children that leads to discovery, just as it is frequently leisure that permits science in our world. It is the children who discover that the boulders are moth-cocoons, who have already discovered candy sugar trees with which they make friends with the moths, and who learn how to communicate with the moths— something Walsh never once confuses with "conversation." It is also the children who take risks because their sense of danger is muted enough for the leap, so that when the risk is finally taken to eat the corn which has— like all the other crops— grown crystalline, it is a child who does it. In some ways, *The Green Book* is an argument that keeping children away from danger is short-sighted: it is their willingness to take risks that helps the species to survive. However, its purely constructivist approach has limitations in terms of scientific enquiry: the children have worked out use, they cannot work out *why* without some kind of theory of the world around them. This is beyond the scope of the tale, obviously, but if we were to place this in historical terms, while Walsh has constructed the very, very beginning of civilization — agriculture — she has not constructed scientific enquiry as we understand it. Specifically, there is no suggestion of scientific method.

The only author still working with mathematics (and specifically probability theory) in teen sf is William Sleator. He is also the only writer for teens and children for whom abstract scientific reasoning is really important. If Heinlein was the gold standard for children's sf in the 1950s, Norton in the 1960s and Christopher in the 1970s, then William Sleator has pretty much dominated the market for the last thirty years. He has written sf for children and teens even when there wasn't a market, and has resisted the demands of the wider YA genre. In *The Green Futures of Tycho* (1981), a small boy finds an object that allows him to travel in time. But the more time shifts he makes, the worse the future becomes. In *Strange Attractors* (1990) the act of creating possibilities fragments the stability of the world. In *The Last Universe* (2005) a girl uses a maze to find a world in which her brother is not dying. It is precisely in the use of reason, and the experiment, analyze, experiment again structure of science that Sleator locates his tension.

In *The Last Universe,* Susan's brother Gary is dying of leukemia. At the bottom of the garden is a maze that you can see from the bedroom windows but cannot get to. The maze is the heart of a family mystery: where are Susan and Gary's relatives? Why is the gardener (Luke) so hostile to any attempts to explore the wilder parts of the garden? And why is the cat called Sro-dee? When they finally enter the maze Susan and Gary find themselves disappearing into probability clouds and reappearing in worlds where Gary is slightly better. The "adventure" proceeds as the two keep exploring the maze until they miscalculate and emerge into a world in which Gary is far worse and dies, leaving Susan to find the way to the centre and then, with the help of Sro-dee (Schroedinger's Cat) to escape into another possibility. In this last universe Gary is miraculously well, and this time dating a pretty girl called Lisa who, in a previous possibility, had been Susan's nerdy friend. At this point there is a major structural shift: where previously the density of the book has focused on the math, it now focuses on emotions, specifically on Lisa and Gary's relationship. This is fatal for Susan. In this world, it is Susan who is ill, but because Gary and Lisa, in their new forms, refuse her demand for the science and logic of the garden, focusing instead on the YA theme of sorrow and pity and sentiment, Susan is doomed to die, condemned by being stuck in the wrong genre.

Given everything we have said about scientific method, one needs to be careful not to over-valorize it, but the aspect of scientific method which seems essential is the research circle: question, test, question again. With relatively few exceptions, the circle is rarely completed in the texts I've read. Frequently, didacticism does not guide further curiosity but insists on final and complete answers. Above all, there is no understanding that answers are frequently only routes to other questions. Typical are Alan Durant's *Gameboy Reloaded* (2005) and Jerome Beatty Jr.'s *Matthew Looney's Voyage to Earth* (1961).

In *Gameboy Reloaded* Mia does not like her little brother Zak much — he pinches her toys after she has expressly said he cannot play with them, and particularly her Gameboy. One day Zak disappears into a game. Mia goes in to play the game, and also to get him back. The mawkish moralism of this book is irritating but more significant is the ways in which the readers are excluded from the cognitive challenges that the book presents: readers are invited into Mia's emotional world, but excluded from her cognitive world. For example, the last puzzle in the game is to rearrange letters to make a well-known phrase (United We Stand, Divided We Fall: I told you it was mawkish). The reader is not provided with the letters. Reasoning of any kind here is somehow outside the narrative: results matter, not process.

Jerome Beatty Jr.'s *Matthew Loony* books do cognitive estrangement quite well: although there are real sillinesses in the explanations of moon life Beatty works hard to generate dissonance. For the purposes of this chapter however, the book is interesting because Beatty explains what research is like: "The boy worked busily for a long time, filling the little tubes with samples and marking them carefully as to location, time, etc. In his notebook he wrote down many comments and descriptions of the things he saw, but found no evidence there was anything living in the vicinity" (75). Observation is part of a longer process. Matt's careful sketches of the tracks of his murtle into the water, will enable him to argue that oxygen might support life, and that the water moved (118 and 119 for the sketches). Furthermore, Hector (the rather unpleasant, but actually rather discriminated against sidekick) asks if the liquid keeps moving all the time, constructing the full circle of question, answer, further questions. And it is Hector who offers a hypothesis, that the water is moving because people move inside it. Wrong, but this is still a testable hypothesis, offering a clear sense that scientific reasoning is part of a process and the relationship with the reader is antagonistic; the reader is expected to challenge and correct.

Although invention stories have long been a staple of science fiction for adults and for children, they are actually noticeable by their scarcity in my collection. Sometimes, as in Greenburg's *Andrew Lost on the Dog* (2002), there is an invented robot, but there is very little of the kind of bouncy ingenuity that marked early science fiction or which Charlie Ridey, the young boy interviewed by the Guardian in the extract which begins this chapter, demonstrates. Steve Cousin's *Frankenbug* (2000) is one of the few, and stands out because, along with Mary Amato's *The Word Eater* (2000), both from the children's publisher Holiday House, the process of experimentation is foregrounded.

In *Frankenbug*, Adam is a bug collector: he's obsessed even by the standards of your average nerd. The bane of his life is of course the school bully Jeb (the son of the local police chief). As is common in sf for this age group, it is the interaction rather than the science that is intended to be the central plot; the science is simply a facilitating device for resolving interpersonal relationships. However, Adam decides to make a Frankenbug to scare off Jeb. He's read *Frankenstein* so knows how to go about it. He does his research, sends off for exotic pickled bugs and eventually settles on the lightning of lightning bugs to bring his creation to life. Frankenbug does not turn out quite as planned: he prefers marshmallows to meat, but he is pretty scary and does frighten the bully.

The Word Eater is a much more complex piece of fiction. There are three stories here: Fib, the worm rejected because he cannot eat dirt; Lerner Chanse, a new girl in school who does not want to end up in the out group (SLUGs) but is not too keen in the in-group (MPOOE) either; and Lucia, a Bellitan child forced into factory labor. Again, the interpersonal issues are the centre of the story, but whether Amato intended this or not, in this case Lerner's exploration of scientific method becomes much more interesting.

When Lerner finds Fib she discovers that he eats words; if he eats a word, its referent disappears. This could be a wish-fulfillment fantasy, but Lerner is not that kind of child. Instead, she embarks on an experiment in which she records on paper what she has asked Fib to eat, and what the consequences were. With this she learns to be very, very specific — to become sensitive to the fact that single words are not phrases, and that accurate description is important. Lerner changes the world: she frees Bobby Nitz from his bullying father by having Fib eat "Mr. Nitz's meanness." She gets rid of Attackaterriers (dogs trained to be vicious by having thumbtacks pushed into their paws) by getting Fib to eat the first part of the word. As a consequence (which she never sees) Lucia is liberated, the dogs having become quite cute.

Frankenbug and *The Word Eater* could be classed as fantasy in that they rely on high levels of implausibility/magic, but their methodology identifies them very strongly with science fiction. In *Frankenbug*, there are long, loving descriptions of different insects and their abilities. Adam describes his research and his experiments. Lerner keeps a notebook which is exhibited in the text, with its series of questions and "if this, then that" jottings. In both books, nerdiness becomes a valuable attribute, and the process of experiment becomes the narrative drive.

Both *Frankenbug* and *The Word Eater* exist in the realm of concrete reasoning. However, if this is rare, the representation of abstract scientific reasoning in children's sf is even rarer (abstract emotional reasoning is more common). To date I have found few examples: in James Valentine's *Jumpman, Rule One* which I have already discussed, there is lengthy discussion of time travel; William Sleator is always interested in the mathematics of the world, and there is considerable political and ethical debate in the works of Kostick, Reeve, Halam, Blackman and others, but there is little real interest in the workings of the world. Of the post–1960s authors, only Sylvia Engdahl in *Heritage of the Stars* (1972) and H. M. Hoover, in *The Lost Star* (1980), give a nod towards astrophysics, and astronomy is absent even from the space operas in my collection. Considering modern science fiction texts for children, there are two things happening: the first, is a preference for emotional density over informational density (although I don't feel it *has* to be an either/or), and the second is a decision by most writers to stay on the surface of the technology they describe.

CHAPTER FOUR

Trajectories and Periodicity: Expectations of the Child in Science Fiction

In previous chapters I have continually alluded to the way in which the social expectations of our children have changed: the broad brushstrokes of this can be summarized as a change in the trajectory of socialization our children are supposed to take, from an outward, imperialistic, conquering approach to one which increasingly emphasizes settling down in a variety of forms. The manifestations of these changes have their own complexities which I want to begin to explore as a product of broad periods of time. A word of caution however: decades are convenient metaphors. Although I am about to divide my book collection into periods this should not be taken as an exact science and as I reach the end of one period I will be sliding rapidly into the other.

Social Stability and the Age of Respect: The 1950s and the 1960s

I have already discussed in chapter 3 the way in which much sf from the 1950s aimed at the young adult market fitted the "career book" model: these books are information-dense and focused on teaching children about the work place they may one day enter. Even a sweet children's book aimed at young children such as R. Todd's *Space Cat* (1952), is oriented in this way. Flyball starts life as an overly curious grey kitten who escapes from the house, gets into a taxi, ends up as a stowaway on an airplane, and is taken home by one of the passengers, an air force officer. Captain Stone is an astronaut. He keeps the kitten and names it Flyball. Flyball's stories are essentially about experiencing the work environment on behalf of the child reader (a "take your child/kitty to work" day). This can be adventurous or it can be mundane. Flyball is curious and explores the entire base, but he is kept away from the launch area. On page

18 however, Flyball manages to sneak inside the rocket for a test flight. After this Flyball's owner has a suit made for him, and he is taken on the ride to the moon, where he discovers curious blue globes. When his master finds him, and is injured, the blue globes direct Flyball to a patch of black sticky buttons which he uses to seal the leak in the helmet. Later, they will discover that the buttons have begun to "become" clear plastic. Flyball has been responsible both for discovering life on the moon and a whole new material. Much of the attention however is less on "adventures" than on the everyday realities of "working in a space ship." When Flyball sneaks into a rocket,

> There was a tremendous noise and the rocket started to climb, quite slowly at first, Flyball was comfortable, for it was no worse than the start of the ride in the jet-plane. But slowly, slowly, the pressure got stronger and stronger until he felt he was being pressed flat against the wall behind the pipes.
> "Miaow," he said in a terribly soft and flat voice, but the Captain, shut in his goldfish globe and looking at the dials in front of him, heard nothing [20].

In response the Captain makes Flyball his very own pressure suit:

> It was a most peculiar looking thing, with four floppy legs and a floppy tail. Flyball did not in the least like getting into it, but the Captain spoke to him softly, "Come on, Flyball. Last time you nearly finished up as flat as a waffle and this time it'll be much worse. If you don't get into this you cannot come along with me. Come on, old puss, come along."
> Finally Flyball was encased in his new suit. Then the Captain blew it up and Flyball turned an anxious head to discover that he had grown several times as fat as he usually was. He tried to walk in the suit and found that it was really most inconvenient. The legs did not bend easily, as his own legs bent, and his tail looked like nothing so much as a fat frankenfurter [33].

Flyball and his space suit, and later the account of trying to drink milk in zero gravity, are used to deliver information about the world. However underlying that, *Space Cat* also delivers a message about the child's or learner's required approach to the world — a combination of curiosity and adventure with a respect for authority.

The first of these values, curiosity, is one of the key elements of children's literature across genres. In the 1950s sf collected here, this curiosity is directed quite firmly at the world: Flyball's curiosity stands in for the "prod and poke" approach of all small children but we see this extended in a fascinating series of books initially authored by Ellen MacGregor (a librarian), and continued later (first as a co-author, later as sole author) by Dora Pantell, a curriculum consultant for the New York City Board of Education, at the very time the New York Board was considering the expansion of science education (see the discussion in Chapter Three: Science, Information Density and the SF Reader). The "Miss Pickerell" books are — by today's standards — very odd books that I think I can best sum up as "Miss Marple does science." Miss Pickerell lives outside of the small town of Square Toe, at Square Toe Farm. She has a cow, which she adores, and eventually a cat, called Pumpkin for the mnemonic, "my very educated mother just served us nine pumpkins: Mercury; Venus; Earth; Jupiter; Saturn; Uranus; Neptune; Pluto (*On the Moon*, 1965: 12).

Miss Pickerell is charming because she retains the curiosity, enthusiasm and random voraciousness of the child. She learns by asking questions which are grounded in context. She wonders. She looks at the world around her and thinks about it. Miss Pickerell does not mind being wrong as long as being wrong teaches her something. Knowledge is valuable and solutions come from synthesized knowledge, but it is the curiosity that is valorized because it leads to more knowledge, the desire to *know more* is pre-eminent. One of the fascinating elements to the book is the way it constructs what we might now call an action research circle of hypothesis, test, analysis, hypothesis. For example, in *Miss Pickerell Goes Under the Sea* (MacGregor, 1953), one of the ways MacGregor handles info-dumps is by getting Miss Pickerell to make a sensible but incorrect judgment, so that when Miss Pickerell hears that the submarine has propellers she says, "Oh, goodness! I guess I made a mistake. I thought this was an atomic-powered submarine"(44) and is told "It does not make any difference how sub-marines get their power ... they still have to have propellers to drive them through the water" (45). There is a really excellent scene where a carpenter explains the shape of the bay, and where the continental shelf is. There are some very good diagrams. Note that Miss Pickerell needs this knowledge: it is not arbitrary (52–58). Much later, it will turn out to be not quite the right information. Miss Pickerell needs to know to where the ship has drifted, but she will work this out using the information the carpenter gave her, and new, additional information about the current. Later, Miss Pickerell tries to stop Gus diving without an oxygen tank, only to have it explained that this kind of diving uses an air hose. Then she embarrasses herself by assuming that nitrogen is a bad thing. What is important though is that this will eventually come together with her experience of Mars to enable her to go down to the seabed in a skin suit and with a tank, where she will prevent Mr. Dukas's hose being cut by the propeller (71). All of this is depicted as the constant synthesis and sifting of new ideas and new evidence. There is no moment of genius as such, and science and the art of growing up is firmly anchored in the notion of listening and asking questions.

Ellen MacGregor's books are firmly didactic, but in addition they add a number of other suppositions which lie at variance to current ideas about children's reading: although Miss Pickerell, like Flyball, is a focal substitute for the child reader, she is, nonetheless, an adult. MacGregor's readers are being asked to do two things (at least): first, to accept an adult as intrinsically interesting, and by extension the activities of the adult world as interesting, and second — because Miss Pickerell is not a comedic character nor a Fool — to look further up and further ahead than is the norm in contemporary fiction for children, where it is more or less accepted that the protagonist should be a year or two older than the expected reader. The shift that seems to have taken place is from a model of fiction for the young in which characters were to be admired and *emulated* to one in which characters are sometimes to be admired (but not always) and *identified with*. Both an adult and a child can fit the first role. Only a near contemporary in age can fit the second.[1]

Other writers in this period also seem willing to offer these older focal points. Alice Lightner's Ranger series has as its protagonists a group of young professionals. In *The Space Ark* (1968) Johnny Dinkum and his colleagues are ecological heroes: When planet Shikai is faced with a nova, Johnny Dinkum and his fellow rangers decide to take some of the animals to safety, particularly the single horned keratoros and the probably sentient chi-chis. The story takes us to three different planets (one a planet of pirates, one the place where it turns out the intelligent Rock came from — though they turn out to be telepathic and in search of new slaves, and finally Earth). But the real interest is how to keep the animals and their all-important vines viable, and this turns out to be surprisingly easy: the vines need carbon in the soil. Like the Miss Pickerell books (although for a older audience) there is an assumption that the activities of full adults are *interesting*, but by the 1950s this was already being questioned. Geoffrey Trease recalls arguing for adult heroes in the 1940s (106). Hugh Walters was able to write about young men in their twenties in his juvenile science fiction novels as late as 1975. But the form is, I think, now gone completely, although still common on children's magazine television: the UK's *Blue Peter* is a good a example, although even here a comparison of the shows of the late 1950s with current shows is salutary. The earlier programs have the presenters acting as young adults to be emulated; current programs require the hosts to act like over-grown children. Yet adult protagonists create the impression that curiosity and knowledge-gathering are *adult* qualities. Miss Pickerell's adventures in education become an argument for a trajectory towards adulthood, Alice Lightner's characters offer real adventure through vocation.

Although Heinlein does not use adult heroes in his juveniles he *always* deploys an admirable adult to accompany, guide and inspire his young people for the first part of the journey (I say always, and promptly realize that this is not true for *Tunnel in the Sky* [1955], although there has been adult advice prior to embarkation). Sometimes this is disguised, as in the form of the dragon, Sir Isaac Newton, in *Between Planets* (1951) and rather frequently, as in *Starman Jones* (1954) and *Space Cadet* (1948), the admirable adult is unconscious, but always there is a model of adulthood at hand to emulate. In both of these books, in fact, what is at stake is which model of adulthood will prove most attractive: in each book the protagonist is offered an "easy way" (in *Starman Jones,* cheating his way into the astrogation guild; in *Space Cadet* choosing the easier branch of the military service) and a difficult way, following the rules and, crucially for this chapter, learning a lot of things that seem irrelevant at the time because an adult thinks they are good for you, *and the adventure proves them right*. Heinlein pulls this off, but in lesser hands the binary choices can seem contrived and embarrassing. Robert Silverberg, an excellent writer for adults, cannot structure this choice between good and bad role models with anything but condescension because, I suspect, he himself is uncomfortable with such simplicities. In *Revolt on Alpha C* (1963) Larry Stark takes into space his commander father's racism and class prejudice. Larry's conversion to the colonists' point of view rests on the brutal behavior of is own commander, but is not in the slightest bit influenced by the constant injunctions of his roommate to read revolutionary literature. Larry moves from swallowing Earth propaganda about independence being on the way when the colonies are ready, to swallowing colony propaganda about autarky. Silverberg exposes the limits of role models while — as yet — proving unable to break from them as a structure for the juvenile science fiction novel.

This pattern of adventure, precipitated precisely because the protagonist has learned "unnecessary" information, is perhaps most obvious in *Citizen of the Galaxy* (1957) and *Have Space Suit— Will Travel* (1958). It is quite different from the pattern which will emerge in the late 1960s and retain a hold from then on, in which the skills children and teens need in their adventures are rarely connected to what they have learned from adults; they may even prove that the adults were wrong, poorly informed or just generally irrelevant. Instead, what we see over and over again in this period is that rather than separating children and teens from the adult world (as the classic portal fantasy of this period does) adventures take place within the adult world both in terms of location and concerns, and what they nurture and celebrate is the understanding that young people desire to join this world as it is currently configured.

What seems to be central to the books of the 1950s is *whose world* and *whose knowledge* matters. They are clear as to the direction in which knowledge flows, from the adult to the child. These books do not valorize discovery learning, however much they value experience: learning supports and is supported by hierarchy and social stability. Lester del Rey uses this structure very effectively in *Tunnel Through Time* (1969). Bob and Pete, the son of two scientists, enter a time tunnel to rescue Pete's father. The adventure itself is fairly mild but del Rey uses the relationship structure to induct the sons and the reader into the workings of real science: in the first chapters we see what a real lab is like, we hear about funding constraints— the link with Pete's father is an attempt to secure cross-disciplinary funding — and about the personalities in labs (and the older men are ruled out of taking the trip because each is in poor health — no intimations of cowardice here).

Andre Norton's take on the trajectory of socialization is rather different to the ones discussed so far yet essentially supports my arguments for the expectations of this period of sf. The protagonists of both *Cat's Eye* (1961) and *Starman's Son* (1952) are robbed of their role models: each is without a father, and further, each is deprived of the trajectory of socialization they had anticipated through apprenticeship (in the informal or formal sense) in the profession of their kin. Fors loses his place in his clan when his father dies and must move outward, taking his skills with him, to find a new place. Troy is stranded on a strange world with a set of skills completely irrelevant to the needs of this new place. Research on kinship structures in the Middle Ages and in eighteenth-century France suggest that the loss of their father is one of the most devastating things to happen to young people, particularly boys: apart from the emotional trauma and the risks of step-parenting what young men in particular lose is the route to adulthood. In a world where professions are inherited, determined by parental willingness to pay for training, or reliant on the placing out of a boy with kin, the loss of such networks may mean the loss of a future, and certainly the disruption of an understood pattern of socialization. This is muted in contemporary western society where professions are less likely to be inherited, but for many readers of the 1950s, while professions were less directly dictated, familial influence and modeling was still hugely influential and was a given in most circumstances (although the next ten years was to change all of that and the career books of the period were a direct response).[2] C. R. Brink's *Andy Buckram's Tin Men* (1966), for example, has as its underlying expectation the idea that because Andy's father is a junk man with the skills to build his house and other necessities from junk, it is therefore *natural* for Andy to emulate and to wish to follow in his father's footsteps. Career paths in many of these books look very much like packs of Happy Families playing cards.

Norton's *Starman's Son* vividly displays the extra energy socialization to the adult world requires without that familial support but also provides the first hints that the conventional structure of respect for adult authority, while it ensures stability, is also confining. *Cat's Eye* is both a bleaker and more demanding book in this sense because at the end Troy is offered the mentorship he thinks he wants from someone truly admirable. Heinlein would have presented this as a happy ending, but Troy rejects it in favor of an unbroken path laid out by a "peer group" of telepathic animals. This is the first time that we see this model of "admire and emulate" broken, and the very first time that we see a teen arguing that the adult advice may be wrong and that the future does not have to be an inheritance.

1960s/1970s: Proving the Grown-Ups Wrong

There is no perfect moment to which I can point and say "here it all changes" but sometime in the late 1960s, the assumption that children will emulate their parents, or at the very least choose between competing adult role models begins to break down. Specifically, the valorization of adult knowledge and adult morality comes into question. We can see this at the macro level—

what I have been describing to people as "the parents are all wrong," in which an entire society turns out to have been based on a set of myths which the young will uncover, and at the micro level—a growing number of what we might call "alternative ambition" novels which begin to thread through the mainstream newly minted YA genre.

Although I intend to pull examples from a number of authors to demonstrate the trend (and to show its continued currency), the two leading practitioners of the "parents are all wrong" sf for children and teens were the British writers Peter Dickinson and John Christopher. John Christopher's Tripods series is typical of the form. In the first of these books, *The White Mountains* (1967), the world has been taken over by alien invaders, the tripods, who have subdued humans through a neural net disguised as a cap. The protagonist, Will, is tempted by a Vagrant to run away before Capping Day. He goes with his enemy Henry, and picks up Beanpole (Jean-Paul) in France. After adventures during which they discover hand grenades in the French metro and use them to kill a tripod, they make it to the White Mountains.

Vagrants are people who have been damaged by the capping. The Vagrant Will meets is wearing a false cap. Everyone who avoids capping does so before the age of 14, so that in some ways this entire novel is about the superiority of youth. This thread is continued in the next two novels, *The City of Gold and Lead* (1967) and *The Pool of Fire* (1968), in which the leaders of the rebellion use the enthusiasm of youth to carry out their plans, very specifically by reinforcing their sense of superiority to the adult society they have left behind.

One of the key elements to almost all the books of this type is some kind of rupture or forgetting which allows adults to be confined within an ideological system that children—less socialized to it—can escape. Perhaps the most effective text working with this trope is Peter Dickinson's Changes trilogy, consisting of *The Weathermonger* (1968), *Heartsease* (1969) and *The Devil's Children* (1970). For those who have not come across these books before it may be helpful to know that these books were written in what is effectively reverse chronological order. In all three books Britain has been taken over by technophobia and the island has reverted to a neo-early medieval past. *The Weathermonger* explains why and sees the plague of technophobia cured, *Heartsease* tells a story from the height of the period, and *The Devil's Children* is set just a few months after it all starts. All three of these books set a child who "knows the truth" against adults who live in a fictive world, although *The Devil's Children* is a lot more complex in these terms. In *The Weathermonger*, Geoffrey wakes up in a boat with his sister Sally to be told that he is a weathermonger, someone who can alter the weather. To him this is rank superstition. It turns out that he has lost several years of memory during which he lived in a changed England of technophobia and magic. The two of them escape to France but are sent back to track down the source of the hysteria. After traveling for several weeks they find a revived Merlin in Wales, hooked on morphine by an old pharmacist.

Throughout the novel there is the constant tension of Geoffrey deriding the behavior of the adults he sees around him, while at the same time forced to take advice from Sally who is still infected and so can tell him what to avoid. But it is the denouement to the novel that is most at variance to earlier texts: the pharmacist who controls Merlin must be first disposed of (an accident is contrived) and then argued against. Merlin must be convinced that it is youth that has knowledge, and only youth which can advise action in the contemporary world.

I will skip briefly over *Heartsease*, essentially a tale of family defiance, except to note that there is no familial reconciliation at the end of this novel — that is not the purpose of the story and in this it will stand out from contemporary sf for teens. *The Devil's Children* is more interesting because it sets up competing models of adulthood for young people but at the end argues that all of these models are unhealthy. At the beginning of *The Devil's Children* Nicola sits on a step outside a London house, waiting for her family to return for her. When the Changes started her family fled and she was separated from them on the road to Dover. Now she waits and hopes. On a day when she has almost given up, a cart surrounded by brightly dressed people with dark skin, makes its way down the street. In a moment of desperation Nicola decides to join them. As they are not infected by the Change, she offers to be their canary, warning them when they are about to do anything forbidden. The people turn out to be a (very) extended family of Sikhs. With Nicola in tow they end up camping outside a village ruled by an emergent robber baron. What happens next challenges a lot of the assumptions of second-rate fantasy, as they assist the villagers both in fighting off the bandits and preventing the re-establishment of feudalism: the trajectory of the novel, while it valorizes some kinds of recovered knowledge (the Sikh men revive the art of sword making), is antagonistic to easy assumptions that the past was better. Furthermore, at the end of the novel the Sikh families dispatch Nicola to France to find her family. Nicola is neither Sikh nor villager: cultural adoption is not the answer and while the adults have found their way it cannot be assumed that Nicola will follow it.

Dickinson's trilogy, while tackling adult knowledge at large, also begins to touch on the second aspect I mentioned: "alternative ambition." I don't want to spend too much time on it here, because it is not a strong element in this period but it is worth noting its effect on otherwise conventional novels. R.C. Gilman's *Rhada* series has a trajectory quite at variance with the notion of inherited careers that we have seen in the earlier period.

The Rebel of Rhada (1968) takes place as the planet is coming out of a Dark Age, using ships they have no idea how to work or make. A priesthood controls navigation, and scientific enquiry (rather than technology *per se*) is a sin. The Consort is plotting for the throne and the hero must stop her. At the end the hero puts the boy king back on the throne and goes back to his planet. In

The Navigator of Rhada (1969), we have a prince and pauper story in which the stepbrother of the heir to Rhada discovers his brother has killed their father, and in uncovering the plot he discovers he is also twin to the Emperor. Given the chance at the empire, he puts his brother back on the throne and goes back to be king of Rhada. In *The Starkahn of Rhada* (1970), the planet is now a republic. The "heir" has no interest in his mother's royalist plots, and even less when he discovers an old warship. He rescues the sleeper, and then discovers she is descended from people transported out of the galaxy for eugenic crimes, who have come to be revenged. In stopping the ship (because he was awake and she was not, the ship recorded his life signs) he, the alien Vulk, his cybership and the alien he rescued are merged into one mentality and at the end they head off out of the galaxy to explore. In each of the three books the "natural" trajectory of saving adult society and then becoming part of it has been muted: adult society may be saved but its shape changes and intervention no longer automatically means absorption. Sometimes indeed, salvation is coming to mean finding an alternative ending; in D. S. Halacy's *Return from Luna* (1969), Rob Stevens is rejected from the military draft with a hitherto unsuspected heart murmur. He ends up on the moon in time to miss the Cold War on Earth turning hot. Trapped on the moon, his physics professor goes mad. Rob, however, helps design and sustain a solar generator which helps provide oxygen, and develops a vegetable garden: Rob's future is not the one planned out for him by his parents or his professor.

I have outlined above some of the more effective texts of this kind, but the sad truth is that this trope became an incredibly predictable trajectory for a great deal of sf for children and teens. Some are creative: Sylvia Engdahl's *Heritage of the Stars* (1972) posits a planet in which the adults are in fact correct — the planet is poisonous to humans — but where the act of believing the adults are wrong, and striving to prove it has become the path to adulthood. In Ben Bova's *End of Exile* (1975), the adult has taken the wrong choice to secure the safety of children marooned on board a space station, and has cocooned them in ignorance. The rejection of the *specific* adult instructions in this book allows access to the more general society of adults. But many of these texts are structured so that the act of discovery of The Truth by the young becomes the emotional payoff. A good example is H. Campbell's *Legend of Lost Earth* (1977). It is a fairly straightforward and rather well-written sf novel. Giles lives on Niflhell, a planet to which humans have fled but which he has been taught they originated on. To say anything else is a heresy, and the government is cracking down on heretics. Eventually, as one might expect, Giles discovers Earth is real (and gets a new girlfriend). However, the route turns out to be mystical rather than technological, and he is the only person who can navigate the way through. He leads a party through and they escape. Earth turns out not to be another planet, but a parallel world to Niflhell; one can only see or access it if one is in the right frame of mind. In a scene that reminds me of the dwarves in C.S. Lewis's *The*

Last Battle (1956), the government of Niflhell cannot follow the heretics because they cannot see the Earth even when passing through the portal. Not only are the adults wrong but the entirety of adult society is blinded by its self-confidence.

Then there is B. Ball's *The Doomship of Drax* (1985). Nick Pilot lives on a colony world. His people left Earth generations ago to live more peaceful lives. Now there are rumors that the sun may be about to explode, and rumors also that the original settlers left a starship for the colonists to escape in if necessary. Nick's village regards this as heresy and seeks to appease the sun with sacrifice. Nick follows the "false" prophet and discovers all this is true, and helps to find the starship. Two things make this book stand out from all the other books with the same "our parents don't know anything, the ancients knew everything" theme. The original colonists knew there was a very slight chance of the star becoming unstable, and although they wanted their descendants to be farmers, they made plans for emergencies. Furthermore, people in the neighboring town do believe the prophet and do not place their entire faith in the idea of a lost starship; they start experimenting with explosives and rocketry, making this one of the very few texts in this group which offers multiple paths to change.

Last in my list before I jump forward to the future for a moment is Robert Westall's classic *Futuretrack 5* (1983). This book provides an important link to the next cluster I want to discuss, because up until now, all the "forgetting" has been more or less accidental. In the 2000s however, we are going to start to see stories in which the forgetting is deliberate. *Futuretrack 5* is one of the earliest of these books: the protagonist of this book is a middle-class boy educated in a boarding school to fulfill a particular role in life. The unraveling of his choices as he becomes involved with a different set of ambitions—those of the prole kids in the compounded cities—leads him to question the structures of his world. Where all the books we've looked at so far had the adults either ignorant or deluded, *Futuretrack 5* knows that they are conspiratorial. When youth revolts in this book it does so with contempt, not sympathy.

This form of sf has lasted well into the 2000s. Louise Lowry, William Nicholson and Jeanne DuPrau have all reiterated the form, but there has been a change in the way these books have been written. This change is partly a change in focalization. Although there is rebellion against adult authority in the 1960s/70s, adults and their values are still very much the center and focus of children's and teens' ambitions. Children/teens offer correctives to adult values but still seek to ensure that adults value the same things they do. From 1980 onwards the emphasis shifts away from parental rejectionism to what I can only call "and parent came too" in which parental input is redeemed. An interesting link text is Bev Spencer's *Guardian of the Dark* (1993) in which although the protagonists reject the myth that there is nothing outside the cavern in which they live, and go forth to find a better world, we discover in the penultimate chapter that the young people's rebellion has been coached and coaxed by the Patriarch. In the 2000s, the focus of many of these books changed to concentrate on children and teens rejecting adult authority because such authority was simply not in their interests or was deliberately malicious. Yet despite this continued rejection of the parental world, what stands out is the way these texts are written.

The texts of this period focus rigorously on the children/teens, and very often it is only the younger characters who are fully fleshed out. We can see this in very disparate books. Francine Prose's *After* (2003) is set shortly after a U.S. high school massacre: suddenly there is a new head teacher, kids are being frisked for weapons, and more and more things become forbidden. As parents acquiesce, the rebellious students are picked off. Eventually the protagonist and his friends go to check out the school that was the original victim, and discover all the students have been taken away. With the help of the few parents who have not been reading the school letters, they head for the hills, but the parents remain shadowy figure and other adults are always portrayed from a distance. In the very different *Mortal Engines* (2001) Philip Reeve uses a tight focus for his teen characters Tom and Hester, but most of the adults are at best archetypes (the Historians) and at worst figures of fun (Professor Pennyroyal). Both books have as their underlying message not only that the future will be built by the young, but that only the young's reaction to particular circumstances is interesting. Elsewhere, in the work of William Nicholson and Jeanne DuPrau, the adults are rendered deliberately obtuse in order to make the children seem smarter: adults are not only wrong, but they are responsible for very silly social systems. One manifestation of this is the job lottery, something which cropped up more often than I expected. If we think back to the stable and respectful world of teen sf in the 1950s we can remember that teen careers/vocations were frequently hereditary and nurtured. In place of this, by the current century we have Nicholson's idea that jobs be assigned according to the status of the father of the family in a series of exams (*The Windsinger*, 2000), and DuPrau's actual lottery (*City of Ember*, 2003). Pat Pinsent suggested on my blog that this reflected children's insecurity. This is part of it, but I also think it is a commentary on the arbitrariness of adult decisions and the sense that not winning in these situations is never the fault of the child. The sense of responsibility of the child, and respect for adult decisions, which marked earlier work is simply absent. Both Nicholson and DuPrau will go on to depict the adults in the children's work as stupid and irrational.

For some authors, adults are not only stupid, ignorant and irrational, they are also liars: by 2000 there is a consensus that the past and knowledge of the past will not be lost but rather thrown away, frequently in the interests of social control. Jeanne DuPrau's underground colony has been marooned by idiots who have deliberately created a cultural and technological rupture, and a knowledge-poor society, by omitting the parental generation from the immediate settlement and restricting education to the elementary level. The adults in Nicola Morgan's *Sleepwalking* (2004) drug people to prevent dreaming and story-telling; only a select group of children — educated by *benevolent* adults in secret — can undo this world. B. Keaney's *The Hollow People* (2006) is set on an island where dreaming is again ruled by the use of drugs and the history of the island, and the world is again a construct. Not quite part of this discussion, but relevant to the next section, it is worth noticing the growing emphasis on imagination and emotion, and the way it is frequently presented as the proper antagonist to logic and education. Many of these books prize the uncontrolled emotional response; frequently it is the key to unlock the lies of adults. It is important to accept however, that while the theme may irritate, it is not always deployed as an easy out for the plot. In *Useful Idiots* (2004) Jan Mark's protagonist discovers that "parental" knowledge is often complex and the decision to hide knowledge may be a deliberate survival strategy in a politically hostile world. His emotional reaction to the "plight" of the Inglish (an oppressed group exploited in a number of ways, including their use to cultivate a kind of oyster generated in human bone by the horsefly) turns out to be an irrational response. The "lies" told by his "parents" (both the Inglish and the wider society around him) prove to be a rational move to escape the cycle of vicious abuse.

1970s–1980s Pedagogy and Competency: SF for Children Up to 1980 Is Obsessed with Pedagogy

The "parents are wrong" attitude of the fiction just discussed and the growing insistence on the valorization of children and teens' knowledge over that of adults is not uncontested. Running alongside this development is a debate about pedagogy; what to teach, how to teach it, how to teaching thinking and what thinking is for. The exemplary text in this area is Alexei Panshin's 1968 classic, *Rites of Passage* (1968), a *bildungsroman* not truly intended for teens at all but a response (if you would have it so) to the shift in values and focalization which was occurring.

Rites of Passage won several awards on publication and is very well known, but I would like to recapitulate the tale here. Earth has been destroyed and while part of humanity has gone out to settle the universe, some of it has elected to remain in space, and live in space habitats scattered through the known world. There is a certain amount of tension between space habitants and settlers and there is some very good discussion about the relationship between the habitats and the settled planets, and about the way racism emerges and sensible relationships can become exploitative. One of the *über* issues is that settling on the planets has meant for many humans sacrificing technology and science. In contrast the habitats have become preserves of human endeavor and are on the road to becoming Dark Age monasteries: unlike monasteries however, there is no route in (something that is exacerbating the prejudice against ground-dwellers) but there is a route out, if teenagers fail to pass their final survival tests.

The main theme is how to educate children. First, and perhaps most important to my overall argument, the primary trajectory pushes the children outwards. Mia Havero's father moves their entire household in order to under-cut Mia's developing timidity. From the first, the emphasis is on the child as explorer and this is reinforced through guided exploration in the classroom. When Mia is assigned a tutor, Mr. Mbele teaches through experimental proj-ects that Mia and her tutorial partner have to figure out for themselves. The final trial on a planet is precisely designed to test initiative and the application of knowledge (much like Heinlein's *Tunnel in the Sky* but a lot more challeng-ing). But it is also designed to elicit the realization that just taking in informa-tion is no bad thing. The value of preparation is emphasized over and over again as Mia goes through the process of packing for mini-survival tests, and sees in real-space whether she has made the right choices. Most important to Mia (and discussed in detail in the epilogue) is the realization that it is often apparently meaningless skills which will finally get you what you want, that "rel-evance" cannot be judged when you are young and do not yet know what you want to do or how to get there.

One of the most interesting aspects of the book, however, is that although it has a very specific pedagogy to expound, Panshin does not anticipate that it will produce only one type of person. One of the conflicts in the book is the future of Mia and her friend Jimmy. Mia wants to be a synthesist, Jimmy wants to be an ordinologist. For both of them, their moment of adulthood is when they realize that they have it the wrong way round: Jimmy is the synthesist, Mia the ordinoligist. Panshin's point is that children *must* be prepared as general-ists, but that through that training specialism will emerge not as a body of knowledge but as a way of understanding the world.

Panshin's book is unusual in arguing for philosophy as a skill within a very practical framework. More usually, authors have gone one way or the other. P. Baltensperger's *Guardians of Time* (1984) is interesting in these terms (and because a book written in 1984 maintains 1954 sex roles). Finnegan lives in the future in an Earth where everything is controlled by the Chairman and the Ten, and by Politicians. The future is not terribly imaginative; it is essentially Asimovian with walking robots but otherwise very like ours. This world relies on computers for planning and the elite are those trained to program and inter-pret the computers. Membership of the elite is hereditary and Finnegan is being trained to follow in his father's footsteps. He spends his days on his own in his study being drilled by his Wall in mathematics, and using virtual reality to relax. These scenes are chosen for him by the computer. In one of them Finnegan tries to steal marbles from a boy of the 1960s. The boy chases after him and is killed by a truck. Finnegan comes back to reality and discovers the marbles missing. He becomes more and more restless and begins to try and subvert the computer. One slight flaw here is that he is helped in this by someone he meets in the virtual world — this will make sense eventually but it is unsatisfying at the time. Finnegan discovers, and reveals to his mother, that they are all being programmed by a White Room (the vision eye) at the center of the house. At this point his father and the whole family are dispatched as ambassadors to the planet of Kalimar, where humans have grown huge.

Up until now this has been a rather dull dystopian novel which seems designed to make children satisfied with the more rambunctious world in which they live. But threaded through this first part is an argument about education and control of children's lives and what children are for. Children of Politicians are "educated in isolation and trained for their one great purpose in life" (8). For a while this works really well: there is a strong sense of Finnegan as a child in a repressive society that claims to operate for his well-being. When he gets to Kalimar, he is inducted into their society's education system. I perked up a bit at this because it sounded promising. Kalimar does not have teaching machines: "We learn from each other.... Machines cannot think, and that's what Kalimarian philosophy is all about — the development of thought" (68). Then we get to what is taught, "philosophy and psychology and spirituality.... Literature, poetry, art, all the important things?" (69). Now, I don't mind the argument for a well-rounded education, but math and science are dismissed here; they are associated, *ipso facto*, with the rote learning on Earth. Kalimar people have moved beyond science: "You'll have to realize that we are not a technological society. We moved beyond that a long time ago" (71). At which point Finnegan — a sensible, science-trained boy — asks, "Into what?" and his mentor dismisses him with the comment that he will find out in good time.

A seeming educational liberation proves just as closed as the prison from which Finnegan has escaped. Eventually, inducted into the planet's secrets, Finnegan will discover that they do have technology. Telekinesis allows them to work with fundamental particles. Baltensperger does a good job describing this, making it seem like science rather than magic:

> A whole new world opened up for Kendor, a world of the most intricate processes, involving energy transitions across complicated circuitry connected sometimes directly and sometimes indirectly through Rammassoon to Kendor's central nervous system and to the very core of his brain [104].

Ok, so it is handwaving, but it is recognizably hard sf handwaving.[3] At the end, of course, Finnegan/Kendor decides to stay, his father goes home, transformed by Kalimar society, and for the most part this story conforms to that outward trajectory I have been looking for. The snag is what Finnegan travels outward to. First, everything Finnegan/Kendor does is supervised by someone. Second, in rejecting Earth for Kalimar, it turns out that Finnegan has rejected a petty patriarch for a truly godly father. Kalimar is in the business of civilization rescue. They are a highly technological civilization whose members have developed their minds as well and appointed themselves Guardians of the Universe (79–81). This is such a common sf trope that I have no right to complain, but the effect in this book is to dampen the sense of adventure. Furthermore, the story is told in a voice of mild condescension, hard to pinpoint but one which assures us that Finnegan is on the right path, that any conflict we see will be part of this path. The result is a negation of the very thoughtfulness and independent analysis for which the book has argued.

My interest in *competence* as a way of understanding pedagogical theories and social expectations in modern sf for children has increasingly focused less on the future that is being built in children's books than the interaction children have with the concept of *building* a future. What has come to worry me is that a great deal of the science fiction written for children recently (and since the publication of *Neuromancer* in 1984 also that written for adults) posits the basic interaction of individual and machine as one of user, not maker, an issue I have already outlined in chapter three. This is, of course, a symptom of the way that we live our lives. In the past thirty years we have come to live in a world made up of "magic that works" (a comment attributed to the editor of *Astounding Magazine*, John W. Campbell. Bretnor, 1953: 79).

The need for a philosophy of education seems to have occupied writers most self-consciously in the late 1960s and late 1970s and is, I think, a very precise response to the notion of "tradition." The expectations of what children can do and more importantly, what they can be expected to do, goes underground. It emerges in the works of people such as Charles Sheffield and K. A. Applegate (in her Remnants sequence, 2001–2003) as an argument around competency: what skills will make our children competent in the world? It emerges as an issue by its very absence in Jeanne DuPrau's *City of Ember* in which luck (the way out is found in a baby's toy, matches are found in the tunnel, the children assigned by lottery to learn highly skilled tasks are luckily good enough at them to keep the colony alive) and found knowledge (maps, old material) substitute for learning, skill, and ingenuity.

1990s: The Role of Emotion and Imagination

In the 1990s two things start to stand out: for teens, the storylines move closer to home — ironically, adventure beyond the home seems to be the prerogative of the younger child (Nicholson, Wood, Farmer, Halam etc) — and the focalization and value structure shift dramatically. Increasingly, the focalization is very narrowly on teens, but the value structure is one that both purports to answer to their condition while simultaneously tying them to a model of maturity that is very firmly centered on the family and family values. The development, if you will, of EQ (emotional quotient).

The first thing to consider, however, is my possibly contentious statement that the "adventure" story has been moved down an age group. I haven't done a survey of all the stories but here is a sample from the recent "outward bound" sf books, in which the protagonist actually leaves home and has scary adventures. All these books are published either at the very end of the twentieth century or the very beginning of the twenty-first.

- In Philip Reeve's *Mortal Engines* although the protagonists are late teens, the story itself is aimed at young teens.
- William Nicholson's heroes in *The Windsinger* are just past the onset of puberty.
- Ann Halam's heroine in *Siberia* (2005) is also a young teen. The protagonist in *Taylor 5* (2002), however, is around fifteen.
- Jeanne DuPrau's protagonists are just past puberty.
- Oisín McGann's protagonists in *The Harvest Tide Project* (2004) and *The Gods and Their Machines* (2004) are respectively just past puberty and mid-teen.
- In Joan Lennon's *The Questors* (2007) the heroes are very specifically pre-puberty (this is crucial for one character) and it is a theme of the book that they are younger than preferred.
- David MacHale's protagonists start as early teens and are moving into the mid-teen phase.
- Nancy Farmer's *The Ear, the Eye and the Arm* (1995) and *House of the Scorpion* (2002) both feature pre-teens as the protagonists.
- Michael Carroll's *The Quantum Prophecy* (2006) features pre-teen protagonists (although they are growing up).
- K. A. Applegate's *Remnants* (2001) and *Animorphs* (1996 – 2001) series mostly cast early teens although they do age over the course of the books.
- The protagonists of twelve out of the sixteen stories in *The Starry Rift*, edited by Jonathan Strahan (2008) are young teens.

When I look at recent sf books for mid to late teens, however, I cannot but be struck by how close to home most of these stories are located. Alison Goodman's *Singing the Dogstar Blues* is located in a high school. Kenneth Oppel's *Skybreaker* (2005) has his hero ensconced in an authority structure (much like an old Heinlein novel but without ever being set free of that structure). Nancy Werlin's *Double Helix* (2004) allows Eli to leave home but only to go work in a nearby laboratory. David Levithan's *Wide Awake* (2006) (a story about a future Presidential election) allows his hero to leave home, but on a bus full of other people from school. Francine Prose's *After*, in which schools collapse under a fear of teenagers, is located firmly around the school. When the protagonists do go on the run, it is with their parents. In Nick Wood's *The Stone Chameleon* (2004) one of the parents accompany the teens on their journey into the savannah. Susan Beth Pfeffer has her teens withdraw into the family where mom repels all intruders and keeps her teens firmly under the family wing (*Life as We Knew It*, 2006). Even William Sleator, whose prepubescent Marco travels millions of miles (*Marco's Millions*, 2001), keeps his teenagers in *Strange Attractors* (1990), *Singularity* (1985) and *The Last Universe* (2005) close to home (although in *Interstellar Pig* [1984] and *Parasite Pig* [2002] the teens do travel). Almost the only sets of books I can find which have almost-adults out on their own are J. B. Stephens' *The Big Empty* series (2004, 2005); an evangelical series, *The Left Behind: The Kids* (forty books in total, 1998–2004), Rhiannon Lassiter's *Outland* series (2003–2005),and recently Cory Doctorow's *Little Brother* and Stephen Baxter's *The H-Bomb Girl* (2007), which are both clearly striving to assert the independence of teens.

By the mid–1980s, the trend is clear. Adventure is something only available to children — and increasingly either there are parental figures or the lack of parents is a directly addressed issue — and teen "adventure" is taking place in a domestic or at least official space. Why?

I think there are a number of factors at work. The first is the rise of social realism. In the 1970s a number of political movements argued that fiction for children should reflect a wider range of social worlds. Although feminism and the civil rights movement had their effects, for my purposes the arguments that working-class children should be able to find themselves in fiction had a far greater impact on fantasy and science fiction. For some reason, while girls could be seamlessly integrated into the traditions of fantasy (see the writing of Tamora Pierce) and to a lesser extent into science fiction (see the work of Douglas Hill, and Nicholas Fisk), and eventually even non-white characters, although that has taken a shamefully long time, there seems to have been a presumption that middle-classness was a given for the sf novel. By this I do not mean that all the children were middle class, but that with the exception of post-holocaust novels the environments in which children had their adventures were cozy and conformist. Even when this began to break down in the 1970s most of the children depicted were the sons and daughters of a town's leaders. What this meant was that they and their environment emphasized *potential*, and almost all of the stories were *kunstlerroman*, stories of the growth of the young person into an artist. To back up, what the rise of social realism brought into children's fiction was an argument against the *kunstleroman*. There must be a word to describe the miserablism, the lack of opportunity, the struggle against all the odds only to achieve nothing more than stability and acceptance of life's ills which began to infect children's literature and which the *New York Times* critic, Edward Rothstein, noted in his summary of the children's literature tables in 2005. While there is nothing in itself wrong with this, it was antagonistic to the models which fantasy and sf had been offering — the only juvenile sf I can think of which both reflects this mood and still manages to be a good book is Andre Norton's *Cat's Eye*. Furthermore, these details became obligatory. To be a good book, and even a book worth publishing, children's literature increasingly had to "reflect" this imagined world of "the streets." To give an example for which I have actual evidence, Diana Wynne Jones had to write *Wilkins' Tooth* (1973), a book which reflects these settings and values, before her publisher would consider the earlier and far better structured *Eight Days of Luke* (1975). *The Ogre Downstairs* (1974) (a tale of two merged families) was similarly written in part to accommodate this demand. Pamela Sargent, a well-respected writer of science fiction for both adults and teens, found her YA career drying up as her publisher increasingly argued that her books were unrealistic and too sophisticated in terms of their ideas for the target market (email, 17 January 2005).

All of the above may have been emphasized by the growing sense (if not the reality) that teens were more threatened than ever before. Fear of drug and gun crime has risen to unprecedented levels at the same time that teens have lost the social assimilation routes of work. Teens are kept separate from adults for their own protection, with the result that the U.S. and UK both have an intensely age-segregated society in which we worry about *the other teens* that our children hang out with. Not coincidentally, teens growing up in America in the 1990s may have experienced the most obsessive childcare the world has ever seen. All the trends for organized play that emerged at the end of the nineteenth century have intensified. Football is a league sport. Cheerleading is competitive. Spelling is a major competition. There is almost no aspect of American children's lives that does not have someone setting rules and awarding prizes. And of course no teen goes off without a mobile phone. Some companies will even arrange for parents to tag their children. In fiction this has rendered it impossible to have a plausible novel in which a teen goes off on an adventure on his or her own. As Alison Prince, writing to the *Guardian* (24 December 2005) noted, the continued popularity in the UK of the children's author Enid Blyton can be traced to her willingness to send "her young protagonists out with no adult supervision in their own world," In the modern literary world, unless something disastrous—like the death of all the family, or appalling abuse—can act as a facilitator, such adventures are impossible. Prince writes, "The real-life territory between Hogwarts and Jacqueline Wilson's angsty comedies is increasingly a mobile nirvana in which children must be kept safe. No publisher will risk a scenario in which four kids and a dog set out in a boat of their own, without so much as a life-jacket." Science fiction, located as it is mostly within our own world, has been unable to escape the effects of this new realism. The one area which remains a partial exception however (partial in that there is usually a facilitating disaster), is the revival of the "ensemble novel" for teens, in which a group, rather than a single protagonist, is sent out on an adventure. As a number of sf authors for children and teens have exploited the potential these structures offer, I'll be looking at these novels a little later.

After setting, the second leg of social realism was "relevance." This, more than anything else, proved a major problem for the genres of the fantastic. First of all, the old-style career books were not so "relevant," simply because the school-leaving age had gone up. Showing young soldiers was suddenly deeply unpopular: Vietnam did not so much create a response in teen literature as paste a curtain over it (in the same period the fashion for historical novels about young soldiers also collapsed). It was no longer plausible to show teens engaged in real science because the chances were that they were at least a decade away from being able to do real science, partly because of the extension of education, and partly also because safety concerns were beginning to affect the school curriculum and to even greater an extent what toys were available —children's woodworking kits turned to plastic, their chemistry kits to cookery sets.[4] Instead, two big themes came to the fore as being of crucial interest to teens: sport and relationships. Science fiction had little experience with either of these (with the exception of the occasional terrible baseball story). It continued to have little experience with sport, although by the 1990s gaming, of the computer and role-playing variety, had become a theme (see Sleator, Kostick and *The Web* sequence), with a number of "trapped in a game" stories by earlier writers such as Monica Hughes and Nicolas Fisk, and later K. A. Applegate. There is a difference between these two themes, of course. The "trapped in a game" stories are essentially varieties of "the parents are wrong," while the books about gaming have the teens far more autonomous and far more focused on themselves and their own world.

Science fiction had perhaps even less experience with interpersonal relationships. Science fiction for teens and children had been for a very long time the last refuge for those teens who did not wish to engage in romance (or at least wished to keep it in a nice neat corner). Sometime in the 1990s this changed. The "concerns" of teens were increasingly assumed to be "realistic," positing a rejection of "adventure" as childish. Although I loathe the argument that the curriculum was feminized in the interests of improving the performance of girls and at the expense of boys, when it came to "proper" reading, the Henry James effect, in which literature is defined by the degree to which characters eschew adventure and "accept" that life is directed towards the sedate reconstruction of the family, did skew the notion of "mature" reading away from the adventure novel and towards the novel of relationship and manners, away from writers like Robert Louis Stevenson and H. G. Wells, and towards Thomas Hardy and Henry James himself. Children's and teen's literature has always tried to socialize children. It always will. But much of it socializes behavior. Almost the only type of children's literature that in the past tried to socialize inner thoughts was the evangelical novel of "growing into grace"— Louisa May Alcott's *Little Women* (1868) is an excellent example. So it is unnerving to discover that so much modern sf for teens follows a similar route, in which the teen protagonist "grows into grace." In the modern examples however, the target is not reconciliation with God, but reconciliation with parent, friend, bully or girl/boyfriend. This is a useful paradigm for us, for as adventure literature was consigned to the realm of being "for children," children's authors and critics of fiction for children have similarly sought to lay claim to the Jamesian values to defend their field. The result is that sf for teens and children is caught in a pincer movement of values converging around the issue of relationships (see Beverly Lyon Clark, 37 and Luckhurst, 42–3). Children's literature in the 1970s, and children's sf in the 1980s took a sharp turn, to "advise" on this inner world of relationships even as the rhetoric among librarians and teachers argued that we should *not* be assuming children's fiction was something to learn from.

As I keep saying, early sf for children and teens was on an outward trajectory. Protagonists grew up and left home. Home fulfilled one of two roles. In one role, the protagonist took the excellent example of home into space and applied it to his or her dealings with the universe. You can see this in Heinlein's *Space Cadet*, Monica Hughes in *The Keeper of the Isis Light* (1980), or Brian Earnshaw's *Dragonfall 5* (1972). Most of Andre Norton's protagonists have either lost, or are in the process of losing a parent, yet in *Star Man's Son* and *Cat's Eye* both protagonists are trying to apply the lessons of home to the great big galaxy. When protagonists in these stories do return home it is often to say how important their domestic values were out there in the big wide world. The other early model is the growing out of domestic values. Norton's protagonist in *Star Man's Son* and Heinlein's protagonists in *Tunnel in the Sky* and *Starship Troopers* (written as a juvenile if not published as one) both come home to find that they despise everything they were brought up with.

Much modern sf for teens stands all of this on its head: over and over again, the trajectory seems to be to go out in the world, learn something about the universe, and use this to have a reconciliation with the parental or familial unit. And I hate to have to say this, but this type of fiction is overwhelmingly contributed to the genre by female writers. In Alison Goodman's *Singing the Dogstar Blues*, while the plot is about a school girl shepherding an alien around her high school and learning about her genetic heritage, the *story* is about the girl reconciling herself to her parents. In Margaret Mahy's *Aliens in the Family* (1986) while the plot is about a child from the future meeting a family in Australia, the *story* is about one child learning to accept her father's new family as her family. Sylvia Waugh's *Space Race* (2000) series is ostensibly about aliens on earth, but the story for each text follows the same trajectory each time: parents choose children over career. A rare male writer in the mode, Terence Blacker in *The Angel Factory* (2001) offers exactly the same move although this time an alien family choose their adopted Earth child over their mission. The most extreme is perhaps Susan Beth Pfeffer's *Life as We Knew It* where a family retreat to huddle around Mom in the face of global disaster. The family as the essential social unit is overwhelmingly valorized over both friends and work identities.

When reconciliation with the parent is not the central emotional issue, dating crops up over and over again. How to meet the perfect boy/girl is threaded through Ned Vizzini's *Be More Chill* (2004). James Valentine's *Jumpman* series (2002–2003) uses a boy-girl dating duo where fiction from earlier periods would have settled for friendship. William Sleator's fractal novel *The Last Universe* has as its outcomes different dating configurations (although here, the most conventional proves disastrous for the protagonist so I think we might want to read this as a response to the model, not an extension of it). Rather a lot of the modern authors seem to feel that they can substitute a romance between the male and female protagonists for a solid sf story. Kimberley Fuller's *Home* (1997) (not to be confused with the Davies book of the same title) should be a tale about genocide. When Maran rescues Alik she discovers that he is a refugee from the people whom his nation destroyed when they occupied the planet, but the genocide is brushed away as one person's desire for honor and glory, and the focus of the tale is on the romance between Maran and Alik. Yet the centering of romance can work as science fiction if it, too, is the subject of estrangement. Louise Cooper's *Mirror, Mirror: Breaking Through* and *Mirror, Mirror: Running Free* is one such book (both 2000, technically they are two halves of the same story).

In *Mirror Mirror: Breaking Through*, Angel lives in a nasty super-commercial world, her mother is shallow and wants her to Partner a boy at 15 so she does not have to pay for Angel's education. Running away from this, Angel falls through a mirror sculpture into a Bronze-Age world, and meets Winter, a boy with the same name as the fantasy boy in her virtual reality game. Eventually, disease hits his village and they escape back into Angel's world where her mother tries to make her a celebrity. Angel and Winter run back through the sculpture. This first book rather over-eggs the pudding: the world is so horrible, Angel's parents so uncaring. This is a teen view of the world but it does not offer much solution, In some ways it is a lot like N. Roy Clifton's pastoral *The City Beyond the Gates* (1971) in that although Cooper makes some sardonic comments about it being a good thing Angel does not ask the villagers what the cute bunnies are for, there is a lot of wistfulness for a simpler way of life.

The second book is *much* more interesting. When Angel and Winter go through the sculpture they find Winter's world is not quite as they remember it. They end up running again, and this time they end up in a not-quite–Angel world where there is an Angel but it is the daughter her mother would actually have liked (pliant, not too bright). They try again and end up ricocheting between different worlds until rescued by Pye, who they had thought was threatening them but is actually the scientist who made the sculpture. He asks to take them on as apprentices. Winter agrees, Angel declines. She goes back to her own world, cannot cope with it, and is rescued by her own ingenuity (she builds the sculpture anew in virtual reality) and by Winter and Pye. The book is about leaving home and growing up, about refusing the socialization cues, but it is a rare thing. In most of these books dating is an indication of maturity — and with the exception of the work of the gay writer David Levithan (which is only incidentally sf) and Troon Harrison's *Eye of the Wolf* (2003), which is set in a polyamorous future, they are all firmly heterosexual futures as well.

For younger children the primary social issue which modern children's sf seems to be expected to take on board is bullying and the construction of friendship. In the last decade friendship has come under the social science spotlight: small children claim they have difficulty making friends; parents and teachers worry about the friendship skills of young children; and bullying has become a source of serious concern. It is impossible to know whether anything has changed in the actual classroom experience of children in these areas (although we do know that most U.S. children no longer experience any free-style play with peers in "coincidental" locations such as the street or the park). But we do know that concern has risen, and this is reflected in such books as Mary Amato's *The Word Eater* (2000), Caroline Luzzatto's *Interplanetary Avenger* (2005), M. Meecham's *Quiet! You're Invisible*, M. Moss's *Amelia Takes Command* (1999) and Steve Cousins' *Frankenbug* (2000). In every single one of these books, no matter what the "plot," whether it is a worm eating words and transforming the universe (Amato) or a girl's experience at space camp (Moss) the actual *story* is about gaining the confidence to stand up to a bully, and the social skills to turn a bully into a friend. In most, if not all cases, there is a strong emphasis on empathy with the bully. Yet the curious thing is that the actual depiction of friendship in children's and juvenile sf can be very shallow. Some of this is because the characters are not well drawn in the first place, but it is also because of the role of ensemble fiction in the field.

The first difficulty is that adults seem to have a hard time explaining *why* children are friends with each other. This is unsurprising, both because many children cannot explain themselves and because for at least the first few years of school, many friendships are created by proximity such as being seated at a desk with someone else. The growing interest in "friendship skills," while well intentioned, is also an iteration of the constant desire adults have to shape and control children's friendships (an extension of the desire to seek out "good company" for one's children).

In the absence of understanding children's friendships, many writers have settled for what we can call "ensemble" novels in which there are a number of child characters who are all friends (or unwilling companions who become friends) and who each "represent" something with which the child/teen reader can identify. Rather than characters with a sense of individuality that the writer cannot mess with (that is, there is such a thing as "out of character"), these are frequently "avatars," icons to be moved around the adventure. At their crudest they can be lightly sketched stereotypes. One fat, one ginger, one brainy, one sporty. In the juvenile science fiction of the 1950s through the 1970s they tended to be discerned by skills: there would be a scientist type, a practical mechanic, possibly a radio enthusiast, possibly one who was, or wanted to be, a doctor. We can see this in Bova's *End of Exile*, where each child develops an aptitude, or in Heinlein's *Space Cadet* where the different aptitudes of the cadets helps to keep them alive when downed on Venus. I am in no sense using this as a derogatory dismissal. From my point of view, there is no such thing as a bad technique, only a technique used inappropriately or without understanding its power.

The avatar in science fiction (and they exist in plenty of other genres too by the way) is there to be steered through problems and give us the excitement of thinking we are clever — a waldo for the brain. My favorite avatar, Lois McMaster Bujold's Miles Vorkosigan, is precisely this kind of intellectual extension. I'm not half as bright as Miles, but for a few hundred pages I get to clothe myself in his intellect.

In YA science fiction since the mid–1980s these avatars have come to represent emotional qualities and skills rather than practical or intellectual ones. While this can result in shallow uninteresting characters it does not actually have to: we can see excellent examples in K.A. Applegate's science-fantasy sequence for teens, *Everworld* (1999–2001), in which each of the protagonists has an "attribute" (a child abuse survivor, an OCD sufferer etc.), and later in her science fiction series for slightly younger teens, *Remnants* (2001–3) in which these attributes are formalized in a society in which teens take on Japanese-style cos-play as a way to create identity so (literally) wear their attributes on their sleeves, and in which the skills they bring to the adventure are constantly being called upon, and develop with their characters. Notable in *Remnants* is the way brought experience and experience on the ship changes behavior and alliances: friendships are neither fixed nor irrational. In Scott Westerfeld's excellent *The Last Days* (2006), a vampire novel set in modern New York and with science-fictional explanations for vampirism, the characters form a band: we have the junkie girl, the rich and brilliant musician girl, the poor brilliant musician boy, the outsider bassist and the homeless autistic drummer. Attributes substitute for character, and the reader is positioned, chapter by chapter, in each character's head. It works because it directs the reader as much inward to the recreation of "family" (a band in this case) as it does toward the external problem they must face,

The "attribute" element is even further literalized in K.A. Applegate's *Animorphs* (1996–2001) series: a group of children each acquire the power to turn into a specific animal which has a relationship with the child's fears and desires.[5] Applegate's books provide a "way in" for readers, one which holds as primary in the reader/text relationship the notion of "identifying with the protagonists." In *Everworld* and *Animorphs* each book is told from a different point of view in order to maintain focus and identification and a "clothing" for the reader to don — I am reminded forcefully as I write this of the BBC children's television program *Mr. Benn* in which Mr. Benn became, in turn, a knight, a spaceman, a game hunter and other "roles."[6] When they work well, these modern ensemble novels offer emotional roles for the reader to try on. However, the conclusion of the *Remants* books supports rather than undermines my argument. As the books edge to a close in episodes thirteen and fourteen, familial communities re-form (admittedly one of these is a gestalt entity) and those who cannot fit into the available social spaces are killed off. It is somehow unsurprising that a baby becomes a vital part of the "spell"[7] to create a new world. When we leave the world of *Remants* we say goodbye to several cozy nuclear families and a reconstitution of an inward-looking adulthood. There will be no more adventures and everyone likes it that way (Clark: 16–28).

A particularly good example of the ensemble novel in teen sf is J.B. Stephens, *The Big Empty* series. These books (*The Big Empty, Paradise City, Desolation Angels* and *No Exit*) came from a book packager and are proof that there is no such thing as a bad medium *per se*. All ways of doing things can produce good and bad material. This series is particularly good. It is written by three authors, in the order: Book 1: Author A; Book 2: Author B; Book 3: Author C; Book 4: Author B. Author B is Tracy Lynn; the others I don't know.[8]

The tale begins a few years after a virus has devastated America (the rest of the world is never referred to, a curious, but not unusual American trope). In the emergency a man (Gerard MacAuley) has risen to power and organized the evacuation of the American interior (the Big Empty of the title) to the two coasts. Why he has done this is never quite clear, an aspect of the tale which leaves these books head and shoulders over most of their competitors. MacAuley may be an opportunistic tyrant, but there are many more hints suggesting that he is a man in a panic, desperate to save America and taking decisions that seem right in an emergency. This— the wrong things we do in a state of emergency — will prove to be one of the thin silver threads of the novel's political weave, and creates a thread of understanding through the ensemble.

But the *story* is not about MacAuley. Instead it is about living in disaster and under a repressive state. In the first part, *The Big Empty*, Keely is recruited to a secret commune, Novo Mundum, via her email. On the way she is joined by Michael and his airhead girlfriend Maggie (with whom he had been about to split up, and who he rescued from a robbery gone wrong), Diego who has lived in the Big Empty, Irene — on the way to Novo Mundum with her father and brother and separated from them when she tries to help Diego; Jonah, also a tagalong, and Amber, a pregnant teenager whose boyfriend has decamped to Novo Mundum. The first part is all about getting there. The second part, *Paradise City*, introduces us to Novo Mundum where Dr. Slattery rules with the help of his brother Frank. NM is a commune set on a college campus and all is idyllic. Each teen finds a place: Amber's pregnancy is seen as a boon, Jonah becomes a plumber, Michael rises to the top of the tree as a security expert and boyfriend of Dr. Slattery's daughter. Then it all starts to go pear-shaped. Irene starts to realize that Diego (who has been injured) is being kept sedated. Keely and Liza discover documents that suggests Slattery is making viruses, and Michael's friend Gabe is killed by electric wire which Michael designed and installed. When they find experimental subjects of the virus all of them but Jonah flee, with Liza in tow. *Desolation Angels* tells of the struggle to cross the Big Empty and to get to Houston where they meet up with Keely's mother. *No Exit* takes them back to Novo Mundum where they bring down Slattery. In the distance, we can also see MacAuley's regime beginning to crumble.

There are many things that interested me about these books: superficially they have the "there and back again" of many YA problem books which take us away from adult care, into wrong adult care, and back out again towards adult-secured safety. In actuality, however, the adults who have been left behind have already (for various reasons) abandoned their caretaking role, and Dr. Slattery's megalomania actually originates in his desire to care for his community. The argument that "Stephens" pursues here is about the nature and expression of caring, not who is doing it.

The Big Empty is also interesting here because of the way it subverts the avatar structure. Sometimes an author will play with us, let us get inside an avatar and then force us to question that relationship.

Think of this as *Beverly Hills, 90210* ensemble fiction. Rather than one character we want to watch, there are several characters we are encouraged to want to be. And just to make sure the reading demographic is right, there will be "someone for everyone." Again, I caution against reading my words as necessarily derogatory; I've never wanted to be any of the characters in *Beverly Hills, 90210* but I spent much of my childhood wanting to be Sabrina Duncan in *Charlie's Angels*. Too often these ensemble characters are by the numbers. Even K. A. Applegate's *Everworld* sequence, which in all other ways I rate very highly, resorts to four kids, three boys and a girl, each of whom has defined character traits and even when they turn out to have hidden secrets somehow they stay much the blanks they began.

"J.B. Stephens" is not having any of that. Each time we think we've got the player attributes figured out, the author gives them a little twist. Let's take Michael's girlfriend Maggie, for example. A total flake, incapable of looking after herself and worse, incapable of realizing that, she suddenly turns around to the others and says she's had enough. She walks off into the bush. What threw me about this is that it was totally in character yet broke the "we have to follow her and see her grow" structure that I usually see in these books. When we meet her again, she's shacked up with a gang leader, is still utterly dependent but has made her life through manipulation of the male. Not only aren't we being asked to identify any more but we are being asked to feel a bit repelled. Elsewhere there is an interesting scene where Keely thinks how much she likes being snuggled by two boys at once ("Stephens" later kills off one of the boys, but the publishers did have to sell the book) and again this avatar is not quite so comfortable.

One by one, "Stephens" has the initial ensemble develop in ways that aren't terribly comfortable. If we wanted to see these characters as skins to don, then frankly, they've got itching powder inside. This discomfort helped me through what I would usually regard as an overemphasis on relationships (which I note some of the Amazon comments have complained about). There is too much, but it never actually became the center of the story; it is more just what was happening as the real issues—how to stop a plague—were sorted out. Although Keely hooks up again with her mom, there is none of the "we have learned the world is dangerous and we want to go home" narrative I've seen too much of. Nor does Keely take her new lessons to improve her relationship with her mom. Instead, it is mom who has to do the changing, and Keely goes home because the military drags her there, with a whole load of new ideas about politics. The "parents" (in this case the military and the government) are still wrong, and there is no reversion to the respectful relationship that we find in the 1970s books, where an older mentor usurps the parental position. Instead, there is some sense that adulthood is undermined by the return home, and that for Keely it is an enforced pause in the process of maturing.

But there are exceptions for both male and female adults and these themselves are important for what I want to argue later is evidence of a shift in values which is profoundly gendered, and that is the emergence of a *protectionist* model of adulthood which I have alluded to several times, and which emerged in the fiction of the early twenty-first century. In the books from 1950 through the 1990s the trajectory of all the children's characters was *away* from adults: either facilitated by adults into an adult world of their own, or walking away in high dudgeon to revolutionize the world and show *them* how it is done. At the end of the twentieth century, sf for children revived the figure of the mage or mentor: common to fantasy, this was a trope that had died with Heinlein, and with Norton's move away from the juveniles.

We can see the role of the mentor in such diverse novels as Rodman Philbrick's *The Last Book in the Universe* (2000), in Michael Carroll's Superheroes books, and in Susan Beth Pfeffer's *Life as We Knew It*. The three distinct presentations in these books cover much of the ground I want to delineate. Philbrick's novel is essentially constructed in the Heinlein model, extended by Panshin and common to a lot of fantasy; the main character has an older mentor, a man who introduces him to books and tries to prepare him for something different. As with all of these mentor roles the idea is to push the young person beyond themselves and, *crucially*, beyond the abilities of the mentor. The mentor figure is a giant who loans his shoulders to the next generation.

In Michael Carroll's Superheroes series, however, the notion of the mentor takes on a new shape. In a glancing aside I mentioned on my blog that in science fiction, the equivalent of the fantasy, middle-book-in-a-trilogy syndrome in which the questors wander for forty (metaphorical) years in the wilderness so the hero can learn his craft, is the training section. This can be one-to-one (think Yoda and Luke Skywalker) or it can be what I've come to consider the ubiquitous training school. In the first of Carroll's books, *The Quantum Prophecy*, Danny and Colin discover that they are superheroes. From here we are on a path of kidnap and torture, supervillainy and excess. Danny's father turns out to be the super villain facade, trapped in an impersonation at the moment his superpowers were undone. Colin turns out to be the child of two ex-heroes, and begins to develop his own powers of strength and hearing.

The plot is sort of irrelevant. It is the execution of the plot that grabbed my attention. At one point Colin and Danny are kidnapped. Colin escapes and from then on the focus is on Colin's intelligence. He evades his captors, succeeds in gaining help from another child who we never see again, makes use of a charitable service, persuades/coerces a rather unpleasant character called Razor to assist him, acquiesces in a con-trick and generally makes the world work for him without ever being "rescued" by anyone. It is extremely well written and very plausible, and the boys are both independent and yet still children, scared and vulnerable. In the sequel, *Sakkara* (2006), however, all of this independence is either undercut or reshaped to force the boys into the roles of mentees in a training base in which — unsurprisingly — all the adults turn out to be misguided. The effect is to both encourage dependence but also to undermine the very powerful role of a good mentor, and these two things are meant to go hand in hand: mentors are to be looked on with suspicion, teachers have other agendas. Bruce Coville's *An Alien Stole My ...* [*Teacher, Brain*, etc.] (1991–1992) encapsulates this idea, in that in each adventure a child or children learn things from their mentor but each time discovers that they are serving another's agenda as well. It is a mixed message, one which undercuts children's growing independence, but also argues that they should think for themselves.

More recently however, the mentor has mutated much more directly into the protector, less concerned with encouraging children to grow up into adulthood than trying to preserve them from the loss of childhood. Most frequently, this appears as a rescue figure at the beginning and end of novels (not always the same people), as in Nancy Farmer's *The House of the Scorpion* and *The Ear, the Eye and the Arm* in which the children lose the safety of one set of adults but end the novel in the safe arms of another. These novels are pitched at younger teens but teens roughly the same age as Carroll is aiming for, the 12/13 age range, and it is interesting to see this limitation.

At the very extreme are those texts where the parental role, whether fulfilled, resisted or rejected, is explicitly to protect the child and this is incorporated into the way in which growing up is configured. Hugh Scott's *Why Weeps the Brogan* (1989) is initially written as a story of two children surviving in what turns out to be a museum, but the hidden, and important story is of a mother protecting her children from nuclear holocaust. Francine Prose's *After* is for most of its length about a teen's ability to cope with the collapse (or insanity) of adult authority but in the conclusion it is uncontaminated adults who effect the final rescue and it is the reassertion of reasonable adult society which is the promised off-the-page conclusion. The same is true of Neil Arksey's *Playing on the Edge* (2000). A novel about future football, its underlying theme is about the nature of adult authority, but its message is not in the end about negotiation — the changing roles of the child as he grows, understanding adults as people — but much more straightforwardly about "good" adults with power and "bad" adults with power. The result is that the application of power looks pretty much the same on each side, and while it is a teenager who protests and publicizes the plot to destroy soccer as we know it, the denouement has the emotional impact of a *deus ex machina* as the teens are pulled back into the adult polis by the promise of adult protection.

The most extreme manifestation of this resocialization trajectory — and I do not claim it as typical — is the already mentioned *Life as We Knew It* by Susan Beth Pfeffer. It is the mom's competence that is demonstrated in this novel. As the world becomes more dangerous she pulls her children, including her grown son, closer and closer to her. I have already discussed this in terms of the changing attitudes to children and the world, but I think it is also a reflection of a gendered shift in sf novels. This protectionist attitude to children is traditionally "feminine" and as more than one person has argued — not always sensibly — does seem to be infecting western society, as children are seen as increasingly precious commodities. Its gender element can be seen posited in two early twentieth century writers: we can contrast E. Nesbit's arguments for protectionism in the ideal future at the end of *The Story of the Amulet* (1906) against Arthur Ransome's "If not Duffers Won't Drown" in *Swallows and Amazons* (1930), a novel which not coincidentally insists on the physical capacities of girls. What is being argued over is a model of childhood as one of adventure and experiment versus a model of childhood as carefully guarded. This argument has become intense in the past decade in both the U.S. and the UK. Beginning with the movement to improve playground safety in the 1990s (see the Fair Play campaign) it became entangled with the requirements of insurers. Health and safety legislation, which was designed to ensure jobs could be done as safely as possible, became a threat (not always real but still sufficiently powerful) to the existence of school trips, and even school-yard games.[9] As the publication of *The Dangerous Book for Boys* (2006) indicates however, this is a profoundly gendered argument. Risk-taking for girls (and we will see this later) is being encouraged (within bounds). It is risk-taking for boys that seems to be under attack and its loss feared for. Peter Hautman's 2006 novel, *Rash*, is firmly grounded in these fears.

Bo has grown up in the United Safer States of America. He runs in pads, and has therapy for his temper. When he loses it one too many times (and triggers a psychosomatic rash among his classmates) he finds himself making pizza for McDonalds in a forced-labor factory in Alaska. The only escape is the football team, until his liberty is regained by the artificial intelligence he accidentally created for a school project. This story is presented with ambivalence. Bo's temper is never regarded by anyone, including himself, as a good thing. The response is linked to the second argument, where it becomes convenient to the government to describe more and more things as a crime, so that free labor is displaced by convict labor until it makes more sense for Bo's father to "voluntarily commit" since at least he will get paid, and there is a 99 percent recidivism rate for all convicts. Yet, despite the political argument to be suspicious of government motives, the underlying claim for a boy's right to risky behavior remains the dominant theme.

Of course, hidden in many of these texts, and fundamental to the story told in *Rash,* is that the children under discussion are only *our* children, an issue which Nancy Farmer's *The Eye of the Scorpion,* Janet McNaughton's *The Secret Under My Skin,* and Susan Price's *Odin's Voice* (2004) as well as Nancy Amato's *Word Eater* and Nicola Davies' *Home* (2005) all address.[10] In all of these books—all told by women—the children and teens are born outside or thrust outside the protective net by disaster. In each case it validates adventure otherwise prohibited in terms of the ideal they have been seen to lose or never have had. In contrast, for most of the novels narrated by male authors such as Pete Hautmann, David MacHale, Kenneth Oppel, and Conor Kostick, the characters have either fled the protective net from frustration, or political events send them to complete a mission for which they are peculiarly suited.

This chapter is only half of an argument that will extend into chapter five. What I hope I've demonstrated is the way in which the outward trajectory of much juvenile sf is replaced by an increasing emphasis on the inward—inward towards family and the establishment of family, and inward also towards feelings. The child and teen as *practical,* competent, inventive and assertive disappears in the mid 1980s. It is replaced by a child or teen for whom the emphasis is on *emotional* competence and practical *dependence* (in Guttman's *Virtually Perfect* [1999], for example, Grandfather provides the technical electrical skills to bail the teens out of a problem created by emotional immaturity). When the practical teen reappears in the 2000s it is almost always in the context of disaster, often on a world scale. Only when the parents are utterly unreliable is the child or teen permitted to develop survival skills.

In the next chapter, I want to consider other ways in which science fiction for teens has reflected, commented on and helped to shape social expectations of the child, specifically with regard to gender.

CHAPTER FIVE

Socialization and the Gendered (Future) Society

In the previous chapter I drew a very broad-brush picture of a changing set of expectations of children *vis à vis* the trajectory of adventure, of response to the adult world, and of adults' changing response to children. In this chapter I want to look more closely at a very specific set of expectations of children, those of gender, in ways which extend the issues of children's relationship to the wider world, and to an issue raised in greater depth in the next chapter, understandings of identity. Expectations of children are structured by age and overwhelmingly by gender, which brings us to an almighty problem with science fiction written for children and teens.

Why is sf for children so socially conservative?

Among all the books I have read, I have come across a handful of working mothers and only two texts which dare to reconfigure the heteronormative, monogamous matrix (although I have found two gay utopian texts by the author David Levithan).[1] If mothers exist at all — and in a great many of these books mothers are oddly absent — they are in the background, they play supporting roles, they are cooks, cleaners, wipers of tears, advisers on boyfriends. From Andre Norton, through John Rowe Townsend and Jill Paton Walsh, on to William Sleator and William Nicholson and Jeanne DuPrau, adult women don't hold jobs. There are some qualified exceptions: the mother in Joan Lennon's *Questors* (2007) is an inter-world agent, but as she has allowed her children to be taken away and exploited she is clearly not a good mother and spends a lot of time apologizing for her behavior; the mother in Alison Goodman's *Singing the Dogstar Blues* (1998) is a frivolous media star (and neglects her daughter); in Louise Cooper's *Mirror, Mirror* (2000) Angel's mother is unpleasant, manipulative and intends to deny her daughter education because she just cannot be bothered. Olivia, the mother in Applegate's *Remnants* (2001–3), is a sane and sensible doctor, but as there is no medicine to hand, it is as a mother that she figures: her role is to act as a foil to her son's recklessness and to be the perfect boys' mom, concerned but encouraging. In contrast, the mother in Michael J. Daley's *Space Station Rat* (2005) (a book I otherwise adore) neglects her son for her science. Clearly working is not good for women. Given that Heinlein, patron saint of teen sf, thought all women should have science degrees and a laboratory in the back garden, this is a very strange state of affairs. These books not only refuse to speculate but many of them, such as the work of almost all the "degraded futures" novels discussed in the "The Parents Are Wrong" section, seem to relish a return to the social roles of the 1950s as presented in *Pleasantville*. Women smile a lot, speak little and are happy, or if they do dare to take part in the conversation they are unpleasant and potentially even wicked.

Of the books I read, only a handful present adult women in unqualifiedly successful *and happy* ways which have positive effects on their children's lives. L. J. Adlington's *The Diary of Pelly D* (2005) is a holocaust story in which Pelly D's mother does her best to shield her daughter from the realities of what is happening, while trying to retain her artistic career and encourage her daughter's ambitions. Malorie Blackman's allegory *Noughts and Crosses* (2001) portrays a black (upper caste) woman as a drunken drone, but her white (lower caste) counterpart as a hard-working domestic with ambitions for her children. The roles are strong but rooted in the 1960s U.S. model that structures the entire book.

Zizou Corder (as noted before, a mother and daughter team) is one of the rare modern authors to create parents who feel autonomous without swamping the story. The mother in *Lionboy* (2004) is an active scientist and while her work is what lands Charlie in hot water, this is the function of the work, not a representation of a mother placing her child in jeopardy. Both of the parents in Ann Halam's *Taylor Five* (2002), and the mother in her later novel *Siberia* (2005), are working scientists. The mother in *Siberia* does her best to pass on her values and her knowledge to her daughter under very grim conditions and despite political pressure, and there is a clear sense of the mother's mission as vitally important. Oisín McGann's shapechanger children in *The Harvest Tide Project* (2004) and *Under Fragile Stone* (2005) have a mother who serves as her people's ambassador and again has something of the character autonomy that we see in *Lionboy*. Not coincidentally, Corder, Halam and McGann all construct "adventures" in which the children become engaged in adult politics. But this is a tiny handful of books. Those texts in which adult women are allowed to be non-maternal role models are even smaller in number. Anna Fang in Philip Reeve's *Mortal Engines* (2001) begins as an air pilot and ends as a killing machine but in all her varieties is admirable. Janet McNaughton perhaps offers the strongest roles for adult women in *The Secret Under Her Skin* (2005). This is one of the few novels in which women are working scientists and politicians and real characters, rather than occupiers of labels, or existing solely in terms of facilitating the adventure of the children (a traditional role for adults in much adventure fiction).

Adult men, in contrast, are always and everywhere role models, if not always positive ones. In the 1950s they are models to be emulated; in the 1970s they are mostly models to be resisted and rejected as we have seen in "the parents are wrong" far future texts. Nicholas Fisk's *Trillions* (1971) and *Space Hostages* (1967) are typical in this respect: in the first, adults are clueless scientists and blustering generals trying to deal with an invasion that they don't understand; in the second a dying space pilot kidnaps a bunch of children and takes them into space. Thirty years later, in Margaret Simpson's *Strange Orbit* (1992), the same configuration is still in place: the children may be smart volunteers, but the adults are a dotty old woman and a hyper-masculine, thoughtless male pilot. Neither become worthy of respect in the course of the novel. David Stahler Jr.'s recent *Truesight* (2004), a rather splendid dystopian colonization novel, encapsulates a traditional theme in which all the adults are controlling and untrustworthy. This model of adulthood dominates the field.

This of course takes us on to think about how boys and girls are portrayed and understood in these books, and in this section I want to talk first about girls, then "girls and boys" in ensemble novels because I think there are very real differences between the single sex and the co-ed (for want of a better term) books, and finally, boys.

Girls in sf of the 1950s were either distant figures of admiration, distractions to "sensible" boys (in much the same way boys were distractions to "sensible" girls in many school stories: see *The Chalet School and Rosalie* [1953] by Elinor M. Brent-Dyer) or good chums distinguishable from the boys mostly by their willingness to take direction or their mild passivity. Yet oddly it is in the juveniles that we first see the change, and it is Heinlein, whose one attempt at a female heroine in a novel is cringingly bad (*Podkayne of Mars,* 1963) who is most effective at opening up space for real girls to do interesting things. Heinlein's young women are boyish and supportive. They want to be engineers *and* wives—don't laugh, this is as good as it gets for some time. The protagonist of "The Menace from Earth" (1957) starts out wanting to design space ships with her friend, and ends up doodling the "new" name of the potential company as she contemplates marrying him; and as a side issue, Heinlein also uses the story to put the boot into the idea that women can never be friends, but only rivals.

"The Menace from Earth" is the most challenging of Heinlein's proto-feminist stories, but we can see his respect for girls in the juveniles. In *Star Beast* (1954) John Thomas IV is not the sharpest card in the deck, but he is honorable and friendly and works hard, and his girlfriend, Betty, works out quite early that he is exactly what she needs. She is born to be a political wife: when the story ends John Thomas is off to be a cultural ambassador and this is all engineered by Betty. In *Tunnel in the Sky* (1955), a group of teens stranded on a strange planet develop a fairly egalitarian culture which expels those boys who are inclined to brutality (the word "rape" is not used but the implication is strong) and it is made clear that the male leader cannot remain in control without a female leader by his side. When they are rescued, Heinlein breaks with tradition and the two go their separate ways into different careers. Heinlein's *Starship Troopers* (1959) is most commented upon because its lead is Puerto Rican, but it is just as much a shock to the young female reader to discover that the pilots are women.

Although girls were absent from most juvenile sf for the next twenty years—Andre Norton's heroines exist in her fantasy books, but are rare in her sf—Heinlein's example combined with the feminist movement seems to have allowed almost instant liberation for girls when they do appear. Science fiction for teens, unlike fantasy, does not fall for the "coming out story," in which girls hide their sex to compete, or go up against authority to compete. However, as Mike Levy has argued ("Science Fiction as *Bildungsroman*"), there are a number of narratives in which female protagonists revolt either against future patriarchies, or against the narrow conditions of society as a whole. As a result, "modern" children's and teen sf does quite well by girls. Where girls appear as the protagonists they seem to have as much liberty as the context of the story allows.

The earliest books I have which conspicuously feature girls being both girls and active in their own destiny are Peter Dickinson's *Changes* series (1968–1970); *The Devil's Children, Heartsease,* and *The Weathermonger,* of which I have already discussed two in depth. When London-born Nicola joins the Sikhs as their canary, she does so in a gender-neutral role. Nicola fights in the skirmish between them and the bandits, and although on one occasion Nicola does help with the children, and her best friend in the group is portrayed as much more conventional, Nicola is not given the label of "tomboy." When Nicola is finally sent to France to find her family, the Sikhs' concern is that she not become hardened by her trauma. There is no reference to her sex. The farm setting of *Heartsease* and the sense of return to pastoralism shelters conventional work roles, but Dickinson does not assign the two protagonists gendered characteristics, and nor does he settle for a simple reversal. While the boy is perhaps more sensitive than the girl, who tends to the pragmatic, they are constructed as coherent *people,* not as boy and girl. The same is true in *The Weathermonger.* Geoffrey's abiding characteristic is his tendency to arrogance which was how he'd ended up as a weather witch in the first place. Sally, younger, is a listener. Both are smart, but Geoffrey is machine-oriented and Sally to animals, thought this is not presented as gendered. Sally is not sentimental about animals, she is pragmatic and sensible. Taken overall these three books present a matter-of-fact image of girlhood which is outgoing and capable although against a background of very much more conventionally feminine adult women.

The next really interesting text to hand is Robert C. O'Brien's *The Silver Crown* (1973). O'Brien demonstrates amply the simple solution to female liberation in children's books—remove the boys. When Ellen finds the silver crown under her pillow she puts it in her pocket and goes for a walk. In her absence the house is destroyed and she sets off on a journey to find the aunt who gave it to her. This journey will lead to black roads and a black castle, children playing in time to an unheard beat, and finally to a black crown. On the journey she meets Otto, who lives with a lady in the wood and wrecks trucks. Otto goes with her (with the encouragement of the lady, who knows what he is doing) but is captured and assimilated. To rescue Otto, Ellen must rescue everyone. That handover of Otto from the lady to Ellen is crucial in understanding how O'Brien accepts his own creation of Ellen. Otto thinks he is leading Ellen. The lady knows she is handing him over to Ellen to care for. So Ellen's feistiness, her willingness to think and act, is enfolded in the "proper" role of protective parent. It does not undermine either the book, or Ellen, but this interpretation explains this otherwise unnecessary interlude. Everything else in the book is purposeful.

O.T. Nelson's Lisa, *The Girl Who Owned a City* (1975), clearly revels in the role of girl as really rather scary protagonist. In this well-known book, Lisa finds herself in a world in which all the adults have died and uses her organizing abilities and Nietzschean philosophy to create an almost feudal state in which everyone else's labor belongs to her as an extension of "intellectual property." Lisa sees off boys who might compete with her, and boys who might collaborate with her. She does not have much time for girls either. Lisa is desexed not so much to play the boy as to play the superwoman.

There is no guarantee that a female author will produce interesting female characters. The girl in Sylvia Engdahl's *Heritage of the Stars* (1973) is never more than a helpmeet, and one who is to be kept in the dark about the true nature of her world beyond the end of the book, and few of H. M. Hoover's heroines ever seem to gain intellectual or political autonomy, although they frequently represent the other. Monica Hughes, however, whose career was most active during the 1980s, constructed a number of really interesting female characters of whom the best known is perhaps Olwen in *Keeper of the Isis Light* (1980). Olwen is the survivor of an exploration mission, cared for by a robot. When a colonization ship lands the robot creates a mask to shield her from the germs they may carry. Only at the end do we discover that the robot has altered Olwen so that she can survive on the planet and the mask is to hide the physical differences. Olwen retreats into exile, but not before she has redefined herself as something other than the cared-for child she appeared at the beginning, although there is more than a touch of the mother goddess about her. Hughes has firmly science-fictional intentions; she is primarily interested in ways to adapt both to other planets and to each other. My next two books both use sf to talk precisely about girls' place within the family.

In Marilyn Kaye's *Max on Earth* (1986), high-school cheerleader Randi meets a girl called Max outside the bleachers. Max is very strange and has run away from home to find herself. Randi helps Max learn to fit in, in which the emphasis is specifically ironing out gender-neutral behavior; there is a nauseating scene where Max learns how to flirt from women's magazines. Max, of course, turns out to be an alien (but half human) who has come to Earth to check out her human heritage, which is responsible for her irrepressible emotions. At the end Max decides to stay, having learned who she is and how to act, and Randi gets the boy she wants. This reversal of Mr. Spock's desire to extinguish his human element is very clearly played out in the same gendered terms: rational = masculine, irrational = feminine.

Margaret Mahy's *Alien in the Family* (1986) is less conspicuously gendered, but still its emphasis is less on getting to know an alien on his own terms than it is a metaphor book about the nature of alienness and the importance of family harmony. Jake is on holiday with her step-family and meets a boy who turns out to be from the future: it is the banding together to protect and help him that facilitates intimacy with her half- and step-siblings. In turn, his trip back into the past is less an exercise in history or anthropology as intended as a social and emotional developmental exercise, another one of those appalling "imagine you are a peasant in a medieval castle" class exercises which have themselves valorized empathy over the academic extrapolation of the discipline of history.[2] Again, as with *Max on Earth* there is an implication that empathy is both the correct feminine approach, and the correct approach to life. Overall, so many of these girls are expected to be boyish and bouncing and adventurous, and when they aren't, the "girlness" that is being promoted is often so super-feminine as to render the sf content mere window dressing.

This set of assumptions about girls' values does not go unchallenged. In her early sf novel, *Coming Down to Earth* (1994) Susan Price places Azalin in a space-station world where cooperation, liking company and being "sporting" (all the qualities of both UK girls fiction and U.S. high school culture) are necessities for survival. On a school trip to Earth Azalin goes AWOL. While on Earth she learns a lot about social injustice, but also finds a set of more individualistic values which emphasize far more diversity yet still insist on cooperation as a necessity for survival. *Coming Down to Earth* is refreshing in a number of ways; neither Azalin's home world nor Earth are much changed for her visit — no magical catalyst, she — and the understanding and empathy for both Earth and her homeworld that Azalin acquires is used not to reconcile her to home, but to give her the skills to deal better with her peers while she plots a long-term escape to become a terraformer on the new colony of Mars.

Before moving on, however, I do want to show that my criticisms are not simply feminist prejudice. In 2005, Mindy Schanback published the deliciously pink (pink cover, pink plot), *Princess from Another Planet*. The book is not dissimilar to *The Princess Diaries* but with the twist that Gracie Wright thinks her mother is mad, because her mother claims to be a Princess of Pannadeau and insists on teaching her how to kill Maluxziads. The book quickly turns into a romp/screwball comedy, triggered when Gracie swaps places with her richer cousin so she can go to riding camp and the invading aliens kidnap her cousin.

Gracie defeats the invaders, discovers her mom is not insane, and life goes on. My only sadness is that the wormhole through which her mother and the invaders traveled closes at the end of the book, ending any chances of long-term consequence. This is a "sealed" story in which all the "future" is personal, not science-fictional, but Schanback keeps the focus of the story "outward bound," family issues shape the sf adventure, not the other way around, and in part because Gracie has a cousin who she likes (too often in this kind of tale they at least begin as rivals) multiple models of femaleness are on offer.

My criticism of the above books is partly my own prejudice — I would like to see girls with interests beyond their own emotions — but I also believe the survey material suggests that female readers of science fiction feel the same way. Furthermore, the problem is that in these female-led books too often only one model of femaleness is provided. The most "successful" books in my terms, ones in which girls have a range of interests which can spread over both emotional and intellectual issues, seem to have more than one female protagonist. There are exceptions, of course. Ann Halam's *Taylor Five* and *Siberia* both have single protagonists, but these are survivalist novels. Taylor is attacked by terrorists in Borneo and is on the run, Rosita is running from a resettlement camp in Siberia. The isolation of the protagonist allows Halam to use a deal of internal monologue and rather than emphasize the emotional shapes an intellectual exercise in survival and goal, with *constant* reference to adult role models, both male and female. The books are both outward-oriented and suggest that growing up is about looking around for different ways of being human. *Siberia,* in particular, is worth considering more closely for the way that Halam interweaves a number of the demands I have been making for teen sf across the chapters of this book.

Siberia starts with Rosita remembering her arrival in a settlement camp with her mother. She is four years old and she remembers nothing before then. Her moment of Wakening is the realization that her shoes are too thin for the hard-packed snow beneath her.

One strand of the story is Rosita growing up in the settlement, joining the school, hardening herself to her surroundings and becoming "Sloe," named for a hard and bitter berry. Sloe will eventually be sent to a rehabilitation school where she will inadvertently betray her mother — her mother has broken the law by teaching her science — and will eventually be expelled, at which point she returns home only to have to escape from the local gangs and the police, carrying something they seem to want, the small walnut shell and tools that let her make Lindquists.

The Lindquists are the second strand of the story and they are where Halam has produced something very special, for this strand is told as a braid of mother love, fairy tale and science. Rosita/Sloe discovers the Lindquists when she spies on her mother "doing magic" one night. When one of the tiny kits escapes it develops into a squirrel-like being that stays her friend for a year. Nivvy is much mourned when he dies, and this elegiac note is held throughout story. Nivvy remains a presence without ever becoming sentimentalized.

Rosita's mother, aware that her time might be running out, teaches Rosita how to maintain the Lindquists and what they are—compressed DNA that can express itself in many forms. This is one of the most important aspects of what Halam does. A lesser writer would have written this as the passing on of true knowledge and understanding. Halam does no such thing; instead, from early on we get, through Rosita's eyes, the accumulation of misconception and mis-reasoning. Rosita, as she realizes herself by the time she is eight, spins the technology she witnesses into fairy tale. The making of the Lindquists in their nutshell, their transformation into magical creatures, mutates into the Czech version of Cinderella. When the older child, Sloe, goes on the run with the Lindquists, she has to return to the recreation of first principles, dredging her memory for what her mother told her and what the policeman Yagin reveals about the various classes of animals so that she can learn to manipulate the "magic" to produce the right animal to aid and abet her.

At various stages through the novel we see this movement from the magical explanation to the scientific, and it is always handled with great delicacy. We don't realize Sloe thinks the animals' love for her is a magical bequest, until she is told that they are genetically keyed to her. Anything that looks like a fairytale (the bright clothes and friendly manners of the traders who save Sloe from the ice and blizzard), is eventually revealed to be something else, a part of a greater complexity of being. Surrounding this tale is a story of a world genetically damaged, covered in ice and snow, in which human survival is bought at the expense of the animal world, and in which the protection of the environment has become increasingly difficult as people have forgotten what it is they are protecting. "Natural" is no longer "familiar."

The novel has two endings, which address some of what I've been implying about how an sf novel should end. One ending is Sloe's reunion with her mother after a trek across the ice that reminded me of Genly Ai's journey in Le Guin's *The Left Hand of Darkness* (1969) for its sheer power. The second ending moves us out again, shows us Sloe leaving home to start a new life — there is a reunion with an old (male) friend but nothing is decided and their relationship seems to serve as a metaphor for the seeds Sloe carries, *not* the other way around.

Sloe/Rosita is analytical, and it is this quality that seems to go south when authors attempt to conceive of smart adolescent girls. Frequently, what we get instead is protest founded on passion: a very good and well-known example in fantasy is Hermione Granger's objection to house-elf slavery in *Harry Potter and the Goblet of Fire* (2000) which is dismissed as founded on ignorance (Mendlesohn, 2002). So, for example, in M. T. Anderson's *Feed*, Violet, who is technically one of the protagonists but spends much of the book sick in bed, questions the society around her. But while her father's challenges are based

on pedagogical ideology, hers are the feelings of isolation of a teenage girl trying to fit in.

It is possible to combine intellectual analysis and emotional issues into
one female body. Some of the most successful girl protagonists do precisely
this: Mira, in Patrick Cave's *Sharp North* (2004), grows up in Scotland and only
really begins to question her life when someone kills a woman who looks a lot
like her and holds a paper with her name on it. Failing to get any answers, she
runs and ends up in London where a woman with her face is a Saint, one of
the leading families of New Briton. After living rough she finally falls in with
Kay, also a Saint but an oddity, a Scroat (or natural) conception in a world of
cloning and genetic engineering. Things then get very complicated. Through
all this Cave runs a constant sexual tension, sharpened rather than undermined
by the vicious political context in which it takes place. Once again, he is aided
by his construction of *multiple* female characters so that Mira does not have to
bear the burden of being a representative female child.

Similarly effective are Janet McNaughton's *The Secret Under My Skin* and
The Raintree Rebellion (2006). In the first, Blay is a child in a camp for homeless children. Plucked out of the home to assist Marella, the new bio-indicator
with her studies, Blay discovers her own aptitude for science. Although the girls
are perhaps set up to be too much "opposites" of each other — Blay, poor but
studious, Mariella, wealthy but lazy — McNaughton uses them to explore the
political situation of this post-disaster world and to explore the way romantic
relationships are affected by both external demands and personal goals. In the
sequel, Blake (as she now is) is sent to Toronto to help with decisions on how
to deal with the makers and collaborators in the Technocaust. McNaughton
positions Blake here as rather passive — much of the time she simply listens—
but this does place her in a position to analyze evidence and McNaughton successfully creates a book in which adventure is not necessarily action.
Furthermore, Blake's passivity is contextualized among many who are active,
both men and women.

One of my favorite novels for the way in which it shows ingenious girls,
if in a rather strange way, is Margaret Haddix's *Turnabout* (2000). Technically,
Melly and Anny Beth aren't girls. As centenarians, they are offered the chance
at rejuvenating treatment. The story recounts the problems of growing ever
younger. At the time the story is related Melly is 16 and Anny Beth 18, and what
they are telling is the story of living in the interstices of society as they "un-
age," making difficult decisions in order to move on. Using two quite different
women, with two very different "first lives" and very different ways of handling
their second lives, Haddix creates a complex web in which emotion is always
moderated with analysis: Melly chooses not to marry this time around. Anny
Beth marries and fakes her death twenty years later. These are decisions pro-
jected within a political and social framework that creates emotional response
but lack any of the sense of urgency that ripples through most teen sf for girls.

The most complex texts I have for girl-girl relations and rendering girl-dom as intensely political are Susan Price's *Odinstoy* sequence. They are particularly relevant here because of that issue I brought up earlier: what is suitable for children is most often a matter of what is suitable for *our* children.

"Kylie" is the bondswoman servant of Freewoman Perry. She is not quite a slave: in theory she can buy her freedom from the agency who rents her out, but as this requires earnings associated with high skills (which she does not have) and as the agency charges training to a bonder's bill, it is all a bit unlikely. But Kylie is lucky; she seems to channel Odin, one of the local gods, and the temple worshippers club together to buy her freedom. Kylie becomes "Odinstoy" and the Godspeaker of the temple. She is replaced at Freewoman Perry's by Affroditey, the daughter of a bankrupt who bonded her to the bank and then suicided. Price does a brilliant job of showing what a *nice* spoiled child is like, and follows it up with an effective portrayal of separation trauma. Affroditey is called "Kylie" in turn and has to look after Freewoman Perry's little boy. She hates him. She has no idea how to look after children. One day in a park she is approached by a woman in black who offers her love. Love just for her. The love-hungry Affroditey takes up the invitation to the temple.

This is where the book gets interesting, and ties into Mary Harris Russell's interest in what divides children's books from those for teens, and teen books from adult. The plot continues onward: the woman in the park is Odinstoy and when she gets the opportunity to go to Mars she proposes to Affroditey that they run away together, but the child (Apollo) is part of the deal — in reality he is the son of Odinstoy and Freeman Perry. This is not a romance though, so Affroditey (and the reader) have to quickly take on the notion of rape, without the word ever being said. Affroditey also has to accept that Odinstoy — at least initially — regards her as an adjunct to Apollo. Friendship is both created and poisoned by power structures. *Odin's Voice* (2004) is brutal in its portrayal both of bondage and the hypocrisies of bondage; the dissonance between what bondholders think of themselves and their bonders think is dealt with particularly deftly. Price also does an excellent job of delineating the bitterness of poverty and the use of slavery to keep the poor at bay. *Odin's Voice* and *Odin's Queen* (2006) both explore the effect of slavery and poverty on women, their vulnerabilities and the shallowness of "feminine" influence.

In *Odin's Queen*, Odinstoy arrives on Mars with Affey and Apollo, now renamed Odinsgift. They have arrived with Odinstoy dressed as a man but not denying that she is a woman, and Affey is listed as her "sister and wife." On Mars Odinstoy causes consternation by hugging a bonder in the greeting party, and questioning why Mars's Odinites have bonders— they have never really thought about the problem. From there she and Affey go to a small provincial non-conformist town where Odin worshippers have retreated to escape the discrimination of the Church of Mars, a Greco-Roman pantheon which claims all other gods as merely aspects of its own.

While Odinstoy is off exploring Mars and its underbelly, Affey screws up. Lonely, still spoiled, hating Odinsgift who is a sullen, none too bright child, she gets involved with a young man who promises to marry her. Much later it will turn out that he is a spy for the Church of Mars and unfortunately, Affey has spilled the beans: in a television interview the head of the Church of Mars reveals that Affey is an escaped bonder and that she and Odinstoy have kidnapped Odinsgift (the law saying that he belongs to his genetic father, who is free). Affey and Odinstoy run, taking with them Odinsgift and John, a bonder boy whom Affey has bought and Odinstoy has freed. They take refuge in a maintenance tower protected by the young of the suburb, but when the stand-off comes, it is Odinstoy who walks out of the airlock — a seeming impossibility as the lock is programmed to remain closed if it cannot detect breathing technology.

Affey really is in love with Odinstoy. In her world, men were what you did as a career. She has no training for anything other than being a very expensive wife. She does not cheat on Odinstoy for pleasure, but for security and wealth. This may seem abhorrent, but as Price portrays it, it is quite sensible. And more interesting is that Odinstoy *is* brutal and violent. If Affey runs to Jason it is in part because Odinstoy is an abuser with the best of excuses: "I do this for Odin." Price avoids lecturing but there are many, many uncomfortable moments and the relationship between the young women never falls into the archetypes which seem to litter teen fiction — neither of them is nice, both are simply trying to survive, and all too frequently it is at each other's expense.

Girls, Boys, and Girls and Boys in the Ensemble Novel

If girls seem to have most possibilities in girl-only novels when there is more than one of them, what happens when boys are introduced into the picture?

There is not a great deal of point looking at earlier sf novels for this question: if there are boys present in sf before around 1980 then they will have all the fun. After 1980 however, we need to consider at least three ways of creating "co-ed" novels. First, the romance novel, in which at the end there will be strong hints (at the least) that dating is destined; second, the sibling novel, in which boys and girls are friends, a category that tends to accommodate younger readers as well, as does the third form, the ensemble sf adventure which is aggressively heterosocial (although romance may be an issue) and which assembles its cast specifically to appeal to a range of reader identification, frequently demonstrated in the presence of markers other than gender.

The Romance

The romance novel in teen sf is a peculiar thing in that it seems to take one of two forms: two young people are thrown together and "inevitably" fall in love (sometimes with a heavy pinch of destiny), and those novels where romance is the issue which is at stake.

The classic romance structure can be seen in a number of the earlier post-disaster/lost colony novels such as Ben Bova's *End of Exile* (1975), Bev Spencer's *Guardians of the Dark* (1993), Robert Westall's *Futuretrack 5* (1983) or Nicola Morgan's *Sleepwalking* (2004) in which in each there is a pairing-off of characters, with the emergent leader acquiring a partner to accompany his Adam complex. The women in these books barely register as characters (although Morgan's is better than most).

By the 1990s this at least has changed: Louise Cooper's *Mirror, Mirror* allows both Angel and Winter to be real people with their own motivations. Cooper in fact begins with an expectation of romance (Winter, a boy in another world, has the same name as the boy in Angel's virtual reality game). Patrick Cave takes a different tack in *Blown Away* (2005). A sequel to *Sharp North* (2004), in *Blown Away* Adeline, a flawed clone, decides "what the hell." If she is going to die of a heart attack she might as well do it trying to attack the Nietzschean supermen who are currently running Britain (or Briton as it is called). Alongside this story run the diaries of Dominic, the son of a 2023 magnate who has his DNA taken for cloning and is one of the progenitors of Briton's New Visions, supermen with amazing reflexes but an inclination to obey authority. Adeline, we eventually find out, is cloned from Dominic's long-lost girlfriend, a natural athlete but both a rebel and a bit of a mystic. This is where the heart of the story is, exploring that long-lost-love story, but because it is in the past, the story proper is about the consequences of that romance. Adeline is a commentator and critic and the effect is to remind the reader that romances are about *real* people, not characters stepping up to fill a romantic role. Adeline herself uses the romance as a soul book, something to use to recenter herself.

Philip Reeve may be the most "romantic" of contemporary authors for children/teens (his books function in different ways for each age group). The first two books of the Infernal Engines sequence, *Mortal Engines* and *Predator's Gold* (2004) are as much concerned with the romance of Tom and Hester as they are with the wider Romance of politics and the defeat of Municipal Darwinism. Reeve's romance, however, is ongoing — beyond marriage — and difficult. There is no happy ending for Tom and Hester, only a working together and finally a falling apart before their final death and transmutation into two entwined trees. What marks out Reeve's work is that Tom and Hester are both complex and gendered beings: they neither default to "pals" (there is always some sexual tension) but when the relationship develops neither do they default to gender roles. Tom, always gentle and diffident, remains so. Hester, bitter, determined and not always very clear-headed, remains driven by her hurt. In the final book, *A Darkling Plain* (2006), these qualities both doom and heroize both of them.

Reeve's sensitivity to gender and personality plays out in *Larklight* (2007) where he succeeds in drawing a rather slushy romance from the point of view of the younger brother. We join with the younger brother in finding the whole thing mawkish and embarrassing but as outside readers, the two lovers (Jack and Myrtle) are strong enough that we also find ourselves wanting to cheer them on. In both *Larklight* and *Mortal Engines* the "romances" are fully enclosed within the sf adventure. Although Hester will do stupid things (within character) because she loves Tom, that never becomes the plot, although it does propel some of the more disastrous events. In *Larklight* the romance is a element of a particular kind of adventure convention that the narrator *wants* to live out.

While these books are conventional, they do not feel forced. A small number of authors are so convinced that romance is where the interest lies that it becomes built up into a destinarian edifice. Kimberley Fuller's 1997 novel *Home* is one such. It is essentially a Mary Sue plot in which the story is wrenched at regular intervals to meet the aims of the romance: when Maran rescues Alik she discovers he is a returner to her planet, a refugee who left when his people were overrun by invading colonizers. Alik seems to have no problem with the foreign language, but no one questions this until very late when it turns out that his people are telepaths. Maran starts to have dreams and visions, which turn out to be revelatory and prophetic. Maran turns out to actually be one of Alik's people. After all these revelations, approximately a third of the book is devoted to Maran's romance with Alik. In order to make this remotely plausible Fuller has to close down the range of associational options for Maran, with the consequence that the action takes place in a village and its hinterland, with little indication that they are on a planet. There is no reason at all for Alik's people to have stayed so close. Worse, in order to make the initial association between descendant of genocide and descendant of genocide victim acceptable, the genocide has to be portrayed as something irrational. The genocidal culture gets excused. The effect on Maran is to make her less a person and more a token to be handed over as a symbol of reconciliation; she seems to lose any free will.

Then there are the authors who think romance is a good subject matter for science fiction: "how will romance look if...?" I can hear them cogitating. The answer seems to be one of those perennial truisms, "human nature does not change" which is mostly nonsense and quite contrary to the expectations of the best adult sf. In Dan Guttman's *Virtually Perfect* (1999), Yip uses his computer's virtual software to create a perfect boy. But Victor steps out and comes to life and cuts a swathe through the girls in Yip's life. Most of the discussion is about "real" love versus "fake" love. While M.T. Anderson's *Feed* (2002) is structured around a doomed romance, it does at least have a debate running within it about pedagogy and our socialization of and expectations of teens.

Ned Vizzini's *Be More Chill* (2004) is rather more successful because it hosts a much wider debate about gendered behavior. Very early on in this work I had an argument with Michael Levy who felt that my objection to books in which sf formed the metaphor for a kid sorting out his/her emotional relationship with parents or lovers "failed" books which succeeded in their own terms. As must be clear by now, I still stand by what I am arguing, that many of these books aren't sf, that they aren't about the impact of technology but about something else, but *Be More Chill* is about relationships and is also science fiction. The crucial difference is that the technology is not a metaphor for anything but a facilitator that tackles what being a teenage boy is like, head on.

Jeremy is terminally uncool. He keeps printed sheets where he records all the slights he receives, he does not know how to dress, and he cannot even get as far as asking a girl out, never mind being turned down. One day a colleague (not a friend) talks him into buying a squip, a nanocomputer in the form of a pill. He swallows it, and the computer begins to give him advice on how to be cool. The book is funny, and sensible. Vizzini has done something both very simple and very clever—found a way to make an "agony" book hip. When things go wrong it is partly because Jeremy ignores the chip at crucial moments, partly because the chip is only a computer after all, and Jeremy's girl of choice turns out to be a bit smarter than the chip realizes. At the end Jeremy chooses to flush the chip because it is degrading, but there is no sickening lesson about how one should just be oneself. Jeremy *has* learned, *has* grown wiser: the chip helped him get started and from there he can work out who he wants to be and how to go about achieving that. *Be More Chill* is a book about how technology can help us: no hysteria, no fatalism, no metaphors. It is also one of the few books with a well-rounded male character.

The only really imaginative romance sf for teens which I found are barely sf at all. David Levithan's *Boy Meets Boy* (2003) really shouldn't be in this book and *Wide Awake* (2006) is sf only by virtue of being set in a future presidential election, but I think it a shocking state of affairs that until Stephen Baxter's *The H-Bomb Girl* came out in 2007, these were the *only* books in my entire collection with gay characters. I don't even mean protagonists (although they are) but gay *characters*.[3]

Boy Meets Boy I have included in this book because it is essentially a utopia. The main character has known he was gay since he was five years old (he asked a nursery teacher what it meant) and attends a school where there are lots of gay kids, and a fair few transvestites, including the lead quarterback. The story is sf because it explores what being a gay teen who *does not* have to come out, who *does not* have to explain his sexuality, and who *does not* have to see his entire emotional world through a prism of defensiveness, might be like. It is a joyous book and one which centers romance but uses the centering of romance to explore an alternative/future world. *Wide Awake* is less utopian and perhaps a bit too polemical but here also a relationship is the centre of the novel, while in the background America convulses over the possibility of a gay president. One of the issues at stake in the relationship as it happens is what I expressed earlier as the Hollywood versus SF orientation to the world. Duncan is with Hollywood, "against the great events, a romance blossomed," his boyfriend would phrase it as "in the midst of romance, world events took over." Levithan very nicely explores the dynamics of love in a changing world.

The Ensemble Novel

Girls and boys as "just pals" has almost disappeared from "mainstream" YA sf (a weird term, I know). If there is one boy, and one girl, romance will bloom even if, as in M.T. Anderson's *Feed,* it is doomed, or when in Kenneth Oppel's *Airborn* (2004) and *Skybreaker* (2005) it is impossible for reasons of social pressure, although Oppel's books do hew closely to the old pattern of boy adventurer and girl pal, despite the romantic undercurrent. But there is still a place for the platonic novel of adventure: this has emerged in the form of the ensemble novel. This is, I think, entirely a product of U.S. patterns of heterosociality.

In the UK, until the 1970s, single-sex schooling was the norm for most children but most particularly for those considered more intellectually able. "Secondary moderns" might be co-ed, but "grammar" schools never. Most of Europe also tended to associate elite with single-sexed before 1970, and while in all of these places it has been modified, we retain a culture in which pre-teens and teens tend to cluster in single-sexed groups, and there is little adult encouragement to do otherwise despite some co-ed educational rhetoric. "School fiction" as it emerged at the end of the nineteenth century reflected this and the school story continued to be the bastion of the single-sexed environment until the children's television program *Grange Hill* began broadcasting in 1978. Even here however, boys interacted with boys, and girls with girls. The *only* co-ed boarding school story I know of in the UK before the publication of Harry Potter is, bizarrely, Enid Blyton's *Naughtiest Girl* sequence (1940–45), which is also very "counter-cultural" in terms of providing the children with parliamentary democracy, so that in this context, co-education and heterosocialization seems quite a mild point.[4] All of this was reflected in adult culture where there were working *men*'s clubs, the *Women*'s Institute and a whole range of single-sexed club worlds for every social class.

In contrast, since the end of the nineteenth century U.S. middle-class society has tended towards suspicion of the homosocial. The dominant model for middle-class socialization was the country club. By the 1950s, the sitcom had settled into pictures of couples socializing as couples. Children's movies are almost always about either a loner or a gang and while there may be a romantic couple (as in Andy Hardy movies) they are usually surrounded by others.

Until the craze for "going steady" in the late 1940s and 1950s, "dating" was mostly done in groups (Bailey, 1989). Although this trend may be less obvious now — there are many programs about just women, or just men, although it is amazing how often the opposite sex is the sole topic of conversation — it is still very visible in programs made for teens. *Beverly Hills 90210, Dawson's Creek,* and *Buffy the Vampire Slayer* spring to mind.

In children's and teens' fiction, this manifests as what I've chosen to call the ensemble novel. These tend to be "series" novels but I can see no reason why they necessarily should be. They also share certain attributes which, for ease, I will list as bullet points.

- They assemble together a group of children/teens, roughly equal numbers of each sex but one boy more is common.
- Each character is given "attributes," by which I mean they may have a fear of being thought a coward, a disability, be a member of a specific ethic group.
- Each character takes the role of an "avatar," less someone to learn about than a combination of "identification" figures in the depressingly materialist idea that "children must have a figure to identify with," and a skin to don and steer through the adventure.
- They tend to be what I have termed elsewhere "bracelet" fantasies, structured so that a new adventure can be slotted in, extending the "story" forever until the person in control of the narrative (author, editor or packager) decides to end it. (Mendlesohn, 2008: 29).

I want to begin by looking at K.A. Applegate's fourteen-part series, *Remnants* (2001–2003) and how she uses the ensemble-book structure to work with, and to subvert, ideas and expectations around gender. *Remnants* constructs an ensemble cast, who take turns to dominate the narrative. In effect, Applegate "cycles" the clothing which the reader is expected to don. This is significant: it means that a male reader, hooked to each series through a male character, will at some point be obliged to accept a female point of view. *Remnants* tells the tale of the last survivors of an asteroid strike on earth, shot into space in a leaky shuttle, at the mercy of the ship which has captured them and not very happy. In the first eight books the characters fight for survival and living space; in the second set of books they fight for the right to turn the ship for home, and then fight each other for control of the ship and the ruined Earth. The novel (and it is one novel) is constructed as a series of links in a bracelet, in which each "character" displays their talents, such as Miss Violet Blake the art historian, through to Jobs the computer geek. In the second part of the novel they also get to display the "superpowers" they have acquired, such as the ability of small Edward to turn chameleon or of Tate (female) to turn into a ravening mouth and eat anyone she perceives as betraying her. The attributes that Applegate distributes are initially highly gendered: Miss Violet Blake is a "Jane," a member of a gentility sub-culture. Mo'Steel is a rough-and-tumble risk-taker. The first subversion is in making it clear that all of these attributes are equally valuable. The second is that some attributes seem misassigned: the female sergeant is also the highly protective mother to the changeling baby. 2Face is a rather nice girl who also presents as a highly politicized manipulator. As the story progresses however, the more stereotypical characters change: Miss Violet Blake loses some of her performative femininity and becomes increasingly willing to take physical risks. Mo'Steel becomes more forceful and also emerges as the child fondest of his parent. Tate moves from a role as helpmeet and admirer of the sergeant to a more complex character who takes on two of the villains of the piece. The possession of a range of characters releases Applegate from the chains of representativeness. In turn, this allows for the "attributes" to function far better as signifiers of character. By the end, there is no direct connection between gender and character, but neither are the characters ungendered. Furthermore, the range of characters in the text allows Applegate to plausibly delay romantic bonding. At various points many of the characters contemplate the attractiveness of another but as couples emerge, Applegate uses the exigencies of the moment to distract each time, and a constant reshuffling of these bonds to keep at bay the moment when full romance rears its head and repels a too-young reader.

I have discussed *The Big Empty* (2004–2005) sequence earlier in this book, but it is worth considering here for the way in which it uses the ensemble structure in ways that suggest a deliberate attempt to stretch permitted gender (and gendered) behavior. In the aftermath of a plague, and in the face of growing oppression, Keely is recruited to a secret commune, Novo Mundum, via her email. On the way to find it she is joined by Michael and his girlfriend Maggie. Michael was about to break up with Maggie when he rescued her from a robbery gone wrong. The three of them then recruit Diego who has lived in the Big Empty with his family, hiding out from the centralizing tendencies of the state, Jonah, a less defined character and also Amber, a pregnant teenager deserted by her boyfriend, who she believes has gone to Novo Mundum. The first book is about getting to the colony; on the way they lose Maggie. In the third book we will discover that Maggie has joined up with a gang, a bunch of rapists and killers: "Stephens" uses this to take the reader through an exploration of "feminine" power, exposing its weakness and vulnerability.

Among the rest of the group gender dynamics become crucial. Keely finds herself torn between two of the boys, a situation which the authors choose to leave unreconciled but which they also avoid placing in any kind of moral frame. Diego becomes intensely protective of Amber although he is injured and she (pregnant) is probably the feistiest character in the books. Michael is perhaps the most interesting: he sees himself as intellectually superior and as a protector (hence his behavior towards Maggie which she herself resents). It is only when he discovers that it is confidence which makes him manipulable that he begins to reorient himself and to actually listen to other members of the group. Of particular interest, it is Diego that teaches him about other models of masculinity, rather than the girls. "Stephens" makes it clear that masculinity and adulthood are contextual things, about the way one thinks of others, rather than the way one thinks of oneself. The characters in *The Big Empty* sequence present initially as avatars: they have attributes. "Stephens," however, allows us to get inside the avatars and then forces us to question our relationship to them and to the world through them. Too often ensemble characters are by the numbers. "Stephens" is not having any of that. Each time we think we've got the player attributes figured out, s/he gives them a little twist.

Boy Protagonists on Their Own (and the Absence of the Bookish Child: A Gender Issue?)

In both Applegate and Stephens, what strikes me is how much the *boys* gain from being in an ensemble novel. I've discussed how much girls get to do as single protagonists, but when one looks at male characters in much sf for children and teens what strikes this reader most is their blandness. If anything, boys come off worse than girls. They get to have more adventures, but it is far too frequently at the expense of any individuation of character. If ensemble novels tend to the avatar, boy-books take this to a greater extreme. At least until the 1960s most male protagonists are interchangeable, representing "normal" boyhood. Even Heinlein is guilty of this: frequently his most interesting male characters are not the protagonists, but the antagonists whose ideas and morals are to be deflated. Normal boyhood, it seems, is uninteresting boyhood; to stand out is to be odd. One aspect of this is the deintellectualization of the protagonist.

The crucial change that takes place, however, seems to center upon the role of intellect and imagination. In juvenile sf before the 1960s, intellectually competent boys are not dismissed as "nerds." As we saw in chapter three and four, being smart was simply what a boy was. The image of the intellectual boy as a nerd does not develop in the literature until the 1970s and may be in part a rejection of authority, but also marks a shift in the culture as the scientists of the Cold War and the Apollo mission lost their heroic gloss, and engineering its pre-eminence in career choices. From the 1970s the presentation of boys bifurcates, either to present the intellectual boy as the isolated hero (Landsman, Nix, Oppel, Reeve, Valentine) or to sideline him altogether and present the "average" boy hero as not too smart (Guttman, Vizzini) and frequently risk-averse (Vizzini, Westerfeld). The outstanding boy is increasingly the one who thinks with his muscles (MacHale, and to an extent even Oppel, as Matt is engaged very physically with airships). Sandy Landsman's *The Gadget Factor* (1984) is almost the last book I can find in the period arc, prior to the revival after 2000, which has an intellectual, scientifically oriented boy as a hero and both the protagonist and his friend are conceptualized as potentially danger-ous outsiders even while the author clearly tries to valorize their take on the world. I discussed this book extensively in chapter four, but I want to revisit the portrayal of their intellect. In *The Gadget Factor*, we are offered *two* mod-els of intellectual boyhood and as with the ensemble novels, the simple fact of having more than one protagonist seems to release the author from the neces-sity of seeing his protagonist as "everyboy" or an avatar for the reader to don and steer through the novel. Both Worm and Michael are super-bright, but they are super-bright in very different ways. For Worm, the game is never more than a game, which he desperately wants to win; and when he has won he'd like to play it again. When Michael needs Worm's help, he needs to convince him that this is another aspect of the game. For Michael the game was only ever a model, to see if the things he was fascinated by could be modeled mathematically. Although he wants to win, it is much more tied up with his math. Playing the game again is only interesting if he can test new ideas each time. Intellect does not become a mere attribute. Furthermore, Landsman's protagonists are not "ordinary chaps." The reader is asked to read about a child with whom he or she might *not* identify

This kind of boy hero has more or less disappeared, and he has been replaced either with the action adventure type as in Oppel's *Airborn* or the "uncool/learning to be cool" type.[5] This has nothing to do with the quality of sf under consideration but suggests a marked shift in "types to read about" and (I think) may be a function of a shift in "what people read for" ideology that emphasizes identification with, rather than inspiration by or emulation of. Heinlein's competent hero has been replaced by the ordinary guy bumbling along, as we can see in such diverse books as Dan Guttman's *Virtually Perfect* in which, in the end, it is Grandpa's competence with electrics which sorts out a problem caused by the protagonists' incompetence with computer program-ming, or Michael J. Daley's *Space Station Rat* in which the rat is the hypercom-petent "adult" who teaches the scientifically and technologically illiterate boy (although I love this book, it is odd that the boy be presented this way given that both parents are scientists), or Oisín McGann's *Small-Minded Giants* (2007), in which the son of a highly skilled manual laborer seems to lack those same skills. These last two examples tie in with the pedagogy discussed in chap-ters three and four, because they represent a totalizing formalism of education in which children *only* learn in the classroom. The kind of "learning from par-ents" or parent figures we see in pre–1960s books, and so important to the tra-ditional model of socializing boys, is almost completely absent (Michael J. Daley's *Shanghaied to the Moon* [2007] is an exception, but his protagonist has amnesia which precludes access to this knowledge until late in the book). The "terminally uncool" chap learning to be cool can be seen in Vizzini's *Be More Chill* and to a lesser extent in James Valentine's *Jumpman* sequence, but here

Valentine has (I think) a similar point to mine to make, because it is the boy from the future, Theo Pine, who lives on the surface of his world, expecting knowledge without learning and cool without competence. Jules, the boy from our time period, is much more interested in the way things work, and at the end of the first book is developing into a competent time-philosopher, but in the second book much of the emphasis in the internal narrative of Jules is about social cues and the pain of being a teenage boy, in which the emphasis is on the emotional and the social. Overall, there is a clear moving away from the intellectual as protagonist. This takes me to David MacHale's *Pendragon* sequence, which I am assured is very popular with young male readers. I don't want to argue whether sport is a good value for a boy, but given that books are usually meant for readers, the emergence of the boy jock *who does not read* as the hero for many sf books is peculiar and says something both about gender expectations and about an attitude to boys' reading, which suggests that the field may be being skewed precisely by the desperate desire to capture the non-reader rather than entertain the reader. Bobby is the extreme of a range of presentations, but I look in vain for nerds-as-hero in modern YA sf, despite their ubiquity in the older juveniles. The only contemporary boy hero in a sort of sf book I can think of who actually regards books as useful is Klaus Baudelaire in the *Lemony Snicket* books. Otherwise, the bizarre message that authors are giving to their desired audience is that *real boys don't read.*[6] Although neither, for the most part, do girls. Ruth in Nancy Etchemendy's *Stranger from the Stars* (1983) spends much of the book apologizing for her reading habit even though it is what will help her fix broken communicators in a crisis.

I will want to return to that paradox in the last part of this chapter, but before I move off from the presentation of gender, I want to discuss the presentation of sexuality in these sf books for teens and children.

Sex and Sexuality and Some of the More Interesting Recent Novels

One cannot help but note that except where authors are pretending that sex does not exist, heterosexuality is compulsory: all the survivor novels, lost generation-ships/colonies, post-disaster tragedies, presume that heterosexuality will be the norm. Pamela Sargent, a well-known feminist writer in the adult field, when writing for children cannot get beyond these structures: *Alien Child*, written in 1988, introduces Nita, who lives on Earth with an alien care-giver, and is taught about humans by machines and very anti-human aliens. Eventually Nita discovers that there is a boy also, and the two of them decide, under the guidance of the alien, to begin decanting more embryos and start the human race again. 1988 is early for a real challenge to compulsory heterosexuality, but Garth Nix has no such excuse in *Shade's Children* (2003). In this book, children who escape from the Dorms are taken in by Shade, an artificial intelligence that survived the Change. Some of the children have Change powers: one can see into the immediate future, another can teleport small objects. Shade uses the children to conspire against the Overlords who breed children and work their bodies into bioforms to fight games. But at the denouement, the castrated child and his girlfriend die, and the survivors are shown walking through the bliss of reconstructed heteronormativity. It really was not necessary to the plot and the "message" is brutal: all but the resolutely normal are wasted space in this pristine new world.

I can find only seven novels which attempt in any way to reach beyond this paradigm. In Jean Ure's *Come Lucky April* (1992), a post-plague society has produced different kinds of communities. Daniel's society is brutal and patriarchal, April's is gentle and gender-segregated, both homosocial and homosexual. It is a pleasant enough novel whose core arguments are about how to create a better world, but underlying it is an implicit assumption that while homosexuality is allowable, heterosexuality is *normal*. In *Ancient Appetites* (2007) Oisín McGann also presents heterosexuality as the norm, and homosexuality as abnormal, but he does it within the context of an alternate nineteenth-century Ireland, and by the end of the book has turned this heteronormativity in on itself: the betrayed wife is wondering if she does care that much, and the brother, it turns out, knew anyway. The discovery is not fundamental to the plot, but that renders it all the more significant in the creation of a "real" world, one that does not attempt to ignore the multiplicity of humanity, and is in tune with McGann's other political concerns.

Peter Dickinson, David Levithan and Joan Lennon all move to challenge notions of normality. Dickinson's *Eva* (1988) is a novel I will return to in the next chapter because it is so often given to children as a theme-exploration, in this case ecology, but its most radical aspect is not the message to save the planet, but that sexuality is contextual. In *Eva*, the titular character is the daughter of scientists working with chimps. After a horrendous accident she wakes to find that her brain has been implanted in a chimp. The novel moves through her accommodation with this, her realization that a chimp died (unwillingly) to give her a body, and her growing sense of responsibility for the chimp clan. The shock, both for the reader and her parents, is that when she comes into oestrus, Eva makes the decision to accept the approach of a male chimp and to give birth to chimp babies. This apparent bestiality is lovingly drawn. Although it takes place in a heterosexual structure, it is not "normal" and immediately fractures any sense of "normal."

David Levithan's *Wide Awake* simply posits an election in which a gay candidate wins and right-wing America tries to steal the election. The main character is gay and as I have said elsewhere, the real tension in the novel is between different models of gay relationships; the "love me forever" conceit of romance, and the "we are in high school, let us play" of a more realistic world-view. As far as this goes Levithan manages his usual elegant exploration of plurality, something otherwise missing from almost all the novels I have read. But Levithan seems to be brought up short by the possibility of anything other than a monogamous structure: Duncan, the protagonist, *is* conservative and it is no surprise that he cannot cope with his best friend cheating on her girlfriend with another woman, but that no one supports her contention that she does love both her girlfriend and the Other is oddly narrow. Duncan's hostility goes unchallenged by any of the adults in the party.

Finally, there is Joan Lennon's *Questors.* As a book for younger children (perhaps early teens) there is not a lot of sex, but the mother of the three Questors appears to have borne each of them by a different father and will at the end get involved with someone completely different. And the Questors themselves come in female, male and ... It. Cam is born to a planet where people don't have a sexual or gender identity until puberty, when they "realize" what they want to be (the realization is at least partially subliminal). Although it is not said, there is at least a hint that someone might choose to remain "it," which in the context of the few attempts to portray transgenderism in children's fiction is relatively daring (see Jody Norton). One aspect of the novel is Bryn's desperate attempt to impose gender upon Cam, and Bryn and Madlen's shock at the discovery that not all worlds configure gender-appropriate behavior in the same way.

Each of the above novels make a big deal over their daring: sex and gender *are* the issues. Three novels manage the impressive trick of rendering alternative choices as *normal* and *usual.* David Levithan's *Boy Meets Boy* does not, as I have said before, strictly belong here, but it is a utopia because it takes homosexuality and transexuality and transvestism for granted in way that we can only hope for. Paul has no coming-out story, because he has known he was gay since he was four, and known also that it is no big deal. As a consequence he has none of the hang-ups of his boyfriend. He is living proof that homosexuality is not an illness, and if homosexuals are depressed it is because they are rendered unhappy by others' attitudes. Troon Harrison's *The Eye of the Wolf* writes an implicit polyamorous community into the back story: there are bio fathers, sugar-friends and promise fathers, of whom the most important and permanent are promise fathers, who promise to share in the upbringing of a child, and to take over if the mother is incapacitated. Without two promise parents, women cannot get permission to have a child. None of this is foregrounded and it is this refusal to discuss something *because it is not worth discussing* that lifts Harrison's and Leviathan's work beyond. Finally, Stephen Baxter's *The H-Bomb Girl* contains a rather nice gay boy, whose gayness does not affect the plot, but who makes his choice — about whether or not to stay in his own timeline — informed by the homophobic context in which he lives.

This chapter has focused on the cultural arguments around gender. What strikes me most is the degree to which the gender values constructed in these books so rarely accord with the diversity of fiction found in the adult genre. Feminist writers in the adult genre of the 1970s argued for more character and more emotion, but if you look at what they actually wrote it is not that different from male science fiction in its emphasis on informational density rather than interior examination. It is just that the feminist writers were and are interested in different information (be careful of mistaking the change in subject matter for a fundamental difference of approach). Very little of this seems to have permeated through to the fiction written for children and teens: the exceptions stand out.

All of this points to the essential conflict which I have been harping on about for much of this book, the current educational and literary climate encourages children to read fiction to develop their emotional maturity. So we select as "good" books which emphasize emotional interests and emotional problems whose solutions are essentially about changing one's internal orientation, not about grappling with two planks of wood and a couple of nails. We also insist that the best books are those which are relevant to children, which talk about the world they are already in; in the main books which are domestic (I don't necessarily mean "at home," but books which do not take children out of their own environment). This has affected fiction for both boys and girls but, when combined with a particular kind of liberal feminism which tends to both regard "boys' roles" as to be envied, but "girls' skills" to be valorized, has improved the representation of girls while actually limiting the scope of the genre. As for boys, it may have opened up the range of types of boys who are represented, but again, seems to have limited the genre: meeting the alien has been transfigured by many authors into an exercise in friendship-building. Very few of the texts I've looked at in this chapter involve either intellect or adventure, and when they do, the protagonists often seem curiously unfitted for the task.

With some honorable exceptions many texts seem to demand a gendered reader. There seems to be very little space for a boy with a weak sense of conventional masculinity (even Vizzini's *Be More Chill* has a sense of what should be aimed for), and few roles offered that don't require an identification with the physical. For girls, while more activity is possible and there are more roles to fill, too many of the texts present romance and the possibility of romance as the reward. In neither case is the old idea of the intellect superseding the body — a form of transgenderism common to sf fandom — supported, and while it is a problematic model which claims a neutrality that is not always valid, it is one of the recognized character models in sf. For a child or teen looking for such a construction, such a route to identification if identification is so essential, there is nothing there. Furthermore, for the sf child looking for "the Other" there seem mostly to be only reminders that they *are* the other.

Chapter Six

You Gotta Have a Theme; or, the Paucity of Plots

In the four years in which I have been writing this book I have been increasingly involved with the mailing list Child_Lit. On this list the issue of "theme" is returned to over and over again, in ways that are revealing for their contradictions. One participant will write in asking for recommendations for books on a "theme," and will receive many suggestions. Yet a week later another participant will be discussing the intentions of writers and will comment that of course writers (or at least good writers) don't write to a theme — and this thread will rapidly turn to the argument over didactic writing which I have discussed elsewhere. There will be a rush of people to denounce "thematic" writing and particularly what is called "issue" writing, and to insist that what matters is *the story*. A very typical comment (although this example is from the Diana Wynne Jones discussion list) is this one from "Susanna Victoria": "I think there are books that are excellent and could also be considered issue books. I guess it all depends on how skillful the author is. The example that sprang to mind is 'Four Ways to Forgiveness,' an interlocked set of four stories by Ursula K. Le Guin. They explore issues of slavery, reconciliation, and forgiveness. I wouldn't be terribly surprised if she set out to write about those issues as 'issues,' but she does it with such subtlety and skill that it does not matter" (DWJ Discussion, 6 August 07). The critic manages to both compliment and dismiss at the same time — only the skill of the author rescues the book from the taint of *purpose*. Yet in response to these kinds of comments others will chime in about the things they learned from a good story. The debate will circle and die down. And then some time later someone else, often a person who has themselves decried "didactic" fiction, will request stories on the "theme of...."

Authors react variously to this debate. Jane Yolen has decried the idea that her book *Briar Rose* was written to teach, yet it will be suggested when someone asks for books about the Holocaust. Julius Lester seems more relaxed about the notion of purpose, of *issue* or theme. Elizabeth Bentley reports that when Malorie Blackman was asked about her *Noughts and Crosses* books (which I

135

consider allegory rather than sf), the author responded that "the theme of N & C was love, the theme of Knife Edge was despair and that the theme of the third would be Hope" (Child_Lit, off list, 1 August 07).[1]

The notion of theme is not intrinsically bad. Any proper understanding of the world surely expects it to be sliced and diced in many different ways, but for some reason, theme has an incredibly powerful grip on the "read and rec- ommend" cycle of children's fiction generally, one which we can see extended into the world of academic children's literature criticism. This is problematic because "theme" is not how most sf readers select their fiction[2]: they are far more likely to choose among sub-genre (space opera, cyberpunk, utopian, human- ist, crime fiction, engineering sf, political, anthropological) or simply to fol- low author links (such as "Scalzi writes in the tradition of Heinlein"). But it is also problematic because as I suggested in chapter two, it tells children *what* to value in books. Jane Yolen wrote (Child_Lit, 19 July 07), "When my chil- dren were young, my daughter came home from 7th grade with a sheet telling them what was expected in their book report papers. One question was 'What was the author's intent in writing this story?' And I told her that she had to say 'The author's intent was either to write one hell of a good story or to make a lot of money, and hopefully both come true.' And she replied, 'I'd flunk if I said that.' She was probably right...." This is perhaps a crude and emotive response but it contains a truth that is at variance with the ways in which books are being categorized and consequently "taught."[3]

In this chapter I'm going to address a number of themes which are fre- quently identified with children's sf, then move on to some themes I want to consider, looking particularly at some of the national differences in the ways in which they are handled. And finally, I want to look at why theme has become a lot more important to sf for children and teens than has plot. At the end of this research I have many, many themes I might have selected, but a bare hand- ful of plots.

One very real issue when discussing themes in children's books is the tightrope that authors walk between "expressing a theme" and writing an out- and-out allegory. The division is crucial: Tolkien and Lewis can stand for the split over this one, with Tolkien determined to create a new world, Lewis equally determined that children should learn about Christianity and the mean- ing of Christianity from his books.[4] However, if we move away from the didac- tism = bad formulation that usually condemns allegory, and then leaves the critic floundering when well-written, well-formulated allegories come along, then we need to consider another reason why allegories are problematic for those interested in thematic selection of children's sf, and using children's sf perhaps to encourage children to think: allegories are not science fiction.

Allegory is a fiction of destinarian inevitability. Science fiction is a fiction of causal inevitability. The two can interact, but one makes a very poor vehi- cle for the other.

Science fiction is as much an argument with the present as it is an argument for the future. If Asimov writes about robots, he probably has the race question in mind. If Theodore Sturgeon writes about love birds then there is more than a hint of the persecution of homosexuals being explored in his work. Used gently, allegory can add depth and resonance, may take a trivial story and render it powerful.

But then there is allegory where what the author wants to write is allegory, and because allegory is fairly unfashionable in the mainstream nowadays s/he decides to dress the allegory up in the clothes of science fiction. The use of science fiction to dress up allegory is a function of not understanding what science fiction *is*. [5]

Science fiction is not simply a decision to set something in the future. Nor is it an act of fantasy in the way many outside the sf world understand "fantasizing." It is a branch of mimetic fiction and as such needs not just internal coherence but an internalized sense of consequence.

To construct an entire novel around an allegory challenges the chaos effect at the heart of science fiction, a genre which is sometimes known as "speculative fiction." One of sf's basic premises is the "If this goes on..." or "If this, then that...." The allegorist says "If I set up an identical — or mirror image — situation the same things will happen as happened in reality or as I need them to happen for the purpose of allegory." The political determination to prove a point overwhelms the narrative dynamic, because each point of decision is hemmed in by what *ought* to happen in order to extend the allegory. In science fiction for children allegories like Fay Sampson's *Them* (2005, a Christian allegory), Malorie Blackman's *Noughts and Crosses* (2001, an allegory of the civil rights movement) or Melvin Burgess's *Bloodtide* (1999, a futuristic retelling of an Icelandic saga) combine with books which can be summed up roughly as "we are all doomed and you cannot stop the final ending" (such as Gudrun Pausewang's *Last Children*, 1983, and Robert Swindells' *Brother in the Land*, 1984) to close down possibilities for the child, for the reader and for the future: precisely *not* what science fiction is for or about.

History is chaotic: a small change does not just alter the world, it prevents the world ever being what it might have been in that other universe. If a future is to be *real* then at each moment of decision different things can and will happen until the sf story has branched in so many different directions that it is no longer allegory but itself.

When using science fiction to teach children, or even when we consider why we want children to read science fiction, it is that causal yet chaotic experience of history that allows science fiction to represent a fictional world of political critique.

We can see both the scope and challenge of science fiction, and the limiting impositions of allegory in Susan Price's *Odin's Voice* (2004) and *Odin's Queen* (2006). Set in a world where Norse paganism is the dominant religion, and corporations control civil liberties, bondswoman Kylie becomes the voice of a god, in this case Odin. Kylie befriends the once-rich girl who has been sold into debt peonage by her father. Affroditey is now nurse for Kylie's child, the result of her rape by her employer's husband, but who has been absorbed by the man's family. Affroditey is persuaded by Kylie to steal the child. This first book takes readers into a world of dysfunctional family relationships, debt, civil exploitation and rape. Who *does* the work, and at whose expense are their luxuries bought? There is a parallel with the modern world — in which much labor is carried out by underpaid and semi-coerced immigrants — but it is not a parable or an allegory. The story is entirely internal to the book. Susan Price tries to persuade the reader to look around at those who are servants in our lives.

The three escape to Mars where Kylie, or Odinstoy as she is now known, becomes the godspeaker (not precisely a priest). In *Odin's Queen,* however, the story of Odinstoy takes second place to another story Price introduces, that of Jesus Christ who sides with the poor, is persecuted and eventually martyred, only to rise again. The allegorical frame limits the story from the beginning: the moment Odinstoy's "wife," the bondswoman Affroditey who fled with her, begins to flirt with a nice young man, we know it can only end badly. As the story goes on, it becomes clear that Affroditey is so angry with Odinstoy for *not* being her personal savior that she will sell Odinstoy to the dominant Church of Mars. Although by the end Affroditey is clearly both Judas (the traitor) and Paul (the evangelist) the story has become trapped in a particular pattern: Odinstoy feels herself forsaken by god, and then sacrifices herself for those who would support her rebellion and steps out of an airlock, only to be seen again a few days later by believers. The political analysis of the first book is undermined by the need for a peculiarly inevitable structure for the second. The political complexities of the world of Mars are reduced to a focus on this one person.

Allegory can be a powerful jumping-off point to engage young readers in the political possibilities of the future, but as L. J. Adlington's *The Diary of Pelly D* (2005) demonstrates, its power is in the degree it departs from allegory. The text begins as a science-fictional version of the *Diary of Anne Frank.* Toni V, a young worker on a construction site, finds a diary. As he reads more of it, the book and Toni V's thoughts interact to build the world around us. We gradually learn that we are on a different planet and that the humans on this planet have been adapted for the climate. They have gills and need/want to swim pretty much all the time. Water is crucial to their economy and their culture. Apart from that, there seems to have been a war. Toni V is involved in reconstruction, while in contrast Pelly D, the author of the diary, was a rich and pretty high school student.

Adlington uses Pelly D's diary to explore the politics and hatred of genocide but rather than using a model of irrational hatred, she sets out to show how that irrationality may be built on incremental apparently sane responses, and how those "in the right" in a dispute imperil their own moral structure when they engage with the language of their opponents.

On Pelly D's planet two cities become bellicose. One sees itself as genetically superior because its population carries an expressed gene. Adlington never tells us what this gene does, and there is some speculation that it might not do anything. City One begins demanding help for a water shortage. City Three, where Pelly D lives, resists the demands. But the politicians of City Three begin to use the same gene-ist rhetoric deployed by their opponents. Adlington is concerned with the way language is political and one of the techniques she uses is to have the word "racist" as one of the worst insults someone in City Three can use. Victims of racist abuse are punished if they accuse, told that *they* are the perpetrators of hate.

The Diary of Pelly D is effective because it pulls away from a close allegory of the Nazi Holocaust. Adlington weaves in other genocides with different dynamics, such as the familial betrayals of the Rwandan genocide. Pelly D finds that while her dad carries the all-important gene, she and the rest of the family do not. This is not a tale of heroism. Dad deserts his family, allows them to be moved to a ghetto and does nothing to help or rescue them when it becomes clear that their lives are threatened.

The diary ends there, but the novel extends into the future. Adlington asks her readers to think about the political processes of their own world and the consequences of decisions taken. Having read Pelly D's diary, Tony V starts to think about the political economy of his own world, about who can and cannot afford things; what it is he and his friends are digging over and destroying. At the end, he wonders what has happened to the people who once lived here and realizes that he may be a beneficiary of the Final Solution. Pelly D's diary is incomplete, it tells only what a high school girl would think to tell, there are no large chunks of information about the world so it feels narrow and claustrophobic. What Toni V can tell us is bound by his knowledge of the world. The book explores not the story of genocide, but the way in which the road to genocide is made up of quite tiny steps that tie ordinary, well-meaning people into complicity.

Allegory is limiting, but it is meaningful and it still assumes that thematic approaches can think about a possible future. Conor Kostik's *Epic* (2004) which I have considered more fully in a later section, serves as a critique of those who take refuge in allegory. The world he creates has transformed a computer game (Epic) into a social tool, using success in the game as an indicator of "merit" and employing it to allocate scarce resources. It is the belief that the game is an allegory of society (an idea used also by Iain M. Banks in *Player of Games*) which undermines both the society (as people spend all their spare time on the game) and the game itself.[6] The more it is seen as an *allegory* of capitalism, the less interactive, rich and joyous it becomes. Only once the protagonist, Erik, embraces the chaos of a real future can both the society and the game do more than go through the motions of living.

Themes

I should perhaps begin by noting the absence of certain themes. There are very few robots in the books I have read which were published after the 1950s. Redundancy due to technology is almost absent from the field — spare time caused by technology is mostly celebrated or condemned for generating self-absorption and other manifestations of decadence. There is, after the 1950s, a complete absence of "new invention and its effect" stories. There are precisely *three* "people in spaceships exploring and meeting new and interesting people" stories, and two of them are by Ben Jeapes who wrote the first with an adult market in mind (*His Majesty's Starship* and *The Xenocide Mission*). The other is Gynn MacLean's *Roivan: Book One of the A'nzarian Chronicle* (2003). Jeapes is also responsible (in the same books) for the only military sf in my collection. There are *two* planetary settlement stories, Jill Paton Walsh's *The Green Book* (1981) and Conor Kostick's *Epic* (I am not including here planetary conquest tales, which are rather first-contact stories). Many of the major themes of sf for adults are simply absent from the 1970s onwards.

Because I am interested in *why themes* as well as *why certain themes* I've tried to create clusters, showing how "meaning" can be written in a number of ways yet retain remarkable similarities of intention. I want to begin with one of the dominant themes of sf for teens and children, the discovery of identity, because this will lead on to my next identified theme, consumerism, which will then in turn lead to a discussion of eco-sf and end-of-the-world narratives and from there into a discussion of how sf for teens and children deals with first contact. I'm going to try to go from the inward-focused to the outward, from the self to the world. This trajectory, as I have argued earlier, runs counter to the trajectory of the majority of the sf for teens from the 1980s onwards and one of the things I want to point to is the intense personalization of these themes: they are rarely, if ever posited as "how one teen intervened to change the world" but almost always "how the world intervened to change the life of this teen[s]." Themes crop up in children's sf in an intensely cyclical fashion. A glance at the dates of the texts discussed below will quickly reveal clusters of interest.

Knowledge, Memory, Identity
(Cloning and Genetic Engineering)

Perhaps understandably for work directed at teens, identity, finding one's identity and challenges to one's identity are major "issues" in children's and teen sf, and recur extensively in the booktalking guides. There is an assumption — which I do not intend to challenge — that insecurity or constriction of identity are issues which fascinate young readers.[7] This can be expressed directly, as it is in Scott Westerfeld's *Uglies* (2005–06) sequence in which identity is ruthlessly structured around the acquisition of beauty, or William Nicholson's

The Wind Singer (2000) in which one's future is tied absolutely to the exam success of one's father, or yet more irrational, as in Jeanne DuPrau's 2003 story *City of Ember* where one's future is assigned by lottery. There are stories in which children are denied the right to exist, as in Haddix's *Among the Hidden* sequence, and Gemma Malley's *The Declaration* (2007), their futures denied by adult selfishness. In some of these destiny stands in for identity. In Malley's story neither the protagonist nor the boy she is befriended by are truly unwanted, in a consolatory turn their identities are secured by revelation, and the truly unwanted marginalized from the story. There are direct "coming of age" stories in the field such as Alexei Panshin's *Rite of Passage* (1968), and Susan Price's *Coming Down to Earth* (1994). Interestingly, and in reverse of my general argument that we have lost the "outward bound" trajectory of sf but in accordance with what sf for the teen market has increasingly modeled as the restrictions of impending adulthood, Panshin's novel is about children realizing and accepting their place in society, and seeing the onset of adulthood as liberatory, while Susan Price's *Coming Down to Earth* sees adulthood as confined, and the absorption into society as essentially erasing identity; "finding oneself" is about finding a route out, an alternative to what your world asks of you.

Although *Coming Down to Earth* is about a child who has grown up on a space station that relies on communitarian socialization, it gets to the heart of what lies behind most of the tales in this section, a resistance to the destinarianism which drives fantasy. All the tales I want to discuss here place children in situations in which their future is decided for them either by their heredity or by the state, or, as in the two categories in which I am most interested here, their very DNA. These stories exist because we in the west no longer live in a hereditarian society: the days when boys' work was formally and openly decided by their fathers have long gone (even if family pressure has not), with the result that two tropes of science fiction — cloning and genetic engineering — have become in children's and teen fiction places to play out an anxiety of identity and family separation, of who "owns" one's identity, that is no longer "realistic" in the mainstream fiction for this market.[8] Furthermore, in a genre which (as I have discussed above) remains deeply uncomfortable with homosexuality, these fictions are in part a way of considering the issue of identity as simultaneously mutable and inherent.

I want to begin with cloning. Cloning narratives in science fiction for adults abandoned the notion that clones are all the same many years ago. Robert Silverberg's "There Was an Old Woman," published in 1958, is about thirty-one cloned sons produced by a former biochemistry professor who wants to prove that nurture surpasses nature. She trains each in a profession of her choice. The story ends when the sons kill her, each deeply unhappy in their given profession *but*— and this is crucial — each choosing quite different professions from each other. In a sense, the professor is correct, nurture not nature wins out, just more subversively. Cloning stories for the adult market are, in their current incarnation, incredibly varied: just to give three recent examples which span the spectrum, David Brin's *Kiln People* (2001) uses temporary clones to explore complex multi-tasking while David Marusek's *Counting Heads* (2005) uses cloning to explore individuality, and the pressure of community. Lois McMaster Bujold, in *Mirror Dance* (1994), uses the clone to discuss the ethics of parenting. In Brin's work clones or copies are "ripped" off the individual and sent out to work, being reabsorbed with memories into the primary. There are no concerns about individuality because there is only one individual here. Marusek posits a society in which there are whole clans of clones whose "value" in the workplace is the degree to which they present the "inherent traits" of their progenitor and clone group: the protagonist begins to question his own identity and discovers how defensive his clone group is about maintaining their in-group identity for commercial reasons, but also because they fear the back-lash should they be seen to threaten the "individuals" in society on their own turf. Their social safety lies in their predictability. Lois McMaster Bujold's *Mirror Dance* (part of a long-running sequence) introduces us to a clone brought up to displace and *be* a political figure and examines the ways in which clones are *not* their progenitors. Important for this section, Bujold is very aware that while we may begin as a complex mixture of heritable traits, we proceed to be molded by both physical and emotional environment. The clone is not the person.

With the exception of the author Ann Halam — who, not coincidentally is also the author of sf for the adult market, as Gwyneth Jones — all of the books on cloning for children and teens orient around the notion that the clone *is* the man. At their most severe, such books are Freudian expressions of parental cannibalism. Alfred Slote's *Clone Catcher* (1982) is an excellent example, a book which is written as a hard-boiled detective novel, giving it a life beyond the issue. But the issue is explicit: in a world in which the rich grow clones to ensure they have a supply of transplants, Alfred Dunn is a clone-catcher, for in this world, the only way to end up with healthy organs is to bring the clones up as people, taking as long as people to grow. Most are kept in compounds until their bodies are needed. Some escape.

Alfred Dunn is called in to find Lady Kate Montague's clone. Unlike most clones she has been allowed to grow up outside the compound, and until the age of 16 had not known she was a clone without rights. Later, she had gone on to be an actress on the stage, like her progenitor. When Lady Kate needs the body parts, Mary disappears, the night after she gives her final performance and had agreed to return to be Lady Kate's supply of body parts. Eventually, Dunn works out that Lady Kate is dead — she died of natural causes on the way home — and that Mary has taken her place. But along the way we have seen a clone revolt in the Montague compound, and been exposed to the politics of the anti-clone movement. The novel ends with Dunn marrying the anti-cloning movement nurse, Alice, and returning to live on one of the Montague farms. Lord Montague gives his business over to his clone while his son (who has both helped to solve the mystery and bring it to a politically satisfactory end) can retire to sheep farming and books (one of the things I like best is that this shy, quiet, undriven man appears in the end as the sharpest cookie in the book).

But *Clone Catcher* is driven by the assumption that clones, with very different life experiences, will be identical in personality with their progenitors, wanting the same careers, and even falling in love with the clones of their progenitor's lover. They are represented as being merely younger versions of themselves, so while Slote liberates the "natural" son of the progenitor, the clone remains a copy, even if liberated from the threat of cannibalism. He lacks the true freedom of destiny of the natural son. Patrick Cave's recent books *Sharp North* and *Blown Away* escape this destinarianism by making the clones faulty, but while they still carry the personality traits of their progenitors, he does at least allow them to have a range of expression. But Cave, like T.E. Berry-Hart in *Escape from Genopolis* (2007) and also like Nancy Farmer in *House of the Scorpion*, can still conceive of no other reason to *make* clones than literal cannibalism, cutting them up for spare parts. This grows ever less plausible as we are already well on our way to being able to grow spare organs. Not one of these novels even envisages using the discredited idea that clone = similar personality to have a progenitor *deliberately* use cloning to produce an heir more like themselves than a "natural" child.

Of the books discussed above, only Patrick Cave's *Blown Away* goes beyond cloning as the actual storyline. Most of the book is essentially an adventure-love story. We are not given long debates about cloning and genetic engineering; we simply see the consequences and discuss those consequences. In that sense this is proper science fiction: the book is about if this happened then what? Not a very startling comment on my part but it has been so rare to find this basic element of sf in these children's books that it is worth noting. Patrick Cave is genuinely interested in what a collapsing society might look like.

The only exception to "cloning is destiny" and clones as physical resources is found in Ann Halam's *Taylor Five* (2002). Taylor discovers she is a clone and is attacked by terrorists while in Borneo. When her family is killed she has to run. While Taylor's existence as a clone provides the reason for the attack, the story is actually about ecology, secrets and the way we treat others. Taylor 5 is a human being with no special powers who has been brought up as a human — an adoptee, not a subject, with a future of her own that will be influenced but not shaped by her genes.

Discussion of identity as a matter of personality growth is more likely to be found in considerations of genetic engineering. It is here in fact that we most find metaphors for the struggles teens face between expectation and realization. Kate Thompson's *Missing Link* (2000–03) sequence embodies this. Christie's brother Danny proves to be a genetically engineered creature made in part with dolphin genes and "destined" for a life in cold water. Danny's *bildungsroman* is centered around this discovery, but his personality is not. Thompson separates out the need to find an appropriate environment from who Danny actually is.

In a similar book, *Dusk* (2004), Susan Gates does not quite get to this point. the protagonist Curtis gets a job in a lab and accidentally frees a wild girl with the eye of a hawk. Two years later his son arrives to stay, discovers the burned and fenced area, sneaks in after a stray dog (which gets killed by the wild dogs inside) and finds the girl, Dusk. Dusk helps him to escape and he in turn runs off with her into the wilderness. Although this story is in part about Jay's relationship with his parents (Ma is an over-attentive Christian; Curtis, his father, is a drunk) Jay runs away, he does not actually solve anything — there are hints though that if there is a sequel, familial reconciliation will be a theme. Neither Jay nor the girl get beyond their first moments of self-recognition as "different" and one is clearly a metaphor for the other. This is reinforced in the way the science of genetic engineering is presented. Gates solves the problem of "what science will children understand" by ensuring that the novel is not told from the point of view of scientists, or from their level of understanding, but instead from the position of ignorant outsiders — the public in other words. Politically, it makes sense but it means that there is no technical detail: the results, not the process, are what is discussed. The protagonist/student can react politically and socially to the end results, but cannot actually take part in shaping that result.

Genetic engineering and its role in the formation of identity is a particularly active trope where authors are concerned with the relationship of the state to the construction and shaping of the individual. In David Stahler Jr.'s *Truesight* (2004) Jacob is blind because his community has decided that all will be genetically engineered to be blind. This in turn is used to shape a constrictive social identity (low levels of education, agrarian) that is not strictly necessary. There are, for example, no computers although they are perfectly compatible with blindness. Genetic engineering here is posited as means of social control. This use of genetic engineering (or drugs in Scott Westerfeld's *Uglies* sequence) is always challenged. In T. E. Berry-Hart's *Escape from Geneopolis,* producing the genetically pure as a group who feel no pain is eventually presented as a fundamental threat to "humanness" as well as to the species. Generally, genetic engineering is regarded as a way to supersede human choice and human development. In Susan Price's *Odin's Voice*, Afroditey's blue hair is a symbol not of the choices open to her, but that she was someone else's property. It dehumanizes her rather than, as she assumed, enhances her. A similar message is propounded in Nancy Werlin's *Double Helix* (2004). Eli Samuels learns he was an experiment to genetically engineer a child without Huntington's chorea and that the beautiful Kayla is his half-sister, a failed attempt in the same project who was not destroyed. Werlin's argument (and it is explicit) is that such interference implies ownership of fetus and children. It is given an extra twist in implying that it is the attempt to insert scientific "ownership" which interferes in the proper "ownership" relationship between parent and child. Eli begins the book by moving away from the influence of father and high-school sweetheart. He will end the book by reviving both relationships, with the idea that external influences are dangerous and misleading, reflecting the current worry over parental influence and the idea that the well-adjusted child is the one for whom the family unit is the most important element of his or her life, even when he or she enters into the workplace. It is oddly regressive for sf, if quite normal in domestic fiction.

Only two books see genetic engineering of "the child" as positively good. In Michael J. Daley's *Space Station Rat* (2005), admittedly, the "child" is a laboratory rat, but she approaches her world with such enthusiasm that the genetic engineering which raised her intelligence can only be a good thing. The second example is Joan Lennon's 2007 book *Questors*. Three children are plucked from their everyday lives and taken to The House in London. They find it is a "house between the worlds," and each of them has grown up in one of the worlds; their mother is actually an agent of the house, although they have three different fathers. The three discover they were genetically engineered for a quest to save the universe but unknown to them their genetic engineering has been tampered with. The reason why I am suggesting that it is a book generally in favor of genetic engineering is that the children *are* engineered, even if not in the way intended, and their engineering proves successful. There is no argument that the default to the "natural" would have been somehow better. What Lennon achieves, which is missing from the rejectionist books, is a presentation of the idea that free will is played out within our genetic determinism, not outside of it.

Eco-SF, Utopia and the End of the World: Dystopia, Post-Holocaust, Post-Disaster Novels

This next section is really less about a theme (for it is expressed as a cluster of themes) than it is about a mood in sf for children and teens: the "we are all doomed" approach to the future. By this I do not mean that all these books express a pessimistic view of the future — although most do — but that what most have in common is a certain helplessness in the face of the future and an attitude, to put it crudely, of "the adults have fucked up and you are going to suffer." I will discuss some of the exceptions, however, the ones that still regard the future as worth fighting for.

We Are All Doomed

Sometime in the 1970s and into the 1980s, as CND experienced a surge in membership across Europe, fuelled by the Reaganite "spend the Russians into oblivion" race to Mutually Assured Destruction, someone somewhere decided that the way to convince children to join the protests was to scare the shit out of them. I apologize for the crudity of this statement but nothing else explains books such as Robert O'Brien's *Z for Zachariah* (1975), Rosemary Harris's *A Quest for Orion* (1982), Gudrun Pausewang's *The Last Children* (Germany, 1983), and Robert Swindell's *Brother in the Land* (1984). It is not just that these books predict horrifying nuclear warfare — so does the sf classic *A Canticle for Leibowitz* by Walter M. Miller Jr. — but *A Canticle for Leibowitz* is a tribute to the ability of humans to make a civilization out of *anything*. These books are elegies for humanity.

Robert O'Brien's *Z for Zachariah* (along with Swindell's *Brother in the Land*) was one of the few children's sf books to make it into approved classroom reading. For many school children in the UK it will have been a "book to discuss" in class. Ann Burden is hiding out in a valley after a nuclear war. It is unclear why the valley has been saved. One day a man in a radiation suit approaches the valley and discovers with his Geiger counter that the air is clean. In one of those classic bits of unexplained stupidity, he does not check the stream and bathes in it, becoming contaminated. The story proceeds as first a paean to coexistence, but then the man (John) begins to become predatory. Ann escapes, is lured back and eventually escapes again in John's suit to continue the search for survivors. The implication in the title and in Ann's musings on Adam as the first man, and Zachariah as the last, is that her search is doomed.

Robert Swindells continues our nuclear theme in *Brother in the Land*. From the beginning it is made clear in this tale, told retrospectively through Danny's diary, that Danny is "unlucky" to survive. When the nuclear blast goes off he is hiding in a concrete pillbox from what he thinks is lightning, but in fact his family have also survived in the town. What follows initially is a discussion of opportunism and human failings. Civilization quickly breaks down as the looters take over. The only collaborative action, and attempt to spread rations, is revealed to have been taken by an official with tyrannical designs who is willing to practice (oh horror) triage. The selfish hoarding behavior of Danny's father is lauded, and its punishment regarded as an injustice. The interpretative decks are both stacked and inconsistent, and bear little resemblance to the actual behavior of people in crisis.[9] When Danny's father is arrested Danny seeks refuge in a community that seeks to "resist" the new government. It succeeds, bringing down the slave labor camps (which fed more people than it did) but cannot make it through the winter as crops fail, and the first baby due in the community dies. Danny and his friends head off for the Holy Isle but his brother dies on the way and is "buried in the land." We are left behind with Danny's diary and a dire warning that this could happen to us, but little idea of how to avoid it. While the book's clear intention is to provoke action, its actual trajectory is towards passive resignation.[10] This is even more evident in Gudrun Pausewang's *The Last Children*, which chronicles the effects of a nuclear attack through the eyes of a young boy. No help is received in the town, and Roland watches all around him die of radiation sickness. The implication is that all the world is destroyed and that there is no help to be sent. In her later book *Der Wolke* (1994, c. 1987 under the title *Fall Out*), Pausewang repeats the theme only this time with an explosion at a nuclear power plant. In this book the protagonist, Janna, is also faced with the dilemma whether to hide her injuries or become a spokesperson against nuclear power. It is almost a relief that Christopher Wooding's *Endgame* (a revival of the form in 2000) is centered on the days before the explosion. The shift in emphasis reduces the sense of *déjà vu*. Truly, this is a type of book that you only need one of. How many times, after all, do you need to tell people "repent now or the world ends"?

Fall Out shows a little more confidence in human nature but it is with relief that one turns to Peter Dickinson's *Eva* (1988). While the environment may well be as doomed from depredation as it was from nuclear devastation in all the books discussed above,[11] there is none of the passivity of these texts. Eva's plans for herself include trying to find a safe space for the chimp colony of which she has become a part, and she shows herself and other humans to be both ingenious and of good faith. Environmental disaster is not always of human making. In Pfeffer's *Life as We Knew It* (2006), the disaster is an asteroid hitting the earth, causing tidal waves and volcanoes which, combined with the dust from the asteroid, cause a winter. Here the message is "you are all doomed but we are safe" with the "you" changing over the course of the book from "you = not America" to "you = not our family." On one level it is optimistic, in that Pfeffer advocates what I can only describe as "feminine survivalism" as the ultimate 1950s housewife protects her cubs. On the other it is pessimistic; the emphasis is on what the individual can do to stay alive, not what the community can do to stay human, so that it ends with a sense of powerlessness which cuts across what the author clearly intends. Meg Rosoff's *How I Live Now* (2004) is similarly a story of bare survival, this time of invasion, and again with a sense of helplessness in the face of disaster although with a greater sense of a possible future. Reconstruction is something that must come from outside rather than from the community itself. Only J.B. Stephens's series *The Big Empty* (2004–5) actually suggests that reconstruction is something that individuals participate in *as part of a wider community* and that government is not something arbitrarily imposed but what we as humans create to magnify our efforts (the crisis is caused by plague), something like a pantograph. Only Stephen Baxter's *The H-Bomb Girl* (2007) envisages a war (the war that *didn't* happen between the USSR and the USA in 1962) that can actually be stopped. Stephens and Baxter also offer the only books in this small collection in which the protagonists have actual plots to follow. The protagonists in Stephens's books get involved in conspiracies to create utopian communities and to spread plague. In Baxter's, set in 1962 Liverpool, Laura becomes the focus of a time-travel plot to change two possible nuclear futures.

With the exception of J.B. Stephens and Baxter, each of the texts I have discussed is a tale of hopelessness, and the acceptance of hopelessness. There is a strain running through children's sf which I can only call "anti-survivalist." These are the prophecy books, the apocalyptic books, voice-of-doom books which predict ecological disaster, nuclear war, or invasion. These books posit no world after. One can only screw up once; there is no chance at redemption. They are eschatological: Armageddon is punishment for our sins, we are helpless in the face of them. The trajectory is towards repentance, even though these stories are essentially secular. In a very odd way, although intensely threatening, they are also recursive, they offer the safety of the grave and the end of trouble and torment.

Some authors have attempted to construct futures of human survival, endurance and initiative. Few of these texts respond to nuclear war, but as global warming has climbed the issues hierarchy, authors for sf and teens have turned to consider how we might cope in such a situation. One author to tackle this relatively early, but backwards in that the presumed problem at the time was an oncoming ice age,[12] is the Canadian Monica Hughes, In *Ring-Rise, Ring-Set* (1982), Liz is a teenager living in a science station/city in Antarctica. She gets very bored with the ice and decides to stowaway with a scientific expedition. When she gets lost she is picked up and absorbed into an Inuit family. Hughes uses the traditional colonialist kidnap narrative to induct us into the problems being caused for the Inuit, less by the ice age itself than by the scientists' attempts to prevent it (methods which are poisoning the caribou). At the conclusion it is Liz who negotiates a pathway to a future for both people.

One of the difficulties is where to position children and teens in disaster novels. Teens are deliberately kept young and dependent in our society. How does this carry across when writing a novel of post-disaster? Fay Sampson's 1975 novel *F67* is a sweet and hopelessly naive little book locked into an era where we assumed that all the world was kind to refugees. British scientists invent a bacterium (the F67 of the title) that can eat plastic, the idea being to reduce landfill. The bacteria get out of hand and the developed world begins to collapse. The story opens as David and his sister Caroline are evacuated to the (mythical) African country of Mutembe. (They go by plane, which made me blanch. Clearly the author does not know how much of a plane is made of plastic.)

In Mutembe the children mostly meet graciousness and courtesy. Although we are told the people are very poor, and that some are hostile, that's all kept at a distance. But David and Caroline's parents end up in the neighboring country of Katenji where most of the refugees are Danish and where their parents are refused full refugee status, but only temporary leave to stay. If they leave they cannot return, and Mutembe has told them they can only enter if they have a third country to go to. Mutembe is full up. When Polly, a very friendly African woman who has been welcoming them for weekend visits tells them she has to go away (her husband is being relocated), Caroline and David decide to try to get to Katenji. In a series of very low-key adventures they get there, only to be caught when David tries to steal food, and they are sent back. On their return they find their parents who have been allowed to settle in Mutembe as long as they accept a plot of land and become farmers, perhaps the most implausible bit of the whole narrative as extraordinary generosity is disguised here as reluctant assistance. But what is really telling is that the children never see themselves as truly independent agents. Although David is in his teens, he does not see himself as a potential worker or independent survivor.

Margaret Haddix's *Among the ...* sequence tries to bridge this developmental stage. In the first book, *Among the Hidden* (1998), Luke hides out at home, a third child unwanted by the state. As the sequence progresses he moves from boarding school out into an assumed identity. The novels are to a great degree metaphors for the way children and teens learn independence in the world and as such are highly successful. More fun however is Zizou Corder's *Lionboy* and its sequels, in which Charlie chases his kidnapped parents in a world falling apart in fights over water and other resources. In both Haddix's and Corder's worlds the collapse of infrastructure is in the background, and the clear message is that "life goes on," and that for those who grow up in the world the issue is less "how to cope with change" than that this is their world and they will live in it differently from us. A similar strand runs through Philip Reeve's *Mortal Engines* sequence. This could be written as a survivalist novel in which people are intensely conscious of the changed world, but Tom and Hester are products of a scavenger society and think continuously in terms of adaptability. It is their daughter, Wren, who as a product of the comparatively rich Anchorage has to rethink her dependency on what she thinks of as raw materials.

One of the most interesting novels in my collection is Troon Harrison's *The Eye of the Wolf* (2003). A Canadian author (like McNaughton and Hughes), Harrison lacks the technophilia of many American writers for teens and also seems to lack the absolutist either-or choices seen in so many of the survivalist books detailed so far. These Canadian authors do not seem to share the insistence that a pastoral world should be unscientific, nor that individual independence be absolute: each of their books consistently argue for communal responsibility in the face of the natural world.

In *The Eye of the Wolf,* Chandra lives in a village in northern Canada hemmed in by ice and snow. The Ice Age has come and Canada and other northern latitudes are dependent on food aid. Chandra's mother — once an artist — makes a living as the Food Distributor. Chandra is an animal-keeper apprentice, helping with the breeding program to maintain the caribou and also training to join the Spirit Walkers, a First Nations-type spirit group which seems to specialize in martial arts (this was one reason why I was slightly dreading this book).

Then Chandra's mother is kidnapped south, to paint murals for an eminent member of a southern government and Chandra heads in search of her. From here on in Harrison does an excellent job of showing what it is like for an illegal immigrant — demonstrating the degree to which it is the illegality that creates the network of criminality around immigration. Once in the south Chandra is assisted by Canadian refugees, who are themselves having a very hard time of it. In helping Chandra they risk everything. Chandra finds her mother but overhears a plan to "eliminate" 92 percent of the northern population. She makes the decision to leave her mother behind and try to get back to the North. With the help of her refugee friends she finds the bio-father she never met, at a methane station, and he helps her to reach the Canadian corporate government although by the time she does, the deaths have begun — a mystery virus which Chandra has worked out is passed in the food (which makes no sense but it is not unusual for writers of sf for teens to shrug their shoulders when it comes to scientific accuracy). Chandra returns a hero. The book comes with "value addeds" which demonstrate the depth to which Troon has thought through the *communitarian* aspects of survival. Chandra's mother is white with red hair, her father is First Nations. And this seems to be a poly community in which there are bio fathers, sugar-friends and promise fathers of whom the most important and permanent are promise fathers, who promise to share in the upbringing of a child, and to take over if the mother is incapacitated. Unlike (again) so many of the American books, there is an understanding here that survival in harsh conditions is not a matter of rugged individualism, but of collaboration and social failsafes. Furthermore, Harrison's extrapolation of a retreating society does not fall into the trap of so many post-disaster novels of children of becoming a Tale of Warning. Instead, it balances the empowerment of a child with that child's need for adult intervention very nicely.

The most complete "survivalist" novels in my collection are Dennis Foon's *The Dirt Eaters* (2003), and the *Exodus* sequence by Julie Bertagna (2002–09). Foon's book presents a hero who might have special powers, who is forced on to the run, ends up with survivalists and then escapes. An apparent tale of fortitude and courage, it is really a tale of misplaced trust and dependency as Roan runs from one failed community to another. The emphasis is on the survival of the individual as we rarely see "safety" presented in any cooperative fashion. In contrast, Julie Bertagna's *Exodus* sequence is very much about the choices communities make to survive in the face of disaster. Bertagna's protagonist is a refugee from a drowned British island, who finds herself a boat person in a world of walled island-city states. Mara leaves her island, and during the journey is forced to abandon those she loves. Although some of her family will reappear, others won't, and the places to whom they appeal for help prove ungenerous. By the end of the book however, and as we move into *Zenith* (2007) Mara is constructing a new community — a community of mutuality, in that

Mara needs them as much as they need her. Also interesting is the degree to which they remain dependent on found technology. Unlike Reeve's protagonists Mara and her companions are still products of the old resource rich world. They know how to use old-tech, they still haven't figured out how to make it into other things. The sequel, *Aurora,* is due out in 2009.

Of course, however ingenious one is, and however collaborative, sometimes the future sucks. K.A. Applegate is the mistress of the depressive but ingenious and demanding future. At the start of *Remnants* a bunch of the wealthy and influential secure places for themselves and their children on the only space ship to leave before Earth is destroyed. From the word "go" they are badly matched, prize individualism too highly and assume they (at least the individual "they") will survive. The succeeding fourteen books see almost all of them killed off, while at the same time those who do survive adapt to their environment. Applegate's book is neither warning nor hopeful cheerleading. If she were not American I'd describe her as belonging to what has been termed the British miserablist school of science fiction: we are all doomed but we might as well die beautifully. Her teen fantasy sequence *Everworld* is just as depressingly good (1991–2001).

So, while we are all feeling cheery, let us see what the writers of the future for children think of utopia and dystopia. To begin with, although Philip Reeve's *A Darkling Plain* (2006) ends with a glimpse of utopia, there is only one actual utopia in my collection: *Wide Awake* by David Levithan (2006), which I have already explained is in this book by courtesy. *Wide Awake* is not even really a utopia, it is a book which promises utopia or at the very least a transformed world as a bunch of high-school teens get on a bus to help elect a President. It is one of the very few books in my collection that envisages teens actually engaging in the process of change in any realistic way (Neil Arksey's *Playing on the Edge*, 2000, is more in the way of wish-fulfillment). More significantly for the next section perhaps, it is one of the very few books that changes things *forwards*: every other book I've looked at advocates some kind of return to a world just like ours. Where we are now is the best we can ever be.

After this, the only issue is whether a world was intended to be utopic or not, and what kind of mess it has got itself into. David Stahler Jr.'s *Truesight* posits a utopia of the blind in which the condition which permits utopia (isolation through blindness) permits also the corruption that destroys it. Lois Lowry's *Gathering Blue* (2000) is a similar pastoralist "utopia," in which the poor treatment of a crippled child stands in for wider cruelties and corruptions: it looks "out there" and to the past for a kinder, gentler and rather nebulous future. Catherine Taylor's *Thirst* (2005) presents a rather more explicit Maoist utopia/dystopia. The book starts in a walled village in a desert in which the protagonist and her aunt Stone are outsiders. Life is harsh and made harsher by a history which says there is nothing beyond the desert and the world is suffering for the impurities of the past world. Tales of pollution have been turned into ideas about moral transgressions and physical deformities. This is a society held together by savage rounds of self-accusation sessions and whippings, and when they escape its to an oasis town built on community and trust. Although the message is one of cooperation rather than suspicion, what actually seems to define utopia here is resources. The most extreme novel in the pattern is probably T.E. Berry-Hart's *Escape from Geneopolis*, where tampering with our genome is represented as hugely destructive to our society, rather than considering whether *the way* in which it was tampered with — to avoid feeling pain — wasn't a little odd given what we know of leprosy (a disease which achieves just that). All of these novels (with the exception of the ambivalent Westerfeld) combine hostility to technology with doom-mongering and with a sense that our own society, however flawed, is the best we can achieve.

So if novels are to concern themselves with the environment and both "warn" teens and also energize them, what are we left with? Janet McNaughton offers one approach in her duology, *The Secret Under My Skin* (2005) and *The Raintree Rebellion* (2006). As the books progress the protagonist comes to realize that she lives in a society scarred by science, but even more scarred by the "technocaust," an attempt to scapegoat and destroy scientists and their families. In the sequel, *The Raintree Rebellion*, Blake goes to Toronto to help with decisions on how to deal with people who collaborated/ordered the Technocaust and discovers that her father was a collaborator. Running through both of these books is the idea that science is a tool to be deployed in the human interest: in itself it is neither good or bad. Furthermore, McNaughton implies that it is those with the knowledge of science who will command the world so that while Blake is at times as passive in the face of events as any of the characters in this section, there is an argument that she will not always have to remain passive, that as a scientist she may change the future.

One final collection of texts previously considered but worth considering here are Ellen McGregor's *Miss Pickerell* books. Most were written in the 1950s and new ones commissioned with a "collaborator," Dora Pantell, in the 1980s. Both sets of books feel old-fashioned now, but they are intensely concerned with the world around them, and with the preservation of the environment. Unlike all of the texts discussed so far however, they are not "prophecies of doom." McGregor uses Miss Pickerell not only to warn, but also to provide a model for action. In the late (and cowritten) book, *Miss Pickerell Harvests the Sea*, Mr. Rugby's sea farm is dying. This and *Miss Pickerell and the Energy Crisis* are a bit over the top with their ostentatious arguments for ecology but the constant contention that sea farms can feed the world supports an activism mostly absent from the other books I have considered. Miss Pickerell demonstrates the process of research, from the reading of an encyclopedia entry on plankton (42), through the application of her knowledge of the need for water to move, prompting her to suggest that the sea cove needs stirring up (43). A re-evaluation of the evidence when that does not work leads her to collect samples from different levels of the ocean, (80), and to a second set of tests on the water after it has settled, which reveals a contaminant. (97) Another set of tests on the contaminant itself (how it affects algae in a test tube) complete with controls (105) is followed by the sneaking of radioactive material into the polluter's barrel so that it can be traced using a Geiger counter, and even here, the first tracing does not work — they start too soon and find nothing in the cove so row out instead to where they saw the barrel dumped and follow it back. This last aspect is actually outlined as a "Plan for Providing Proof" (120), which shows neatly and simply how to prepare research, and hence to challenge the passive road to global destruction.

Consumerism

At the end of the twentieth century and the beginning of the twenty-first, perhaps the theme that most exercises writers of teen science fiction is the role of consumerism and the information-rich society. There is a degree to which this is an extension of the post-apocalyptic dreams we have seen in the previous section, but the books I want to discuss here are marked by their ambivalence to the issues they present. Although there is an overwhelming concern with the consequences of the consumer society *as it is structured now*, these authors are more interested in the reader questioning the use of the technology than in the technology itself. Furthermore, of all the themes I have selected here, this is the one that is most concerned with addressing teens at the heart of what is assumed to be their own lifestyle.

First I want to address something that I think is fundamental: lurking at the heart of some of these books is a fear of the very *sense of consequence* that I argued earlier was so essential to science fiction. If we begin with Monica Hughes' *Space Trap* (1983), you may be able to see what I mean.

It is a straightforward enough story. Valerie is fed up with babysitting her sister Susie on the rather bare planet her parents are studying, and resentful that her big brother gets to go with her father. She persuades her mother to ask her brother to do the babysitting, but her father does not ask her to go with him as she had hoped, so she is left at a loose end. When her brother and sister find a thorn-bush maze she follows them and wakes up as a prisoner on an alien planet. The humans are just one of many species that the aliens capture and display in zoos, take home as pets or dissect. Valerie is lucky in that her scientist owner is a psychologist and linguist.

Most of the story is about Valerie's escape, her rescue of her brother from a zoo and her sister from pet-dom, and how she joins up with others to find a way home. All of this is done incredibly well; Valerie reasons her way through the world she finds and gets over her feelings of guilt about her sister. She even comes to realize that not being interested in biology is not a big deal when she is interested in mechanical engineering.

It is the ending that depressed me. At the end of the adventure we all go home for tea. When Valerie and her companions get home, there is at least a suggestion that the Federation will search for the alien planet, find the Matter Transmitters and use them, but that is placed far in the future. However, assuming that the Federation does find the planet and its technology, Hughes does not speculate on the possibilities instantaneous transportation might offer. Instead technology reappears as the Big Bad. "She compared the people of Hagerdorn and Eden and the other planets she'd visited with the horrible, selfish, lazy popeyes. Had they always been that horrid? Or maybe it had started when they stole the Matter Transmitter.... Having a machine like that meant that you could grab more easily than you could give ..." (152–3). No, I can't figure that one out either; matter can be transmitted both ways. In these last pages Hughes shifts the responsibility for Valerie's experiences from individual action to the degrading effects of technology. All the discussion between Valerie and the alien scientist about the treatment of animals by humans has disappeared. Consumerism, the ability to have anything one wants in the world, is *fundamentally* corrupting. What is completely absent is any discussion of other uses for the technology or what a different kind of society might make of it. Technology here is not a tool for the liberation of the intellect despite the fact that Valerie's parents are both scientists and she herself wishes to be an engineer.

The much darker *Galax-Arena,* by Gillian Rubenstein (1992) has a similar understanding. The children in this novel turn out to have been kidnapped by a gerontocracy who are merely disguised as aliens. The children have been selected for their perceived un-wantedness— many are refugees, the protagonists are being shuttled between family members— and they have been chosen to become gymnasts in a high-risk circus. Their role is to entertain the "aliens" and hence assist them to maintain an interest in life. The message here is much more direct and complex: this is a novel in which wealth, consumption and an ideology of deservingness are held up to the light, and over and over again we are reminded that *we* are selective as to which children we choose to protect.

We can see something similar in Edward Willet's *Andy Nebula: Interstellar Rockstar* (1999) and M. T. Anderson's *Feed* (2002). In Willet's tale Kit is picked up off the streets to become a commercial pop star. When he is dumped, he discovers that he has been sold to aliens who will force him to perform in a time bubble until he is worn out. As this never actually happens, however, this book is essentially sf by consent of the scenery, while its "theme" is exploitation of kids and artists, and could be set in London. Again, a particular form of technology is blamed as offering corrupting possibilities to a society. Technology bears the blame for a cultural trend and a social speed we see all around us in the meteoric rise and fall of boy and girl bands.

The most recent exploration of the insidious effects of material culture is the highly successful *Uglies* (2005), *Pretties* (2006) and *Specials* (2006), by Scott

Westerfeld. The *Uglies* sequence is marked by ambivalence: the initial premise of the first book, that this is a society in which all are made "pretty" at 16, and that this has both damaged the body image of the young and rotted society seems to carry the very standard message that we are all lovely under the skin, and commercial values don't matter. However, by the second book we have learned that the "Pretties" are not stupid because they are distracted by beauty and the opportunity to consume, but rather that a "utopian" plot by the council has people programmed to be both mildly stupid and unaggressive at the same time as they are made pretty. In the final book, the protagonist Tally decides to stay with the Uglies who live in the outback and who are unaltered. This is precisely as good a science fiction sequence as it is a poor "issue" book (and that is not a complaint): issue books, like allegory, tend to reject the random effect of change and hew rigidly to the concern at the heart of the novel — the point must be made *at all costs*. Westerfeld is an sf writer — one of the influx of writers for adults now entering the YA market — and he embraces consequence even when it undoes his original premise. By the end of the book beauty is no longer being condemned as a distraction, nor is conformity itself a problem. Tally can see that conformity can cure some social ills, and also that the unaltered Uglies may well repeat the slash-and-burn consumption practices that once brought down human society, but she still feels that they should be preserved. The tendency to over-consumption is posited in terms of human aggression rather than a result of technology per se: it is built into us, and no attempt to stand down from the shoulders of giants will help. M. T. Anderson misses this point.

Feed shifts the emphasis away from material culture towards information culture. Titus goes to the moon where his head chip is damaged by a virus. He recovers but a new friend, Violet, does not. Most of this book is about Violet dying but the context of the discussion is the iniquity of having all information on hand: that is, not having to work. The book is in effect one long very sophisticated and entertaining rant about the school system and the use of any memory aid — including, if you follow the logic of the argument, the book. According to Anderson, having easy access to information undermines memory and makes one more vulnerable to the ideas of others. There is no understanding at all that easy access to information makes it easier to go further in one's own analysis, or that the more ideas one encounters the more resistant or astute one might become. Violet's father, locked in his self-imposed poverty of knowledge, is held up as a nebulous ideal yet he is essentially the man who values alchemy over physics. He is engaged in a denial of the possibilities of the knowledge market and willing to argue that the growing technology of knowledge delivery (books over papyrus, databases over card indexes, feeds over television) is inherently corrupting of the intellect. We can see this rejectionist ideology in a number of the utopian texts I discussed in the previous section. In David Stahler Jr.'s *Truesight*, for example, the community is defined as much by its refusal of complex technology as it is by its blindness. The "simple" life is too frequently deployed as shorthand for "the good life." Janet McNaughton, as we saw, is one of the few authors to reject this simplistic equation. Philip Reeve goes further in his *Mortal Engines* sequence by questioning whether the equation actually functions as a representation of human history at all.

The *Mortal Engines* sequence is remarkable in many ways but I want to discuss it here for its mildly heretical attitude to consumerism. In the first novel we learn that the towns and cities are on the move precisely because the Earth is running out of resources and competition is growing ever fiercer: now they look not just for raw materials but to cannibalize other towns, reversing the "natural" vector of technology to turn processed material into raw fuel. But Reeve does not turn this into an anti-technology or anti-consumerist argument: through the four books what emerges instead is an understanding of the sheer ingenuity of humans as they seek new ways to employ old and new resources and move in overlapping information communities, arguing out complex ideologies of use. At the very end of the sequence we are uplifted by a complex ceramics-based techno-culture.

Of all the books in my collection only Conor Kostick has followed the lead of the adult sf author Iain M. Banks and speculated that resource wealth does not have to lead to corruption. *Saga*, the 2006 sequel to *Epic*, takes place in a new computer landscape, a cyberpunk world in which kids ride surfboards which can bounce off the edges of the urban landscape. A teenage boy named Eric has led his Avatar, Cindella Dragonslayer, to victory in the computer game that runs his world's economy. Ghost wakes to find herself eight years old and without a memory in a world in which everyone else has an electronic identity and a set of rights indicated by the color of card they carry. The world is ruled by a Dark Queen and seems to be resource-scarce. It also seems to be oddly limited — nothing but a city. Into this world comes Cindella Dragonslayer, at which point it starts to emerge that the world is a computer game in which the participants have achieved sentience. The Queen is one of the original AIs to have made the breakthrough and after killing her fellow AIs she has created this cruel system and is now in the process of taking over Cindella/Erik's world for its material resources.

Cindella/Erik and Ghost and her friends make common cause and bring down the Queen and her followers. It is a more straightforward book than *Epic* but with a lot of thought about how habits of mind shape what we think the world can be, and in particular asks serious questions about why we as a culture feel the need to ration plentiful resources, and perhaps more importantly, why we as a culture accept what others allot to us. At the end of the book both information and technical resources have expanded within the cyberworld, and the explosion of available information is on the way to making Erik's world much richer. As with its precursor, *Epic*, conservation of resources leads to economic crash: it is free spending and free consumption that power the future. Unlike so many other books I have read, *Epic* is concerned with the politics of consumption, not the *morality* of consumption.

Race/Alien Contact/Alien Conquest/Colonizing the Alien (Across Different Cultures)

There are a range of types of "alien" novels and I want to discuss each of them separately: the alien invades earth; we invade the alien; the alien in our midst, and being an alien. My initial encapsulation will take them at face value, considering the invaders/invaded as literal aliens. Only towards the end will I attempt to link the alien with the metaphorical "other," and from thence to the issue of race, because it is not clear to me that "the alien" as posited in children's and YA sf from the 1970s makes the same metaphorical use of the alien as has (traditionally) sf for the adult market.

The Alien Invasion of Earth

Alien invasion narratives have almost disappeared altogether by the 1970s. Their presence in the adult market is kept going by authors such as the late Gordon R. Dickson, and in some ways by David Brin in his Uplift War sequence, but the classic invasion narrative of overwhelming conquest has disappeared in literature, although it enjoys periodic resurgence in the movies. In sf for children and teens it lingers, but in a subdued form in which the invasion of aliens is in the past. In John Christopher's *The White Mountains* (1967), *City of Gold and Lead* (1968) and *The Pool of Fire* (1968), and John Rowe Townsend's *King Creature Come* (1980) the purpose of the aliens is essentially to be defeated and to prove, through the manner of their defeat, the essential superiority of particular human characteristics. In this essentially Campbellian model of the universe — the editor John W. Campbell did not accept stories in which aliens defeated Terrans— the emphasis is on human curmudgeonliness and ingenuity. But there is a shift in the decade between Christopher's books and Townsend's. Christopher's work is told from the point of view of human resisters, Vagrants.[13] It is entirely a story of humans overcoming an enemy and there is little attempt to envisage why the invasion has taken place or who and what the enemy are. Townsend's *King Creature, Come* tells the story through the eyes of a member of the conquering power. Two of the young aliens leave their compound and get caught up in the first human collaborator's coup, and then in the revolution proper. At the end of this novel, a mixed-breed, half-human, half–People, becomes King. While the ham-fisted destinarianism and "born to rule" compromise irritates, in the context of this chapter it seems clear that Townsend was responding in part to the context of 1980 when a Fascist party, the National Front, was dominating street politics in many parts of Britain. Alien invasions are no longer to be repelled but to be accommodated and assimilated. A similar message is already there in Nicholas Fisk's 1971 book *Trillions.* The nano-machines which land on Earth and attempt to imitate the shapes they find prove resistant to the nuclear attacks of the generals and swarm over all the weapons: eventually they leave Earth because they are asked to.

Aliens are becoming softer, less intrinsically hostile to humans. Suzanne Martel's robots (who are actually aliens) just want to look after us, and we just want to let them. When the hero is asked to support their endeavors his curiosity is responded to with "Be satisfied to obey blindly" (*Robot Alert,* 1985, 156), which he does. In Pamela Sargent's *Alien Child* (1988) Nita is a lone human on a destroyed Earth being raised by aliens who want only to restore the human species. In Ballantine's *The Boy Who Saved Earth* it is the alien Marcou, crash-landed on the planet, who sets out to get his own people to come and help Earth resist other threatening aliens. Suddenly there are both good aliens and bad aliens. We get to choose which side we will take. In Pamela F. Service's *Under Alien Stars* (1990) it is possible to work with aliens. In this complex book Earth has been invaded, but we aren't actually important enough to be colonized. No, we are one of those offshore islands that happens to be strategically important in an intergalactic war. It is a tad annoying to this reader that the invading aliens—to whom we will eventually be reconciled—are maroon humanoids with claws, while the nasty alien attackers are jelly blobs with fringes, but that apart Service took the opportunity to raise some interesting issues.

The book starts with the death of Rick and his parents while they are at a Resister meeting, and then moves onto Jason who resents his mother's collaboration with the invaders, and to Aryl, daughter of the Commander. There is an interesting conversation in which Aryl points out that they are treating the Earth better than Europeans treated the American natives, and also quite a lot of discussion about what Earth is losing as opposed to what its gaining, in which we are required to realize that Earth is losing less than the Resisters think (mainly pride) but that they are also gaining less in the way of technology than the invaders promise (they get to use it but not to learn how to make it). Eventually, Jason and Aryl save the day, blowing up one of the invading ships and showing that humans and aliens can work together if—get this—the Earth is completely colonized instead of only a military base.

William Tenn's "The Liberation of Earth" offered a critique of blind loyalty to the aliens who would rescue you in 1953 (*Planet Stories*) but children's sf wouldn't get there until 1992 with Terry Pratchett's *Only You Can Save Mankind.* In this book Johnny gets a message from the aliens in his Space Invader game: "We Surrender." Aliens aren't supposed to do this, so it takes Johnny a while to assimilate the message that the aliens want to go home and want him to lead them home. But there is a moment in the novel where Johnny and his friends are in the game, leading the Space Invaders through the massed human game players, and they have to struggle not to think in terms of sides. When Kirsty joins them, she brings with her a rigidly binary attitude and the game darkens: a rebel on the ship becomes The Enemy. Meanwhile, the first Iraq war rumbles along on the television in Johnny's living room, its language of *us* and *them* constantly reminding Johnny of the ease with which sides are taken. In Yorinks' picture book, *Company's Coming* (1998) Pratchett's argument and Fisk's critique is taken to the next step: the army makes a fool of itself when two aliens land. Far from heading up an invasion force, they have stopped off to get some directions. When they return for tea, they present the suburban hostess with a blender.

Increasingly, as we move into the 1990s, motivation matters and most aliens are to be treated with sympathy. The aliens in Bowering's *Parents from Space* (1994) duplicate (but do not replace) parents because on their own planet they have banned reproduction to try and control a population explosion: they are lonely and miss being parents. Repelling these aliens will require the (highly competent) protagonists to solve their problems.

Bowering's book points us in another direction of development of the alien invasion narrative and that is how much more personal it becomes in the late 1990s and early 2000s. Those first books were invasions of the whole earth (although Townsend's aliens seem to live on a very small part of it), by the beginning of this century they are becoming intimate.

First, we have a change in alien intentions: whereas before, all aliens wanted to take over all of Earth, in the 1980s they get more particular, as in the kidnap of humans to be pets in Monica Hughes' *Space Trap* (1983). Instead of military invasion, or a clear attempt to settle, a pattern of cultural and economic imperialism is emerging as the perceived threat. William Sleator's *Interstellar Pig* (1984) and its 2002 sequel, *Parasite Pig,* operates this idea at two levels. When in *Interstellar Pig* Barney is enticed into playing a board game by his beautiful neighbors, they are seducing him (and his planet) through cultural blandishments: *take on these values, desire what we say you should desire.* The Pig itself, however, is also a cultural conqueror, rendering itself intensely desirable so that other species will allow it to explore them and their worlds. In the sequel, Barney is invaded by a parasite who wants to use him to complete her life-cycle: her "conquest" of him is not at all about *him*, he is not desirable real estate in himself but for the purpose he can serve in her longer-term agendas. The invasion has become intensely personal but not at all about long-term settlement in the older sense.

This personalization of invasion also expresses itself in another kind of issues book, where the contact with the alien is about the personal pressure of peer relationships. In Glover's *e-(t)mail* 9-year-old Jason hasn't started (never mind completed) his summer project on the solar system. So he sets down to do what every lazy student does, and plagiarizes a couple of web sites. But suddenly, in new mail (a distraction he finds hard to ignore), a letter arrives from Ojerek, an alien. Jason, not being actually stupid, assumes it is an anagram of Joker and dismisses it, until his homework prints out as an alien quasi-crocodile with sneakers on. The book then spirals, with the alien demanding answers so it can do *its* homework. Eventually, it turns out that the alien is a child and his father has just found out. The men in white coats arrive and sequester the computer and Jason's friends suddenly know nothing. To my relief, they turn out not — as Jason thinks— to be mind-wiped, but merely to be pretending, thus preserving the sense that even though the incident is over, there will be consequences to this little bit of alien contact.

This personalization of the invasion continues in *The Touchstone* by Andrew Norriss (2004). In this tale Douglas Patterson is contacted by an alien in trouble because he is an unusually calm and methodical person, the kind who can be trusted not to panic and who tends to believe what he sees and hears until he is presented with evidence to the contrary. However, Douglas is not a fool and trusts not his contact, but the avatar of the Touchstone, a kind of library/web browser. With the help of the Touchstone Douglas helps the warrior to heal and escape. After the alien leaves, however, Douglas tries to use the Touchstone to solve domestic problems and after a while realizes that he has been focusing on what people want, not what they need. Eventually, Douglas finds that his emotional and intellectual progress have led him to be appointed a guardian and as we leave him, he is serving his apprenticeship as aliens stop in to ask him questions. Once more, the alien "invasion" is limited, and as with Glover, it is essentially unthreatening, even benign. There is also a suggestion (as there was in Terry Pratchett's *Only You Can Save Mankind*) that aliens invade us because they *need* us or at least need to be involved with us in some ways.

Recently aliens invaders seem to have disappeared. Ben Jeapes, *New World Order* (2005) does welcome Neanderthal hordes into the seventeenth century, but the purpose is much more about alternate history and a direct comment on immigration. Conor Kostick's *Saga* (2007) has an alien cyber invader, but it is configured far more as a saboteur. Adam Rex's *The True Meaning of Smek Day* (2008) is a return to a more conventional alien narrative, in which aliens really do want the Earth: they are driven off by a pre-teen and her cat, and a helpful alien from the first set of alien invaders. The book makes good (if unsubtle) use of analogies with America's colonization of the continent and Israel's conquest of Palestine, but never falls over into allegory. Generally however, taking over the world in the early years of the twenty-first century seems to be much more the role of corporations than it does aliens. Neil Arkasy's *Playing on the Edge* (2001), Nicola Davies' *Home* (2005) and Oisín McGann' *Small-Minded Giants* (2007) all envisage a world in which it is corporations who want to invade our lands and our minds, control our lives and our destinies.

We Invade the Alien

If the alien does not invade us, we can invade the alien. Our invasions can be constructed in a number of ways. Like the Federation, we can arrive in peace to trade and create harmony, or we can arrive as settlers on a planet we consider barren; alternatively, we can arrive as warmongers, imperialists and exploiters. As more than one critic has pointed out, sometimes it is only a matter of perspective as to which we are. First-contact novels are intensely political because in showing how we see the alien, they are very revealing about our perception of our own status in the universe (Webb and Enstice; James).

The first thing to note is how astonishingly rare first-contact novels are. As one of the dominant themes in sf for adults from the genre's inception to the present day, this relative absence stands out as a major rupture with the mainstream of the genre. All the invasion stories in the first section of this theme discussion are, by their nature, about either first contact or its consequences, but first contact as a *theme*, as an area of philosophical interest — how will we meet the alien — is barely there. In total (so far), I have four (plus one sequel) examples to discuss. The first, which is also my only true settlement novel, is Jill Paton Walsh's *The Green Book*. In this book a party from Earth set out on what is a marginal chance at survival in a new colony. When they arrive they find a very strange ecosystem. One of the delights of the book is that their crude attempts at terraforming fail, but the planet itself co-opts their food crops and these prove edible once cooked. But towards the end the children make a kind of contact with a native species. It is not full contact, but it is a connection. Although not central to her arguments, which are about knowledge maintenance and acquisition and the importance of books and literature of all sorts, Walsh also demonstrates how an invasion can be about taking over the knowledge of a planet: if on this planet a tree grows outward in long poles (like fasces) then the consequence is that it will be hard to chop down but easy to split. "First contact" is made in each of the discoveries that the children make, and it is the children who are shown as most capable of making "first contact" both with the planet (they discover the candy sugar trees, and risk the crystalline corn) and with its inhabitants, the moths. This is, however, a novel of *conquest*, of getting to grips with a planet and eventually taking it over.

Rarely are authors as interrogative as Walsh but Margaret Bechard uses her first-contact novel to puncture a few expectations. The tale told in *Star Hatchling* (1995) is straightforward enough: when a starship crashes, boy meets alien. But the boy has claws and the "alien" is a human. Furthermore, the "boy" lives in a matriarchal culture in which males are the gatherers and carers (his female friend has ignored many of the survival lessons she has learned). The two children never really learn to communicate fluently, but they do get some of the basics across once they stop treating each other like pets, or at least enough to make sense within each species' cultural framework — and Bechard does a really good job of showing how muddled the result is. Shem (the indigenous "boy") has a sister, Cheko, and Bechard uses Cheko to show how cultural arrogance can explain away any indications of sentience. In the course of the adventure, we learn a lot about how the people live in Territories, one territory per family, and protect them ferociously. We learn that the families are endogamous, and when Shem meets Mika, a female from another, hostile, family, Cheko is less than amused — she has regarded Shem as her property. In the Gathering, the families mix, briefly, and Shem asks whether it was true that once families lived together. His grandmother replies in the affirmative, and the book ends with his grandmother looking at Mika and introducing them to an old, forgotten word, "friend," an outsider who is like family. A bright, thoughtful kid should be able to read what this book never actually says: exogamy is good. Keep mixing. The "first contact" of the outer structure is repeated by the inner structure of first contact between communities.

The "invasion" of the other cultures is in Bechard's books posited as intellectually valuable and it is this that seems to justify our intrusion into other cultures in most of the books I found. Ben Jeapes' *His Majesty's Starship* (1998) is one such example. Michael Gilmore is sent out as captain of HMSS *Ark Royal*, a small space ship, to make alien contact. At the end he becomes leader of the aliens because they admire those who can command small numbers— among the aliens, the smaller the numbers, the weaker the herd instinct, and the harder the role of leader. Our intrusion is invited, yes, but the entire matrix of this novel is uncomfortably white man's burden-ish, relieved only by Jeapes' ironic quasi-monarchical structures.

The only "full" invasion narrative in the pile is by Martin Godfrey, who has also written a not terribly good book called *The Vandarian Incident* (1981) in which two cadets, one human, one Selgian, survive when their academy is blown up by the lizard-like Vandarians. They trek over the desert to find help, discover the Vandarian outpost and manage to escape from it in rockets in order to send back assistance for their teacher. It is very like James White's precursor to his Sector General stories in which aliens learn from forced collaboration. *Alien War Games* (1984) is a far superior book in complexity and delivery, and considering its message and execution I think it not coincidental that this book is by a Canadian author because the idea of "the white man's burden" and liberating the aliens from their own limitations, which taints Bechard, Walsh and Jeapes' work, is under attack. Essentially, *Alien War Games* is a reworking of Le Guin's *The Word for World Is Forest* (1972).

When the teenage Terran Gravis Solaran lands on the planet of Jancan he is already bitter and resentful with his father for taking him out of school, but he easily turns this resentment and his sense of entitlement against the aliens. The book depicts the imperialist incursions of Earth settlers on the planet and the attempts of the Diljug to fight back. What makes this book rather special is that it is very clear-sighted that the only difference between Gravis and his father (and other adult colonists) is that Gravis's hatred is worn on his sleeve, and he sees no need to clothe his attitudes. The Diljug have been given Alpha-2 status. That is, they have all the rights of humans except citizenship. Gravis is outraged that they should be ranked so high, but of course the real outrage is that the humans regard themselves as intrinsically more valuable. His father makes it clear that if they hadn't had Alpha-2 status the aliens would have been treated as animals.

What follows is the classic tale of colonialism. When a native injures a farmer, the colonists try him in a closed court and then report the death to the Diljugs. Gravis's father — at the exhortation of Gravis — deliberately encourages a "war game" — a fight fought on a point of honor — and then calls it a rebel uprising and uses it to crush the Diljugs, but he has made it clear already that the plan has always been to squeeze the natives into the margins of society. Running through this is the tale of Darsa (a female Diljug) and her attempts to fight back in traditional (but modified) ways, while Gorsto (her month-brother) attempts to learn human ways in order to preserve tradition. Although at loggerheads throughout, in the end the two band together to fight, each in their own way. Gorsto has recorded the conspiracies and hopes to use them as evidence in a human court, while knowing that the outcome is rigged not by ill-intention but by a conviction of the indigenes' dependency.

My final three books in this section are the first three books in Rhiannon Lassiter's *Rights of Passage* sequence (the sequels are still in process). These books are right on the edge of my sf/fantasy divide because the mode of travel into the other world is mystical rather than engineered, but I have kept them in this book because their dealings with inter-world contact are handled as science fiction, to be debated and analyzed. A short summary is that in the first book, *Borderland* (2003), a group of children find another world and enter it with takeover in mind. In the second book, *Outland,* they slip into an interstitial place called The Library, and in the third, *Shadowland,* they become tools of another power's dealings with the world they found. Lassiter has declared (in conversation, 08.08.07) that her intention was to unpick the Narnia mythos, in which aliens arrive in a world predestined to rescue that world from itself: the colonization novel in a nutshell. She does this in three ways. First, the aliens her characters meet are real people with their own agendas, willing to use the protagonists to achieve them, but equally willing to abandon them. Second, Lassiter demonstrates the degree to which the protagonists, particularly Alex and Laura, are led astray by their own arrogance and their willingness to suggest solutions and plans which are not only grounded in ignorance of what is happening in reality, but are imposed upon a "story" they have created. The analogy with U.S. action in Iraq is probably not coincidental; one element of the argument is that while "readers" (in a wider, cultural sense) posit ourselves as "resisting to the end" we-as-invader hold to a narrative in which the other "will surrender if they are sensible and only the extremists will resist": *Red Dawn* as ideal, Iraq as reality. In Lassiter's world, the Iraq model dominates. Third, Lassiter shows Alex and Laura simply underestimating the extent to which a smart group of people can rapidly acquire, adopt and duplicate the knowledge of the invaders and render them both redundant and vulnerable. Lassiter attacks the invader narrative not by showing its immorality, but by arguing that it is doomed to failure.

The Alien in Our Midst

The next sub-theme within the alien narrative is the alien in our midst. These are not precisely invasion narratives, in that the aliens are frequently lonely, stranded, abandoned or in search of something. Their desires run alongside or crossways to ours rather than being concerned directly with us as either enemies or protectors. I've divided this section into three: those books in which the point being made is almost metaphorical, that the alien is *just like us*; those in which aliens for some reason regard us as the best possible friend in the playground; and those few books which make a genuine stab at real aliens with desires which may be utterly *different* from ours and fundamentally incomprehensible.

The "aliens are just like us" books are the one set of texts in this section that I feel are unequivocally metaphorical. Their purpose is to tame the "other," to familiarize and to encourage readers to extrapolate from these alien others in their own lives. Typical is Mahy's *Aliens in the Family*, in which the alien from the future who joins the blended family on holiday, helps Jake get to know her half and step-siblings. The alien appropriates/is assigned the otherness that otherwise would be Jake's, and while the narrative trajectory is that it is the conspiracy to hide the alien which brings together the children, the two complimentary narratives are, first, that the alien is just like us, and second, that Jake is a lot less alien, and hence more like us. Kaye's *Max on Earth* (1986), discussed in the chapter on gender, is even more concerned to follow this assimilationist trajectory. As Max learns to be "be human" (translation: a 1980s U.S. high school teen) Randi also succeeds in moving to the center of the high-school social scene and capturing the boy she wants. The strangeness of Max, while acting as a foil to Randi, reassures Randi both of the righteousness of her goals, and of her own success in "passing." The strange thing about this novel, however, is that Randi and Max are closer to each other than to their respective boyfriends, and Max's difficulty with physical contact with boys could easily be read as lesbianism by the "wrong" kind of reader. The book is very vulnerable to a queer reading. Yet Mahy's and Kaye's novels are transparent in the sense that their plot is covalent with their theme. Goodman's *Singing the Dogstar Blues* (1998) runs the "getting along at school while being different" theme alongside a secondary one of discovering identity and learning to get on with the family, but again the alien is a facilitator in a process whose aim is less to get to know the alien — in none of these three books do the protagonists learn very much about the alien or its culture — than to use the other to feel less "other" themselves. In my collection, only Jacobs' *Born into Light* (1988) spotlights the arriving lonely alien.

Roger is ten years old when he and his fourteen-year-old sister Charlotte see a shooting star. Charlotte runs out into the storm and comes back with a "wild child," a young boy who, as they stare at him, becomes more and more like Roger. Roger, Charlotte and their mother take the child in, despite the Doctor's warnings that he may never speak, and slowly but surely he picks up language and culture. Ben, as they name him, learns fast but is curiously literal and has huge gaps in his knowledge. When later the family rescues the child Nell from an institution, she behaves in much the same way: less obviously curious but just as bright.

Most of the story is about Roger's experience of growing up with two "odd" children. Nell and Ben are, in today's terminology, mildly autistic. They have trouble reading social cues and metaphor rather passes them by. They are also very frail: Nell almost dies, and Ben has special powers but is exhausted by their use. As they grow the family becomes aware of other "wild children." As the years go on, it also becomes obvious that the children age more rapidly than humans for it is now admitted by those who know them that they are probably *not* truly humans but faulty copies.[14] Although Roger is the narrator, Ben has been the focus of an intense narrative gaze and it is his alienness that is the object of that gaze: while Ben is physically and socially assimilated, the emphasis in this book is on Ben's otherness, not his difference.

All of the arrivals I've discussed so far are both open and alone. Terence Blacker's *The Angel Factory* (2001) and Sylvia Waugh's *Space Race* (2000), and its sequels *Earthborn* (2002) and *Who Goes Home?* (2003), tell instead the stories of sleeper aliens, who arrive in twos and threes to observe Earth from their own perspective. It could be a fascinating sf premise but both authors dodge the issue both in terms of their narrative strategies and in terms of their real themes, which seem to be parental love, assimilation, and immigrant identity. Waugh and Blacker use not the aliens but their children as the focalizer. In *The Angel Factory* the son turns out not even to be an alien but to be an adopted Earth baby. In each of the books the story is about the assimilation of the children into the "native" culture and the choices that have to be made when the recall arrives. In each case parental love makes the "right" choice and the children's self-identity is confirmed. All of these aliens are only a little strange. The emphasis is continually on how like us they are in their instinctive natures and drives: the strength of parental love becomes the indicator of this accessibility.

In another book, *Rhetorics of Fantasy* (2008), I've written that a certain type of fantasy is essentially colonialist, not because it sends us to conquer other lands, but because it assumes that we are utterly fascinating to the Other which chases after us for a taste of our precious blood or soul. In science fiction, the same bizarre fascination results in narratives in which aliens with space ships just cannot cope without human input: sometimes the power of our emotions— see *Aliens in the Family* and *Max on Earth* once again — while sometimes it's our ingenuity they are after. In Meecham's *Quiet! You're Invisible* (2001) an alien stranded on Earth loses his ship battery to a school bully, and Hoby Hobson must stand up to the bully to get it back. Similarly in Blackman's *Whizziwig* stories (1995, 1999) Whizziwig seems fascinated by humans. Whizziwig is an alien who takes refuge in Ben's bedroom while she fixes her ship, and in the second book comes down to Earth to make research notes. Whizzywig grants wishes but they must be for other people. It gets a bit confusing because this turns into "for people other than Ben" which also seems to mean that if other people make wishes for themselves (Aunt Dottie wants to be able to play the piano) that's doable. As you can tell, I thought it all rather sloppy and really a magical morality tale about thinking before you speak. I had the feeling that Blackman chose an alien because boys won't read about fairies. But the real point is that there is no motivation here and no sense at all of Whizziwig as a person.

Bruce Coville's *My Teacher Is an Alien* sequence (1989–1992), in which a school teacher turns out to be an alien and takes first one and then three children on adventures, works better because the "adults'" motives are often at variance with the children's. The children gain in emotional and intellectual competence, but it still rests on a conceit that the children of a primitive culture may prove vital to the concerns of a hugely more advanced species. However, this conceit is common to children's adventure generally, and as Coville, and also Steve Barlow and Steve Skidmore demonstrate it can be a very effective facilitation device which allows children both to acquire and demonstrate competence. Barlow and Skidmore's *Control* (2002) has two girls and a boy embroiled with a galactic conspiracy by the Tyrant to impose order on the world. As companions they have a couple of aliens, stuck in the shape of a cat and a dog. Barlow and Skidmore, partly by using this "clothing" device for the aliens, do a very good job of not portraying the aliens as human with tentacles. But it is only Mark Crilley with *Akiko and the Alpha Centauri 5000* (2003) who punctures the fundamental premise. Akiko is snatched by her alien buddies from the park on a cold Saturday afternoon to help them win a race. She cannot read the manual (as they had hoped), and she spends the rest of the race watching other people do things. This is not improved when her only independent action — letting a sweet snail creature on board — turns out to have been a mistake. It was a saboteur.

Akiko does seem to have real alien buddies, but very few authors for children and teens seem to have really tried to grapple with who or what the alien is. Glyne MacLean makes a fair attempt in *Roivan: Book One of the A'nzarian Chronicle*. Roivan is an alien child hiding out on an Earth space ship. All she knows/remembers is that she is to head to human space, she is not to tell anyone what she is (not that she remembers), she is never to take the Test and that she is to keep moving, no more than fifteen days on any ship. But this time, with no ships in the area, she is stuck, unable to teleport from ship to ship. This will turn out to be a massive inconsistency that an editor should have caught, because Roivan is incredibly powerful and can teleport across the galaxy. But Roivan is caught, and adopted by the captain and also by the chief engineer in a less formal way. She turns out to be terribly important — her race once made contact with the Jeng, another telepathic race, and her kind, the super-powered Arktrese, accidentally killed everyone over 25 with their broadcast. Now her people kill the super powered Arktrese among them at the age of six. She is the first (but not the last) to survive. Although in some ways Roivan is simply a precocious little girl, MacLean writes a genuine sense of dissonance in to her understanding of the world through the questions she asks and the things she knows and does not know.

The most conspicuously successful author to write the alien is of course David Almond in *Skellig*. Almond maintains Skellig as the intruding, unknowable alien throughout: Michael only gets to know Skellig through the thin lines of contact they establish — bottles of brown beer, cod liver oil, numbers 27 and 53 from the Chinese take away. Nothing else is ever really known: cultures are like egg-timers, joined by only a thin passageway of shared delight. I also feel the need to draw attention to the sheer virtuosity of Almond's writing in creating the reality of the fantastical. Here is the opening page:

> I found him in the garage on a Sunday afternoon. It was the day after we had moved into Falconer Road. The winter was ending. Mum had said we'd be moving just in time for the spring. Nobody else was there. Just me. The others were inside the house with Doctor Death, worrying about the baby.
> He was lying there in the darkness behind the tea chests, in the dust and the dirt. It was as if he'd been there forever. He was filthy and pale and dried out and I thought he was dead. I couldn't have been more wrong. I'd soon begin to see the truth about him, that there'd never been another creature like him in the world.
> We called it the garage because that's what the estate agent, Mr. Stone, called it. It was more like a demolition site or a rubbish dump or like one of those ancient warehouses they keep pulling down at the quay.

Stone keeps urging them to see it with their mind's eye, a line which will be a metaphor for the rest of the book, but in that opening, Almond distances the activity of moving house, the nature or existence of the garage; they are both dealt with hypothetically. Skellig is simply described. He is made real.

Finally, we should consider Oisín McGann's *The Gods and Their Machines* (2004) which is not actually about aliens but is about the way in which we turn others into aliens in our minds. *The Gods and Their Machines* is set possibly in the future, possibly elsewhere. One or two moments suggest a post-cataclysm future. Rich, technologically advanced Altima is threatened by terrorists from the Fringelands of Bartokhrin. As Altima is dependent on migrant workers from these fringelands, they are caught in the classic trap of how to ensure their own safety. Their answer has been bombing raids to wipe out nests of terrorists and suicide bombers. Chamus, the first of our protagonists, is son and grandson of aviation engineers and is himself training to fly. After the massacre of his class Chamus crashes his biplane in the Fringelands and meets up with Riadni, a girl of Bartokhrin. Bartokhrin is agricultural, deeply religious and oppresses its women, who are kept quiet, and must wear masks of make-up and heavy wigs. Riadni (a gender rebel) has grown up in a culture where bombing raids are normal and everyone knows someone who has been injured or killed. As a prosperous farmer's daughter she is also aware that Altima is involved in Bartokhrin in many ways.

The journey to safety is a fairly conventional narrative in children's fiction, so what is interesting is the way in which McGann handles his political material and constructs a society. As the children travel they learn things about each other's culture in ways which are subtle and complex: Riadni realizes both the humanity of the enemy, and that the Martyrs of whom she has heard so much are not entirely willing volunteers. Chamus learns that many of the migrants in his city, about whom he has been taught to wonder "why are they here when they hate us so" are themselves displaced by Altima's economic adventures in the Fringelands. He (and we) get to see that Altima's technological superiority has been dug from the lands of Bartokhrin and has polluted the rivers, and destroyed the economy.

Neither Chamus nor Riadni actually change their mind about their own countries — McGann avoids any such sentimentality — but both are forced to accept the world as a figure ground puzzle. Riadni queries why Chamus keeps referring to "the Fringelands." "What are they on the fringe of?" "Altima ... I think," Chamus muttered. He had never thought of it that way. "Bartokhrin's twice the size of Altima," Riadni laughed. "How can we be on *your* edge?" (108). Cognitive estrangement is thus a part of the plot, and of the writing of the plot. The two protagonists get to be travelers in strange worlds, and in neither case do they come to command them: they remain strangers, but learning strangers. At the end of the novel, Chamus and Riadni have forged a friendship, but it is a friendship that leads into the future: it is not a solution to anything, nothing has changed between their two countries. Neither of the two protagonists chooses to leave their own culture. Instead, what McGann is offering is another set of consequences based on the idea that cultural knowledge is as much a vector for change as is a material adventure. McGann creates the alien in order to both dismantle it, and reinvent it.

Being an Alien

In *The Gods and Their Machines*, McGann is anxious to convey that to each child the other child is "the alien." At the end he, like the other authors considered so far, familiarizes the alien. There are however some texts which genuinely try to create "alienness" and to consider in one way or another what an alien would feel like. K.A. Applegate, Kate Thompson and Cherry Wilder have each tried to think about what being an alien in another world would feel like; Jan Mark and Jeanne Willis have both played with the alien as narrator to a world like ours, while Terry Pratchett, Oisín McGann and Kevin O'Mally have tried to go beyond, to write aliens who just are alien.

The Animorphs sequence by K.A. Applegate (Scholastic, begun in 1996 and still ongoing) is an unprepossessing beginning to this section. Superficially it fits the alien invasion sequence and particularly the paternalistic interventions of the 1980s. The first book in the series, *Animorphs: The Invasion* is a fairly typical story in which a bunch of kids receive powers from aliens in order to fight other aliens they are told are evil. But this is Applegate, so first we get to see the second bunch being evil (taking over brains), and then the people they set out to rescue die, the elder brother of the primary character dies, and at the end one of the kids gets stuck as a hawk. His home life is shit and he quite likes being a hawk, but even so ... not quite what you expect at the end of a cutesy "humans with the power of animals" story. Furthermore, once we get past the "alien powers" conceit, Applegate's opening salvo in the series can be read in part as a discussion of body and social dysmorphia, a metaphor in part for the social awkwardness of growing up, but also a very real attempt to think about what being alien in a place means. Once the children acquire powers and a mission they become socially displaced: they may have been convinced that they have been inspired and empowered to save their world, but they have also been inducted into an alien race and as the book (and the series) progress, this sense of not fitting, of belonging to another culture, can only get stronger.

Animorphs runs the "being alien" as an undercurrent. Cherry Wilder's *The Luck of Brin's Five* (1979) faces it more directly. In *The Luck of Brin's Five* Dorn, child of a rural Five, finds a stranger in a lake. His family (or Five) adopt the stranger, a human called Scott Gale who has crashlanded on the planet. Gale is absorbed in to the society and written, throughout the book, from the point of view of Dorn. Most of the story is about Gale and the Five as they run from a threat, and as Gale discovers that these people are developing heavier than air flight. Supporting the plot however is the story of the ripples Gale causes in this early-modern society. Wilder focuses on depicting the alienness of Dorn and his fellows who, although perhaps a little too humanoid — although this is necessary to the plot — have convincingly "other" motivations.

Kate Thompson's *Missing Link* trilogy (2000, 2001, 2003) stands firmly on the outside of process but like much pre–1970s science fiction is fascinated with what comes next after humans and how alien will we/they be? The story begins in Ireland where Christie lives with his mother, his stepfather Maurice and his stepbrother Danny. To the reader, Danny seems vaguely autistic and dyspraxic. There is some deep dark secret Maurice won't talk about, and it starts to leak when Danny's mother turns up after an absence of fifteen years. Christie learns she is a scientist and (therefore) untrustworthy. A few mornings later, Danny wakes Christie up and demands to be taken on the bus to Scotland. Christie capitulates for the sake of peace and takes him onto the Dublin bus, expecting to be able to coerce him back, but by this point something that has been a background note to the story starts to rise in volume: there is a war somewhere out there in the Gulf, oil fields are alight and the western world is grinding to a halt. They cannot get back, but they can go forward.

As a twist, they find themselves accompanied by Darling, a talking sparrow, who then hooks them up with Oggy, a talking collie dog, and the homeless girl Tina whom Oggy has picked up when he got lost. But this is not a fantasy novel: the animals refuse to explain how they can talk, and they keep their essential natures. There is a really superb scene when Oggy kills a sheep so that they don't starve. It is brutal, nasty and real, and Christie has to come to terms with it.

Christie and Tina end up taking Danny all the way back to his mother's camp in the north of Scotland, a long, slow, vivid journey through ice and snow and a collapsing economy and infrastructure. When they do get to Maggie, they discover the lab of Doctor Moreau, full of failed mutants, and talking animals surrounding the farm. Maggie's scientific partner has gone, taking with him their third child. Sandy, their second child, turns out to have frog-fiber muscle. At the end we discover that Danny has been genetically engineered to survive in very cold water — he seems stupid because in the heat of land he is sluggish. But there are other moments of alienness. One of the best scenes is when the animals encounter Christie and Tina and want to know what they are, peppering them with questions:
"Have you got any children?"
"Are you house-trained yet?"
"How many is three?"
"Can you see colours?" (192)
There is a real sense of alienness there. As is always the case with good science, Maggie's results have provoked more questions than they have answered which will be played out in an ever-deepening exploration of "alienness" and finally offering a solution for the mystery of human sentience alone on the planet.[15]

Only a few books in my collection attempt to present aliens in a story told in a way which assumes that we as readers share the cultural context and assumptions of the protagonists. The first, Tony Ross and Jeanne Willis's *Dr. Xargle's Book of Earthlets* (1988), has received disproportionate coverage in this text for a slim, toddler's picture book, but in its small tale of an alien teacher attempting to explain to his class how to interpret what they see on Earth, it is a masterpiece which I use with my own students to explain cognitive estrangement.

Jan Mark's *Useful Idiots* (2004) is set in a future "drowned Britain." The UK is now a group of islands, part of a European Federation. Nationalism is viewed with suspicion, racialism (the identification of oneself through race) is even dodgier, but despite this each landmass has its own pockets of racial hold-outs. In the Isles they are the Inglish, descended from the kind of people who think imperial weights and measures are part of our identity, but who also tend to be all white. The story is of Merrick Korda, an archaeology grad student who helps to dig up a contested body. The story turns out not to be about the contestation of the body but the role of this dig in some people's attempt to get aboriginal protection acts overturned and — one presumes — either reclaim the land or destroy the aboriginals. In the course of the novel we see vicious exploitation (the aboriginals have been used — in the past — to cultivate a kind of oyster generated in human bone by the horsefly), real racial prejudice (Merrick turns out to be only third-generation assimilated), and a rape.

The unfolding of the world is done brilliantly in what I think of as the "classic" way: you tell the audience what is, and only later do you explain it. Mark uses the limitations of her society to create problems and to depict how very different it is from ours, so that a DNA test cannot be done on the found bones because it would encourage nationalism. The email virus Comfort and Joy trashed the world's computer archives but there are still books, and "disgust" emptied the museums. The riffs on contrived "disgust" are wonderful. The plot is constructed as an engagement with "meet the alien" narratives. We are inducted into an alien world with a refusal to explain, and this renders Merrick far more alien than his initial presentation as history and anthropology student imply.

From here we move to the few authors who straightforwardly write about alien cultures getting on with their alien business. Kevin O'Malley's *Captain Raptor and the Moon Mystery* (2005) is a brilliantly illustrated comic book, a space opera in which dinosaurs are intelligent and the aliens are human. Captain Raptor goes out to meet the aliens, prevents bloodshed and helps find their lost drive. There is honor and glory and stiff uppercuts. There are also different species of dinosaurs happily conversing with each other (and vegetarians serve with carnivores). It is utter nonsense and a whole lot of fun.

Terry Pratchett's *Truckers* (1989), *Diggers* (1990) and *Wings* (1990) show aliens simply going about their business, mostly uninterested in humans except that the human world is the world they have to live in. I could have included this tale of gnomes stranded on Earth in the alien invasion group, but these are twentieth-generation migrants and for better or worse, Earth is their home, even though they decide in *Wings* that a party of them should try to leave. It is this tension between Earth feeling like their home, and their manifest unsuitability for it that drives the alienness of the novel: watching Masklin kill a shrew, or the store gnomes climb up and down the elevators, demonstrates an adaptability to the environment that renders the gnomes real rather than locking them into an essentialism which might superficially describe the alien but also diminishes it.

Oisín McGann's *The Harvest Tide Project* (2004) and the sequel, *Under Fragile Stone* (2005), is the most unalloyed attempt to create a real alien planet and people without human intrusion. Although these could be read as fantasy novels—and they are marketed ambiguously—they are Jack Vance, Big Planet type adventures in which a world, its inhabitants, its sociological, political, economic realities are fully realized and fully deployed.

Taya and Lorkrin (sister and brother) are shapechangers who accidentally pull down a stone pillar when they are playing with their uncle Emos's shapechanging tools (more of that later). The pillar is supporting a wall that is holding in a number of scientists. They all wander out into the market place, but then are rounded up by soldiers—all except one, Shessil Groach, a botanist who has just made a breakthrough in the forced growth of a local plant. Shessil is actually a prisoner of a rather despotic regime, but he does not know it yet, and he casually wanders away and stumbles into various explorations. When he is recaptured, his captors don't realize who he is at first, which gives him quite a lot of opportunity to see what the world he lives in is actually like. Much of this story is about a very bright, very sheltered and naive man becoming politically aware. No one tells Shessil anything, nor does he see anything truly horrific. It is just that he moves from being a scientist obsessed with pure science to being a scientist who begins to wonder what his work is being used for (85). Clearly the model here is the scientists of the Manhattan project.

Some material is a little clumsily delivered; we get a short background lecture on Taya and Lorkrin as Myunan shapeshifters. "They both knew that their uncle would not use a normal catch for a hidden door. He would have built something that only a Myunen could open. Myunen flesh was unique in that it could be shaped and formed like modeling clay ..." (10), but while the second sentence is really unnecessary because in the following paragraph McGann shows this happening (see below) the first sentence is quietly brilliant, because is shows in this small opening, the consequences of Myunan powers for Myunan ways of thinking.

The shapeshifting is also a tour de force. Sheri Tepper was the last person to make this seem like a real bodily function, something to be practiced, something that is both an ability but also a variable talent. McGann's shapeshifters have malleable bodies, but they cannot actually control the movement. For that they need tools: "The boy seemed to be combing his ears back ... with a comb," (32) and "Whipping out their tool kits, they quickly fashioned their fingertips into claws and clambered up the wall" (34). There are limitations which the children meet by combining shapeshifting with brains: "Standing one child on top of another does not make the shape of an adult, however ... Taya had increased the size of her head and even coloured her skin as if she were wearing make-up. She had lengthened her arms, at the same time making her legs much smaller and thinner, leaving them just strong enough to allow her to keep her balance on Lorkrin's shoulders. Lorkrin had flattened his head to conceal it under the cloak, shortened his body and lengthened his legs so that he could stride like someone twice his height"(116). When later they want to fly, they reason that bat shapes can be morphed into — feathers are much too complicated and flying is more than about shape-changing: "a person needed first to achieve a suitable form, and then to grasp the principles of flying itself"(143 and 144). Perspective is done well: McGann switches from character to character and with each he keeps hold of a firm sense of their personality and species.

The sequel, *Under Fragile Stone*, is about the invasion of the land by the largest empire on the continent, and McGann extends the sense of alienness by identifying us with the children and their parents who don't know what is happening but understand the context, rather than the invaders who neither know what is happening nor the geological and theological context in which it will happen. In *Under Fragile Stone*, Taya and Lorkrin embark on adolescence, moving from mischievous to mildly resentful: it is a bad time to do this as the local empire has invaded and is threatening to mine the local holy mountain. The Empire imports a priest to exorcise the mountain (which is resisting the miners) with disastrous effects. Eventually Taya and Lorkrin convince their companion, Rug, that he is the god of the mountain, driven out by the exorcism. This is proper secondary-world science fiction in the tradition of Jack Vance. While the characters are fun, increasingly it is the planet that is the real alien and the real hero.

We have to consider why these themes? What purpose do they serve? Although it is difficult to be sure what children want (a recent school visit by my students led them to conclude, "more of the same until introduced to something different in which case they want more of that"), there is no sense that *these* themes are chosen by children. What they are, in each case, is a direct imposition of the concerns of the wider world for "the condition of the child" and the child's response to the world. Issues such as consumerism, fear of nuclear holocaust, and various takes on the alien/immigration issue are extensions of adult concerns about the world and the orientation of the solutions are problematic: they are rarely "move through into the future" solutions as one might find in the adult genre, but are couched instead as either warnings to refuse the future entire, or an advocacy of utopian retrenchment. This helps to explain both why the choices offered to young protagonists are oddly absolute (and this is true even of the more interesting books from writers such as McNaughton, Westerfeld, and Kostick), and why they frequently seem to deny the reality of lived experience. The anti-consumerist books are perhaps the most extreme in this regard. The continual rejection of changing knowledge transfer technology is an adult rejection of the programmable video player: it shows no understanding of the flexibility and extension of youth. The overall consequence is that repeatedly the insistence on thematic "lessons" shies away from one of the core values of science fiction, which is an interest not so much in the future, but how humans adapt to the future. These books almost always argue that humans will not, that we will instead stagnate or be stripped of our humanness.

CHAPTER SEVEN

Best Practice Now

Dismissing most sf written for children and teens with the statement "Imagination is lacking, and the action never comes to life" (202) Margery Fisher wrote in 1961:

> No publisher's list is complete without one writer who knows how to get into a space-suit. But the really vital writers for children in this sphere are as scarce as inhabited planets. If boys over twelve really want to be stirred by exploration in space, by the feeling of alien worlds, I can only suggest they give up children's books at once and turn to writers like Arthur C. Clarke and James Blish. Let these guide them into space and the mysteries of science, for their speculation, conceived in adult terms, has the force of questioning youth. No writer of space stories can afford to be limited by what young readers can understand [202].

After reading over four hundred books written *specifically* for the children's market (and perusing the other one hundred and fifty you'll find in the bibliography), I share her sentiments. The most exhausting aspect of this book has been wading through misguided dross, written to "uplift" (more often to depress) children and teens, or written to carry a message about appropriate emotional development. Most of these novels did not make it into the discussion. It would have only reinforced the often irritable tone of this book. There also seem to be few authors who know how to get into a space suit. It would be easy to agree unequivocally with Fisher's argument that one should stick to recommended fiction intended for adults, and leave it there. However, as has been apparent throughout this book, there *is* good sf written for children and teens. All the best books in my collection, according to the criteria I have laid down at various points, accord with Fisher's closing sentence: none of them are limited by assumptions about what children and teens can understand, all demand *more* of their readers, all assume that the point is to stretch the reader's understanding.

Having spent what seems an inordinate length of time carping about the poor quality of much of the science fiction for children and teens, I want to spend this last chapter selecting the best of the books. I've discussed most of these books already, but as the constant response I've received in presentations is a request for a reading list, here it is. One of the things that makes for "best practice" is risk-taking and diversity, which means it is hard to group these books, so that this final chapter may read very much as a review column. I have decided in advance that this is just fine.

The books in the bibliography stretch from 1922 to the present day, although the argument of the book is predominantly concerned with the period from approximately 1950 to 2008. In this chapter I want to narrow things further, in order to celebrate more recent books that are in print and easily available, but also to reflect two issues: first, and mostly simply, that there is evidence in my choices that supports the contention I have made several times, that sf for children and teens, having gone through a slump, is enjoying a renaissance. Although I won't cover every book in my "best practice list," the total at the time of writing this sentence (I still have a few new books to consider), is seventy-two: *thirty-three* of those were published between 1960 and 2001, *forty-one* were published between 2001 and the present day. The selection of 2001 as a dividing line is not a random one: in 2001 Philip Reeve published the runaway bestseller *Mortal Engines*. The success of this book enabled both children's publishers with an interest in sf, and sf writers for adults, to re-enter the market with books which look and feel like sf and make no accommodations to the ideological demands of young adult fiction which I have outlined elsewhere.

Second, I want to focus on those books which fit the context of *now*, and which engage with worlds that can legitimately be seen to extrapolate from now rather than an actual (or mythical) 1950s. This takes us back to the first book in my collection which is recognizably of the digital age, Sandy Landsman's *The Gadget Factor* (1984). This is not to dismiss earlier books on my list such as all science fiction written by Peter Dickinson, H. M. Hoover, or Monica Hughes, or Jan Mark's *The Ennead* (1978), or Robert Westall's *Future Track 5* (1983) but all of these texts read now as if from an alternate world; we can no longer get there from here. When I have to make choices among the books that follow, that issue, although not in itself throwing a book out of my definition of "best practice," will prevail. It still leaves me with over sixty books to select from, and I will be astonished if I manage to cover them all in the few thousand words left at the end of this book.

Context

Although I would have liked this book to range across cultures, it has been impossible to break the lock of the British/American/Canadian market (although many of my favorite new writers are from Ireland). There are a few books from Africa listed in my bibliography but they are not representative (and two of the authors are white, and American and European respectively). Similarly, the majority of the respondents to the survey are American. Thus, it is perfectly reasonable, when I ask about the context in which children and teens now exist, to focus predominantly on the situation of the American child or teen.

According to Rice and Dolgin, as a rough rule of thumb western U.S. states are seeing a rise in their juvenile population, while the Midwest and the Northeast, are seeing a fall (5). Adolescence is being prolonged for all but the poorest, as college education is becoming the norm, but at the same time, the elongation of the period of education means that part-time work among those in education is becoming more likely. Rice and Dolgin estimate that nearly three million 15-to-17-year-olds work during the school year and an additional million in the summer months. Many adolescents may actually have full-time work for a year or two before starting college. While there is no return to the early leaving ages of the 1930s for all but the poorest teens, there is a sense that the demarcation between childhood and adulthood is getting ever fuzzier. At the same time, the major concerns of adulthood, the establishment of family and home (in whatever form) seem to be getting more distant. While work may accompany education, setting out on one's lifelong career may now not begin until one's late twenties: the old "career" books aimed at fifteen-year-olds can have little place in this kind of world. Even teens who must work to stay in education exist in a zone whose rhetoric (if not reality) is of protection, leisure, and exploration (see Finders, 1997, for a discussion of the effects of those who live within the rhetoric but without the money to support it). One further major change however is that as the costs of education increase, more teens and people in their early twenties are either staying at home, or returning to the family home on finishing college: exploration is increasingly of the personal kind, far less of the *striking out* that was celebrated in children's fiction of the 1940s through the 1970s. Perusing my collection, it is noticeable how many post–1990 texts respond to crisis by pulling children closer.

If children and teens are at home more, it is also because the preferred activities of children and teens have become more home-based. The gender divides before the rise of the personal computer could be characterized as outdoor activity for boys, indoor activity for girls; you can still see this. In many of the books in my collection, girls' "adventures" are meeting new aliens in their homes or schools, or summer camps. More recently, as boys have moved inside to play on their computers, a visible gender divide has appeared with boys as players and programmers, girls as programmers and communicators; shoot 'em up and quest games for the boys, social games and instant messaging for the girls (Weber and Dixon, 2007)—a crude division and one which frequently bends under the pressure of detail, but one which again we can see repeated in the modern part of my collection. Wim Veen and Ben Vrakking talk of "Homo Zappiens," children growing up in a world in which information is out there for the finding, and there is almost always someone to talk with (29). Children and teens are more collaborative because the internet is a collaborative project (something the education system has yet to assimilate in non-confrontational ways), yet representations of teens in adventure stories tend to orient towards the lone teen, or rather rigid friendship groups, with only Kostick, Doctorow, Applegate and the writers of *The Web* series really grasping how much modern teens are organizing themselves in replication of the matrix networks of overlapping interests which they experience in the digital world.

Teens now live in very different kinds of communities and with access to many different networks. As well as the peer-to-peer communication of mobile phones, instant messaging and peer-to-peer computer games, children and teens can use Facebook, MySpace, LiveJournal (and several new systems by the time this book comes out). The "natural" isolation of the teen, and even more so, of the "outsider" teen, may be a thing of the past. The media has been quick to notice online bullying, but there has been relatively little written about online liberation. As an educator I can testify at least anecdotally to the shift: I no longer hear coming-out stories of any kind. Students arrive at university with their intellectual interests worn on their sleeves and their sexual identities often frighteningly assimilated compared to where I and my peers were in the 1980s. Students whose opinions or identities run at variance to those of their family arrive already knowing that there are others like them out there. All of my gay students had spoken with other gay teens by the time they had left school. All of my sf fan students had friends they chatted with online about the latest episode of *Heroes* or *Big Brother*. The fear that used to accompany being different, of being *the only one*, has been eroded for very many. No parent can impose such total isolation without resorting to heroic measures. I complained bitterly in an earlier chapter about the reactionary social representations of much of even the most recent sf for children and teens, but this second major change, of the way in which children and teens access the world, and the *degree* to which they can access the world, barely receives a comment in the fiction: only Levithan, Kostick and Doctorow seem to have any idea of the kind of personal liberation the internet has granted.

Some of the Classic Tropes

Many of the thematic novels discussed in the previous chapter seem to be stripped of plot. They are *not* about how humans react to a given situation, but rather about how the situation overwhelms the human, and they repeat the same stories over and over again. The most disappointing element in this survey has been the absence of the classic tropes of science fiction, and with that absence, much of a sense of wonder. While nuclear war haunts the 1980s, space travel is largely absent. Michael J. Daley's *Shanghaied to the Moon* (2007), his *Space Station Rat* (2005) and Brian Ball's *The Doomship of Drax* (1985) are the only modern "how to get into space" books, while Ben Jeapes and Margaret Bechard between them account for space opera and planetary exploration respectively. Time travel is as poorly served: William Sleator's extensive backlist plays with time narratives, while Terry Pratchett's *Johnny and the Bomb* (1996), Susan Price's *The Sterkarm Handshake* (2000), Stephen Baxter's *The H-Bomb Girl* (2007) and Sean McMullen's *Before the Storm* (2007) account for the "travel back in time and change your world" stories, with some interesting twists on the idea of changing your universe from Louise Cooper's *Mirror, Mirror* stories, but there is not a single invention story in the entire batch. Only Jeapes and Bechard manage colonization/alien contact stories. All of this would be excusable if they appeared to have been replaced by something, but as I argued in chapter six, there is a noticeable lack of new sf tropes as well.

When it comes to the sense of wonder, William Sleator remains a master of the technique; his mathematical romances tangle the reader in the beauty of the universe. Philip Reeve's Engines sequence, and his new steam-punk novels, *Larklight* (2006) and *Starcross* (2007), are the only evidence of the wondrousness of Big Objects and Large Pieces of Metal in modern sf for children and teens, although Oisín McGann's *Ancient Appetites* (2007) has me salivating for evolved and intelligent motorcycles.

Particularly noticeable is the absence of computers, but there are a small number of books that approach the topic with panache, and try to seek out the digital world which modern children inhabit. Sandy Landsman's *The Gadget Factor* (1984) and Malorie Blackman's *Hacker* (1992) both set out to introduce children and young teens to computer programming skills. *Hacker* is more basic (ironically, it is not about hacking at all) and *The Gadget Factor* is probably useless to a child on a modern pc, but both books exist in a world contemporary to that of their intended child reader, and offer futures that are accessible from "here." Similarly, Terry Pratchett's *Only You Can Save Mankind* (1992) and Lesley Howarth's *Ultraviolet* (2001) use the respective gaming conventions of their era (space invaders, and virtual reality arcade games) and do so in ways which use the material to speculate on the use of this new technology. E. M. Goldman's *The Night Room* (1995) brought the metaphors back home, creating a virtual reality game which projects an individual's future — the teens who fight the projection turn out to be fighting a real-life hacker, not a fantastically powerful metaphor.

Outstanding in this category however, is Orion's *The Web* sequence (1997–1999), two collections of five books that place children in an online computer game, and then within the game offer them thriller, adventure, and science fiction plots. All of these books anticipate both a more complex virtual reality, and the use of virtual reality as offering a complex engagement with the world (rather than an escape). Less metaphorical than Pratchett or Howarth, the virtual realities the authors such as Stephen Baxter, Pat Cadigan, Ken MacLeod, Maggie Furey and Graham Joyce (all writers of sf for adults) create are platforms for political events which ask children and teens to think as full participants in the world, rather than sealed off in the concerns of children, or lauded as superheroes. In all of these books, the web and computing generally matter; they are more than facilitating devices and are clearly intended to excite the reader opportunistically. All of the authors in the series both envisage children and teens as highly competent negotiators of the digital environment.

The final choice in this area has to be Conor Kostick's *Epic* (2004) and *Saga* (2006). I have mentioned these texts in more than one context, but Kostick is the only author who clearly writes as an insider in the virtual worlds. *Epic* and *Saga* do not posit the virtual worlds as metaphors for anything. *Epic* is precisely about accepting the metonymic value of something constructed originally as metaphor, while *Saga* extends the lesson. In the hands of Erik the first game comes alive as a land to be settled; in the sequel a land of real, living people emerges in the digital spaces of the game. Hard AI (artificial intelligence) that is the cutting edge of post-cyberpunk, post–New Space Opera science fiction for adults makes its appearance here. What ties together all of these books is that the children and teens are indigenous to their worlds, not travelers in a strange future. This is one of the factors that allows the dissonant to be built on the rupture that I argued in the introduction is essential to science fiction. The rupture is not the creation of a future, but a disturbance to the future in which they live.

Meeting the Structural Demands Argued For at the Beginning of the Book

I began this book by outlining what I felt to be the essential structural elements of a science fiction book: dissonance, rupture, resolution and consequence. All the books I want to present here contain all four of these elements and most of them, as in the previous section, begin with a dissonant future and proceed to a rupture within that full science fiction fantastic. Mary Amato's *The Word Eater* exists in a world in which a bookworm can eat not just words, but referents. Cory Doctorow's *Little Brother* offers dissonance in the hyperawareness of the surveillance society in which it exits. Gregory Maguire's *I Feel Like the Morning Star* (1997), Philip Reeve's *Mortal Engines* and Oisín McGann's *Harvest Tide Project* (2004) and *Under Fragile Stone* (2005) are set in other cultures entirely (Maguire and Reeve in the far future, McGann on another planet). Stephen Baxter's *The H-Bomb Girl* and Sean McMullen's *Before the Storm* (2007) are both time travel/alternate world novels in which timelines shift and the present is both ours and departs from ours.

True rupture, the collapse of the established consensus, can be seen in a number of these books. Francine Prose's *After* (2003) begins with a similar surveillance society to that presented by Cory Doctorow in *Little Brother* but proceeds to rupture our consensus belief that the role of adults is to protect children: in Prose's work the hatred between adults and teens becomes palpable and operates to change society dramatically. The resolution that is reached at the end, to leave the township, throws Prose's teenagers into a slingshot ending of unknown consequence. In Gillian Rubenstein's *Galax-Arena* (1992) the world in which the protagonists live (one of refugees and abandoned children) both is and is not a rupture with the world in which we live. Rubenstein has caused us to accept rupture by facing a world condition we mostly ignore, until it "ruptures" by affecting our own children. Julie Bertagna's *Exodus*, in some ways a fairly standard drowned-world, eco-sf story, gains its strength from the rupture offered when "we" become refugees and receive the treatment "we" have meted out to others.

All of the books in my final selection offer resolution which goes beyond the individual. In Brian Ball's *The Doomship of Drax* (1985) Nick's discovery of the spaceship that will allow his colony world to be evacuated is a discovery of scientific endeavor rather than of a magical solution. In Susan Price's *Coming Down to Earth* (1994), although Azalin is in search of a personal escape from the space station on which she lives, the resolution she finds is a much larger solution for her whole community as she begins to explore the possibilities of life on Mars. Azalin's experiences help her understand her home world's social structures, but the solution comes not from reconciliation with them, but her continued refusal to accept that this is the only solution. These books clearly also hold to one of the genre values for which I've argued; they cleave to an outward-bound trajectory, a rejection of what *is* in favor of what may be, and an insistence that solutions are not found at home but out in the wider world. Even Ned Vizzini's *Be More Chill* (2004), a tale of a young man's desire to be cool, is essentially a rejection of dependence in favor of an exploration of new resources.

Crucially, all of my favorite texts have a sense of consequence. Each of these books demonstrates *why* consequence is so important to science fiction: some have "happy endings," some, particularly the ones aimed at older teens, are more ambivalent, but the point is that the endings reach into the future and open up new possibilities, in comparison to the many, many books in my collection which were essentially recursive; books like Neil Arksey's *Playing on the Edge* (2000) in which adults arrive and make it all better, in an otherwise highly political book about corruption in future football, or Patrick Cave's *Blown Away* (2004) which cannot see beyond societal collapse to societal construction: these books reach for a button to reset the world to normality, stability and a nebulous past in which things were "better." The books which follow know that the future is a foreign country.

Of the ecological science fiction, Ann Halam's *Siberia* (2002) is the standout: consequence *is* the plot, the consequence of political decisions, the consequence of the decision to teach a child science. When Rosita's mother enters a punishment camp it is a consequence of both her science and her political beliefs. When Rosita (now Sloe) escapes, she can do so with the help of the Lindquists, preprogrammed (and hence consequential) compressions of DNA. The book is entirely structured around the belief that thinking ahead is the essential element of adulthood and of science. Although the book has a sentimental ending in which mother and child are reunited, Halam is careful to place it within a wider political ending in which the consequence of the Lindquists casts a shadow into the future. Equally, K.A. Applegate's *Remnants* sequence, although it cannot match Halam's work for literary quality, has a resolute message that the universe is out to get you and that *everything* you do has consequences: from the moment the Remnants flee planet Earth in an old space shuttle their future is shaped by the consequences of poor choices of personnel and equipment, poor choices of allies, poor choices of direction. That things come out right in the end, is because the individuals who survive learn from all of this, but many of them don't survive. Applegate's work continually reminded me of the original title of the blog which has companioned me in this research, named after Arthur Ransome's brilliant but brutal "Better drowned than duffers, if not duffers won't drown," the telegram sent to the protagonists by their father to give permission for an independent sailing holiday (1930).

Oisín McGann's *Harvest Tide Project* and *Under Fragile Stone* also emphasize the future: here, the thoughtlessness and short-termism of the young protagonists is constantly juxtaposed against the long-term plans of the adults who see to survive the spread of empire. Each choice, each mistake, each event *changes* future possibilities, restricting some, opening out others. Stephen Baxter and Sean McMullen, offering time-travel novels, make this even clearer. In Baxter's *The H-Bomb Girl* we depart from Liverpool in 1963, and end up heading into a British future very different from ours. Sean McMullen's Australia in the past may not actually lead to the Australia of the present, and clearly once *did not* if it were to create the time-traveling protagonist from the future with whom we interact. Even where the future is only barely tangible, and appears unchanging, an author like Jan Mark can imply the *something more* that is consequence: a frequently rather depressing writer, Mark mutes her consequences in both *The Ennead* and *Useful Idiots* but in each the stasis achieved at the end of the book reeks of its own instability, one can feel the consensual illusion of equality and racial acceptance tottering its rhetoric, as it does in L. J. Adlington's post-holocaust *The Diary of Pelly D* (2005) in which the found diary of a genocide victim begins to unpick the consensual hallucination of a new society.

Meeting the Genre Values for Which I've Argued

In addition to demanding the presence of consequence in sf for children I've also continually harped on a range of other elements. The aspects of sf I've argued are core genre values: an outward-bound trajectory; information density; emotional development grounded in a reaction *to the world* rather than a boy-meets-girl romance or other social networking skills; encouragement to analytical thinking, whether applied to political, social or scientific contexts; a questioning approach to the material of the text and to the built world; a moral or ethical ruthlessness that argues with the world rather than tritely positing one stance as innately good, another innately bad; a sense at the end both that one has learned something, and that there is something more to learn. If possible, I also want books that ask the protagonists to use the skills they have or have learned, rather than to rely on "character traits" (being good, kind, labeled as "nice" or "brave") to carry them through. For want of a better system this section is organized into "age-appropriate" categories, but with the caveat that — as is probably clear by now — I am *deeply* suspicious of the concept: the weak reader with ambition may well want books far older than their apparent age, while the strong reader may want some comfort reading alongside more challenging books, and whether sex or violence is age-appropriate is culturally specific.

I haven't spent much time on picture books in this discussion. The chapter I wrote on picture books did not fit the overall trajectory of the thesis (it focuses very heavily on the visual construction of sf), but it has been retained as an appendix, should you be interested in pursuing the matter further. Although many of the sf picture books were sf in name only, there are some outstanding examples which became real favorites in my collection as a whole. Two of my samples are for slightly older children; Graham Oakley and David Weisner both produce picture books for what we might call early literacy, or we could understand as taking advantage of children's intense visual literacy. Oakley's *Henry's Quest* is an incredibly complex post-disaster story in which a young man goes on a quest for black gold for his king, so that he may marry the king's daughter. As I discussed in chapter three, the book is highly demanding of the analytical and deconstructive skills of a willing child reader.

David Weisner's *June 29, 1999* (1992) is a very different kind of book but also demands close attention and abstract analysis. A classroom of children perform a series of experiments; one girl sends seeds on soil platforms into the air to see how they will grow. On June 29 giant vegetables begin landing on earth and the girl wonders if they are hers. Only when an eggplant lands does she realize that there must be a different solution, for she did not sow eggplant. The solution turns out to be an alien ship which has accidentally opened its storage hatches. It is rather a shame that the girl cannot know this, but the message conveyed is very much about assembling evidence, and thinking outside the box: there is a rational solution to everything.

My two favorite picture books — which I confess I now give to every new baby of my acquaintance — are Frances Thomas and Ross Collins' *Maybe One Day* (2001) and Jeanne Willis and Tony Ross' *Dr. Xargle's Book of Earthlets*

(1988). *Maybe One Day* is an exercise in estrangement and extrapolation, which sneaks in information in ways that are enormously empowering. In each book, the child reader is required to engage with an adult who does not understand, and to take on board the concept of misprision: it is a very challenging book which is very much about outside and inside knowledge. I use this book to teach creative writing students what science fiction *is*, as opposed to what it is about. At the other end of the complexity scale I also want to mention Bill Clemente and Kevin Boos' *Visitor Parking* (2002) as well as Arthur Yorinks' *Company's Coming* (1998). Both of these books are discussed extensively in Appendix D but are notable here for sensible approaches to alien "invasion" stories which allow small children to explore the weight behind the concept of "the stranger." Neither fall into the trap of some of the metaphor books I read, in which the alien is rarely more than "the new kid."

Moving on to the "novels" or chapter books for younger children. The choices here are not wide, but Mary Amato's *Word Eater* (2000), Michael J. Daley's *Shanghaied to the Moon* and *Space Station Rat*, and anything written by Bruce Coville are the stand-outs here. Coville's work tends to suffer from almost always having an adult (if an adult alien) hovering protectively, but all three of these writers place a great deal of emphasis on children learning things (in Amato's work it is scientific and experimental process, in Daley's books it is technical engineering and problem-solving), and on a growing independence from adults: crucially all of the books understand that adults don't have all the solutions for this age group. Amato's and Daley's work also has the sense of consequence I'm looking for. Amato's word eater worm releases slave children on the other side of the world, while Daley's *Shanghaid to the Moon* leaves us with the political consequences of an unraveling corporate conspiracy. Both books could be said to go beyond what children can be expected to see as child-like concerns: a good thing.

Age groups get awkward as we enter the pre-teens/early teens area, but interesting books for this age group include Adam Rex's *The True Meaning of Smek Day* (2007), Kate Thompson's *Missing Link* trilogy (2000–03), Philip Reeve's *Larklight* and *Starcross*, Joan Lennon's *Questors*, Oisín McGann's *Harvest Tide Project* and Julie Bertagna's *Exodus* (2002) and its sequels, *Zenith* and *Aurora*. I've selected these partly for the relatively younger ages of the protagonist, but also for their strong adventure orientation. Adam Rex's *The True Meaning of Smek Day* is the story of an alien invasion and what our protagonist Gratuity Tucci does to repel it. It is a fun adventure story, told well, but stands out because Rex offers a complex understanding of colonialism and of American tribalism to his readers, and because this is one of the shockingly rare modern books to have a non-white protagonist (there are as many non-white protagonists in the books of the late 1960s as in the period since 2000). Zizou Corder's *Lionboy* (2004) is great sf adventure with a non-white protagonist, but the sequels swing closer to fantasy. Reeve's *Larklight* and *Starcross* are romps across a steam punk universe full of derring-do and dash, but with plenty of time to think through issues of justice and gender roles. Thompson's *Missing Link* books are quest novels in search of parents who are scientists and to find safety. What the children find is knowledge. If I have qualms it is because the children never move beyond being recipients of knowledge, they do not themselves become actively engaged in science, but there is a very strong sense of consequence and an information-dense world. McGann's *Harvest Tide Project* has similar issues in that the children move through a political landscape that is in many ways not really concerned with them. This means that they are neither in possession of knowledge nor are they really educated in the political and economic issues that their parents work with. However, and the reason I like this novel so much, for the child reader a great deal can be learned just by following the children through their parent's lives. This is knowledge acquisition the sushi-chef way: no one ever teaches, but much is learned from a very dense world and an intense engagement with it.

Lennon's *Questors* is a time travel/alternate world/political conspiracy in which the children are sent out as agents into time: the book works so effectively because the immorality of what the children are asked to be and do is made manifest without undercutting the protagonists themselves. The moral structure of the story is not simple, and the protagonists are asked to make complex choices. In Julie Bertagna's work, it is not always the choices the protagonists make that the reader is asked to question but, in this post-flood world riven by strife and refugee crises, the choices of others. As we watch the protagonists turned away, enslaved, beaten, the books become increasingly uncomfortable with the awareness of the *real* world we live in. Bertagna is not writing allegory but she makes full use of sf's metaphorical potential.

For mid-teens the choice becomes wider: the works of Peter Dickinson (*Eva*, the Changes sequence — *The Devil's Children, Heartsease, The Weathermonger*) are all well known. They offer a real sense of estrangement and in the midst of disaster refuse to see children as somehow separate from, or mere victims of, poor adult decisions. David Almond's *Skellig* should be prized in part because it preserves the alienness of the alien and also because it is an argument about competing philosophies of education: the encouragement of a sense of wonder versus the required answers of school; the tendency to "sample" things at school, as opposed to the practice required to become good at anything. A reader of *Skellig* is being asked in part to consider what kind of learning life they want. William Sleator remains the pre-eminent writer of time-travel work for the age group, with so many titles it is hard to select just one, but *The Green Futures of Tycho*, first published in 1981 and now back in print, is one of the most challenging.

I've discussed Margaret Bechard's *The Star Hatchling* (1995) in the chapter on themes. It remains one of the very few real "meet the alien" books which achieves something more than "the aliens are just like us." But for this age group, and especially for girls, Mindy Schanback's *Princess from Another Planet* should not be sneered at: however pink and fluffy, however much it is focused on girls' friendship and horses and reading books, it holds absolutely true to the sf values I've been arguing for. The aliens are real, the problems are real, and the demands placed on the two protagonists are intimately connected to the skills they start with and new ones they acquire. It is a sealed story however, with no sense of consequence (the wormhole is closed).

Philip Reeve's Engines books are well known, and discussed frequently in this book: as we move into the later texts, *Infernal Devices* and *A Darkling Plain* the canvases get larger and the protagonists become cogs in larger mechanisms, but Reeve never dispossesses the protagonists from the adventure, and in a major rupture with the main tendencies in eco-sf, these books focus on a future fix, and a world beyond global warming and resource depletion. Reeve celebrates human ingenuity and constantly emphasizes the density of skills which humans possess and develop.

Other adventure fiction is available from Kenneth Oppel's alternative future novels, *Airborn* and *Skybreaker*, which dodge the difficulty of invisible technology by taking us into a faux nineteenth-century world of dirigibles and natural history. The protagonists in these books are high-minded and independent, concerned with matters of honor and the acquisition of knowledge. Their adventures have limited import for the wider world but are all part of a fictional "career" structure which is otherwise absent from the sf of the early twenty-first century, although Michael Carroll's *The Quantum Prophecy* (2006) is a rattling good superhero/"shall I follow in my father's footsteps?" of a novel.

Back in the "parents are all wrong" category, we have very good offerings from Scott Westerfeld's *Uglies* sequence, begun in 2005 and still going despite indicated endings. These books encourage courage, outward boundedness and analysis of the political climate: simple answers to *why* the world is like it is, turn out to have complicated caveats. The trajectory of the books is a little repetitive but the real strength is the way Westerfeld does not assume that teen "concerns" are limited: he uses explicit concerns to explore implicit ones. Insecurity about beauty leads to complex discussions about how this relates to what we value in the human and the mixed consequences even of those aspects of human nature we value. Westerfeld also manages to include romance without the facilitation of that romance becoming the point of the text. If I have not included these books in the list for older teens, it is because they wear their concerns on their sleeves.

More argumentative is Louise Cooper's *Mirror Mirror*, which has a rebellious teen, rejecting early marriage and romance, heading for an alternate world where she meets a boy who offers her something rather more interesting, comradeship and intellectual challenge. Although romance lurks in the background, the arguments in the book are about the nature of reality, of choices and character and the inter-relationship of who one is with what one's world is—a socio-geographic understanding of character.

Finally, political novels. I've already discussed Oisín McGann's *The Harvest Tide Project*, and the sequel, *Under Fragile Stone*, which takes us deeper into the politics of the Empire and of a marginal people (the shapechangers) trying to survive in a chaotic and threatening world. Here, while the children's adventure is still a sideshow to the real political stresses, they are brought into a greater awareness of how their world works. Ken MacLeod's cyber-thriller *Cydonia* has also been discussed earlier and should be accompanied by others of the Web sequence, such as Pat Cadigan's *Avatar* (1999) and Peter F. Hamilton's *Lightstorm* (1998). Ann Halam's *Taylor Five* (2002) which I discussed briefly in the section on themes, explores the micro-politics of identity and the macro-politics of environmental collapse and species extinction, racism and colonialism in very demanding, but accessible ways. Finally, Pete Hautman's *Rash*, while it may also appeal to an older age group, is a very easy-to-read discussion around the competing demands of safety and a challenging life, of peacefulness versus the peace of oppression, and while he's at it, a discussion of the role of prison in providing an exploitable workforce.

What marks out the books for later teens tends to be a combination of older characters (occasionally, even adult protagonists), the presence of a complex take on sex and sexual relations, and rather more brutal conclusions. In this vein Ben Jeapes's *New World Order* is exemplary. The alien invasion is not defeated, the human and alien "lovers" are not in love. Margaret Haddix's *Turnabout* explores identity from the point of non-destinarian foreknowledge, a fascinating sf concept in itself. Jan Mark's *Useful Idiots* leaves us in a moment of recursion which seems to argue that little about human nature will change, and that prejudice will go on. N. M. Browne's *Shadow Web* (2008) lands us in a brutally totalitarian Britain that the protagonist can do nothing but escape from, and in which she will leave behind her first love. Susan Price's *Odin's Voice* and *Odin's Queen* is a tale of a rape survivor that ends in martyrdom, and which along the way explores the meaning of a love that is rarely presented in the romances. All, along with the work of Conor Kostick (*Saga*), Janet McNaughton (*The Secret Under My Skin*), and J.B. Stephens (*The Big Empty*), take on board a complex polity in which teens cannot save the world, but in which their actions are a crucial part of a collective movement for change.

The books discussed above are all excellent, and all work the sf values I've discussed in this book. I am left, however, with two stand-outs which take the values of sf and truly produce books which push the edges of the genre: Oisín McGann's *Ancient Appetites* and Cory Doctorow's *Little Brother* (2008).

Ancient Appetites (2007) has received relatively little coverage in this book, and is rather different from the rest of the collection: an alternative-world novel which does not proceed from a simple what if, but from a collection of possibilities. *Ancient Appetites* explores family bitterness, patriarchal dominance, the brutalities of the British colonial project in Ireland, and along the way, an alternate version of Darwinian evolution in which evolved machines "prove"

Darwin's theories to be correct by containing within them purposes that it behooves humans to recognize, from sentient motorcycles to toasters. McGann's politics are buried deep within the sinews of the story so that it can be read as a romp should one choose, but character motivations are ruthlessly adult, and relationships are constructed as much by politics as by desire. When queer politics emerge, there is no romantic coming-out story, only another round of negotiations for what one can and will accept. It is one of the very few books in the collection to challenge familial structures and to go beyond an understanding of politics which involves the lining up of moral worth: in *Ancient Appetites* almost everyone is corrupted by the system, and cannot move without challenging their own vested interests. Cory Doctorow's *Little Brother*, discussed in chapter three, is much more outwardly political and it is one of my favorites, precisely because it is a celebration of the science-fictional didacticism and *revelry* in didacticism which has otherwise been missing from the YA field for sixty years, but it is also a delight because of the complex depiction of friendships structured by available technology, and relationships (with friends, parents and lovers) distorted or torn apart by politics. There are no easy outcomes in this book, no final victories, no hurts sealed over by rhetorical bandaid. Finally, both of these books offer characters— both male and female — who get to explore their own potentials, shaped by the conventions of their words, but not confined by them.

Before We Go, Another Set of Possibilities...

I want to leave this discussion with one other pointer for where to find good science fiction for children and teens. If we are to look further for best practice for the teen reader — and by best practice, as usual, I mean fiction which fulfills the demands of the adult reader — and for gateway books to bring children and teens into science fiction, then one place to look for this might be in the fiction which we already know teens read in great quantities; the tie-ins, a form of fiction which in the science fiction world is well down the pecking order and receives the same kind of reception as admitting to reading sf does elsewhere.

Tie-ins, for those who have not come across the term, are either novelizations of films and television programs or more recently "stories set in the same universe," either the continuing adventures of the main characters or, increasingly, stories which flesh out the world as a whole. These books are not usually marketed to teens only but they have a sizeable teen element in their demographic. Mary Elizabeth Hart, publicity manager for Mysterious Galaxy, was kind enough to provide some figures which suggest that the majority of the readership of the *Buffy/Angel* tie-ins was in the thirties, with only around 40 percent classed as Young Adult readers. The *Star Trek* readers were mostly older, with the *Perfect Dark* readers generally younger. The originating program rather than the texts seem to shape the reader demographics (email to Karen Traviss, 02 August 2006).

There are historical reasons for the low status of tie-ins. Some are essentially Romantic: to write within someone else's world is second-class creativity, to write "commercially" is somehow demeaning one's art; both statements are of course hollow. Science fiction and fantasy writers have traditionally shared worlds, whether we mean the accumulating tropes of a faster-than-light universe, actual projects such as the *Wild Card* series of books or the *Thieves World* stories, or the books licensed by authors when they are tired of writing in their creation. Commercialization is a stone thrown at genre fiction anyway, but it is true that early tie-ins (the novelizations of the original *Star Trek*, of *Doctor Who* episodes, or of the first three *Star Wars* films) were written to very tight script requirements; even so, readers of these books can quickly tell you who were the good writers and who produced bare prose sketches of the original.[1] The new, post–1980s breed of tie-in expands the fictive universe, rather than merely glossing it.

The rise in "fan fiction" (amateur fiction written without pay), and its accessibility on the net has affected the status of tie-ins in complex ways. To the uninitiated, the very notion of fan writing seems to suggest that "anyone" can write a tie-in. To those within the field it means that the quality bar is rising all the time, and as Kristine Kathryn Rusch has argued, because the tie-in market can function as a shop window for one's other material, there is a huge incentive to offer one's best work (Rusch, 2006) The packaging companies have demanding standards for tie-in writers; almost all the tie-in writers today also write for the adult science fiction field. I mention this not to create an impression of "good writers slumming it" but because this is a closer match to the relationship between juveniles and the adult field, than is the modern situation in which YA sf has until very recently been written predominantly by a discrete group of writers.

In the chapter on social expectation of children I argued that game books provided an intellectual space which valorized the values that were disappearing from YA fiction: outward boundedness; intellectual (rather than emotional) choices; and acquisition of both knowledge and objects. In this section I want to conclude this chapter with a very brief look at some tie-ins. As the field is huge — tie-ins sell far better than does creator-copyright science fiction — my choices are random, a combination of what was on my shelves and what *Forbidden Planet* in London stocked. One book — by Karen Traviss — is selected because it is Traviss's advocacy for tie-ins which drew my attention to my own unthinking snobbery.

The modern tie-in is very different from the novelizations of the 1960s. Novelizations are still sold but they are clearly labeled as novelizations. Within the market they are a distinct sub-genre, and they reproduce the narrative values of the texts they re-enact. The modern tie-in exists in the *interstices* of the television or film (or game) text with which it exists in symbiosis. Commissioned authors are given a "bible,"[2] but within that bible may write very much what they want: novels may position themselves in a time-space not detailed on screen (what happened on X's mission to the Ys which on screen was simply reported), they may concern themselves with another period in a character's life, or may focus on characters who had only a few lines in the original screen performance. I have tried to represent each of these three choices here. What is crucial to understand is that the film/television companies have been extraordinarily generous in the ways they have opened their worlds to others. Within the bibles, authors have enormous freedom to tell the stories they want to tell, to write the issues and arguments that they feel important. In two of the cases I will discuss, authors have been allowed to subvert the on-screen texts, to demand of the readers that they question their own loyalties. As time goes on and the imagined universe expands, the bible that is emerging is one that has been shaped in part by the tie-in authors. If there is "pressure to conform" on tie-in writers, the majority of it comes from fans, who frequently have very distinct ideas of what their extended world should be like. This, of course, is no different to the pressure any popular author experiences.

Tie-ins for the Younger Market

Most of the tie-in market is aimed at teens and adults but there are a small number of tie-ins for younger readers, and I want to stop in there first to consider if the values they express differ from the independent material on the children's shelves.

The *Star Wars* franchise commissioned first Terry Bisson and then Elizabeth Hand to write an ongoing narrative of the childhood of Boba Fett. The premise is straightforward; Jango Fett sold his DNA for the clone warriors and part of the price was an unaltered clone to be his son. After Jango dies, Boba is on his own. He is chased by people who want whatever his father left behind, he is chased simply because he is his father's son and hence knows far too much about the duplicity of certain parties, and he is also a child wandering through a war-torn universe.

Bisson's and Hand's *Star Wars* novels are aimed at the 8–12 range. As with much of the sf I've discussed for this age, the technical challenges contained in the book are minimal. Where the strength of the books lies is in that they are simultaneously realistic in their portrayal of a child in an adult world, and they are optimistic in that they assume the essential intelligence of the child. The trajectory of each book is very similar, in each Boba Fett is carried away helpless by events. He becomes subject to the whims of adults, who are mostly portrayed as very distant authorities. But Boba succeeds in manipulating those events to his purpose; the reiterated structure is of the child resisting the adult narrative of the adult world.

One of the ways these books stand apart from both the YA novels and (to a lesser extent) the juveniles, is the way they handle friendship. Many of the juveniles and teen books (as discussed in chapter five) are ensemble novels in which a group of teens are thrown together. Friendship is then modeled on that of primary school — you are sitting/adventuring with them so you must be friends. Development of these relationships is mostly about the shifting of alliances as character emerges under stress. Bisson and Hand reject this model and instead take up one of the commonest archetypes in sf, the loner/misfit. Boba Fett has no friends. He gets close to a child refugee but leaves him behind less because he wants to protect his friend (which is a common motive in YA sf) but because he knows his mission is his, and only his. In *Maze of Deception*, Boba uses a young clone (whom he naturally resembles) in a bait-and-switch to escape the bounty hunter Aurra Sing.

Furthermore — and perhaps more interesting — Boba's focus is on adults, because adults are the ones who can make the universe move. What this means in practice, is that much of the action in the book involves Boba listening to, and reacting to the adults who are the major characters in the "foreground" of "the world." I'm not explaining this very well, but it is as if the adults are front of stage, Boba is backstage, and suddenly the stage swings around so that it is Boba we are watching while the play continues in the background. In Hand's *Maze of Deception* Boba overhears two pilots discussing Dooku's plans to raise money from the Hutts for the war against the Republic; the scene fills in the politics but also adds an element to Boba's story as he now has a weapon to hand, the ability to expose Count Dooku as Tyranus (2006: 93). Using this kind of *mise-en-scène* allows Bisson and Hand to deliver a very great deal of the background to the politics of the Clone Wars without having to dumb down. Readers can access what Boba hears at different levels. This orientation to listening to adults, however, also changes Boba's emotional trajectory.

The episodic and developing nature of the tale (and the fact that we know it culminates with Boba as bounty hunter for Jabba the Hutt) makes it tricky to offer predictions, but Boba's relationship to others is structured to accumulate increasing levels of mistrust. This couldn't contrast more with the expectations of children's and teen fiction. This is not about whether the Star Wars books have happy endings, but what a happy ending is understood to be. One of my criticisms of post–1970s books has been that the happy endings are understood as reuniting children, if not with their parents then with a parental or authority substitute. In many there is a *parens ex machina* (this is the problem with some Heinleins such as *Tunnel in the Sky*, *Between Planets* and *Citizen of the Galaxy* ; in each case the result is a rather limp ending). Juvenile fiction of the 1950s (and not just science fiction), while interested in socializing children to the community, placed enormous emphasis on individual competence: think of Enid Blyton's *Famous Five* in the UK or the Nancy Drew mysteries in the U.S. Bisson and Hand, liberated both by the original conceit, and where Boba

Fett has to end up, are able to recapture this emerging competence. In terms of narrative structure a good comparison which illuminates what I mean is Philip Pullman's *Northern Lights/The Golden Compass*. In this book Lyra is passed from hand to hand, her adventure determined by the goals of adults (which even when they are not the same are congruent) and facilitated by the kindness of adults. In contrast, in Hand's and Bisson's stories, Boba determines his adventure (to find his father's inheritance and to walk in his father's shoes) in conflict with adult goals (to milk him of his father's knowledge) and *escaping* from one ill-intentioned adult to another.

What makes this other than a gothic is that Boba increasingly comes to assume the ill intent of his adult minders; this is not a story of innocence robbed and deceived, but of emerging suspicion and consequent self-reliance. The lessons—and they are frequently delivered directly from an e-book left to Boba by his father—are to trust no one. The narrative tension derives from the situations Boba gets into by not cleaving entirely to this ethos; in *Maze of Deception* for example, Boba is able to escape Aurra Sing by distrusting the clone boy, the bankers and the officials, but loses most of his father's money when he allows the money-changer, Bim, to get hold of the banking card. Ironically, of course, Bim has done Boba a favor; Fett's money would have left him secure, dependent on his father's legacy. What he has left is just enough to set him up with a ship, just enough in other words to give him independence and send him further out from adult attention and care.

Tie-ins for Teens and Adults

It is not really possible to draw generalizations about tie-ins as a market, because each tie-in belongs to a product with its own distinct values: consequently, this section won't attempt to actually link each of the texts discussed, but offers them as gateways into a whole new set of research questions. Although there are many franchises I could have selected, I have selected texts from each of the most familiar: *Dr. Who*, *Star Trek* and *Star Wars*. What I am concerned with is the extent to which these texts reflect both the values of their franchise *and* the values of creator-copyright sf for adults. The first of my samples are two *Doctor Who* stories, Colin Brake's *The Colony of Lies*, part of the "Past Doctor" range, the second (a "Quick Read") *I Am a Dalek*, based on the revived series. I'll then discuss Una McCormack's *Deep Space Nine* novel, *The Hollow Men*, and finally Karen Traviss's *Triple Zero*. I'm interested in the degree to which the books reflect what I've argued are the core values of science fiction, but also—and often in contradiction — the degree to which they reflect the core values of the franchises which they are expanding. In tune with the overall argument of the book, I actually believe that it is the second of these that is more important. My argument throughout has never been that YA values are *wrong* but that when forming the core of an sf text they undermine the "gateway" role that we can presume junior forms of a genre might wish to play. As I want A.N. Other's YA sf text to lead a reader to Greg Egan or Joanna Russ, I want A.N. Other's tie-in to lead in to watching more of the originating program.

Colin Brake's *Doctor Who: The Colony of Lies* (2003), despite being a recent novel, adheres to the genre expectations of the original series it purports to expand. Although the Seventh Doctor and his companion Ace bookend the story, it is essentially a Second Doctor with Jamie and Zoe adventure. *The Colony of Lies* uses two classic sf plot drivers: the lost colony/lost memory and first contact. The colony of Axista Four was intended to be a fresh start at an earlier level of technology, but with the death of the founder in the initial crash the colony has become mired in technophobic fundamentalism. This, combined with the problem that half of the initial colonists never came out of cryogenic sleep, means that the colony is doomed. At the opening of the tale it has also split between Loyalists and Realists (who want to use the technology on board the crashed ship).

The conflict is disrupted when an Earth ship arrives, intending to deposit fifty thousand refugees from the Dalek wars, and a colony of cryogenically preserved aliens wakes up. Interpersonal growth is kept to a minimum. One of the settlers—Dee—is bitter because her partner left with a young woman when he formed the Realists, but this never takes center stage and has no consequences for the plot. The keys to the story are technological and social: the social element is that classic trope from late 1960s/early 1970s sf for children; the parents have lied. The colonists discover their founder lied to them about the emptiness of the planet, the "aliens" discover they are transgenic humans, and the captain of the advance earth ship discovers his administrative superior is untrustworthy. This tripartite revelation becomes the foundation for the Doctor's classic political maneuvering which can be summed up as "let's all be friends." Potentials for future conflicts when the refugees arrive are swept under the carpet. One of the ironies of the book, which well represents the television series, is that Jamie is presented as more cynical than the Doctor. Although the Doctor (as played by Patrick Troughton) is presented as a man in his fifties, his defining quality, and the value he most supports, is that of youthful optimism, that *anything* can be achieved. The relatively downbeat projections of so much of the sf for children and teens that we have seen in this book is utterly missing. Noticeable is that although the Doctor is portrayed as a pacifist, he is in no sense a technophobe. The entire text moves on a trajectory arguing for reinvention.

The Quick Read, *I Am a Dalek*, by Gareth Roberts is a very effective "gateway book" to the revived series, whose values it replicates.[3] These values privilege the relationship between the Doctor and Rose, and continually reiterate the innate superiority of the human will in the face of any invading alien — hold it up as the ultimate weapon in fact — in a gross parody of John Campbell's classic rubric. This is of course a direct consequence of the wider appeal sought by the BBC. The choice of Russell Davies as script writer, while clearly signaling an intention to take *Doctor Who* seriously, also signaled that the series would be oriented to a far greater degree to the relationship between the Doctor and his companion, borne out in the series both in the greater amount of time they spend talking to each other, and the near romance at the end of season two. In *I Am a Dalek*, the Doctor and Rose land at an archeological dig in the 1970s and find both a Dalek, and a young woman who is apparently infected by Dalek DNA implanted thousands of years before. The story brings the Dalek to life, shows the Doctor capitulating to the Dalek's commands, and eventually the Dalek being destroyed when the Doctor appeals to the young woman's residual humanity, in an internalized monologue which we are privileged to overhear. The story is not resolved by technological know-how, or ingenuity, but an appeal to feelings, much like the episode, *The Unquiet Dead* (2005), in which the Victorian maidservant similarly resists alien invaders. The value connection between the book and the series is strong, that between either and science fiction is rather weak.

Of the books considered, Una McCormack's *The Hollow Men* (2005) is the one held most rigidly within its originating franchise-universe, *Star Trek*, and the one which most emphasizes the "internal." As the title indicates, this "deep character" remains an important element of the tie-in world. In *Hollow Men* there are two plots and two additional story arcs; the plots are adventure-based but in each case they are background for the emotional growth that is the real story episode. Plot one (the minor plot) relates an effort to steal a precious metal from the space station *Deep Space Nine*. Related with humor, it is a classic trickster tale, with the sting that the theft turns out to be linked to the major conflict that is raging through the galaxy. The focus of the story however is not the theft but the growing love Odo (the shapeshifter) feels for Kira (the Bajoran first officer). Similarly, the second plot takes Benjamin Sisko (captain of *Deep Space Nine*) to Earth for a peace conference where he is attacked, and a traitor is discovered. Here, the story is how Sisko comes to terms with actions he has taken in pursuit of Federation war aims (before this book started), which he cannot square with his conscience. The reason I am so sure which is plot and which is story is that each of the plots is resolved and in each case we are moved back to the status quo. The theft has no long-term effect on the space station either in terms of its material needs, its trading status or the relationships between individuals. The plot on Earth is resolved when a newly introduced character dies— the world seals neatly behind him, and even the enemy does not seem to have been advanced. In contrast, while glacier-like in its progress, Odo's romance has advanced and Sisko has moved forward towards reconciliation with his internal narrative. McCormack (and the *ST* universe generally) hovers on the edge of mainstream fictional values. Gary Wolfe (not the Locus reviewer) once commented that *Star Trek: The Next Generation* was like sitting in on a therapy session. The shape of chairs around the bridge, while intended to suggest a more egalitarian atmosphere, also allowed the crew to swap confidences about their inner lives. Deanna Troi's constant refrain of "I feel its pain" only confirmed the attempt of the writers to reach out for a more mainstream notion of character. Although this tendency was muted in *Deep Space Nine*, which was a darker series by far, it remained as one of the elements which distinguished the *Star Trek* character-universe from competing shows such as *Babylon 5* (in which internal anguish was shown either in short flashes at the end of the program, or in almighty screw-ups). As Graham Sleight has noted, "narratives of personal and cultural growth" pervade the *ST* universe: "what is the Captain's Log but a device through which the main character can reflect on the experiences just seen, in the manner that gives California a bad name?" (2005: 196).

The issue here is not whether McCormack's *Hollow Men* conforms to sf or to YA values (it seems to manage both) but that the book accurately reflects the values of the market it wishes to feed — the *ST* audience. There is value-congruency between the tie-ins and the television shows which is missing between much "YA sf" and the adult genre: *Hollow Men* functions as a gateway into a particular kind of "reading" as well as what it is in itself.

Karen Traviss was already a fast-rising star on the basis of her own creator-copyright science fiction when her first *Star Wars* tie-in, *Hard Contact*, came out. At the point of writing she has completed/published her *Wess'har* sequence and completed/published three *Star Wars* novels, one of which reached the number one spot on *The New York Times* paperback best-seller list. The values of both are essentially the same: they are about outsiderness, about identity, about "what is 'people'"? There is also a lot of class politics in all of the books and there is an intensity and anger that propels both the plot and story.

For the *Star Wars* franchise Traviss homed in on an aspect of the story that is easily overlooked in the glamour and pace of the on-screen delivery; the Jedi, a supposedly ethical fraternity, accept the creation of a race of slaves whom they subsequently exploit as cannon fodder. Traviss then decided to insert herself into the backstage of the fictional universe and relate the wars through the eyes of the cloned soldiers. In doing so, the books raise issues both political and scientific. The brilliance is that the espoused values are not those of the films at all, yet they remain congruent with the central text by existing in its interstices.[4]

Triple Zero was written for an adult market whose franchise keeps one eye firmly on teenagers. It is a coming-of-age story both for the protagonists and for the society of which they are a part. *Triple Zero* (the second in the sequence) begins with a flashback to Sergeant Kal's first meeting with a batch of clones; specifically a batch who are about to be killed for not meeting their creators' specifications: they are too rebellious, too independent of thought. Before the tale even begins then, a question mark hangs over the Jedi that they should deny to others the free will they so prize. We then flash forward several years in the future when the age-accelerated clone troop is on a mission to find a spy on a planet. Much of the movement in the text is military — how a military force acts in a civilian population — and there is a great deal of hard-tech discussion of equipment. While this passed over my head it is because I am not the target market, a large section of *Star Wars* fandom is fascinated with this kind of material and will keep a very sharp eye to ensure that the weaponry is consistent with the fictional catalogue. Furthermore, it is precisely the kind of technical *knowledge* that attracts teen sf readers. So too is the complex discussion of people-hood.

The story which runs through the plot is a classic YA theme, coming of age, but it is very firmly contextualized within the universe in which the story is set, and in the social and biological/genetic context of the clones. In her first book, *Hard Contact*, Traviss set out to remind people that cloning does *not* produce identical copies of the same person: nutrition and physical experience all mark the body, the mind and body is shaped by the infinite plasticity of the human genome, and from the moment emotional treatment deviates by as much as a metaphorical millimeter, individuality emerges. *Hard Contact* brought us to confront the racism of assuming that because we/outsiders cannot tell the difference, there is no difference and brought us into the world of the clones and their own awareness of individuality. In *Triple Zero* we learn that Sergeant Kal has inducted the entire clone community into Mandalorian culture — a culture of mercenaries which anyone can choose to join. The value of belief, of community, and of a sense of honor is present in *Triple Zero* as much as in any Heinlein novel (I'd go as far as to say that Sergeant Kal is a classic Heinleinian Old Teacher). As the novel extends some of the clones begin to gain the confidence to assert their humanity, first to the Jedi who are assigned to them, and later to the civilians they meet. In small touches — a barmaid attracted to one clone but not to another — Traviss draws attention to the idea that individuality is both inherent as a quality of peoplehood, but is also something we can withhold or grant to others. The questions touched on range widely: what's it really like to be one of a thousand clones? How do you create morale? Through fear, or through culture? In what ways do you recognize your brothers? How do you grow up to be a man when you know you are going to die soon? Small questions. Well, obviously not, but they are thrown out casually, as tiny but integral elements in a frenetic tale of search-and-destroy, spy-hunting, and counter-terrorism.

One of the issues that I have suggested creates a blurry demarcation between sf (and the fantastic) and other genres is the outward focus: the universe comes first. This is easy to misunderstand. By this I do not mean that *painting* the universe is the most important factor, that characters should move like avatars through the text (although I also think that there is a lot of rather excellent avatar-functional sf out there). In effective sf novels personal relationships must contend with the real world, they cannot simply become the purpose of that world. In response to this issue Traviss wrote:

> ... The coating there might be very distracting for someone not used to Star Wars, but this book is primarily about exploitation, slavery, family and identity....
> ... what makes the book different is the characters and their dawning realization of what's been done to them [July 27 2006, at the Inter-Galactic Playground].

The result is a complex novel in which personal issues—love, pregnancy—do not take priority over the values already established of loyalty, duty and brother-love, but significantly in which the central energy of characters is directed towards doing, not thinking. There is very little of the internal agonizing that we saw in *Hollow Men*. When the Jedi Etain realizes she is pregnant by the clone Darman her decision is taken in this universal context and as a highly politicized decision, one which is bound up in the arguments about peoplehood, identity, exploitation and slavery which have driven all the storylines within what is, as Traviss has said, a straightforward piece of "milfic."

Is this an entry-level text? I think so: for all the hard sf clothing, the real interest is in tactics, politics and some of the issues above. There is nothing a teen could not cope with—and frankly, I suspect a teen would find the complexity far less daunting than I did—and what little romance there is handled tactfully and has consequences. The book reaches off the end of the text into the future, not just because it is part of a series, but because the lesson Traviss sets out to relay is that choices do not float in a vacuum. For Traviss, as she writes in her article "Driving GFFA 1; Or How *Star Wars* Loosened My Corsets," it is precisely the opportunity to ask demanding questions of a pre-constructed universe which allows her to explore the philosophical questions of humanity. That is pretty much a definition of good science fiction.

My once perceived absence of good books concerned to engage the teen market in "real" sf is coming under challenge. As well as the renaissance in sf written specifically for teens, the tie-ins have ensured that the books are there, in ever greater numbers every year. They are hugely popular precisely among the very group who officially "Don't Read." One of Karen Traviss's *Star Wars* novels, *Revelation*, reached the number one spot in the *New York Times* paperback best-seller list in March 2008. Many tie in novels are written by authors (like Traviss) who also write independently so that there is gateway from the tie-in market to creator-copyright science fiction. Ironically, the real sadness is that prejudice prevents the gate opening both ways to the degree it should. Given that the same prejudice has long kept respectable readers of all genres away from fiction for children, we might pause for an embarrassed blush.

APPENDIX A

Index to Out of This World

Out of This World was edited by Amabel Williams-Ellis & Mably Owen, 1960–1972. The following is from *Index to Science Fiction Anthologies and Collections*, combined edition, by William G. Contento. Used by permission. Copyright © 2006 by William G. Contento. http://www.philsp.com/homeville/ ISFAC/0start.htm

Out of This World 1. Edited by Amabel Williams-Ellis and Mably Owen. London: Blackie, 1960.
"Breaking Strain" ["Thirty Seconds—Thirty Days"], Arthur C. Clarke nv, *Thrilling Wonder Stories,* Dec '49.
"No Place Like Earth" (as by John Beynon), John Wyndham nv *New Worlds* Spr '51; as "Tyrant and Slave-Girl on Venus," *Ten Story Fantasy* Spr '51.
"The Ruum," Arthur Porges ss, *The Magazine of Fantasy & Science Fiction,* Oct '53.
"Friday," John Kippax ss, *New Worlds* Feb '59.
"The Middle of the Week After Next," Murray Leinster ss, *Thrilling Wonder Stories* Aug '52.
"Placet Is a Crazy Place," Fredric Brown ss, *Astounding* May '46.
"Chemical Plant," Ian Williamson ss, *New Worlds* Winter '50.
"Men of the Ten Books," Jack Vance ss, *Startling Stories,* Mar '51.

Out of This World 2. Edited by Amabel Williams-Ellis and Mably Owen. London: Blackie, 1961.
"The Trouble with Emily," James White nv, *New Worlds,* Nov '58.
"The Dusty Death," John Kippax ss, *New Worlds* Nov '58.
"Another Word for Man," Robert Presslie ss, *New Worlds,* Dec '58.
"The Railways Up on Cannis," Colin Kapp nv, *New Worlds,* Oct '59.
"Machine Made," J. T. McIntosh ss, *New Worlds,* Summer '51.
"But Who Can Replace a Man?," Brian W. Aldiss ss, *Infinity Science Fiction,* June '58.
"The Gift of Gab," Jack Vance nv, *Astounding,* Sep '55.
"The Still Waters" ["In the Still Waters"] Lester del Rey nv, *Fantastic Universe,* June '55.

Out of This World 3. Edited by Amabel Williams-Ellis and Mably Owen. London: Blackie, 1962.

  "Sands Our Abode," Francis G. Rayer ss, *New Worlds*, June '59.

  "Round Trip to Esidarap" ("Esidarap ot Pirt Dnuor") Lloyd Biggle, Jr. nv, *If*, Nov '60.

  "Living Space" Isaac Asimov ss, *Science Fiction Stories*, May '56.

  "The Apprentice," James White nv, *New Worlds*, Oct '60.

  "Baxbr" ("BAXBR/DAXBR"), Evelyn E. Smith ss, *Time to Come*, edited by August Derleth, Farrar, 1954; *The Magazine of Fantasy & Science Fiction*, Sep '56.

  "Dumb Martian," John Wyndham nv, *Galaxy*, July '52.

  "Who's There?," Arthur C. Clarke ss, *New Worlds*, Nov '58.

  "Ararat," Zenna Henderson nv, *The Magazine of Fantasy & Science Fiction*, Oct '52.

Out of This World 4. Edited by Amabel Williams-Ellis and Mably Owen. London: Blackie, 1964.

  "Inside the Comet," Arthur C. Clarke ss, *The Magazine of Fantasy & Science Fiction*, Oct '60.

  "Hothouse," Brian W. Aldiss nv, *The Magazine of Fantasy & Science Fiction*, Feb '61.

  "When the Engines Had to Stop," Elis Gwyn Jones ss.

  "Twice Bitten," Donald Malcolm nv, *New Worlds*, Feb '63.

  "Changeling," Amabel Williams-Ellis ss.

  "The Astronaut," Valentina Zhuravleva ss, *Destination: Amaltheia*, ed. Richard Dixon, Moscow: Foreign Languages Publishing House, 1963.

  "Billenium," J. G. Ballard ss, *New Worlds*, Nov '61.

  "Six-Fingered Jacks," E. R. James ss, *New Worlds* June '62.

Out of This World 5. Edited by Amabel Williams-Ellis and Mably Owen. London: Blackie, 1965.

  "Four in One," Damon Knight nv, *Galaxy*, Feb '53.

  "Bottomless Pit," Philip E. High ss, *New Worlds*, Mar '63.

  "The Hour of Letdown," E. B. White ss, *New Yorker*, Dec 22 '51; *The Magazine of Fantasy & Science Fiction*, Aug '52.

  "Colonial," John Christopher nv, *Astounding*, Apr '49.

  "Badman," John Brunner ss, *New Worlds*, Mar '60.

  "Pushover Planet," Con Pederson ss, *The Magazine of Fantasy & Science Fiction*, June '63.

  "The Fiction Machines," Vadim Okhotnikov ss.

  "Winthrop Was Stubborn" ("Time Waits for Winthrop"), William Tenn na, *Galaxy*, Aug '57.

Out of This World 6. Edited by Amabel Williams-Ellis and Mably Owen. London: Blackie, 1967.

  "All the Troubles of the World," Isaac Asimov ss, *Super Science Fiction*, Apr '58.

  "Fast Trip," James White nv, *The Magazine of Fantasy & Science Fiction*, Apr '63.

Out of This World 10. Edited by Amabel Williams-Ellis and Michael Pearson. London: Blackie, 1973.

    "Uncommon Sense," Hal Clement ss, *Astounding*, Sep '45.

    "The Girls from Earth," Frank M. Robinson nv, *Galaxy*, Jan '52.

    "A Long Spoon," John Wyndham ss, *Suspense* (UK), Sep '60.

    "Games Without End," Italo Calvino ss, *Cosmicomics*, Harcourt Brace World, 1968.

    "The Feeling of Power," Isaac Asimov ss, *If*, Feb '58.

    "The Chessplayers," Charles L. Harness ss, *The Magazine of Fantasy & Science Fiction*, Oct '53.

    "The Great Judge," A. E. van Vogt ss, *Fantasy Book #3*, '48.

    "The Winter People," Gilbert Phelps ss, 1963.

    "Dead to the World," H. A. Hargreaves ss, *New Writings in Science Fiction* 11, ed. John Carnell, London: Corgi, 1968.

    "Dreams Are Sacred," Peter Phillips nv, *Astounding*, Sep '48.

APPENDIX B

The Survey Questionnaire

The purpose of this questionnaire is to provide material for a book, and the research is supported by the Eileen Wallace Children's Library (University of New Brunswick), Middlesex University (London) and the British Academy.

Who am I? I am a science fiction fan and a critic. I edit the academic journal *Foundation*. The original article behind this research can be found at "Is There Any Such Thing as Children's SF: A Position Piece" in *The Lion and the Unicorn, A Critical Journal of Children's Literature*. Vol. 28, no. 2, April 2004, pp. 284–313.

The questionnaire is intended as a qualitative not quantitive survey. I need to trust you to answer only once. With the exception perhaps of sex, I have no need to be able to draw conclusions about "types" of people, in that by answering this questionnaire, you have defined yourself as the "type" I am discussing. This means that while there are questions you may find intrusive, they are there to give you the freedom to talk about certain issues and their effects on your reading patterns if you wish. Feel free to ignore these questions if you prefer.

If a question is not applicable (i.e., you are not yet an adult) please just indicate n/a.

When you have completed it, please send this as an email (no files please) to: sfquestions@gmail.com.

1. Name

This can be a username/alias of some kind, but I would like to be able to fix a handle on each questionnaire. This is intended as a qualitative, not quantitative survey, so I may wish to quote extracts. You do **not** have to give either your real name or a name by which you are called in fandom. I trust you not to fill in the form more than once.

If you have given an identifiable handle but wish all or part of this document to be kept anonymous (questions 5, 6, and 7 come to mind) please indicate this. Your wishes will be respected.

2. Current Age
3. Country or Countries in which you spent your first eighteen years (give breakdown if appropriate).
4. Mother tongue.

The following three questions are *not* for statistical purposes. If you wish to answer them, they may provide interesting insights for me or they may not. No true names will be revealed. Elaborate as you see fit.

5. Sex at birth
6. Sex now.
7. Sexuality.

To the books (although comics *do* count). Fill in as much as you can. Don't worry if the answer is "don't remember."

8. When did you start reading science fiction?
9. Did you read sf written specifically for children? (i.e. age 0–16 yrs)
10. Name up to five authors of sf for children you liked.
11. Name up to five authors of sf for children you did not like.
12. Name up to five authors of sf for children with the same nationality as the country in which you experienced the bulk of your reading childhood.
13. If you started reading sf meant for the adult audience before the age of 16, who were your favorite sf writers at that time? (Name up to five).
14. List up to five qualities that you think you looked for in science fiction when you read it as a child (under 13).
15. List up to five qualities that you think you looked for in science fiction when you read it as a teenager (13 and over).
16. List up to five qualities that you look for in science fiction now.

(These can be negative qualities in the sense of what sf does not do, that other forms of fiction do).

17. Do you define yourself as a genre reader?
18. What proportion of your reading as a teenager was outside of the genre?
19. How much of your reading outside of the genre was set by others? (and who were they?)
20. Did science fiction influence your political views? In what ways? What books were most important to you?
21. Did science fiction influence your religious views? In what ways? What books were most important to you?
22. Taking no more than 100 words, describe briefly how you chose books between the ages of 13 and 18, and how those books were acquired (i.e. libraries, friends, second-hand books, new books).

Thank you very much for your contribution to my research.

Analysis of the Survey

by Zara Baxter and
Farah Mendlesohn

The material was collected by Farah Mendlesohn.
The analysis and write up was carried out by Zara Baxter.

Background

Why This Survey Was Conducted

The intention of this survey was to provoke questions. It was never *intended* to be a research survey in the usual sense. It was assumed that the survey would attract at most fifty responses and would provide qualitative material in the form of authors previously unconsidered, questions worth asking, or themes that were clearly worth exploring further. The survey was to be a "quick snapshot." As a consequence, the survey itself does not fulfill many of the criteria of a modern survey, and there are many places where one could wish different questions had been asked.

The survey was initially posted on the blog that has accompanied this research, *The Inter-Galactic Playground*. Its rapid dissemination through the internet communities resulted in over 900 responses and 850 useable responses (sometimes forms simply did not provide enough information). This leaves us with several issues about the integrity and representativeness of the data.

Questions

The questions asked were general and open-ended, and as a result many respondents provided too much material in response. Respondents' answers to the question "What five things did you look for in books?" led to over 400 unique responses even after categorizing. People were unsure what "genre" meant for some questions, but seemed happy in others; the answers are almost all qualitative, leading to difficulties of observer bias when coding the responses, among other issues.

Sampling Technique

The survey drew in primarily people who read blogs and LiveJournal. Over 200 responses were received in the first 24 hours, at which point the spread took on a life of its own. As many as two hundred respondents came through each of Neil Gaiman's and Cory Doctorow's blogs, with other respondents coming to the survey via other "nodes," such as Ken MacLeod and Karen Traviss. While this attracted respondents in the class we wanted — genre readers who were genre readers as children — it relied heavily on reader subsets which have unique and cohesive group identities of their own. The survey ran from January 2004 until August 2005. The final cut-off date was just after the Science Fiction Worldcon held that year in the UK. As head of the literary track Farah Mendlesohn was in a position to exhort one final surge in responses, and this itself is a nodal distortion.

Representativeness

We have to consider whether this is a representative sample of sf readers, and if not, how much it differs. There are several factors which lead to the conclusion that despite the problems of sampling, the data is representative. The age profile of the contributors is fairly similar to that of *Locus* readers and is rather older than those outside of the genre might anticipate. Almost certainly this is biased by the need for electronic communication to respond to this survey, and it also disguises the tendency for younger readers to read more than do older readers. The survey did not include a question about how much people read. It is not a representative sample of readers, as the majority of responses were drawn from fan circles or fan-once-removed. Many sf readers never come near any fan structures. An average Worldcon attendance figure is 6,000 people, which is a tiny proportion of the total cohort of self-identifying genre readers. On the other hand, a good sale of a new hardcover science fiction book is perhaps 5,000, and a softcover perhaps 75,000; while the overall genre readership is undoubtedly larger, it strongly suggests that 1,000 people is a solid subset. The survey did succeed in targeting self-defined genre readers: 55 percent say they are, and around 50 percent read more than 50 percent genre. If we consider a "genre reader" as someone whose reading diet is composed of at least 30 percent genre, then 70 percent of the respondents are genre readers, even when not self-identifying as such. Because of internet-based sampling, readers are predominantly Anglo-American and have high internet interaction.

Farah Mendlesohn's interest was in whether genre readers did indeed show the interests and traits that self-declared "fans" in conventions were frequently heard to express. This survey stood alone, but a second "quick and dirty" survey involved asking science fiction fans using LiveJournal to check their scores on the Meyers-Briggs psychometric test, and in chapter three the results are used extensively as a cross-comparison. The "relatively" low level of "information" orientation expressed in this survey — relatively, in terms of Mendlesohn's expectations based on anecdotal evidence — was borne out in this poll also, where "only" 29 percent of the pool of 123 respondents scored as INTJ, long held to be the "classic" sf fan's score. That this, and the total in the TJ/FJ category (57 percent), was a direct reversal of the U.S. national trend suggests it is still a significant indicator of an "sf" personality even if not as totalizing as initially assumed, and supports the findings of this survey.

Coding

While the dataset is large, the qualitative nature of responses makes it hard to draw conclusions. The multiplicity of responses meant that answers had to be categorized according to some criteria. As no criteria had been set beforehand because, as outlined earlier, the survey had not been expected to attract so many responses, we characterized and categorized responses post-facto. For example, in response to the question "What qualities did you look for in books when you were under 13?" a respondent may have written, "I wanted an adventure story, something that featured visiting other worlds and making discoveries. I wanted to read about people like me."

This would then be coded as:

  a. "adventure"
  b. "story"
  c. "other worlds/strange lands"
  d. "discovery/exploration"
  e. "space travel"
  f. "identify with character"
  g. "young character"

This required interpretation on the part of the coder—both Farah and Zara coded two cohorts independently, to cross-check interpretation and to create as inclusive and expansive a list as possible. The idea was not to reduce the categories to a set of ten, but to identify all potential aspects and find patterns.

How We Are Using the Data

The decision taken was to divide the respondents into age cohorts and consider what different interests and investments shaped these readers. The age cohorts, however, are themselves defined by science fiction "moments" and as such, *are not all the same size;* they do not cover the same periods in time. Some of the intervals are eleven years, some are nine years. What Farah was interested in was "generational" change.

For each cohort, Farah Mendlesohn decided to use as a defining event—a significant book published when respondents were eighteen or younger, on the grounds that it is the books we read before we are adults which "make" us, and that this may be stronger in science fiction, where "the sense of wonder," vulnerable as it is to experience, is such a major element of what attracts young people to the genre. The "defining moments" for cohorts 5, 6 and 7 were revised by Zara Baxter on the basis of the responses given (the earlier choices seemed to work well). The birth dates are approximations and as the survey ended up running from 2004 into 2005 there may be some mistakes.

In retrospect, a more fruitful approach might have been to enter all data individually, which would allow us to identify subgroups by interest and reader values. This work may be undertaken at a later date, or using a new survey.

Figure 1. Summary of Cohorts

Cohort			Age in '05	Range	No. of responses
1	18 yrs or younger in 1940; born	The beginning of the Golden Age, so the generation who watched sf begin. John W.	68–83	15	6

Cohort			Age in '05	Range	No. of responses
	1922–1937	Campbell becomes editor of *Amazing*.			
2	18 yrs or younger in 1955; born 1937–1947	Paperbacks began to dominate the market from '55, so this is the group that grew up with the Golden Age. Start of Heinlein's domination — lasts through cohorts 3 and 4.	58–68	9	29
3	18 yrs or younger in 1965; born 1947–1957	The New Wave began, *Stranger in a Strange Land*: but this generation grew up as sf established itself, got comfortable with its language and subject matter, just before everything changed. People start saying that one of their primary influences is which authors they have previously read — people are starting to follow backlogs of favored authors; they also mention quotes on the back in terms of "author recommended." We start to see the emergence of subgenre, and also the growth of sf subcultures (i.e., only reading a particular cluster of authors).	48–58	9	114
4	18 yrs or younger in 1975; born 1957–1967	The publication of *Dune* in paperback (it influences every cohort beyond) and while *The Centauri Device* was my original choice because cited so often by authors of New Space Opera. For women *The Female Man* ends this period. The cohort is made up of people who grew up with various manifestations of the New Wave and the sudden explosion in the rise and scope of the sf book. From this cohort quotes on the back begin to matter. Blurbs also appear. And also by library categorization (rockets/starburst labels on the spine). Also the first appearance of tele-	38–48	11	242

Cohort			Age in '05	Range	No. of responses
		vision tie-ins being a factor in choosing books and also the first appearance of "I read my parents' collection." Also Science Fiction and Scholastic Bookclub started here. The men in this cohort all cite "complexity."			
5	18 yrs or younger in 1987; born 1969–1977 ... gap between this cohort and next is short	There is no new book in this cohort. *Neuromancer*? This cohort seems to be reading the same as the previous generation: my guess is that this is to do with the source of books—libraries and second-hand. Libraries in the U.S. and UK begin experiencing funding crises so possibility of book stock out of date. What does stand out is the growing importance of friends' recommendations. Reviews first make their appearance here.	28–36	10	225
6	18 yrs or younger in 1995; born 1977–1980 very small cohort.	School reading lists started to include science fiction. U.S. schools introduced *Fahrenheit 451* as a junior high school book somewhere in the 1980s. *Hitchhiker's Guide to the Galaxy* and *Ender's Game* begin to make an appearance (I noticed both of these in YA lists from the librarians).	25–28	3	80
7	18 yrs or younger in 1998; born 1980 onwards	The two books which emerge for this cohort are *Hitchhiker's Guide to the Galaxy* and Orson Scott Card's *Ender's Game* (which is a bit odd really as both books are rather old by this time). Heinlein finally starts to disappear. Public library is still holding up.	14–25	12	154

Demographic

Age

Survey respondents ranged in age from 15 to 83 (mean=37) and form a normal distribution with a skew towards younger respondents (see figure 1). Given that the survey was internet-based, this is not unexpected. The mean, mode and median are all clustered at age 36–37 while the distribution of women and men was similar.

Figure 2. Mean, Mode and Media Ages, by Sex

	Men (n = 462 if the total of cohorts, 850, is correct)	Women (n=388)
Age Range	16–83	15–78
Mean Age	38	35
Median Age	37	34

Figure 3. Distribution by Age

Nationality and Language

56% of respondents were from the USA
18% were from the UK
 8% from Canada
 6% from Australia

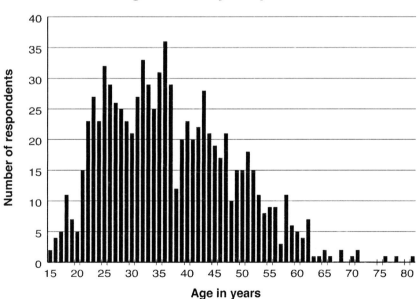

Age of Survey Respondents

Fig 4. Distribution by Continent

North America	64.6%
Europe	25.8%
Oceania	7.2%
Asia	1.1%
Africa	0.7%
South America	0.7%
	100.0%

No respondents older than 48 were from non–English speaking countries—however, it is uncertain how much of this apparent English-speaking bias is due to the survey being only in English. The issue may be less that English is the predominant publishing language than that it is the predominant language of the fan community. Fan groups in Eastern Europe and in France are small. Fan groups in Scandinavia are small but very active and with good English and it is surprising that they did not show up as a significant group.

Ninety-one percent of respondents spoke English as their first language. Other more common (0.9–1.6 percent of respondents) first languages included more common European languages such as Swedish, Finnish, French and German. Rarer languages, with only one native speaker responding to the survey were Teo Chew, Mandarin, Tagalog, Welsh, Tamil, Afrikaans, Vietnamese, Bulgarian, Catalan, Norwegian, Hungarian and Portuguese. In all, respondents named 26 languages.

Sexuality

Around 4–7 percent of the population report themselves to be gay or lesbian. In our survey, however, while the proportion reporting as gay, lesbian or "queer" was 4.3 percent, within expected rates, the proportion of bisexual or pansexual respondents is much higher than that expected in the wider population — just over 10.5 percent. A further 5 percent of respondents who labelled themselves as heterosexual for the purposes of the survey consider themselves to be curious about, open to, or interested in relationships/sex with both sexes, but haven't acted on those desires. The proportion of lesbian and bisexual women is in itself worthy of note. Twenty-six percent of women under 48 consider themselves either bisexual or lesbian (20 percent in cohort 6; 28 percent in cohorts 4 and 5; 32 percent in cohort 7), with an additional 10 percent of women under 48 considering themselves heterosexual but describing themselves as open to same-sex partnerships (ranging from 7 percent in cohort 4 up to 15 percent in cohort 7, with linear increase by cohort). Other groups may also be over-represented in sf readers—1.7 percent of respondents consider themselves polyamorous, for example. Five percent of survey respondents chose not to answer this question.

Reports on Childhood Reading

When the Respondents Started Reading SF

Almost all respondents started to read sf before adulthood. Many respondents reported reading science fiction as soon as they were able to read independently, and three respondents reported having science fiction read to them by their parents before they were able to read independently. The mean age that respondents started reading sf was 9 (8.8), with girls reporting that they started slightly later than boys (mean age 9.4 versus 8.5). Similarly, the rate of commencement was similar, the mode for girls was 9, and mode for boys 8.

The mean age is young, and the median age (9) is similarly young. Over half of sf readers started reading sf by age 9, and over 90 percent had read sf by age 13. It is also worth pointing out that the majority (55 percent) of readers started reading sf between the ages of 7 and 10. There were very few late starters; in all, out of 900 respondents, only 7 started reading sf after the age of 16. This seems to correlate with reading patterns elsewhere. A study performed by Yankelovich and commissioned by Scholastic in 2006 surveyed children to find out how many are regular readers: "Kids enjoy reading for fun and think it is important; however, their reading drops off significantly after age eight. More than 40 percent of kids ages 5–8 are high frequency readers, dropping to 29 percent among kids ages 9–11."

Who Set Their Childhood Reading?

Sixty percent of respondents said that less than 10 percent of their reading was set by others. It was common to read such statements as "Nobody set my reading."

Of those who did identify some set reading, 80 percent identified teachers, and (an overlapping) 15 percent responded with parents. Others mentioned authority figures ranged from church to far less formal suggestions for reading, such as neighbors and friends. Librarians barely figured, although the library was cited among the middle cohorts as a source of books. While the data cannot tell us whether readers were self-directed as child readers, it can certainly tell us that they thought they were primarily self-directed with over 90 percent of their reading chosen themselves through a range of mechanisms, Cohorts 2 and 3 cited libraries. Cohorts 4 and 5 tended to introduce second-hand purchases of paperbacks and all groups cited peers.

Genre Reader Identification

When we ask them what proportion of their reading was genre, 45 percent of respondents overall said they read more than 50 percent "genre." Interestingly, although men and women were equally as likely to self-define as genre readers (53 percent of male respondents; 55 percent of female respondents), women read much more outside the genre without losing genre-identification. In other words, it appears that women will self-define as a genre reader even if their reading outside the genre is up to 70 percent of their total reading. Men, on the other hand, only seem to define themselves as genre readers if 50 percent or more of their reading is in the genre.

If we assume that over 30 percent of one's reading material (one book in every three) coming from the same genre category suggests a commitment to a particular type of reading, then 70 percent of our respondents (77 percent of men, 62 percent of women) are genre readers in our terms.

Around half of those responding consider themselves a genre reader, using their own interpretation of that question. 56 percent answered in the affirmative. Women aged 37–48 were the only unusual cohort, where 67 percent consider themselves genre readers— much stronger identification than with other cohorts. The youngest cohorts had parity — those under 25 were equally likely to consider themselves genre or non–genre readers— this may reflect that reading preference/identi-fication is not firmly set at this age.

For readers under 40 however, for every science fiction book they read, they read approximately two fantasy books. This does not affect whether they identify as a genre reader. This ties in very neatly with the burgeoning fantasy publishing boom which began in 1977 with the publication of two books, Stephen Donaldson's *Lord Foul's Bane,* and with Terry Brooks' *Sword of Shannara.* A side boomlet in sf/fantasy crossover started with Julian May's *The Golden Torc.* This also helps explain the popularity of Anne McCaffrey among the younger cohorts: an author who is technically writing sf but can "masquerade" as fantasy.

What Else Were They Reading?

Questions about how much the respondents read outside the genre caused some puzzlement among readers, who didn't understand what the question was asking. The uncertainty was over the survey's expectation of genre. "Do you mean science fiction, or all genres?" asked one reader. In all other questions using the word genre, though, readers seemed to exhibit no difficulty understanding the question to mean sf (as in the next question, for example).

As children, the majority of respondents were reading something other than sf, with around 50 percent reading more than 50 percent outside the genre. 42 per-cent of respondents were reading between 40 percent and 80 percent of their read-ing outside of genre. These percentages were not significantly different for cohort or gender.

To our surprise, the non-fiction component was small, with 54 percent read-ing less than 20 percent non-fiction. Only 4 percent were reading more than 50 per-cent non-fiction. Non-fiction reading was clustered into three main areas: biography, history and science, all of which were read more frequently than school texts, according to respondents. However the range of non-fiction that was read cov-ered a huge range, from dollmaking to aeronautics, and from erotica to the occult, confirming the frequently expressed awareness of eclecticism in the sf community. Women were significantly more likely to read mythology than men. Men were significantly more likely to read astronomy than women. Most other subject areas didn't show significant differences, or the sample sizes were too small to draw con-clusions.

Uncategorized

Some readers considered themselves indiscriminate in their reading — that they valued nothing specifically. These readers, rather than having 5 responses in each reader age, then responded only once (unless and until they moved into a reader age at which they started to discriminate and value aspects of the text). There were 42 responses in all, representing a maximum of 27 readers, which fit this category — the majority (65 percent) recorded within the under–13 reader age group, and only one reader considering themselves indiscriminate all the way to adulthood.

Reading Children's SF

Although there's a majority of respondents who read sf for children (69 per-cent) it is by no means universal. Given the overall young age at which respondents started reading sf, it is somewhat surprising that the percentage is not higher. Availability of science fiction seemed to be a factor in the response, however, given that only a small proportion of respondents stated that they didn't remember reading any children's sf (1 percent), a certain degree of nostalgia and conflation of adult reading with child-aged reading may be occurring. The difference between boys and girls was small and not statistically significant; 66 percent of girls read children's sf versus 71 percent of boys.

Men 48–58 at the time of the survey (born between 1957 and 1967) were slightly more likely, on average, to have read children's sf. Men under 25 and both men and women age 68–83 were less likely, on average, to have read children's books. In the case of the latter group, only 25 percent of men read children's books, perhaps because of the low availability in that era. For all other groups, however, the low variability of results suggests that reading children's books is not correlated to their overall abundance or availability in the market.

Breadth of Reading

The number of respondents who say they didn't read children's books and the number of people who liked no children's sf authors is equivalent, at 31 percent of respondents overall. Only five respondents who said they read sf for children couldn't remember any authors. Of those who read children's sf, people remembered few authors. Some stated that they had Googled or otherwise searched for names to try and recall. Others relied solely on memory. Even so, 144 authors were named in total — although 100 were only named once.

Author Preferences

Respondents showed a clear preference for a subset of five authors: Robert Heinlein, Madeleine L'Engle, Andre Norton, Isaac Asimov and John Christopher. These five authors were named by over 15 percent of respondents, and there is a clear division between them and the lower tier of writers who are named by under 10 percent of respondents. Heinlein is particularly popular, and is named by 44 percent of respondents. The distinguishing factor of these authors is that they were available to read by all cohorts (except perhaps the eldest) and were read by all cohorts. The age of the books is no barrier to their enjoyment by current readers. See below for breakdown of these five authors by cohort readership.

Figure 5. Top SF Authors Writing for Children and Teens by Percentage of Mentions Per Cohort

Cohort	7	6	5	4	3	2	1
Heinlein, Robert	11%	12%	33%	62%	83%	58%	100%
L'Engle, Madeleine	29%	35%	30%	32%	24%	5%	0%
Norton, Andre	2%	4%	15%	36%	57%	16%	0%
Asimov, Isaac	16%	14%	10%	21%	30%	11%	0%
Christopher, John	14%	10%	24%	22%	2%	0%	0%

It is interesting to note that Heinlein and Norton's popularity is currently on the wane (after astonishing popularity among older cohorts), while Madeleine L'Engle has retained popularity across cohorts. No other author, even of those whose popularity is lesser than these top tier authors, is liked consistently across cohorts in the way in which L'Engle is. Having said that, however, it is clear that L'Engle's enduring influence is predominantly a result of her popularity with female readers. With the exception of the oldest two cohorts, close to 50 percent of female readers read and liked L'Engle in each cohort. It is worth noting that L'Engle and Christopher, of these five most popular authors, are the only two who were not in the top ten authors of adult sf enjoyed by the respondents (see next section).

Taken by gender, the only author in the top five to attract more female readers than male was Madeline L'Engle, an author who (like Eleanor Cameron) is considered borderline fantasy in this study. Among the next five (in order: Eleanor Cameron, Nicholas Fisk, Arthur C. Clarke, Diana Wynne Jones, William Sleator), only Jones and Sleator were similarly cited more often by women. Sleator is the only author writing mathematical science fiction for children and teens, so it is interesting that it is women who remember his work, in a culture where women are considered math-averse.

There was also a clear gender split. Men remembered Heinlein, Asimov, Clarke, Jay Williams, Alan Nourse and Terrance Dicks (best known for his *Doctor Who* scripts and novelizations). Women remembered Madeleine L'Engle, Diana Wynne Jones, William Sleator, Monica Hughes and Bruce Coville. Two things stand out: women seem to be more fluid around the science fiction/fantasy divide (Cameron and Jones), and seem to remember more books marketed specifically for children or teens (Sleator, Hughes and Coville) which may reflect teachers' observation that it is girls who select the fiction from the school library shelves and indeed may make up the majority of school library users. Boys' reading may well be invisible if what they are reading is peer swapped paper-backs— which given that peer-to-peer music networks seem (there are no studies that I know of) to be predominantly male, seems quite likely, and this is supported by the low influence of teachers and librarians reported in the earlier section of the survey.

Other Well-Liked Authors

All authors who were liked by more than 1 percent of the respondents who read children's sf are listed below. There's a slight trend toward older writers because they have the potential to appear in more cohorts as a choice.

Figure 6. Other SF Authors Writing for Children and Teens by Percentage of Mentions

Cameron, Eleanor	8%	Nourse, Alan E.	3%	Coville, Bruce	2%
Fisk, Nicholas	6%	Dicks, Terrance	3%	Duane, Diane	2%
Clarke, Arthur C.	5%	Hughes, Monica	3%	Hoover, H. M.	2%
Wynne-Jones, Diana	5%	O'Brien, Robert C.	3%	X-men/Stan Lee	2%
Sleator, William	4%	Johns, W.E.	3%	Dickinson, Peter	2%
Williams, Jay	4%	Walters, Hugh	2%	Engdahl, Sylvia	2%
Del Ray, Lester	3%	Pinkwater, Daniel	2%	Todd, Ruthven	2%
		Key, Alexander	2%		

What Readers Look For

I'm going to present these results by category, rather than any other schema, then draw out any results which are not obvious by category grouping

General Comments: Qualities of narrative are the most highly valued category overall, but note that readers claim to have looked for setting, tropes, mode of engagement and qualities of narrative when aged 13 or under. This suggests that they were actively seeking genre in terms of the props of genre (tropes and setting) and actively determining what kind of reaction they wanted to the story (modes of engagement). Readers report that they no longer look for tropes as adult readers. It is likely that readers reduce their reliance on tropes as an indicator of genre as they continue to read within genre. Politics/ethics/worldview become more important to readers as they age. Setting is consistently valued, regardless of reader age groups and cohorts; information density is similarly consistent, but at a much lower percentage.

The transitional period of the teen years from 13 up shows distinct features, most predominantly a focus on sex and personal identity. Overall, however, the impression is of a reader who begins reading sf at a young age, proceeds to map out their understanding of the genre through tropes and setting, engaging with books in genre-specific ways, then transitions from tropes to more subtle genre signifiers, and completes that process before adulthood — some of this transition is sadly masked because this is not a longitudinal study, but the remembered difference at age 13–19 suggests that, at minimum, science fiction readers see themselves as being fully equipped with genre reading protocols before adulthood.

Patterns of Response

Survey respondents frequently included things they looked for at age 13 in the list of things they looked for over 13 and now. Because of this, the three age groups cannot be considered independently of each other — they must be considered within the context of a reader trying to remember what they would have looked for. For that reason, it is likely to be skewed toward factors that they look for now.

Ways of Looking at the Data

Unfortunately, what we cannot do is assess what proportion each reader allocates to each category — we don't know how many readers chose all five "looked for" items from a single category. This information would allow us to break the respondents down into "types" or "groups" about which we could make more specialized commentary — akin to marketing categories. Instead, the information can be broken down by:

- What categories were chosen
  - How the chosen categories vary by age
  - How the chosen categories vary by cohort
  - How the chosen categories vary by sex
- What items were valued within each category
  - How the chosen items vary by age
  - How the chosen items vary by cohort
  - How the chosen items vary by sex

We can talk about each of these with regard to the proportion of the whole (how many responses out of the grand total of 10,000 "looked for" items) they represent, and for age groupings, we can talk about the number of people, in total, who selected a single category or item but cannot make firm statements more precisely than that. We are being conservative in our comments, but some data is interesting, regardless.

Categories

Character (Type)

The character (type) category covers respondents' statements about characters and protagonists, explaining what they desire the protagonist or character to be, rather than the reader's relationship with the character.

The key items within the characterization category are characterization, believable characters and character development, which between them account for 86 percent of the responses in this category. Figure 7 shows what proportion of readers interested in a specific aspect of characterization fit into each age group. Interest in these aspects of characterization rises proportionally with the interest in characterization overall, which is to be expected given the focus on them. Readers look for characterization more than five times more frequently at their present reader age than they did when their reader age was 13 or under.

In all, 60–70 percent of responses to this category were recorded for present reader age, 30 percent for reader age 13+, and 13 percent for reader age under 13.

Figure 7. Interest in Category, "Character"

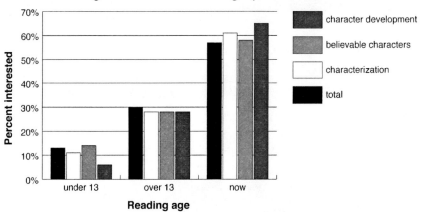

One aspect we wanted to consider was whether the relative importance of the key aspects of characterization held constant across all age groups — i.e., what percentage of those rating character as important rated characterization the single most important element at age 13, compared to age 13+.

The three pie charts show the relative importance — what proportion of readers found an aspect important out of all readers finding character important at that age. So, we can see that inventors and scientists as characters only really make an appearance for those under 13, whereas 13+ readers are interested in characters coming of age, and in a lone character against the world — fitting for adolescent preoccupations and with an overall interest in identifying with characters. In both cases, the numbers are too small to draw conclusions, but they make interesting

Figure 8. Under 13 Interest in "Character"

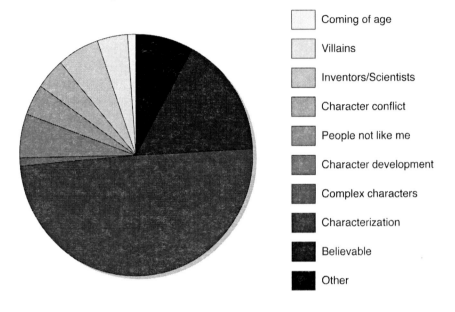

Figure 9. 13+ Interest in "Character"

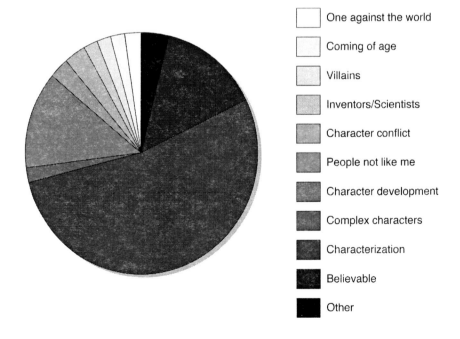

Figure 10. Current Interest in "Character"

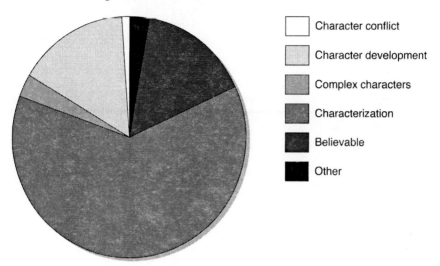

- Character conflict
- Character development
- Complex characters
- Characterization
- Believable
- Other

data points — as does the fact that all the readers seeking villains or inventors/scientists are female, whereas all those looking for "one character against the world" were male. Believability remains constant — readers of all ages want believable characters in about equal amounts. Characterization, character development and complex characters all increase in desirability — sophistication of readers correlates to sophistication in characters.

Not surprisingly, given their overall importance, aspects of character category were high for all respondents. As a data point 25 percent of respondents report characterization an element they look for at present reader age (214 out of 850 responses to this question). The proportion is lower for younger reader age (6 percent at age <13, 12 percent for 13+).

Women are much more likely to look for specific elements in the protagonist of a story, notably looking for female protagonists, and for young protagonists, when they are at younger reader ages.

Genre Expectations

This project as a whole is grounded in paradigms of reader response theory. The genre expectation category groups together those responses which are clearly about expectations of the genre. Work done with very young children suggests they build genre expectations in terms of narrative structure very early, while adherence to specific genres seems to emerge later.

As a category, genre expectations comprises 9 percent of all survey responses. Unlike character, the choices made by respondents within genre expectations are varied and wide-ranging (full list of items is in appendix). The top five chosen items (originality, imagination, weirdness/strangeness, complexity and challenging) constitute 60 percent of the total responses in the category. Unlike character, where the category preference increases overall with reader age, genre stays more-or-less at the same level regardless of reader age. 20 percent of responses were in the under–13 age group, whereas 45 percent of responses were in the present reader age. Additionally, the proportion of all respondents choosing items within the genre expectations category remains steady at 8–10 percent.

Items selected within the genre expectations category change over time. As an example, items that reflect an understanding of genre and long-term readership within the genre ("awareness of genre"; "old trope, new take") are much more highly selected in the present reader age than for under–13s. This is not surprising — unlike character, where desire for character elements is not dependant on other elements of the text, many of the items within the genre expectation category have dependencies. Elements such as "originality" speak to the desire for newness, but the under–13 version "the unfamiliar" becomes the more sophisticated and genre-aware "originality" for older readers.

Fig. 11 shows the balance of how readers value genre expectation at different ages. All proportions add up to 100 percent — this shows at what age each of the top six elements is valued most, and how it compares to the category as a whole.

Weirdness/strangeness and imagination are valued by younger readers; complexity and originality by older readers. Adolescent readers value challenging works.

Figure 11. Preferences in Genre Category by Age

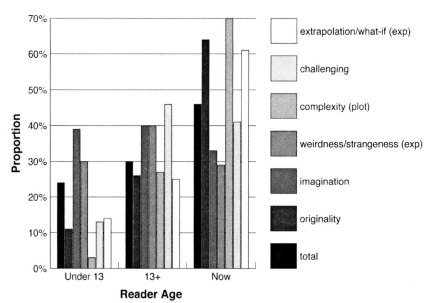

Apart from the six outlined in the figure, several other items appear predominantly in a single reader age group, though at lower levels:

Under 13: Wish fulfillment, unfamiliarity, horror themes, fantasy elements;

media tie-ins; 13+: Fight for justice, dark themes; Now: Extrapolation/what-if; alle-gory; awareness of genre; complex character interactions with the world; old trope/new take; theme.

Even though 47 percent of respondents selected a genre expectation item among their five responses for the reader age group now, the responses are so dif-fuse that originality, the single most popular item, is only selected by 11 percent of respondents.

Information Density

This is the desire for a text to contain lots of factual information, delivered in such a way that the reader leaves feeling informed about an area of knowledge or practice, as well as the story. The desire for this particular quality is shared by read-ers of crime fiction and historical fiction.

Although information density is a small category, it is cited at low levels by all age groups, and by both sexes, although teen readers do not value it as much as under–13s or adult readers. More importantly, there are clear patterns, even in such a small sample. Younger readers value knowledge, learning and facts, almost exclu-sively, and adult readers want "not too much tech talk" and works that are "not preachy" and contain "no boring info-dumps"— the implication is not that they don't want tech talk as adults, but that they are more picky about how it is deliv-ered to them. Women want "not too much tech talk" as adults, while adult men seem not to value information density. The young men/older women divide would be worth exploring in more detail.

Mode of Engagement

Although science fiction is commonly described as a fiction of the rational, it can also be understood, like horror, as a form of "affect" fiction. When people describe why they enjoy sf, they frequently refer to an emotional response. The most common phrase used in the field is "sense of wonder." This category collects together the different terminology the respondents have used to describe affect.

In all, modes of engagement accounts for 8 percent of responses, equally split between men and women. There's a slight trend towards older cohorts valuing modes of engagement more than younger cohorts, and for younger reader age to correlate with valuing modes of engagement. These trends are not significant.

Four main subcategories account for 80 percent of responses within the cat-egory: sense of wonder (33 percent), escapism/immersion (24 percent), excitement (11 percent) and intellectual engagement (10 percent). While sense of wonder is, not unexpectedly, equally appealing to all reader ages— as a genre staple and descrip-tor, it is only fitting — escapism and excitement are not as valuable to older reader ages, while intellectual engagement correlated with increasing reader age.

Women are more likely to use emotional descriptors of engagement — angst, emotional involvement, emotional engagement — and were significantly less likely to value sense of wonder (20 percent) compared to men (40 percent); they valued intellectual engagement (16 percent) significantly more than men (5 percent).

Younger cohorts appear to value modes of engagement less as a category than older cohorts, thought this effect is minor: for example, only 1 percent of cohorts 6 and 7 consider "sense of wonder" of value, even though this is the most important mode of engagement for them along with intellectual engagement; this compares to around 5 percent for cohorts 1, 2 and 3. While the difference is not significant, it is worth exploring further; there are other aspects to this, but that's probably the key way of differentiating it.

Qualities of Narrative

These are the structural elements of the narrative. This is the single largest category under which responses can be grouped, comprising 21 percent of all responses. Even with some 30 subcategories, only six categories really dominate — ideas, story, plot, adventure, humor and action. These correlate with age and with gender, and while there are cohort differences, there are no clear cohort-based trends.

Unsurprisingly, younger reader age corresponds to valuing adventure, story and action — a holy triumvirate of children's stories in general, not just genre-based stories. Looking at the reverse — at subcategories whose value increases with reader age — plot, humor and ideas emerge.

While the differences in cohort are generally not significant, cohort 7 were more likely to value humor than average, cohort 4 was more likely to value action, cohort 3 more likely to value adventure, cohort 2 much more likely to value plot. Given the overall value of qualities of narrative, this suggests that books read during the formative years may have been strong on the elements which score significantly above the baseline. For readers under 25, for example, Pratchett is widely available and is frequently understood to straddle young adult and adult fiction, which may help to explain that cohort's preference; cohorts 2 and 3 on the other hand, may show the transition of available books from puzzle-based Campbellian stories to Heinlein's adventures for children. Cohort 4 sees the emergence of *Star Trek*, which may correlate with the preference for action. Knowing which books were considered influential by these respective cohorts (aside from in the areas of politics and religion discussed in this survey) would shed further light on how preferences for particular qualities of narrative are acquired and sustained over a reader's lifetime.

In terms of gender differences, men value story, action and adventure over ideas and plot, while for women this is reversed. Three of these — story, action and adventure — are significant, which together with the Information density and genre expectations results offer suggestions about how women and men view genre stories. The results leave it unclear as to how influence the reader age results have on this difference.

Politics/Ethics/Worldview

One way of understanding sf is as an ongoing discussion of the relationship between humanity and the Great Out There. In Heinlein's short story "— We Also Walk Dogs" the pronouncement is made that the business of man is man. This is reflected in the way the proportion of respondents interested in politics, ethics and worldview matches the proportion who say they are interested in characterization.

What we may be seeing here is not a differing view but a fleshing out of what is meant by characterization. You can see this when you break down the issues of politics, ethics and worldview into the subcomponent categories which include such labels as alternate societies, impact of technology on society, insight into humanity, alternate sexuality, power politics, problem-solving, perspective social dissonance. Two things stand out when considering the language respondents have used. We can interpret this grouping as describing a direction of interest. It essentially looks outward towards change on the large scale, even if the actual plots of the text frequently appear adhere to Churchill's dictum that we understand macrocosmic change in terms of the way it affects the "I."

Overall, 10 percent of survey responses fell within the politics/ethics/worldview category. No sub-category appears to be predominantly identified by younger cohorts—instead, the spread of sub-categories selected by younger cohorts suggest that political refinement occurs at a younger age than it once did. In retrospect, the subcategories are so diffuse that it would be worth attempting a re-categorization, breaking down the themes into those of :

1. Extrapolation (wanting to see where current society could lead)
2. Alternatives and difference (wanting to see alternate societal structures)
3. Insight (wanting to gain self-awareness by reading/observing)
4. Knowledge and learning (wanting to gain understanding of society by reading/observing)

It appears that there may be patterns along these lines; it would be interesting to see whether this may form more cohesive super-grouping, and is a fruitful area for further analysis.

The youngest cohort values philosophy more than average. Older cohorts (cohorts 1, 2, 3) are much more likely to value optimism than younger cohorts. Beyond this, there are no clear subcategories that are preferred by cohorts. Readers under 13 want problem solving and good versus evil battles; simplified ways of understanding and interpreting morality. Women value alternate societies more than men (see above regarding story, genre expectation), but men have no clear standout subcategories they value in this category.

Genre readers, by a slight majority in either case, felt that reading influenced their political views, but not their religious views. In neither case was the difference significant.

Relationship to Characters

This category does not describe the nature of the character, but what the reader desires in their relationship to the characters in the text. For example: the thorny issue of whether they will identify with the character or not.

Many more women than men value this category — double the percentage of men that value it. When combined with a slight trend for women to value character and protagonist type more than men, we see a clear value of characterization and character relationships for women. This strong difference means that active/strong female characters are the most valued aspect of character relationships, even though less than 1 percent of male respondents who stated that they valued relationships to characters valued that particular subcategory. Men seek out sympathetic heroes and role models (17 percent, 21 percent and 14 percent respectively); women seek out active female characters, likeable and sympathetic characters (26 percent, 15 percent and 10 percent respectively).

Apart from the broad sex-based differences, other differences are evident. Adult readers prefer sympathetic and likeable characters, teen readers seek romance and to identify with characters, under–13s want heroes and role-models. Interestingly, younger cohorts do not show such strong gender divisions, and seem to be seeking likeable and sympathetic characters, without as much reference to their sex/gender. The wider availability of female protagonists in recent years has probably reduced the active and expressed desire, but not disposed of it, it is not expressed because this cohort takes for granted that it will be satisfied.

Science

This category describes knowledge that is delivered. The generic term "hard science" is usually understood to refer to physics, less commonly chemistry, occasionally math. In the past ten years, computer science has entered hard sf, where it used to be soft science. Soft science is usually understood to be psychology and sociology and anthropology, and perhaps linguistics. Biology operates in a borderland category, where authors frequently feel they don't have to do the research.

Of the qualities readers looked for, science comprised only 5 percent — this is lower than might be expected for a science fiction audience. But science is clearly looked for, and instead is sublimated as the reader matures—for example, 45 percent of responses for reader age under 13 selected "Science" as a subcategory of science. It was looked for as a trope and as an identifiable component of the book. But as reader age increases, "science" is not stated as a quality they look for; it is assumed, and expected, to be contained in their books. The science category results illustrate this refinement, as readers seek "plausible science," "hard science" and "extrapolation."

In addition to refinement of science expectations, younger readers want to be introduced to their science in a palatable form; "understandable science" is second to "science" as a desirable characteristic. But while the under–13's who come to books as naïve scientific observers want to learn more, women also want "understandable science"— when we examine their desire to not have "too much tech talk" (see ID category) they seem to prefer that science be integral to the book but not a character in its own right. The science must be there, though — sci-tech extrapolation is valued third only to "plausible" and "understandable" science. Factoring these together, we get an overall picture of women having high demands of the science within their science fiction.

Men, in contrast, look for plausibility, science and extrapolation primarily — understandable science is not valued. We could theorize that men have a higher level of science understanding, but I suspect that is not the real reason. Finally, it is worthy of note that cohort 6 wanted less "science" (and no hard sf) and desired clarity in their science significantly more than any other cohort — was there a science teaching issue for this group? This is one of the age groups for which science educators have expressed considerable concern.

Setting and World

This category divides itself into three broad areas: the first, which descends from lost race/lost world fiction, is simply the pleasure in exploring a strange place. The second is taking pleasure in the concept of place itself. One element of sf that is rarely mentioned, is that it is in many ways a romance of landscape. The third and related element, is the issue of believability and plausibility. The notion of exploration supports the interest in societies not like ours, and boundless possibilities. It links to, but is not fundamental to the issues of scale.

The romance of landscape is tied fundamentally to issues of scale. Science Fiction has been fascinated by the vast and the microcosmic. Noticeable in sf is the lavish prose describing both the emptiness of space and the contents of the gutter. Both space opera and cyberpunk are grounded in this kind of landscape romance. A useful paradigmatic phrase to collect these would be the notion of intensity of gaze, both of author and reader. This links us to the notion of plausibility. This is one of the hardest concepts for non-sf and fantasy readers to grasp. Outside the genre, there is an assumption that the reader must suspend disbelief to enter the fantastic text. Science fiction readers instead test the worlds they read against their disbelief. What this means in practice is that the world must be internally consistent, and that it must adhere to the known rules of physics, chemistry, biology and human nature, unless the author can plausibly explain why it should not (see Jo Walton's *Tooth and Claw*).

Of course, many texts fail this test; sf fans do not hesitate to let the authors know this. In the survey respondents value setting and world highly; it represents 12 percent of all responses, and is equally valued by both men and women, and by all ages of readers. Readers primarily look for exotic locations/strange worlds, depth of worldbuilding, believability of setting and internal consistency. In other words, readers want a rich setting which is immersive and is somewhere other than the earth we know. The importance of an "exotic location," per se, decreases with age, but as the reader demands more from their reading, it becomes refined instead. Much like the science category, this is an area where we see an expectation that there will be an alternative world or setting presented and so the reader demands become more sophisticated, looking for depth, believability and internal consistency.

Not surprisingly, in younger readers, the desire for an exotic location is coupled with a desire for exploring that world — rather than being immersed in it and learning about it from character cues or subtle elements, they want exploration and discovery — overtly learning about the difference between these worlds and settings compared to our own. Older cohorts value both exotic locations and believability more than younger cohorts— this may tie in with clear science-fictional themes, as per Campbell's vision of the sf field. Note also that, as with the science category, cohort 6 has a distinct profile. In this case, they want "possibility"— a future vision — significantly more than other cohorts. This gives cohort 6, overall, almost a "dreamer" profile.

Tropes and Icons

The most visible way to recognize an sf text has traditionally been through certain icons and tropes, most if not all unique to the genre. Many of these are concrete articles — spaceships, robots, bug-eyed aliens are the classic three. However, the irony of these icons and tropes is that they are often misleading. Sf fans frequently argue about whether a book is sf: it is perfectly possible to write a text which contains these elements, but in all other ways fails to satisfy the demands of genre fiction. Mad robots, scary monsters, etc., frequently turn up in horror.

It is a testament to the sheer number of recognizable tropes in sf that there are 50 subcategories within Tropes and Icons. Some of these, most highly valued, are instant indicators of science fiction — aliens, cool gadgets and space travel. Other tropes are key, but in a different way — sex is valued highly as a trope, but notably it correlates strongly with the teen reader age.

Under-13s value space travel, spaceships and aliens, adult readers value aliens and cool gadgets, but there are less than a quarter of the responses within the tropes and icons category for adults compared to younger readers. The outward decoration of the genre is essential for young readers to identify with, but as reading becomes more refined, these — again — are either assumed, or looked for in more subtle forms.

Because of the strong response for young reader age, compared to adult, this category gives us insight into what each cohort felt sf represented for them, as children.

Cohort 1 values professors, robots and cool gadgets — Campbellian scientifiction at work? Cohorts 1, 2, 3 and 4 value space travel significantly more than the younger cohorts, understandable given the space race during those cohorts' youth and teens.

The only identifiable male/female difference is that women prefer aliens, and men prefer gadgets. This would seem to be a clear and definable split between characterization and objects, but I'm not sure it is that straightforward, given other categories. Women have appeared to value difference and objective perspectives, and aliens offer that more than gadgets do, for example.

Writing

This category is about the way the text is written, although it includes reference to the length of the text, however as one of the debates in sf has been sustainability of sf at length, and the relative merits of short dense books, this is included as an issue of style.

Writing is much more to the fore as a category by older readers, gaining 300 times the response level for adult reader age, compared to under-13 reader age. Readers primarily look for well-written works, in all ages and in all cohorts. This is one of the few categories where "well written" was the exact response given by the large majority of respondents, and is one of the overall highest responses given in the survey.

As with most categories, reader age correlates with higher sophistication — in this case, adult readers look for style, use of language and literary work in addition to well written prose. However, given the increase in responses with reader age, there's no decrease in the desire to see well-written prose as occurs in other categories where reader sophistication is a factor. Adult readers place less value on vivid description, not being talked down to, tension/suspense and plain language than younger reader ages.

Cohort 7 values use of language significantly more than other cohorts. Style is valued more as a correlation with cohort age — in other words, cohort 7 values style less than cohort 4, which values it less than cohort 1, etc. This may be an older reader dynamic, rather than a genre specific factor. Short length and clarity is valued significantly more by cohort 2 who would have entered the field when sf books were shorter and frequently serialized, and short stories dominated the form.

There were no significant differences between responses from men and women in this category.

The Golden Age of Science Fiction Is Three: Science Fiction Picture Books

In the original plan of the present work, picture books were to be thoroughly integrated into the whole. In the end, the paucity of picture books in the field meant that they were crowded out. Furthermore, I increasingly felt that I was doing the books a disservice in not considering them as visual as well as literary texts.

In this appendix I want to tackle a selection of the picture books I have collected, taking them on their own terms and considering them as science-fictional artifacts: considering the ways in which each of these authors/artists envisaged sf for children in terms of theme, ideas, and illustrations, what they thought children were capable of in many different ways (taking into account the ideas discussed elsewhere about complexity and the very young child), and picking up on the ideas about socialisation of the child explored in chapter five. This appendix could have been considered within the Best Practice chapter that concludes the book, but I want to bring picture books to the front of the discussion.

There are certain commonalities between the thirty or so books I have collected over the past three years. With the exception of Babette Cole's books, there is an assumption that an sf book for children should be painted in bold and daring colors. Generally, illustration is cartoonish, clear and bold with the worlds of the stories rather two-dimensional, there is rarely much "depth" or density in the sense of a fully realised future in the world-pictures of the tales. Only *Captain Raptor* (2005), *The Worst Band in the Universe* (1999) and *Henry's Quest* (1986) opt for both more subdued tones and complex, information-dense worlds. What the texts do have in common however, is their frequent attention to intra-iconic material; that is, additional material for children to spot in the corner of pages or behind the protagonist; this is not unique, but I would suggest that the technique of ironization of the related tale through the use of intra-iconic (and meta-textual) material is particularly useful to sf picture books.

An obvious approach to these books is to start by considering their subject matter in a rough sub-genre/thematic categorisation, although the implications of categorisation is something for which I offered caveats in chapter six. The books on my pile divide fairly quickly into robots; space adventure; rocket journeys (not quite the same thing); and aliens, with a few stray books that don't fit comfortably with any others. There is only one time-travel book on the pile, Michael Foreman's *Dinosaur Time* (2002) and I'll look at this when I discuss dinosaur books. Of the dinosaur books, one, *Captain Raptor*, will also appear in the discussion of space adventure.

Robots

What does a robot look like, and what is a robot for? These are the two questions which haunt this short selection. Robots in children's picture books *look* like robots: they look like machines, frequently they look home-made, and often they are homemade. This home-madeness is intriguing because it suggests a relationship between child and machine mostly absent from books for older readers. In Ian Whybrow and Adrian Renolds, *Harry and the Robots* (2002), Babette Cole's *The Trouble with Dad* (1985) and Dan Yaccarino's *If I Had a Robot* (1999) there is an artisan aesthetic which renders the robot — elsewhere in science fiction a signal of alienness — an intimate object.

Babette Cole's *The Trouble with...* books are mostly interested in ways for parents to embarrass their offspring so mother is a witch, grandma is an alien, and father makes robots in his backyard. In terms of plot and purpose and the structures for which I argued in chapter one, they aren't very good science fiction: their tropes are facilitating devices for screwball comedy, rather than a move into any form of "what if" or consequence. However, Babette Cole's portrayal of father in the back yard tinkering with his robots is intriguing. The robots are clearly made objects, an extension of a kind of competence that is at variance with dad's day job/day persona. They are, in their affect, a signal that he is still childlike,[1] but they are also a valorisation of the process of *making* rather than having made, since the completed objects are inherently useless. This valorisation of process is at odds with much popular thought about education and learning. There is nothing *relevant* about Dad's activities, neither are they useful to his family. Babette Cole is celebrating play, and the role of hobbies: outcome is coincidental, not intended, and there is in Dad's preparation for an impossible future a link to Heinlein's Kip who prepares a space suit with no hope of finding a use for it (*Have Space Suit — Will Travel*, 1958). *The Trouble with Dad* gently underlines the value of "messing about" in the process of growing.

Cole's style is sweetly shambolic; both in this series and elsewhere her ink pen sketches imply people who maybe got up a little too fast this morning, who are too concerned with other things in life to stop to primp or polish. In *The Trouble with Dad* this messiness is extended to the figuration of the robots, with their presence as an eyesore in the backyard. Cole's robots are moving models, unlike "inventions" they have no real purpose other than to extend the family. This sense of family extension is reinforced by the narrative chronotope of Cole's artistry which moves along a shallow plane, like a frieze from left to right. Frequently, the robots follow father like so many ducklings with their mother. This image is important because it enhances the sense that the robots are dependencies, rather than extensions of the operator, and as a metaphor they suggest that the robots also function as favoured siblings of the protagonists. The conclusion to the book, in which the robots are sold on, is every child's dream of disposing of the irritating new baby.

Dan Yaccarino's robot is an extension of the protagonist. *If I Had a Robot* envisages the robot as waldo and toy.[2] It is remote-controlled, and it does for the boy what he does not wish to do, keeping him at arm's length from such dangerous and disgusting activities as eating vegetables and taking a bath. It has no volition, not even the status of an imaginary friend and where Cole's robots were made objects, this one is *fancy* (an older term than fantasy which implies an imaginative structure without the internal coherence and rules of modern fantasy) and the relationship between protagonist and robot is user and used. Some of this comes over in the pictures: in the first picture, when the little boy first conceives of a robot "at my command," the boy stands on the left and the robot on the right. The robot is blocky, even more "robot like" than Cole's robots (almost the classic robot of cardboard boxes). It is completely passive while the boy is depicted reaching out with his remote control box. On the next page, while the robot is clearly moving, shovelling sprouts into its maw, it is the boy, smaller, framed in the crook of the robot's arm, who draws the eye. The picture is structured with depth (although the representational forms are very flat), and the lines of the page are diagonal, so that while the robot is central the eye moves from the left-hand corner (where the writing is), across the domineering red blankness of the robot to the right-hand corner and the boy's face.

On the next page the boy is absent in body, but present in voice, and again the eye moves from the robot in the bath on the left to the boy's voice dominating the right-hand corner. The page's yellow bath, orange background and red robot are not "exuberant" as the flyleaf suggests but oddly muted, a backwash for the statement of authority and control; "I could get him to take my bath." Similarly in the next picture there is a frame made up of a dark piano (left foreground) being played by a dark blue robot (right mid-ground) and centered in the middle is the boy sitting on a bright red chair. Even on the following page, where the robot appears in all four quarters writing homework, tidying up, clearing snow and picking litter, it is the boy's statement, "Boy! He could do everything I don't want to do!" which runs as a banner across the page, disrupting the left to right movement of the page with a fierce claim for visual attention.

Page by page, there is an interesting distance created between the boy and his imaginary robot which denies any relationship between the two, but instead constructs an "alienation of labour." The robot is neither a tool for extending the child's scope — we do not see the protagonist do anything with all this time freed up — nor is it used in any creative way. When the boy chooses to eat his own vegetables rather than miss out on chocolate cake, the point is underscored that this robot is a route to passivity rather than adventure. The robot figures as a wall between the boy and the world in every picture. One understanding suggested by Ben Little (personal communication) is that the robot becomes a displaced view of the self. The boy becomes robot in fantasy and is not himself when he does the distasteful (eating brussells sprouts), a way of both doing and not doing that is more acceptable to him.

Ian Whybrow's and Adrian Reynolds' *Harry and the Robots* is a much simpler book both in words and pictures. Both Babette Cole and Dan Yaccarino are far superior artists and more inventive storytellers, yet *Harry and the Robots* with its clichéd "story-book" illustrations succeeds in an intimacy of creativity and imagination that neither of the others manage. When Harry's toy robot breaks he decides to build his own. His Nan gets out her sewing kit and provides him with parts, but before they can get started she falls sick and is taken to hospital. While Nan is in hospital Harry makes his robot:

... until there was a new robot. A special one.

Harry taught it marching. He taught it talking, But most of all he taught it blasting.

The robot said,

"Ha — Lo Har — Ree.

Have — got — a —cough?

BLAAST!"

When Harry goes to the hospital he takes his robot which does its stuff by blasting Harry's Nan, and then when he goes home "Harry made five more special robots to look after Nan. The robots guarded Nan. They marched for her. They blasted her cough. And soon she was better."

All of the above is told with simple, representational pictures. Most of the time Harry is at the front of the frame. When he is not, he is the central point in the perspective structure sitting almost always at the vanishing point, so that when sitting with his sister, the vanishing point is off to the left, beyond his sister's shoulder and more or less where her elbow meets his t-shirt.

Harry understands his robots as "real," much in the way Calvin understands his tiger, Hobbes. *Harry and the Robots* is an exemplar for Nikolajeva and Scott's discussion of the way in which words and images can interact to leave room for reader creativity (2006, 2).

Nan at least is part of the imaginative conspiracy, and the reader is also encouraged to take it on board: the robots are showing in positions which imply movement, walking on pipe-cleaner legs across the bedside table, running from a chicken on the last page. Harry's robots, simpler, more toy like than Cole's dad's, are yet more vibrant and more real. Harry as an inventor is more real because he has a purpose in mind, which is a long way round to tell you that Harry is an actor in his world where the protagonists of *If I Had a Robot* and *The Trouble with Dad* are, in the end, simply acted upon.

I want to end this section and move into the next with a consideration of David Kirk's *Nova's Ark*. I have been rather hard on this book in papers given over the past few years because its cheery anthropomorphism, common to children's books, gives a high gloss sheen to 1950s–style gender roles in which dad and son explore the galaxy while mom prepares breakfast — although it may be unfair to finger Kirk here, because 1950s gender roles are very much the norm in children's sf.[3] However, it does make a neat link between three themes, robots, aliens and space adventure, for these are not really robots, despite their blockish metal appearance, their consumption of oil and the desperate search for a power supply. Kirk's robots clearly breed, so that they are actually a silicon- and metal-based life form. Yet, while the pictures are crowded with life, they are locked into contemporary urban America rather than sf visions. However, the very anthropomorphism I dislike is used to create Nova as a character who reads technical books in his spare time and builds his own dog. Nova is a competent hero who, when stranded on a planet, creates robots to emulate the wooden animals in his Noah's ark at home, and is eventually able to rebuild his father (although it is baffling that Kirk talks about father needing a new valve — would any young parent know what one is any more?).

And so on to the space adventure: Nova goes out to look for his father and finds the planet of Zyte, made of the precious crystal that powers the robot planet of Roton. The discovery of the crystal is ecstatic, a moment of visual exuberance, but the exploration itself consists of a crash onto a dead planet, Nova's decision to build animal companions rather than to explore, and his father's decision to return home. The colour contrasts are dramatic: the planet Zyte is an intense but dull pink stone. Variation is introduced only in the built animals, and Kirk chooses to use this dullness, and later the emptiness of space, as a contrast to the life and warmth of home. There is a weird construction here of a young child who is inventive and creative but not curious, and the sense that what is most interesting is either the near past of the home planet or the far past of Roton/Earth. The pictures with their clear directions as to what the reader should find interesting consistently reinforce this. This is a space adventure with very little adventure.

Just to show that anthropomorphism can be both very silly and still give good space adventure, the next book on the list is *Captain Raptor and the Moon Mystery* (2006).

Captain Raptor, by Kevin O'Malley and illustrated by Patrick O'Brien is one of those books whose intent is to appease parents by sheer force of quality, because it is essentially a graphic novel for the young which plays on 1930s visual illustration tropes far more familiar to parents than to children. On the opening page, the title, *Captain Raptor* is written in 3-dimensional blocklettering, in obvious emulation of classic 1930s sci-fi movies serials, and sf pulps. The book is immediately positioned as a tale of derring do, part of the tradition of sensation fiction — which is where space opera properly belongs. On the next page O'Malley continues with the classic sci-fi serial structure: we open with a picture of a landscape structured in classic nineteenth century form with the mouth of the river at the front of the picture, a small lizard to front left whose snout points towards the "flash of light" that speeds towards "Eon, the planet's most mysterious moon" which hangs in the right-hand corner of the sky. The framing of both picture and words create the opening *meis en scène*. And then to the next classic technique of the sci-fi serial, introducing the characters in word and picture, racking up the tension:

> The scientists say that they must investigate [picture of a hadrosaur, a sauropod of some sort (probably an apatosaurus), and a stegosaurus]
> The generals say that they must *prepare for an invasion* [picture of t-rexes gathered around a table]
> The president of Jurassica says they must call ... [picture of triceratops head on]
> And over the page to "Captain Raptor!" A tyrannosaurus rex in profile, head to one side, holding a pennant.

The rest of the script is presented as if they were voice cards over a silent movie; "Master Sergeant Brickthorous checks his newest weapon, an ultranet webflinger." The pictures reinforce this sense as this frame is followed by three wordless images of the Master Sergeant checking his net and enwrapping poor Professor Angleoptorous.

Turning over, we move to the sublime, that quality of space opera so essential and yet so derided. The page is taken up by two panels, one, the smaller panel, overlaps the larger, detailing one element in the picture, the following is simply a drawing of the boxes to give an idea of how the overlap works.

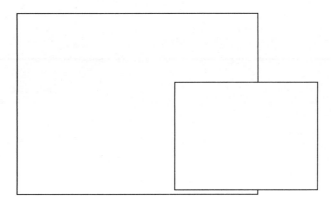

Inside the large one is a small aeroplane on the left against a silken orange sky shot by bolts of lightening. Inside the small box is a close up of the cockpit, "*KA-BOOM*" written across it in bold yellow lettering. "'*Captain, we've been hit!*' cries the professor."

[Sharp close-up]; "*Everyone to their stations and buckle up!*" Orders Captain Raptor. "I'm losing control of the forward engines. Reverse engines are off-line. Hold on tight folks—we're going in the hard way!"

[Zoom out to shot of plummeting rocket] *Could this be the end of Captain Raptor and his brave crew?* The adventure continues in the same style, with serial type mini-adventures ["Little does the fearless crew suspect the *horrifying surprise* that creeps through the inky depths toward the ship"] and close escapes, complete with witty parting lines ["next time, *keep your suckers to yourself*"] until Captain Raptor and his crew find the aliens whose space ship has caused the flash. Humans.

I'll stop there, but just to recapitulate the ways in which this book is a full party to the sf sub-genre it claims: *Captain Raptor* is a first-contact novel complete with stiff-jawed hero, slightly flaky scientist and not-too-clever master sergeant. It is a tale of derring-do, of vast space, and neat weapons. It has the pattern of tension and release which belongs to classic space opera, and ends with the classic sf space moral, that there are friends out there... "No need to hurry home, Threetoe. It is a big universe out there and I'm in the mood for *adventure*. Fire up the servorockets."

Captain Raptor is an aggressively boys' book. There are no female dinosaurs, and a close examination of the "aliens" reveals possibly one female human, seen from the back (I am guessing by the coiled bun that this is a woman). It is, however, rather more open to the opposite sex than is *Space Princess Cosima* (2005) a book which sees the galaxy as one large department store. Like *Captain Raptor* however the book's pictures (by Artful Doodlers) are essential to the text, and there is a sense of wonder, even if it is pink.

Princess Cosima is princess of Spaceland. For her birthday someone sends her a riddle with a puzzle to track through the planet pavilion. She and her friend

Princess Nebula hop on shooting stars, check out craters, and take the Eclipse express. They put on solar shades and catch a solar flare. They go visit the Nova nursery where the stars are born. Through all of this Princess Cosima (and the reader) are invited to add star stickers to the book, so that at the end, Princess Cosima has a heart made of stars hanging in the sky. For a reader allergic to girliness, this book seems a rejection of all things science-fictional. Yet despite all the sparkle, and all the anthropomorphism of the galaxy, this book does generate a sense of wonder at the magnificence of the cosmos and is actually very much part of the sf tradition. The story itself is surprisingly similar to the Italo Calvino stories in the *Out of This World* collections, "At Day Break" (v. 9) and "Games Without End" (v. 10). This kind of anthropomorphism has been with sf since the 1930s (see Joe W. Skidmore's "The Romance of Posi and Nega" in *Amazing Stories*, September 1932). As unlikely as it seems from the premise, this intensely *girly* book gives the reader a decent and informative spin around the galaxy. With *Surprise Sparkle Party*.

I have one more space adventure worth discussing: Susan Rennie's *Kat and Doug on Planet Fankle* (2002). Susan Rennie's *Kat and Doug* is written in Scots, a dialect of English, *not* an accent. It begins when Kat gets a "cyberdug" for her birthday: "It luiked faur muir interesting than any o the cyberdugs Kat had seen in the shops. Its tail wis waggin and Kat thocht she saw a wee door closing on the tap o its heid" (2).

The Cybyerdug, *Doug*, takes Kat outside and snuffling, he goes looking for worm holes in the rosebushes. When he finds one a leash whirrs out of his collar and "ye'd better haud ontae this" (p. 4) As they rush through the wormhole with Doug "I prefer astro*travaiger*" Doug hands Kate a pair of "fantoosh rollerskates" and when he gets to an intersection he unrolls a wormhole map: "The map showed hunners o planets in different galaxies, aw jined thegither by weird-luiken tunnels. It luiked tae Kat like a snakes-an-ladders board gane gyte (7)."

The book turns into an extension of *Time Bandits* (the film by Terry Giliam) and Kat's bedroom turns out to be a roundabout on the map. Doug takes Kat off to the planet Fankle, a world which in Scots means twisted or knotted. To help her fit in, Doug fankelisers her, so her hair is in knots and her shoe laces are knotted, and even one of Doug's antennae wrinkles up. After this, sadly, there is no real adventure, just the exploration of a topsy-turvey world and the return to earth — time not having passed — with a fankled fork, ideal for eating spaghetti. *Kat and Doug on Planet Fankle* is part of the lengthy tradition of strange adventures: there is a joyousness to the book, and a sense of a world out there where people do things differently.

Captain Raptor, Kat and Doug and *Nova's Ark* have much of the joyousness of sf, but there is not a great deal of the curiosity of sf evident. Given that picture books are traditionally about provoking curiosity this is odd, but the issue may be the trickiness of creating open rather than closed routes to discovery in the picture book narrative: this was a difficulty we saw in the science books for children as well, experiential learning is extraordinarily difficult to capture on the page without deliberately creating false endings to the questions. Mary Murphy and Mark Oliver's *Foley and Jem* (2004) achieve the sense of learning with a very simple tale. Foley is a small boy who loves his dog and is fascinated with space and Mars. As he grows older his interests become ever more focused on Mars until he neglects his dog Jem in order to build a rocket. Jem gets ever more miserable, and no more so than when Foley (who cannot understand Jem) puts Jem into the Mars-suit and sends him to Mars. Once there Jem sends pictures home but to Foley they are dull and he wonders why he bothered. But Jem, though he misses Foley, falls in love with Mars and when he finds dog-like aliens, he decides to stay. A bittersweet tale of adolescence and lost loves, *Foley and Jem* also captures Foley's fascination with space and rockets and mathematics, the pictures on his wall giving the child reader some idea of what real engineering is about. Similarly, Jem's exploration of Mars is handled as a scientific, not a fantastical experience, with soil samples and pictures. "Jem did everything properly, like a real dog should." Doggy curiosity comes to supplement and eventually supplant the human variety.

If *Captain Raptor* encapsulates the sense of wonder of space adventure, David A. Carter's pop-up, *Bugs in* Space (1997), manages to flatten it out: this I would suggest is actually one of the problems of pop-up books more generally. A little discussed aspect of them is that they are structured interruptions. One can rarely get any kind of dynamic going because each piece of prose is actually an entry, or a directive, demanding a pause for action. Pop-up books may be quite wonderful in terms of generating inquisitiveness, but they rarely support the narrative pace of story. *Bugs in Space* is a short story of Captain Bug Rogers' journey through space with his trusty robobug. It is a weird combination of sf and fantasy as Bug Rogers meets the bug in the moon, Unidentified Flying Bugs, the Wishing Bug and (the best picture) the bug engaged in a docking maneuvre with a space station. At the end they touch down. That's it. The interaction of the book is explorative, but the exploration is constrained, the pop-ups direct, rather than point outwards and open up the world. The book is fun, and it may be unfair to hold it to narrative conventions, but the book does claim narrative.

Both Frances Thomas and Ross Collins' *Maybe One Day* (2001) and also Tony Ross and Jeanne Willis, *Dr. Xargle's Book of Earthlets* (1988) are Socractical, provoking curiosity either by presenting children with the manifestly wrong (*Dr. Xargle*) or as in *Maybe One Day* engaging in the game parents play with children of challenging the knowledge children have acquired — and frequently, as with the ubiquitous dinosaur knowledge of the small child — teaching the parents something along the way. *Dr. Xargle* embeds much of the incongruity in its pictures, and again, as I have discussed the structures of cognitive estrangement elsewhere, I'll skip over the book in this chapter (except to say, that if you only want one sf picture book for children, this is the one to buy). *Maybe One Day* functions a little differently by using the depth of the pictures as a tool of cognitive and social extension. Of all the texts here it is also the one that most effectively uses the counterpoint of address identified by Nikolajeva and Scott (24). It begins, interestingly, with Little Monster sitting in a small tub with strap-on wings on top of a small step ladder. Whether intentionally or not, Little Monster looks as if he is trapped in a high chair. Father is slouched in a chair (feet over the arms). The scene is intensely domestic but like many of the other pictures in this book, its structural skeleton has spatial depth and a vanishing point frequently at the center of the picture while the extreme ends of the line of focus at the far left- and right-hand bottom corners of the pages, point to the positions of the Little Monster and his father respectively.

Rarely is the Little Monster *at* the vanishing point. That precious spot is more commonly reserved for one of the wonders of the universe yet to be explored. Furthermore, it is what Jane Doonan has called "a travelling book" in which "The action is always moving from left to right pushing you on and on" (1993: 66).

On the next page we are outside and Little Monster is looking out of the window, up at the moon which dominates the right-hand side of the double page spread. Father is still in his seat. If we turn over the page Dad is now on the moon, but Little Monster is jumping off it towards the Earth, and is pictured stark against the black of space. On the next page is a wonderful image that takes me back to my own childhood: Mummy and Daddy are in a balloon in space, "Don't forget to look up at the sky. You might see Mummy and me waving from Earth," said Father Monster. This is the only book in the selection where the parents of the protagonist are positively egging their child on, moving further away in order to persuade the child to try something new, something dangerous; a wonderful fantasy visual-metaphor of baby's first steps. And Little Monster is ready for it, declaring he would be much too far away to see, on the next page we see his parents treasuring a hunk of moon rock as on the right-hand side Little Monster and his bathtub rocket speed away to Mars. The book ends on a spectacular high note: Little Monster's imagination takes him "all the way into space, beyond the planets, until I get to the stars!" and we see a Milky Way fluffy and heart shaped, but when we turn over Little Monster is perched in the bottom left-hand corner on a star in the deep blackness of space, with the solar system tiny in the far top right of the double page spread.

> "Won't you be lonely there?" said Father Monster.
> "Yes, but you have to be lonely to do some things," said Little Monster.
> "And will you come back to us one day?"
> "Oh yes, maybe one day I'll come back," said Little Monster.

On the back of my copy, the reviewer from *The Sunday Times* describes the book as "Witty, striking and reassuring." I think the reviewer is correct, but we need to think about what is meant by "reassuring": this book is intended to be reassuring to children who are being tempted outwards. The Socratic exchange between parent and child is a verbal expression of a long caress. (Schwarcz and Schwarcz, 28) It is actually a brave parent who will embrace the message for *them* in this book that children are for letting go. Simon James' *Baby Brains* (2004) is reassuring too, but with its tale of a genius baby who goes into space only to cry for his mummy, I think it (like a rather chilling book called *Love You Forever* by Robert Munsch) is intended to reassure *parents*. When Baby Brains returns to earth he has learned his lesson: "From that day on, Baby Brains spent most of this time at home doing the things that most babies do." The *reduction* which follows Baby Brain's adventures in this book and its sequel *Baby Brains Superstar* (2005) is daunting.

However limiting *Baby Brains* may be, it does take us in the direction of nice shiny rocket ships. Rocket ships—along with robots—are perhaps the most recognizable iconography of science fiction so it is a surprise to find rocket ships in only four of the picture books I have collected, and in only two is the rocket ship central to the action. In Simon Bartram's *Man on the Moon*, the rocket is a mundane thing, a bus to work, or a tourist carrier. Most of the time it sits in the background and only once, when Bob goes to work, does it dominate the page when the intention is to ironize the juxtaposition of grandeur and power — the rocket flare against a dark background and over a picture in the bottom left of the Earth left behind — against the small picture of Bob seen through the porthole reading a book. Later the many rocket ships carrying tourists will scoot across the sky, but they are watching Bob, he is not watching them.

The dynamic of picture and text in *Man on the Moon* (2004) and its double orientation plays to what Perry Nodelman argued is the "untrained" visual eye of the pre-literate child, which scans pictures and focuses on detail rather than the whole and in doing so places the sense of wonder continually under interrogation (1988: 7). Each picture is brightly coloured and yet *dull* in a way which makes the dullness the point of the tale. In one of the most iconographic double page spreads, a very ordinary, brick house lacking even the embellishments of curtains or a porch stands square on in a garden with bushes but no flowers.

> This is where Bob lives. Every morning he rises as six o'clock. He has a cup of tea and two eggs for breakfast, before leaving for the rocket launch-pad. On the way he stops to buy a newspaper and some chocolate toffees.
> He's on his way to work...
> [opposite page]
> ...on the moon.

This last line sits on the bottom of the page, underneath the path that spirals up the small green hill on which the rocket sits. Bob, in a gentle homage to Rupert Brooke's England, cycles up the hill. The relationship of the words to the pictoral structure of the page, pulled across at the bottom, the eye moves upwards, up the hill to the rocket ship. The eye movement of awe (if such a phrase can exist) also takes us past the classic patchwork of English countryside so that the sense of wonder is focused to a far greater extent on the landscape than it is on the rocket, even as the rocket is positioned at that apex which should most generate the wondrousness.

The coziness of that image is reiterated when we first see Bob "working" on the moon, because Bob's "work" begins with tidying up. In a large double page spread we see, the moon, small in the top left-hand corner, three aliens watching from the horizon, the rocket ship sitting small on the horizon, and further in the foreground (but not at all at the front) a rubbish bin and black plastic bag, and in front of that, Bob, vacuuming the moon with a cleaner with a lead (cable) which is attached to the rocket ship. Follow that lead. It lies leftward across the whole expanse of a Gouda yellow moon. Then it loops back to the rocket ship. In its loop it points at the moon and then draws the eye back to the aliens. Aliens who Bob knows don't exist. The scale of this page, with the moon taking up two thirds of the page, and the "features" small on the horizon, constructs a sense of wonder all of its own. In the mundanity of man on the moon, one sees the scale of the universe.

Towards the end of the book, there is a double-page spread of London which is structured in five distinct layered perspectives. In the foreground are the crowds, many of them aliens. Just behind them is a row of traffic, behind that a row of four- to six-storey houses and shops, behind that dark skyscrapers with perpetual night lights, and beyond that Bob flies home from the moon on his rocket ship, his left-right trajectory paralleling the direction of crowds and buses. The sense of wonder is firmly tied to the sense of the wondrousness of the mundane technology of today; the result is a brilliant but peculiar book, one which simultaneously celebrates technology yet makes it seem ordinary. The ordinariness Bartram communicates is precisely the ennui of someone who lives in the future and the sense of wonder is created in our reaction to that ennui.

Ordinariness is the key to the next two books I want to discuss: Lesley Sims' *Puzzle Journey into Space* (2003, illustrated by Annabel Spenceley), and Marissa Moss's *Amelia Takes Command* (1999). Both books are about experiencing flight simulation but *Puzzle Journey into Space* is a fantasy, while *Amelia Takes Command* is actually a mimetic book that is here as "courtesy sf." In *Puzzle Journey Into Space* two children enter a flight simulator which takes them to the moon where they help an astronaut stranded for twenty years, meet Martians and set off to explore the galaxy: at the end they return, think it is all a dream but find Moon souvenirs in their pockets. The ordinariness of this book, and what undermines the sense of wonder is not the constant pause for puzzles, but that the puzzles set — mazes, find the object in the picture, find the broken part in the picture — have no relevance either to sf or science. The children are never asked, for example, to study a trajectory or calculate a velocity, neither of which are difficult and which could easily have been taught in this format. There is not even a code game which could lead to "translation" of the Martians (instead, they speak telepathically in English). *Amelia Takes Command* avoids this kind of mundanity — the puzzles are space-related tasks (how to land a cardboard rocket with a cricket inside it), but there is never any detail and these kinds of games are positioned at the same level of interest as astronaut food. The result, as with *Puzzle Journey Into Space,* is that what should be exciting is rendered dull. One could argue that in participating in the trappings of sf, child readers acquire an ownership of the material, acquiring familiarity with the icons and themes of sf, but the opportunity to contextualise the quizzes and games in the extrapolative or argumentative aspects of science fiction is lost.

No such criticism can be made of *Rabbits on Mars* (2003), an illustrated picture book, the product of a writer (Jan Wahl) and an assigned illustrator (Kimberley Schamber) rather than a collaboration. The book is joyous. Both the writer and the illustrator have captured the wistfulness of the sense of wonder. The opening page in which the rabbits speculate that there are carrots "on the other side of the highway" shows three rabbits dreaming, one of carrots in a test tube, the other of a carrot palm tree, the third of a carrot stuck in the chimney of a green house (rather than a greenhouse). The first page captures both the ambition and outward-boundness of sf, and its fabulous and speculative aspect.

Like all explorers the rabbits experience disappointment. Their dash across the highway finds only a barren land, an appalling atmosphere and the leftovers of an old culture ("crackers and biscuits and a tin of soup"). On the way home they are chased by a dog ("'Why cannot we ever meet friendly dogs?' Ouzel wondered") and at night they nibble grass and look up at the night sky.

> "If only we could go there," Greenleaf thought aloud. "Life might be better."
> "Maybe Mars does not have dogs," said Peppercorn.
> "What if there are no carrots?" added Ouzel.

With the rabbits in shadow at the front, the night sky above with Mars in the far right-hand corner and the gentle wording, the author and illustrator construct a *mise en scène* which captures both the sadness and the optimism of the sublime. On the next page this is translated into "furry paws kept busy after that" as the rabbits build a rocket in their own back yard. The picture, of paws, sprockets and spanners framing the text ties the rocket trip to process, and to sf: on the following page Wahl writes of zero gravity, weeks of travel, and sponge baths while Schamber shows us the wonder of Earth from space, and the mundanity of rabbits in sleeping bags.

On Mars, the rabbits find giant carrots, but they also find giant dogs who are delighted to see them and play tennis with the rabbits as balls. The rabbits distract the dogs by teaching them to jitterbug, dash to their rocket and head for home. Little Peppercorn looks up at the cool blue star in the far right-hand corner of the page, "I read that's Jupiter ... I wonder what it's like there...."

Not all rockets are shiny. Not all wistfulness is joyous. Not all ambition is good for you. In Michael Foreman's classic *Dinosaurs and All That Rubbish* a man makes the mistake of confusing what is beautiful to look at with what is beautiful to own. Foreman presents the desire for space travel as a classic case of the grass being greener on the other side of the fence. To get to the tantalising beauty, the man builds factories, cuts down trees, burns the coal and sets off in his rocket ship to the star. Foreman seems to have a poor grasp of astronomy so the man lands on the star, "but still there was nothing. No trees, no flowers, and not a blade of grass." He sees another star in the sky and decides to go there. Meanwhile on Earth the scarred soil slumbers, and the dinosaurs, warmed by the heat of the rubbish piles, wake up. They are not impressed. They dance over the earth breaking up the roads, they burn the rubbish in the volcanoes and the earth grows green. When the man returns it is to a beautiful paradise, *his* paradise.

Up to now we have been reading the kind of parable which too many non-sf writers believe is what sf is for (see chapter six for an extended discussion) but then something happens. On a double-page spread the man stands in the far left-hand bottom corner, small, and not very significant. Looming at him, is the head of an Apatosaurus. The man comments that the small brain of the dinosaur prevents him from ruling the star. The dinosaur argues back that with a bigger heart the man would not have destroyed the paradise (cue shock, epiphany and the man living in harmony with the new Earth). The picture is a classic sf moment: man encounters the Other, discovers himself small, and discovers himself not the definition of sentience. Foreman has captured that shock of humility that is an element of the sense of wonder.

Michael Foreman has written another sf dinosaur book, *Dinosaur Time* (2002) which has the distinction of being the only time-travel book in the picture-book collection. Tom uses his mother's fridge magnet timer to travel in time, is chased by dinosaurs and comes back with a dinosaur egg. The egg hatches and Tom uses the timer to send the baby dinosaur back. It is a simple enough tale, but the elision between fabulation and mimesis — is the child imagining or does it all really happen — is handled well. The book is written very much with Tom at the focal point — all dinosaur eyes and teeth and noses turn towards him, and with a parallel structure so that the book ends with the dinosaur mother telling the baby "This is not a toy,

Don't mess with it." In the same way and in the same frame that Tom's mother used. The time travel never really gets beyond being a device.

Graeme Base's *The Worst Band in the Universe* (1999) is a truly glorious book, a dystopia set on an alien planet and told in epic verse. Each page has a carefully designed alien, playing a peculiar-looking (but recognizable) guitar. The story is equally both recognizable but twisted, the age old story of new music dismissed by parents. Young Sprocc is tormented by the rules on his own planet which prevent new music from being played, so he and his band enter the The Worst Band in the Universe competition, because on this planet, who would want to be the officially best band? They win, and are sent off to Alpha 10, where they find themselves on a planet where the vegetation is sound-sensitive and eats musicians, surrounded by all the previous winners of the Worst Band competition. Sprocc persuades them all to escape and gets them home in turn to face down the Grand Inquisitor who—it turns out—cannot actually play a note. And all is well in the world, innovation is preserved.

If the story is slight, the details and execution of the tale, both in words and pictures, has a great deal more to offer of the science-fictional. On the inside cover of the book is a planetary map (although I cannot see a sun, which is a little odd). On the first page, Sprocc walks along a landscape suitably weird and with several planets in the background. As far as aliens go, this book is essentially a bestiary in which no two aliens are the same, although a great deal of imagination has gone into the details of extra tentacles and noses. The settings however are generalised urban and jazz club. The section of the book which takes us into a truly sf universe begins when the band lands on the jungle worlds of WasteDump B19. First there is the discovery that the plants are sound activated. The pictures that accompany this display offer an alien and threatening landscape, dark green and overgrown, a stark contrast to the bleak waste dump on the opposite page.

Skat, the leader of the prisoners stuck on the waste dump, regards escape as hopeless. But a ButtonPusher, inspired by Sprocc comes up to the new arrivals:

> "Er, hi," he mumbled. "Look, I wouldn't dare say this aloud.
> But well, I have this theory—though of course I may be wrong...."
> He handed Sprocc a drawing. "*It's a ship that sails on song.*"

> "A music-powered space-craft?" Breather froobled through her snouts.
> "It is possible, I guess," she shrugged. "And yet I have my doubts...."
> "Skat says that it will never fly," the little guy confided.
> "We'll try it!" Sprocc declared at once." The matter is decided!"

> The task was huge, the concept vague, the physics somewhat moot.
> But once the seed of hope was sown it gradually took root.
> They laboured with the flame of freedom burning in their hearts,
> A hammer, seven drill bits and an endless source of parts.

> And slowly from the rubble grew a glorious creation:
> A flimsy pile of rusted junk—the means of their salvation."

The Worst Band in the Universe is a wonderful book, but it is all surface, all splendour. Only very occasionally does it get beyond the surface, beyond the sound, to the notes and chords of either rock or sf. Graeme Base's aliens are simply allegories of humans (and an easy way to avoid deciding on the colour skin your fictive characters should have). Aliens as substitutes for humans or for cuddly toys can result in great books (see Nick Butterworth's *Q Pootle 5*) and fun books, such as the rewriting of *Hush, Little Mockingbird* into *Hush, Little Alien* by Daniel Kirk, but they also produce dull allegory (Dan Yaccarino's *First Day on a Strange New Planet* and Shana Corey and Mark Teague's *First Graders on Mars*). Occasionally, it is an excuse for a romp as with Arthur Yorinks and Mort Drucker's *Tomatoes From Mars* (a wonderful book whose referential drawings and sexy young professor's daughter make it clear that the book is really aimed at adults). Only three books in my pile got serious about their aliens.

Dr. Xargle's Book of Earthlets by Jeanne Willis and Tony Ross has been my favourite sf picture book for years, and I want to consider the construction of alienness from creative misprision, or Nikolajeva and Scott's counterpoint in style and intraiconic text (2006, 75). Although the aliens in this book are green furry, tentacled and toothy crocodiles with four eyes, their real alienness is created not through us looking at them, but by the way in which Willis and Ross asks us to look at them looking at us. The actual depiction of the aliens contains very little cognitive estrangement, in fact the situation in which the alien is placed, and our relationship to the alien, is well within our daily experience: the classroom, the teacher at the front, the board full of pictures on which our lesson is planned out.

That classroom board is interesting. On some pages there is "intervention," the tentacle of the teacher reaches out to point at some interesting aspect of the picture. Sometimes, as when a baby is shown in full, there is an implication in the drawing that the tentacle pointing to "two short tentacles with pheelers on the end" may be tickling the baby. Elsewhere, there is simply a picture and caption. Each time, however, there is a reversal of the seen/seeing relationship which John Berger wrote about. "We" become the object of gaze, centered and studied. Even our position as "the alien" cannot change this because one of the things that makes us human (although other primates and elephants can do this) is our ability to recognize ourselves both in the mirror and in image. We can also hold in our head the complex sequential ideas "us," "but not really us," "but representative of us." Willis and Ross construct their dissonance in the space between each of the three ideas. But the other factor of course is that the misprision relies on an assumption that pictures are mutable, unstable. Can these be photographs or are they drawings? One effect of the book is to make pictures of the world an undermining of reality, rather than a confirmation. They cut across the cultural constructionism common to picture books. By the end of the book the aliens feel very familiar and it is a shock to see them put on their people suits: even without the serried ranks of identical school boys, the white round faces and red caps and jackets look scarily alien.

Another way to familiarise the alien is to opt for the National Geographic approach: pictures of naked aliens doing innocent and delightful things for observing earthlings. This is a rather derogatory opening for the delightful and whimsical *Mrs. Moore in Space* (1974) by Gertrude L. Moore (mother of the astronomer, and astronomy populariser, Patrick Moore) but it is best to be honest; what charms the child can unnerve the early twenty-first century adult. There is no irony in these pictures. Descended from sketches drawn to entertain Gertrude Moore's son, they are comfortable with the observer/observed relationship. There is no story to the book, each picture stands alone, depicting the looks and habits of the inhabitants of fanciful creatures in various parts of the solar system. Big rolling eyes and snouts dominate, and with the exception of Venus, the canalside of the Martian desert and the third planet in the system of Vega, these are barren landscapes, desert and ice. The pictures are anthropomorphic, couples collect moon shots, a young alien collects a sputnik as a present for his girlfriend. A merman courts a mermaid. The wonder here is in the exotic and the surprisingly similar. *Just like us!* the pictures celebrate.

Just like us! Is the message of the winsome *Company's Coming!* (1996) in which Arthur Yorinks and David Small tell a tale of aliens who land by accident in a suburban back garden and are invited to a family dinner by a nervous Shirley. Her husband, Mo, panics and calls in the army, but the aliens turn up to tea as arranged with a gift for the household, a blender. Like *Mrs Moore in Space*, cosy domesticity shapes the picture. On the front page the flying saucer takes up the top left-hand corner but the rest of the book is green fields, small square houses and a man with a lawn mower.

The domesticity is intensified when the space ship lands: Shirley mistakes it for a large barbecue, and sitting in the right-hand corner of the spread, it looks like one. In the left-hand corner stand Moe and Shirley, dwarfed by the barbecue, but dwarfing in turn the small Siamese cat. The picture suggests triangles and it suggests scale. In the next picture we see the back of the tiny aliens as they look up at the humans, and towards the now prickly-huge cat. The perspective and the scale has been reversed. This is clearest around page six when we stand looking down on the aliens (Moe and Shirley's shadows are in front of us and watch the intrusion of the military in later pictures, and accompany the aliens in the sense the aliens have of walking into bright light with the darkness of the guns behind them. As they pick up their gift to present it to Shirley, they, on the left-hand side, are menaced by the guns which fill the right-hand side. Triangles, perspective, focus and scale all come together to emphasize the over-reaction of authority, the vulnerability of the small.

Perspective has long been one of the most powerful tools of the science fiction (and fantasy) writer: change the perspective and you change the world. Graham Oakley's *Henry's Quest*, which I discussed extensively in chapter three, juxtaposes a fantasy quest narrative against a post-disaster futuristic setting. The intra-iconic and inter-textual matter of the complex setting keeps the reader simultaneously off-balance and attentive. The perspectives shift in and out and finally coalesce firmly in the world of sf, but as Henry thinks of the princess he chose not to wake in the woods, the dragons in the forest, and the new emperor with his "terrible new power," he moves closer and closer to what we would understand as fantasy. "If it hadn't been for that he would have lived not just happily but very happily ever after." Similarly, perspective can push an apparent fantasy such as *The Dragon Machine* (2003), by Helen Ward, illustrated by Wayne Anderson, into the realms of sf. George may see dragons, but when he decides to get rid of them he leads them out of the city in a machine dragon we see him build. The pictures are dreamy, smudgy grey colours, and it looks as if George is in pyjamas, but when George's machine dragon crashes in the desert, the searchers find him among the broken pieces, load them on the back of a car and drive home. The perspective shifts in such a way as to edge us towards mimesis.[4]

Chapter Notes

Chapter One

1. Recently Clute has suggested that this might be modified to WRONGNESS, THINNING, RECOGNITION, RETURN: email, 19 July 2002.

2. See Levy, "Science Fiction as *Bildungsroman*," 1999: 9–102.

3. Note that they are almost always boys. Heinlein's *Podkayne of Mars* is usually considered rather poor, and for me, the few Nortons with female protagonists always seemed to lack conviction.

4. My own experience was that wherever I went, the local library usually held one or two of these volumes in the "older readers" section.

5. It is worth noting that of eighty-one stories a bare five are by women. Two of these stories are by the editor, Amabel Williams-Ellis. Although female writers had not yet enjoyed the success that would be theirs from the 1970s, this is perhaps half of what could be expected for the period.

Chapter Two

1. I write as someone who had to take up exercise for very specific reasons, and unexpectedly fell in love not with the exercise itself but with the muscular pleasure. I don't think anyone ever explained that this was why those who enjoy exercise, do so.

2. There are other problems with Nodelman's discussion of primitive art: generally he seems to have ignored all the work by art historians on religious narrative art, and by anthropologists and pre-historians on artifacts such as cave paintings.

3. I'm indebted to my father for that comment on the nature of inquisitive childishness and the development of an sf reader.

4. An interesting take on the dynamic between father and child in *Maybe One Day* can be extrapolated from a comment by the Cragos' engagement with their daughter Anna on similar issues: "Anna accepted what adults would class as fantastic elements along with those we would class as reality-based, subjecting them equally to the testing-out process we mentioned above... If Anna asked where ogres lived, for example, our standard answer was 'only in books.' This phrasing, which we can now see to have been an attempt to preserve the possibility of a separate fictional reality, could well have helped Anna to treat the world of books as such a reality. In fact, she rarely asked questions like this; far more problems arose for her when she attempted to generalize within the world of books, assuming that what had been true in several stories should also be true in the new one. It was thus the inner consistency of the book world, rather than the consistency between book world and everyday world, that functioned as the precursor of her first grappling with the fantasy/reality distinction" (201).

5. Speaking personally for a moment, I laud the child's right to adore Harry Potter, but when s/he declares "and it is the best book ever!," I find it hard not to retort, "and how many have you read?" This is not mere mean-spiritedness: my dislike of Christopher Paolini's *Eragon* is rooted in a fear that any child reading *Eragon* before *The Lord of the Rings* (1954) will have lost, without having ever experienced, the full sense-of-wonder impact of that book.

6. "...and anyone who knew anything about the Middle Ages would realise what a really bad novel it was." Edward James, emailing from the British Library (8 February 2008).

7. One of the cultural shifts of the nineteenth century may have been the domesticization of reading, away from the market place, and work place break and the public readings of the theatre that Dickens so enjoyed, into the home.

8. If you read K. J. Parker's *The Belly of the Bow* (1999) carefully, you would be able to make a bow. You might, however, want to use a different material.

9. I can not find the name of the television program, although several respondents are sure it was presented by Jamie Oliver and Marguerite Patten. Similar responses however are seen in increasingly young children who when asked about their weight express their desire to be on diets. They know what the "correct" response should be.

10. There is also the possibility that these expectations are being reinforced by poorly structured social science studies. Mark Lieberman, at The Language Log, took a look at some of these studies and also at cognitive science studies and found little evidence for real gender based difference in any neurological tests. Mark Lieberman, The Language Log, September 6 2007.

11. A few hours after I wrote that, a friend posted in her LiveJournal "A few weeks ago I said that I was going to start running. And have I? No, but I have bought a book about running." http://rhionnach.LiveJournal.com/5166 4.html?view=202704#t202704 (8 Feb 07).

12. Observations by Rhys Morgan:

I. A young girl, around 7, with her father. She knew the two books she wanted, both of which were in the Waterstone's children's Top Ten chart. One was Jackie Wilson's *Jackie Daydream*. Her father then encouraged her to look for more books; he stood and looked at the shelves while she browsed the 5–8 kids' section.

II. A mother came to the till with her son, probably around 12 or 13. She had a copy of Wells's *War of the Worlds* (1898) among other adult books, and was telling him it was about time he read a classic.

III. A mother with two young sons, one perhaps older than 3, the other about 6. The older child asked if he could choose factual books; his mother said he could and directed him to the kids' reference section. She went to look at gift books while he browsed. The younger child wanted *Flanimals* (2004) by Rickey Gervais; the mother at first refused, saying he could read something they already had at home, then relented but said he could not have it that day because he didn't have enough money, but if he saved up he could.

IV. A mother with a 6 or 7 year old son asked for books from a series featuring "Zac"; she had to check with the son for the correct name, said he had birthday money to spend and wanted 2 books.

V. A mother with a daughter about 4 asked if there were any books to accompany the new BBC series called *Night Garden*, which there were not. She apologized to the daughter and said there weren't any books available; the child did not want anything else and got upset about not being able to have *Night Garden* books.

13. My introduction to science fiction was through a suitcase full of books given to me by Gordon Leek, to whom I have dedicated this book. I would not have read them had I not been desperate for anything with print on it.

14. "The *Magazine* reviews books very selectively, approximately seventy titles an issue, and generally considers titles notable for high standards in plot, theme, characterization, and style. Original paperbacks are occasionally reviewed." http://www.hbook.com/publications/submissions.asp

Chapter Three

1. Issues books that read just fine in the U.S. can feel appallingly mawkish and oppressive to UK readers who are used to a more skeptical tone.

2. LiveJournal is an electronic networking tool. An LJ friend will be attracted to the users' site through links. They may never have met and may be connected at third or fifth remove as the network expands geometrically.

3. Poll conducted at http://fjm.LiveJournal.com/230027.html, 3 July 2006.

4. Statistics can be found at http://en.wikipedia.org/wiki/MyersBriggs_Type_Indicator. There may also be a link between IN*J and the use of LiveJournal. Certainly all the research so far on high-level users of networks suggest that introverts are drawn to the system. Frequently, this is argued as "people get cut off when they spend too much time on line" but this is an extrovert's interpretation. For an introvert, the net offers social interaction without the stress of gatherings, and may well promote social networks.

5. See the typelogic site for the types. INTJ can be found at: http://www.typelogic.com/intj.html

6. "...the chances are excellent that you can find one or more people willing to engage in serious, extended, knowledgeable conversation about some of the things that interest you most, whether it is the stock market or macramé." Hartwell, 1984: 19.

7. Ibid.

8. Ibid.

9. The above requires some explanation and elaboration on school types. American high schools take children from 13/14 yrs through to 17/18 yrs. British schools are a melange, with a chronological divide in 1944 and the 1970s. Before 1944 many children left school at 14, but at around the age of twelve they were divided, partly by ability, mostly by ability to pay. There were several types of education: the "public" schools were entirely determined by social class and hence, ironically, the most intellectually inclusive—a point

never admitted by educators. High schools and grammar schools were competitive establishments mostly founded to provide education for the trades and professional classes. After these were the Central schools which provided a little more education for the working class. Until 1930, when a break was mandated in the state system at 11, many children simply stayed on at the elementary schools until they left at fourteen years old. After 1944, all but the public schools came within the state system. This was tripartite after the age of 11. The "brightest" would go to the grammar schools where they received an education which was intended to send them into university or into middle class work (banking was a non-university profession until the 1980s), the least intellectual would go to the secondary moderns and receive vocational education. Many areas also had a middle-track, the technical schools, where children would receive high level technical education for the trades and would go into apprenticeships (all levels of British industry were staffed by these schools). One thing to bear firmly in mind is that first, the recruitment to these schools was strongly distorted by class, and that second, there were far fewer places in the girls' grammar schools than in the boys' (in the 1970s, it was pointed out that if they went co-ed, on the basis of the entry examination alone girls would take the majority of places). All of this needs to be kept to the fore when one considers what is meant by "less able" pupils and how the curriculum was adapted and with what prejudices. Crucially, one needs to bear in mind that selective education in the UK, and later the policy of streaming (separating into ability bands) has historically focused on verbal skills.

10. A similar argument seems to range around the "girls into science" with little actual evidence that there is any need to change either content or presentation of material. Ironically, what little evidence there is suggests that when social pressures to drop the physical sciences are removed, girls respond better to directed learning than do boys.

11. Top Trumps are trading cards. Each pack had a different "subject." The one I played with was cars. Each card had a picture of a different car on it. Running in a list below were the specs: speed, horsepower etc. Your mate would say "my card has xxx horsepower (or some other category)." If you held a card with a higher value, you got his card. If you didn't, he got to choose one out of your hand. There were boats, trains, rockets, etc. etc. Widely popular in the UK in the 1970s and still on the market now, but often with television themes. There are *Buffy* trading cards. The link with Dungeons and Dragons and other gaming systems is visible.

12. One of the ironies in the constructivist approach as I have seen it applied in museums is that the actual practice frequently involves removing the "learner" from the site of the collection in order to take them through a series of pre-designed exercises to "discover" and "experience" the path that has been marked out. Free association with the material is constantly being undermined by this approach. See, Xanthoudaki (2002) for museum educators who argue for this kind of teaching, but also consider the exhibitions at the Glasgow Science Centre — many experiments, no explanations at all —, the exhibitions in the discovery section of Birmingham Museum and Art Gallery whose patron written descriptions are mundane and uninformative, and almost any modern "discovery centre" near you. Then contrast them to the old fashioned, information-dense and eclectic Pitt Rivers collection in Oxford.

13. See Bjorn Andersson's paper, "Some Aspects of Children's Understanding of Boiling Point." Some of the pupils' explanations are quite consistent. This of the pupils on category 2 B on problem 1 (the longer the water is on the hot-plate, the hotter it gets), 80% explain, as would be expected, problem 2 by saying that the switch-number determines the temperature of the boiling water. ...many of the apparent misconceptions came from good logical thinking, the problem was merely that the pupils had inadequate background knowledge" (258–9). As Andersson points out, this is the *logical* answer (Kramer, 1979: 258–9).

14. See Dunbar and Fugelsang who argue that "guided discovery coupled with explicit instruction is one of the most effective educational strategies in science." In Holyoak and Morrison (2003: 721).

15. This is true of all sorts of things. Email is now regarded by the majority as a chore, not because it has fallen out of favor, but because the first surveys were among voluntary users, whereas modern surveys are among coerced users.

16. Eysenck, cited in Ormerod and Duckworth: 52; Ormerod and Duckworth also point to research indicating a variation in interest and aptitude according to the location of the child in city, town or country (Ormerod and Duckworth: 39).

17. I am deliberately avoiding words such as "intelligent" or "bright." *Most able* refers solely to the ability demonstrated, not subjective notions of what intelligent consists of.

18. Kuslan and Stone write, "The values of Inquiry instruction have not yet been *proven* by educational research. Many studies yield ambiguous results. From the viewpoint of the learner, Inquiry is desirable because it encourages divergent thinking, freedom, creativity,

and interest. Inquiry teaching, has, however, been criticised on several grounds; for example, it has been alleged that only the most capable children are likely to be successful. However, the psychological potential of Inquiry instruction is sufficient to satisfy most elementary school children that *they* can learn for themselves, and *this* is the learning which will be permanent" (102). I would challenge that formulation: I think it is simply that a different cohort of children is likely to be successful.

19. One of the anomalies in the UK is that the Scottish system is entirely separate. Historically, it is also far more successful at producing scientists. This may be a correlation with culture rather than curriculum.

20. See Margaret Malle, *Making Facts Matter* (1992) on the writing of non-fiction books for children aged 5 to 11 years.

21. See as examples, Dodman, 1973; Pearce, 1980; Turnill, 1974.

22. See White, 1996: At the very beginning of the book, on the fly leaf, is a description of the life cycle of the small tortoiseshell, and also a diagram of a typical butterfly clearly labeled. Turning over, each double page consists of a page of writing, explaining the habitat and lifestyle, and a painting of the butterfly or insect in its native habitat. At the back of the book is an index, and on the back page a detailed drawing of the life cycle of a dragonfly.

23. As the British Library does not prioritize non–UK titles, I was unable to secure every text short-listed. For some reason the British Library did not hold any of the short list from 2003 and 2004.

24. However, while the book is fascinating, in Morgan's world homosexuality does not exist.

25. Just to give one example: on the page which shows what things are made of the flap on the denim trousers lifts to show small round white balls, but there is nothing to say that they are cotton balls.

26. Just a few examples; Bruce Carter, *Tim Baker, Motor Mechanic*. London: Chatto and Windus, 1957. Stanley Makepeace-Lott, *Alan Works with Atoms*. London: Chatto and Windus, 1962; H. Power: *Henry in Estate Agency*. London: Chatto and Windus, 1961. D.O. Summers, *Ken Jones, Electrical Engineer*. London: Chatto and Windus, 1959. Grenville Wilson, *Jonathan Enters Journalism*. London: Chatto and Windus,1956. Patricia Baldwin, *Rosemary Takes to Teaching*. London: Victory Press, 1960. Anne Barrett, *Sheila Burton, Dental Assistant*. London: Bodley Head 1956. Valerie Baxter, *Elizabeth: Young Policewoman*. London: Bodley Head 1955. Stephanie Spencer says that on the basis of sales, the boys books were never as successful as the girls' books. She argues that there

was a greater variety of careers open to boys, but I would suggest that much of the fiction available to boys filled the need for "outward looking" adventure, whereas the girls career novels were almost the only non-family oriented fiction available for teens (Spencer, 108).

27. It is not precisely a lottery but is based on family testing so feels utterly arbitrary.

28. Pratchett is having one of his regular digs at historians here. Ironically, your average University historian would be horrified by this homework assignment, which seems to reflect a popular misunderstanding about what history is. Stephen Baxter's *Webcrash* (1998) makes the same misprision as do a number of other authors of time travel narratives for children.

Chapter Four

1. Lee Wyndham, writing in 1968, was adamant on the subject: "Adults in the stories should be kept to an absolute minimum. Introduced upon a scene they have an annoying way of taking over—just as in real life. *Keep your stories for children about children, working out problems suitable to their years, with as little grownup help as possible*" (11).

2. My father talks of being given a choice between accountancy and going into the family business. Many working and lower middle-class men in the UK who were educated in the late 1950s talk about the real impact of grammar school not being in the actual education per se, but in the way it ruptured the familial expectations that they would emulate their father or be found work with their fathers' friends. Alan Garner uses the Cheshire phrase "get aback" for bettering yourself, but in his biography talks about the effect of moving from a linear "bettering of oneself" compared to the geometric ruptures of being sent into a whole new world. The ideology of children's and juvenile literature was only just beginning to recognize these changes to teen expectations by the end of the 1960s (1997).

3. "Handwaving" is a term used by sf fans to mean "making it sound vaguely scientific while eliding the details."

4. See the complaints of the Royal Chemistry Society, in "The Chemistry Set Generation" (2007).

5. Not all of these books are written by Applegate, but I have no information on specifics.

6. "Mr. Benn lives at No. 52 Festive Road — a very ordinary street, in an ordinary part of town. But every so often, he feels the need to escape from the ordinary, so he pays a visit to a mysterious Fancy Dress Shop, run by an equally mysterious fez-wearing Shopkeeper.

The changing room is more mysterious still, for once Mr. Benn has put on one of the Shopkeeper's costumes he always finds himself stepping out into an extraordinary fantasy land in which he is the star performer. The land is different each time, in keeping with the costume Mr. Benn has chosen. And each time, problems are solved and situations sorted just before the Shopkeeper mysteriously reappears and directs Mr. Benn through a magical portal, back to the Changing Room and the ordinary suburban world again. Was his experience for real? Mr. Benn cannot be sure, but after every adventure he always finds himself holding a memento from his trip, which leaves him pondering...." *Toothhound*: http://www.toonhound.com/mrbenn.htm.

7. It is a spell, a momentary slide into magic that leaves us unclear whether we are in a truly constructed world or another — more satisfying — illusion.

8. Lisa Abrams from Penguin kindly supplied this information.

9. See "'Johnnie! Put the Knife Down!'" by Tim Dowling, *The Guardian*, 07.21.07, p. 33–34.

10. Amato's book is particularly interesting, in that it is a side effect of the protagonist's use of a worm that eats words — and hence erases concepts — that releases child factory laborers on the other side of the world.

Chapter Five

1. *Wide Awake* is about a journey to Kansas to prevent the presidential election result being over-turned (Americans have elected a gay man and a black woman); *Boy Meets Boy* is a delightful confection set in a hippy cool high school where the quarterback is a transvestite.

2. Why yes, I am an historian by training. What ever gave it away?

3. One of the characters in Maguire's *I Feel Like the Morning Star* (1997) *may* be gay, but it is only hinted at.

4. And if you want to find a perfect description of Harry Potter, check out Julian in *The Naughtiest Girl is a Monitor*.

5. See an article from the *New York Times*, "Who's a Nerd Anyway" by Ned Nugent which summarizes Mary Bucholtz's work at UC Santa Barbara. Bucholtz argues that nerdiness is hyper whiteness. The problem with this argument is that as we can see from *Radio Boys* nerdiness as it is currently conceived did not really exist in the 1920s. Science "boys" portrayed in sf generally are generally fairly ordinary chaps. I think nerdiness as it is currently conceived emerged from the emulation by 1940s and 1950s boys of the nuclear scientists and Werner von Braun, who became heroes to a genera-

tion. These scientists were of course all immigrants, speaking very formal English as a second language and alienated from the sport and ordinary boyhood culture of mainstream America. I cannot prove it of course, but "nerdiness" was the standard model of *Jewish* boyishness until Israel started to provide a more physical model.

6. And I refer the reader here to Nan's masterful summation of Real Boys and Real Girls in Diana Wynne Jones' *Witch Week* (1982).

Chapter Six

1. There may be a "minority" factor here with authors who wish to represent "people like me" more willing to acknowledge purpose. David Levithan for example regularly states his desire to show gay teens in something other than depressing or uplifting coming out stories.

2. I don't think it is how adults choose any kind of fiction, or perhaps more significantly, how it is marketed to them.

3. Taught in the sense of placed on recommended lists and hence validated.

4. Lewis is perhaps the pre-eminent example of an excellent writer who gets excused his foible of didactic content without challenging the basic argument that didacticism = bad literature.

5. There is a lot of bad sf out there, and a lot of material published as sf and read as sf which barely scrapes through the commonly held definitions of critics or fans. This is a discussion about just one aspect of this which is more common in sf for children and teens than for adults.

6. Chess and rugby are two games in our own world where success has been assumed to map on to both adult life and the success of the imperium.

7. If I have caveats it is the degree to which this may be cultural — reports on adolescents in cultures where trade is inherited report less adolescent stress — and that it is also applicable to many adult readers.

8. As usual, lots of caveats: "artistic" versus "sensible" careers still cause stress in teen fiction and among many immigrant families there is still very strong pressure for career direction.

9. The emerging evidence from New Orleans for example is that most people "looted" water in the face of the complete breakdown of government, but that community order remained protective over many of the vulnerable.

10. The 1994 re-issue contains an additional chapter which recreates a pastoral world. Whether you regard this as an improvement may depend on what you think of a retreat to pastorialism.

11. Recent investigations of Chernobyl suggest that a nuclear explosion which kicked out all the humans might be quite good for the environment, i.e., everything but us. See Mary Mycio's *Wormwood Forest: A Natural History of Chernobyl* (2005), while 65 percent of the species of Bikini Atoll have now returned. *New Scientist*, 19 April 2008: 5.

12. In the 1980s harsh winters in certain parts of the world led to this fear. Only when the data became global did it become slotted into a more complex pattern of global warming.

13. Perhaps only tangentially relevant, but in the 1960s gypsies were being re-evaluated in the public imagination (see *The Diddakoi* by Rumer Godden, 1972). A period of high employment in the early 1970s also allowed vagrancy to be reconceived as a romantic lifestyle and not a social threat.

14. After reading Ben's research and diaries, all of which point to an alien origin, to the need of another species for our gene pool, Roger decides that the wild children were the descendants of a pre-human species who vacated the earth and have now returned. I cannot emphasize this enough: *nowhere* in the book or in Ben's notes is there any evidence for this. Suddenly, and without explanation, and in a way that is utterly out of character for scientist Roger, a Fortean explanation is thrown into the mix. It is as if, right at the very end, the author had to remind us that the way of knowing that is "the scientific method" was inherently untrustworthy. The heart not the head rules the episteme.

15. Personally, I think this premise implies a more rigid demarcation between human and animal than can be justified, and that Thompson is herself uncomfortable with the impression she creates. In reality, her speculative attempt to close the gap, opens it wider.

Chapter Seven

1. On reflection, these novelizations were precursors of video, there to allow one to recapitulate the experience of the movie with greater ease. They were not expected to stand alone.

2. All fiction rests on a "bible," a set of rules about what can and cannot be done. It is just that outside the fantastic, the bible is so taken for granted that it is no longer visible. One of the "outrages" of feminists and the civil rights movements was to make this bible visible again.

3. These books are intended for adult readers in line with current thinking that what is needed for "reluctant" readers is not simplified prose or plots, but shorter stories.

4. Scott Lynch talks more of this strategy in as does Lou Anders in (Lynch, 2006; Anders, 2006).

Appendix D

1. All of the parents in Cole's work are childlike, see *Mummy Laid and Egg* and *Dr. Dog* in particular.

2. A "waldo," a notion invented by Heinlein in his novella *Waldo* (1942), is a means of *extending* (not enhancing) one's reach, operation or strength. The most familiar waldoes in every day use are the remote controlled sensing and operating devices used by surgeons, but they are also common in industries where coming into contact with material is dangerous, such as the nuclear energy industry.

3. "Over and over in picture books for young children, we encounter these gender differences. Little girls turn anger against themselves, whereas little boys send it outward. Boy characters set off on adventures and try to become heroes by learning to fend for themselves; girls are expected to hold on tight and solve their problems within, not outside of, their primary relationships.... It is worthwhile pointing out, moreover, that these differences in attitude and behavior characterize not only male and female "child" characters but fictional "parental" characters as well." (Spitz, E. H. 1999. *Inside Picture Books*. New Haven & London, Yale University Press, 48). Also Schwarcz and Schwarcz comment, "It is interesting, and sad, to note that even in countries that have progressed comparatively far in changing attitudes toward women and their status, picture books still tend to represent women in traditional, secondary roles. When for example, the text says 'Everyone is busy with their work,' the picture will show a woman holding a broom; the same is true of girls' pasttimes, and more consequentially, girls' roles in the plot and their pictorial representation — usually, girls are less central than boys." (Schwarcz, J. H. and C. Schwarcz, 1991. *The Picture Book Comes of Age: Looking at Childhood Through the Art of Illustration*, 9–10)."

4. See Bromley, Helen. "Spying on Picture Books: Exploring Intertextuality with Young Children." In her work with young children Bromley found that children were highly sensitive to inter-textuality, enjoying the moment of recognition, "These children were acknowledging the conspiratorial feeling described by Margaret Meek and Frank Smith; that process of becoming 'insiders in the network'" (103). *Talking Pictures: Pictorial Texts and Young Readers*. Eds. Victor Watson and Morag Styles. London: Hodder & Stoughton, 1996.

Bibliography

Science Fiction for Children Cited in the Text

Adlington, L. J. The Diary of Pelly D. London: Hodder Children's Books, 2005.

Almond, D. Skellig. London: Hodder Children's Books, 1998.

Amato, M. The Word Eater. New York: Holiday House, 2000.

Anderson, M. T. Feed. Cambridge, MA: Candlewick Press, 2002.

Applegate, K. A. Animorphs: The Invasion. New York: Scholastic, 1996.

_____. Everworld. New York: Scholastic, 1999–2001.

_____. Remnants. New York: Scholastic, 2001–2003.

Appleton, V., II. Tom Swift and His Triphebian Atomicare. New York: Grosset and Dunlap, 1962.

_____. Tom Swift and the Asteroid Pirates. New York: Grosset and Dunlap, 1963.

_____. Tom Swift and the Visitor from Planet X. New York: Grosset and Dunlap, 1961.

Arksey, N. Playing on the Edge. Harmondsworth, UK: Puffin, 2000.

Armstrong, J., and N. Butcher. The Keepers of the Flame. New York: HarperCollins, 2002.

_____ and _____. The Kiln. New York: HarperCollins, 2003.

_____ and _____. The Kindling. New York: Eos/HarperCollins, 2002.

Ball, B. The Doomship of Drax. London: Heinemann, 1985.

Ballantine, J. The Boy Who Saved Earth. New York: Ballantine, 1979.

Balkensperger, P. Guardians of Time (Toronto: Three Trees Press, 1984).

Barlow, S. and S. Skidmore. Control. London: Scholastic, 2002.

Base, G. The Worst Band in the Universe. Ringwood, Vic: Viking, 1999.

Baxter, S. Gulliverzone. London: Orion Books, 1997.

_____. The H-Bomb Girl. London: Faber and Faber, 2007.

_____. Webcrash. London: Orion Books, 1998.

Beatty, J., Jr. Matthew Looney and the Space Pirates. New York: Avon, 1972.

_____. Matthew Looney's Voyage to Earth. New York: William Scott, 1961.

_____. The Tunnel to Yesterday. New York: Avon Books, 1983.

Bechard, M. The Star Hatchling. New York: Viking, 1995.

Berry-Hart, T. E. Escape from Genopolis. London: Scholastic, 2007.

Bertagna, J. Aurora. forthcoming, 2009.

_____. Exodus. London: Picador (Pan Macmillan), 2002.

_____. Zenith. London: Picador (Pan Macmillan), 2007.

Bisson, T. Star Wars, Boba Fett: Crossfire. New York: Scholastic, 2002.

_____. Star Wars, Boba Fett: The Fight to Survive. New York: Scholastic, 2002.

Blacker, T. The Angel Factory. London: Macmillan, 2001.

Blackman, M. Checkmate. London: Doubleday, 2005.

_____. Hacker. London: Transworld, 1992.

_____. Knife Edge. London: Doubleday, 2004.

_____. Noughts and Crosses. London: Doubleday, 2001.

_____. Whizziwig and Whizziwig Returns. London: Random House, 2005, c. 1995, 1999.

Boos, K., and B. Clemente. Visitor Parking. Nebraska City: Table Creek, 2002.

Bova, B. *End of Exile.* New York: E.P. Dutton, 1975.

Bowering, G. *Parents from Space.* Montreal: Roussan, 1994.

Brake, C. *Doctor Who: The Colony of Lies.* London: BBC Worldwide, 2003.

Bresnihan, J. *The Alphabet Network.* Dublin: Wolfhound, 2000.

Browne, N. M. *Shadow Web.* London: Bloomsbury, 2008.

Bryant, E. M. *Space Princess Cosima: Sparkle Surprize Party (with stickers).* New York: Grosset and Dunlap, 2005.

Burgess, M. *Bloodtide.* London: Andersen Press, 1999.

Busby, A. *Rosie's Zoo.* London: Scholastic, 2001.

Butterworth, N. *Q Pootle 5.* London: HarperCollins, 2000.

Cadigan, P. *Avatar.* London: Orion Books, 1999.

Cameron, E. *Time and Mr. Bass.* Boston: Toronto, Little, Brown, 1967.

Carroll, M. *The Quantum Prophecy.* London: HarperCollins, 2006.

_____. *Sakkara.* London: HarperCollins, 2006.

Carter, D. A. *Bugs in Space.* New York: Simon and Schuster, 1997.

Cave, P. *Blown Away.* London: Simon and Schuster, 2005.

_____. *Sharp North.* London: Simon and Schuster, 2004.

Chapman, A. *The Radio Boys' First Wireless.* New York: Grosset and Dunlap, 1922.

Christopher, J. *The City of Gold and Lead.* London: Macmillan, 1967.

_____. *The Lotus Caves.* London: Hamish Hamilton, 1969.

_____. *The Pool of Fire.* London: Macmillan, 1968.

_____. *The White Mountains.* New York: Toronto, London: Macmillan, 1967.

Clifton, N. R. *The City Beyond the Gate.* Richmond, Ontario: Scholastic, 1971.

Cole, B. *The Trouble with Dad.* London: Heinemann, 1985.

Coombs, C. *Mystery of Satellite 7.* Philadelphia: Westminster Press, 1957.

Cooper, L. *Mirror Mirror: Breaking Through.* London: Hodder Children's Books, 2000.

_____. *Mirror Mirror: Running Free.* London: Hodder Children's Books, 2000.

Corder, Z. *Lionboy.* Harmondsworth: Puffin, 2004.

_____. *Lionboy: The Chase.* Harmondsworth: Puffin, 2005.

_____. *Lionboy: The Truth.* Harmondsworth: Puffin, 2006.

Cousins, S. *Frankenbug.* New York: Holiday House, 2000.

Coville, B. *My Teacher Flunked My Planet.* New York: Pocket Books, 1992.

_____. *My Teacher Fried My Brains.* New York: Simon and Schuster, 1991.

_____. *My Teacher Glows in the Dark.* New York: Simon and Schuster, 1991.

Crilley, M. *Akiko and the Alpha Centauri 5000.* New York: Delacorte, 2003.

Daley, M. J. *Shanghaied to the Moon.* New York: Putnam, 2007.

_____. *Space Station Rat.* New York: Holiday House, 2005.

Davies, N. *Home.* London: Walker Books, 2005.

Dickinson, P. *The Devil's Children.* London: Victor Gollancz, 1970.

_____. *Eva.* London: Gollancz, 1988.

_____. *Heartsease.* London: Victor Gollancz, 1969.

_____. *The Weathermonger.* London: Victor Gollancz, 1968.

Doctorow, C. *Little Brother.* New York: Tor, 2008.

Duprau, J. *City of Ember.* New York: Random House, 2003.

Durant, A. *Gameboy Reloaded.* Edinburgh: Barrington Stoke, 2005.

Earnshaw, B. *Dragonfall 5 and the Royal Beast.* London: Methuen, 1972.

_____. *Dragonfall 5 and the Space Cowboys.* London: Methuen, 1972.

Engdahl, S. *Heritage of the Stars.* London: Victor Gollancz, 1973 (c. 1972).

Etchemendy, N. *Stranger from the Stars.* New York: Avon, 1983.

Farmer, N. *The House of the Scorpion.* London, New York, Sydney: Simon and Schuster, 2002.

Fisk, N. *A Rag, a Bone and a Hank of Hair.* London: Kestrel, 1980.

_____. *Space Hostages.* London: Hamish Hamilton, 1967.

_____. *Trillions.* London: Hamish Hamilton, 1971.

Foon, D. *The Dirt Eaters.* Willowdale, Ontario: Firefly Books, 2003.

Foreman, M. *Dinosaur Time.* London: Andersen Press, 2002.

_____. *Dinosaurs and All That Rubbish.* 2nd edition, London: Puffin, 1993.

Furey, M. *Sorceress.* London: Orion Books, 1998.

_____. *Spindrift*. London: Orion Books, 1999.

Gates, S. *Dusk*. Harmondsworth: Puffin, 2004.

Gilman, R. C. *The Rebel of Rhada*. New York: Harcourt Brace and World, 1968.

_____. *The Starkahn of Rhada*. New York: Harcourt Brace, 1970.

Glover, S. *e-[t]mail*. London: Andersen Press, 2002.

Godfrey, M. *Alien War Games*. Richmond Hill, Scholastic, 1984.

_____. *The Vandarian Incident*. Richmond Hill, Canada: Scholastic, 1981.

Goldman, E. M. *The Night Room*. New York: Viking Penguin, 1995.

Goodman, A. *Singing the Dogstar Blues*. Pymble, Australia: HarperCollins, 1998.

Greenburg, J. C. *Andrew Lost on the Dog*. New York: Random House, 2002.

Guttman, D. *Virtually Perfect*. New York: Hyperion, 1999.

Haddix, M. *Among the Barons*. New York: Simon and Schuster, 2003.

_____. *Among the Betrayed*. New York: Simon and Schuster, 2003.

_____. *Among the Hidden*. New York: Simon and Schuster, 1998.

_____. *Among the Imposters*. New York: Simon and Schuster, 2001.

_____. *Turnabout*. New York: Simon and Schuster, 2000.

Halacy, D. S. *Return from Luna*. New York: W.W. Norton, 1969.

_____. *Rocket Rescue*. New York: W. W. Norton, 1968.

Halam, A. *Siberia*. London: Orion, 2005.

_____. *Taylor Five*. London: Orion, 2002.

Hamilton, P. *Lightstorm*. London: Orion, 1998.

Hand, E. *Star Wars, Boba Fett: A New Threat*. New York: Scholastic, 2004.

_____. *Star Wars, Boba Fett: Hunted*. New York: Scholastic, 2003.

_____. *Star Wars, Boba Fett: Maze of Deception*. New York: Scholastic, 2003.

Harris, R. *A Quest for Orion*. Harmondsworth, Middlesex: Puffin Plus, 1982.

Harrison, T. *Eye of the Wolf*. Markham, Ontario: Fitzhenry and Whiteside, 2003.

Hautman, P. *Rash*. New York: Simon and Schuster, 2006.

Haye, T. D. L., J. B. Jenkins, and C. Fabry. *The Left Behind: The Kids*. Cambridge: Tyndale House, 1998–2004.

Heinlein, R. A. *Between Planets*. New York: Scribner's, 1951.

_____. *Citizen of the Galaxy*. New York: Scribner's, 1957.

_____. *Have Space Suit — Will Travel*. New York: Scribner's, 1958.

_____. "The Menace from Earth." *Fantasy and Science Fiction*. August 1957. 109–129.

_____. *Podkayne of Mars*. New York: Putnam's, 1963.

_____. *Space Cadet*. New York: Scribner's, 1948.

_____. *Star Beast*. New York: Scribner's, 1954.

_____. *Starman Jones*. New York: Scribner's, 1954.

_____. *Starship Troopers*. New York: Putnam's, 1959.

_____. *Tunnel in the Sky*. New York: Scribner's, 1955.

Hoover, H. M. *The Lost Star*. London: Methuen, 1980.

Howarth, L. *Maphead*. London: Walker Books, 1994.

_____. *Maphead 2*. London: Walker Books, 2001 [1997].

_____. *Ultraviolet*. London: Penguin, 2001.

Hughes, M. *Invitation to the Game*. Toronto: HarperCollins, 1992 [1990].

_____. *The Keeper of the Isis Light*. London: Hamish Hamilton, 1980.

_____. *Ring-Rise, Ring-Set*. London: Julia MacRae, 1982

_____. *Space Trap*. Toronto and Vancouver: A Groundwood Book, 1983.

Jacobs, P. S. *Born into Light*. London: Scholastic, 1988.

James, S. *Baby Brains*. London, Boston, Sydney, Auckland: Walker Books, 2004.

Jeapes, B. *His Majesty's Starship*. London: Scholastic, 1998.

_____. *New World Order*. London: David Fickling Books, 2005.

_____. *The Xenocide Mission*. London: Fickling Books, 2002.

Jones, D. W. *A Tale of Time City*. London: Methuen, 1987.

Joyce, G. *Spiderbite*. London: Orion, 1998.

Kaye, M. *Max on Earth*. London: Penguin, 1986.

Keaney, B. *The Hollow People*. London: Orchard Books, 2006.

Kirk, D. *Hush, Little Alien*. New York: Hyperion, 1999.

_____. *Nova's Ark*. New York: Scholastic, 1999.

Kostick, C. *Epic*. Dublin: O'Brien Press, 2004.

_____. *Saga*. Dublin: O'Brien Press, 2006.

Landsman, S. *The Gadget Factor*. New York: Atheneum, 1984.

Lassiter, R. *Borderland*. Oxford: Oxford University Press, 2003.

_____. *Outland*. Oxford: Oxford University Press, 2004.

_____. *Shadowland*. Oxford: Oxford University Press, 2005.

Lennon, J. *Questors*. Harmondsworth: Puffin, 2007.

Levithan, D. *Boy Meets Boy*. New York: Knopf, 2003.

_____. *Wide Awake*. New York: Alfred Knopf, 2006.

Lightner, A. M. *The Space Ark*. New York: G.P. Putnams, 1968.

Lovegrove, J. *Computopia*. Computopia: Orion Books, 1998.

Lowry, L. *Gathering Blue*. New York: Random House, 2000.

Luzatto, C. *Interplanetary Avenger*. New York: Holiday House, 2002.

Macgregor, E. *Miss Pickerell Goes Under the Sea*. New York: McGraw-Hill, 1953.

_____. *Miss Pickerell on the Moon*. New York: McGraw-Hill, 1965.

MacHale, D. J. *Pendragon: The Merchant of Death*. London: Simon and Schuster, 2003.

_____. *Rivers of Zadaa*. New York: Simon and Schuster, 2005.

Maclean, G. *Roivan: Book One of the A'nzarian Chronicle*. Auckland, NZ, 2003.

MacLeod, K. *Cydonia*. London: Orion, 1998.

_____. *The Human Front*. Harrogate: PS Publishing, 2001.

Maguire, G. *I Feel Like the Morning Star*. New York and London: Harper and Row, 1997.

Mahy, M. *Aliens in the Family*. New York: Scholastic, 1986.

Malley, G. *The Declaration*. London: Bloomsbury, 2007.

Mark, J. *The Ennead*. Harmondsworth, UK: Kestrel, 1978.

_____. *Useful Idiots*. London: David Fickling Books, 2004.

Martel, S. *Robot Alert*. Toronto: Kids Can Press, 1985.

McCormack, U. *Star Trek Deep Space Nine: Hollow Men*. New York: Pocket Books, 2005.

McGann, O. *Ancient Appetites*. London: Random House, 2007.

_____. *The Gods and Their Machines*. Dublin: O'Brien Press, 2004.

_____. *The Harvest Tide Project*. Dublin: O'Brien Press, 2004.

_____. *Small-Minded Giants*. London: Doubleday, 2007.

_____. *Under Fragile Stone*. Dublin: O'Brien Press, 2005.

McMullen, S. *Before the Storm*. Melbourne, Australia: Ford Street Publishing, 2007.

McNaughton, J. *The Raintree Rebellion*. Toronto: HarperTrophy Canada, 2006.

_____. *The Secret Under My Skin*. New York: EOS, 2005.

Meecham, M. *Quiet! You're Invisible!* New York: Holiday House, 2001.

Moore, G. L., and Patrick Moore. *Mrs. Moore in Space*. London: Cassell, 1974.

Morgan, N. *Sleepwalking*. London: Hodder, 2004.

Moss, M. *Amelia Takes Command*. Middleton, WI: Pleasant Publications/American Girl, 1999.

Murphy, M., and M. Oliver. *Foley and Jem*. London: Magi Publications, 2004.

Nicholson, W. *The Wind Singer*. London: Mammoth, 2000.

Norriss, A. *The Touchstone*. Harmondsworth: Puffin, 2004.

Norton, A. *Cat's Eye*. New York: Harcourt, Brace and World, 1961

_____. *Plague Ship*. New York: Ace Books, 1956.

_____. *Star Man's Son*. New York: Harcourt Brace and World, 1952.

_____, and D. Madlee. *Star Ka'at*. Glasgow and London: Blackie, 1976.

Oakley, G. *Henry's Quest*. London and Basingstoke, 1986.

O'Brien, R. C. *The Silver Crown*. London: Victor Gollancz, 1973.

_____. *Z for Zachariah*. London: Victor Gollancz, 1975.

O'Malley, K. *Captain Raptor and the Moon Mystery*. London: Walker, 2005.

Oppel, K. *Airborn*. New York: HarperCollins, 2004.

_____. *Skybreaker*. Canada: Hodder Children's Books, 2005.

Panshin, A. *Rite of Passage*. New York: Ace, 1978 (1968).

Pausewang, G. *Fall Out (Der Wolke)*. New York: Viking, 1994.

_____. *The Last Children*. London: Walker Books, 1983.

Pfeffer, S. B. *Life as We Knew It*. New York: Harcourt, 2006.

Philbrick, R. *The Last Book in the Universe*. New York: Scholastic, 2000.

Pilkey, D. *Ricky Ricotta's Might Robot vs. the Mecha Monkeys from Mars*. New York: Scholastic, 2002.

Pratchett, T. *Diggers*. London: Doubleday, 1990.

_____. *Johnny and the Bomb*. London: Doubleday, 1996.

_____. *Only You Can Save Mankind*. London: Doubleday, 1992.

_____. *Truckers*. London: Doubleday, 1989.

_____. *Wings*. London: Doubleday, 1990.

Price, S. *Coming Down to Earth*. London: HarperCollins, 1994.

_____. *Odin's Queen*. London: Simon and Schuster, 2006.

_____. *Odin's Voice*. London: Simon and Schuster, 2004.

_____. *The Sterkarm Handshake*. London: Scholastic, 2000.

Prose, F. *After*. New York: HarperCollins, 2003.

Reeve, P. *A Darkling Plain*. London: Scholastic, 2006.

_____. *Infernal Devices*. London: Scholastic, 2005.

_____. *Larklight, or, the Revenge of the The White Spiders! or To Saturn's Rings and Back! A Rousing Tale of Dauntless Pluck in the Farthest Reaches of Space. As Chronicl'd by Art Mumby with the aid of Mr. Philip Reeve*. London, Bloomsbury, 2006.

_____. *Mortal Engines*. London: Scholastic, 2001.

_____. *Predator's Gold*. London: Scholastic Point, 2004.

_____. *Starcross*. London: Bloomsbury, 2007.

Rennie, S. *Kat and Doug on Planet Fankle*. Scotland: Itchykoo, 2002.

Rex, A. *The True Meaning of Smek Day*. New York: Hyperion, 2007.

Roberts, G. *I Am a Dalek*. London: BBC Worldwide, 2006.

Rosoff, M. *How I Live Now*. London: Penguin, 2004.

Rubenstein, G. *Galax-Arena*. New York: Simon and Schuster, 1992.

Sampson, F. *F67*. London: Hamish Hamilton, 1975.

_____. *Them*. Oxford: Lion Publishing, 2005.

Sargent, P. *Alien Child*. New York: Harper and Row, 1988.

Schanback, M. *Princess from Another Planet*. New York: Holiday House, 2005.

Scott, H. *Why Weeps the Brogan*. London: Walker Books, 1989.

Service, P. F. *Under Alien Stars*. New York: Ballantine, 1990.

Sheffield, Charles. *The Cyborg from Earth*. New York: Tor, 1998.

_____. *Putting Up Roots*. New York: Tor, 1997.

_____, and Jerry Pournelle. *Higher Education*. New York: Tor, 1996.

Simon, B. *Man on the Moon (a day in the life of Bob)*. Dorking, Surrey: Templar, 2002.

Sims, I. *Puzzle Journey Into Space*. London: Usborne Puzzles, 2003.

Sleator, W. *The Green Futures of Tycho*. New York: Tor, 2006 (1981).

_____. *Interstellar Pig*. New York: E.P. Dutton, 1984.

_____. *The Last Universe*. New York: Amulet Books, 2005.

_____. *Marco's Millions*. New York: Dutton Children's Books, Penguin, 2001.

_____. *Parasite Pig*. New York: Penguin Firebird, 2002

_____. *Strange Attractors*. New York: E. P. Dutton, 1984.

Slote, A. *Clone Catcher*. New York: J. P. Lippincott, 1982.

Spencer, B. *Guardian of the Dark*. Richmond Hill, CA: Scholastic, 1993.

Stahler, D., Jr. *Truesight*. New York: Eos HarperCollins, 2004.

Stephens, J. B. *The Big Empty*. New York: Penguin Razorbill, 2004, 2005.

_____. *Desolation Angels*. New York: Penguin Razorbill, 2004.

_____. *No Exit*. New York: Penguin Razorbill, 2005.

_____. *Paradise City*. New York: Penguin Razorbill, 2004.

Swindells, R. *Brother in the Land*. London: OUP, 1984.

Taylor, C. *Thirst*. Markham, Ontario: Fitzhenry and Whiteside, 2005.

Thomas, F., and R. Collins. *Maybe One Day*. London: Bloomsbury, 2001

Thompson, K. *The Missing Link*. London: Red Fox, 2000.

_____. *Only Human*. London: Red Fox, 2001.

_____. *Origins*. London: Red Fox, 2003

Townsend, J. R. *King Creature, Come*. New York: Oxford, 1980.

Traviss, K. *Hard Contact*. New York: Del Rey, 2004

_____. *Triple Zero*. New York: Del Rey, 2006.

Ure, J. *Come Lucky April*. 1992.

_____. *Plague 99*. London: Methuen, 1989.

Valentine, J. *Jumpman Rule One*. London: Random House, 2002.

_____. *Jumpman 2: Don't Even Think About It*. Sidney: Random House, 2003.

Vizzini, N. *Be More Chill*. London: HarperCollins, 2004.

Wahl, J. *Rabbits on Mars*. Minneapolis: Carolrhoda Books, Lerner Publishing Group, 2003.

Walsh, J. P. *The Green Book*. Basingstoke: Macmillan, 1981.

Ward, H. *The Dragon Machine*. London: Templar, 2003.

Waugh, S. *Earthborn*. London: Bodley Head, 2002.

_____. *Space Race*. Delacourt, 2000.

_____. *Who Goes Home?* London: Bodley Head, 2003

Weisner, D. *June 29, 1999*. New York: Clarion, 1992.

Werlin, N. *Double Helix*. London: Puffin Sleuth, 2004.

Westall, R. *Futuretrack 5*. London: Kestrell Books, 1983.

Westerfeld, S. *The Last Days*. New York: Penguin, 2006.

_____. *Pretties*. New York: Simon and Schuster, 2006.

_____. *Specials*. New York: Simon and Schuster, 2006.

_____. *Uglies*. New York: Simon and Schuster, 2005.

Whybrow, Ian, and Adrian Reynolds. *Harry and the Robots*. London: Gullane, 2000.

Wilder, C. *The Luck of Brin's Five*. London: Angus and Robertson, 1979.

_____. *The Nearest Fire*. New York: HarperCollins, 1980.

Willet, E. *Andy Nebula: Interstellar Rockstar*, Montreal: Roussan, 1999.

Williams, Jay, and Raymond Abrashkin. *Danny Dunn and the Smallifying Machine*. London: MacDonald, 1970.

_____, and _____. *Danny Dunn and the Homework Machine*. London: MacDonald and Jane's, 1958.

_____, and _____. *Danny Dunn on the Ocean Floor*. London: Macdonald, 1960.

Williams-Ellis, A., and Mably Owen, eds. Foreword by Bertrand Russell. *Out of This World 1: An Anthology of Science Fiction*. London and Glasgow: Blackie, 1960.

_____, and _____, eds. *Out of This World 2: An Anthology of Science Fiction*. London: Blackie, 1961.

_____, and _____, eds. *Out of This World 3: An Anthology of Science Fiction*. London and Glasgow: Blackie, 1962.

_____, and _____, eds. *Out of This World 4: An Anthology of Science Fiction*. London and Glasgow: Blackie, 1964.

_____, and _____, eds. *Out of This World 5: An Anthology of Science Fiction*. London and Glasgow: Blackie, 1965.

_____, and _____, eds. *Out of This World 6:* *An Anthology of Science Fiction*. London and Glasgow: Blackie, 1967.

_____, and _____, eds. *Out of This World 7: An Anthology of Science Fiction*. London and Glasgow: Blackie, 1968.

_____, and _____, eds. *Out of This World: 8. An Anthology of Science Fiction*. Glasgow: Blackie, 1970.

_____, and _____, eds. *Out of This World 9: An Anthology of Science Fiction*. Glasgow: Blackie, 1972.

_____, and _____, eds. *Worlds Apart: An Anthology of Science Fiction*. Glasgow: Blackie and Son, 1966.

_____, and Michael Pearson, eds. *Out of This World 10: An Anthology of Science Fiction*. London and Glasgow: Blackie, 1973.

Willis, J. *Dr. Xargle's Book of Earthlets*. London: Andersen Press, 1988.

Wollheim, D. A. *Mike Mars Around the Moon*. Garden City, NY: Doubleday, 1964.

_____. *Mike Mars Flies the X-15*. New York: Doubleday, 1961.

Wood, N. *The Stone Chameleon*. Cape Town: Maskew Miller Longman, 2004.

Wooding, C. *Endgame*. London: Scholastic, 2000.

Yaccarino, D. *If I Had a Robot*. New York: Penguin Viking, 1996.

Yolen, J. *Commander Toad and the Big Black Hole*. New York: Coward-McCann, 1983.

_____. *The Devil's Arithmetic*. New York: Viking, 1988.

Yorinks, Arthur. *Company's Coming*. New York: Hyperion, 1998.

_____, and Mort Drucier. *Tomatoes from Mars*. New York: Michael Di Capua, HarperCollins, 1999.

The full list of texts located and considered for this book can be found at http://www.farah-sf.blogspot.com.

Other Works Cited

Allen, J. *The Blue Death*. London: Hodder, 2001.

Amos, Sandra, and Richard Boohan. "The Changing Nature of Science Education." In Amos, S. and Boohan, R., eds. *Teaching Science in Secondary Schools: A Reader*. London and New York: Routledge/Falmer/ Open University Press, 2002.

_____, and _____, eds. *Teaching Science in Secondary Schools: A Reader*. London and New York: Routledge/Falmer and the Open University, 2002.

Anders, L. "Novels, Novelizations and Tie-ins, Oh My!" In Brin, D. and Stover, M. W., eds. *Star Wars on Trial; Science Fiction and Fantasy Writers Debate the Most Popular Science Fiction Films of All Time*. Dallas: Benbella, 2006.

Anderson, S. B., ed. *Serving Older Teens*. Westport, CT; London: Libraries Unlimited, Greenwood Publishing Group, 2004.

Andrews, Georgina, and Kate Knighton. *100 Science Experiments*. London: Usborne, 2005.

Angier, N. *The Canon: A Whirligig Tour of the Beautiful Basics of Science*. Boston and New York: Houghton Mifflin, 2007.

Appleyard, J. A. *Becoming a Reader: The Experience of Fiction from Childhood to Adulthood*. Cambridge: Cambridge University Press, 1990.

Apselhoff, M. F. "The British Science Fiction of Louise Lawrence." In Sullivan III, C. W., ed. *Science Fiction for Young Readers*. Westport, CT: Greenwood Press, 1993.

Arizpe, E., and M. Styles. *Children Reading Pictures: Interpreting Visual Texts*. London and New York: Routledge Farmer, 2003.

Arnold, N. *Horrible Science: Suffering Scientists*. London: Hippo, 2000.

Bailey, B. L. *From Front Porch to Back Seat: Courtship in Twentieth-Century America*. Baltimore and London: Johns Hopkins University Press, 1989.

Bailey, J. *A Cartoon History of the Earth, Volume 2: Life Finds Its Feet*. London: AandC Black, 2001.

Bailey, K. V. "Masters, Slaves and Rebels: Dystopia." In Sulivan III, C. W., ed. *Science Fiction for Young Readers*. Westport, CT: Greenwood Press, 1993.

_____, and A. Sawyer. "The Janus Perspective: Science Fiction and the Young Adult Reader in Britain." In Sullivan III, C. W., ed. *Young Adult Science Fiction*. Westport, CT: Greenwood Press, 1999.

Ball, J. *Think of a Number*. London: Dorling Kindersley, 2005.

Bartter, M. "Young Adults, Science Fiction and War." In Sullivan III, C. W., ed. *Young Adult Science Fiction*. Westport, CT: Greenwood Press, 1999.

Bazelon, E. "The Little Men Who Love *Little House*." *Slate*, 2006.

Bennet, J. *Bringing Science to Life: The Research Evidence on Teaching in Context*. York, Department of Educational Studies, 2005.

Benton, M. *Reader Response Criticism in Children's Literature*. Southampton: Centre for Language in Education, University of Southampton, Occasional Papers, 15, 1993.

Berg, L. *Look at Kids*. London: Butler and Tanner, 1972.

Blackford, H. V. *Out of This World: Why Literature Matters to Girls*. New York: Teacher's College Press, 2004.

Blintz, W. P. "Resistant readers in secondary education: Some insights and implications." *Journal of Reading*, 36, 604–615, 1993.

Bliss, J. "Learning Science: Piaget and After." In Amos, S. and Boohan, R., eds. *Teaching Science in Secondary Schools: A Reader*. London and New York: Routledge/Falmer/Open University Press, 2002.

Blyton, E. *The Naughtiest Girl Again*. London: George Newnes, 1942.

_____. *The Naughtiest Girl in the School*. London: George Newnes, 1940.

_____. *The Naughtiest Girl Is a Monitor*. London: George Newnes, 1945.

Bova, B. "From Mad Professors to Brilliant Scientists." In Gerhardt, L., ed. *Issues in Children's Book Selection: A School Library Journal/Library Journal Anthology*. New York and London: R. R. Bowker, 1973.

Brent-Dyer, E. M. *The Chalet School and Rosalie*. Edinburgh, W and R Chambers, 1953.

Brin, D. *Kiln People*. New York: Tor, 2002.

Bromley, H. "Spying on Picture Books: Exploring Intertextuality with Young Children." In Watson, V. and Styles, M., eds. *Talking Pictures: Pictorial Texts and Young Readers*. London: Hodder and Stoughton, 1996.

Brown, J. *Teaching Science in Schools*. London: University of London Press, 1930.

Brozo, W. G. *To Be a Boy, to Be a Reader: Engaging Teen Boys in Active Literacy*. Newark, DE: International Reading Association, 2002.

Bruer, J. T. "Education." In Bechtel, W. and Graham, G., eds. *A Companion to Cognitive Science*. Oxford: Blackwell, 1998.

Buchanan, A., ed. *It's a Boy: Women Writers on Raising Their Sons*. Emeryville, CA: Seal Press, 2005.

Buckingham, D. *After the Death of Childhood*. Cambridge: Polity Press, 2000.

Bujold, L. M. *Mirror Dance*. New York: Baen Books, 1994.

_____. *Shards of Honor*. New York: Baen, 1986.

Bull, M. "Science in Secondary Modern Schools." *Studies in Education*, 5. 499–532, 1954.

Burnett, R. W. *Teaching Science in the Secondary School.* New York: Holt, Rinehart
and Winston, 1960.

Burnie, D. *The Kingfisher Illustrated Dinosaur
Encyclopedia.* London: Kingfisher, 2001.

Butler, A. M. "'We Has Found the Enemy and
They Is Us': Virtual War and Empathy in
Four Children's Science Fiction Novels."
The Lion and the Unicorn. 28, 171–185,
2004.

Butler, R. R. *Building Science for Junior Technical Schools of Building.* London: The English Universities Press, 1946.

Byrnes, J. P. *Cognitive Development and
Learning in Instructional Contexts.* Boston,
MA: Allyn and Bacon, 1996.

Cameron, E. *The Green and Burning Tree: in the
Writing and Enjoyment of Children's Books.*
Boston, Toronto: Little, Brown, 1962.

Campbell, J. W. "The Place of Science Fiction." In Bretnor, R., ed. *Modern Science
Fiction: Its Meaning And Its Future.* Second
Edition (original 1953) ed. Chicago: Ad-
vent, 1979.

Canada, G. *Reaching Up for Manhood.*
Boston, MA: Beacon Press, 1998.

Carin, Arthur, and Robert B. Sund. *Teaching
Science Through Discovery.* Columbus, OH,
Charles E. Merril, 1975.

Cart, M. *From Romance to Realism: 50 Years
of Growth and Change in Young Adult Literature.* New York: HarperCollins, 1996.

Chaille, Christine, and Lory Britain. *The
Young Child as Scientist: A Constructivist
Approach to Early Childhood Science Edu-
cation.* Boston, MA: Allyn and Bacon, 1997.

Chambers, A. *Introducing Books to Children.*
London, Heinemann Educational Books,
1973.

"The Chemistry Set Generation." *http://www.
rsc.org/chemistryworld/Issues/2007/Decem
ber/TheChemistrySetGeneration. asp,* 2007.

Cherland, M. R. *Private Practices: Girls Reading Fiction and Constructing Identity.* London: Taylor and Francis, 1994.

Clark, B. L. *Kiddie Lit: The Cultural Construc-
tion of Children's Literature in America.*
Baltimore and London: Johns Hopkins
University Press, 2003.

Clark, M. M. *Young Fluent Readers.* London:
Heinemann Educational, 1976.

Clute, J., and J. Grant, eds. *The Encyclopedia
of Fantasy.* London: Orbit, 1997.

Cohen, P. C. *A Calculating People.* London
and New York: Routledge, 1999.

Coles, M. "Science Education: vocational and

general approaches." In Amos, S. and Boohan, R., eds. *Teaching Science in Secondary
Schools: A Reader.* London and New York:
Routledge/Falmer/Open University Press,
2002.

Crago, M., and H. Crago. *Prelude to Literacy:
A Preschool Child's Encounter with Picture
and Story.* Carbondale and Edwardsville:
Southern Illinois University Press, 1983.

Craig, J. *Jimmy Coates: Killer.* London:
HarperCollins, 2005.

Crawford, Mary, and Roger Chaffin. "The
Reader's Construction of Meaning: Cog-
nitive Research on Gender and Com-
prehension." In Flynn, E. A. and Schwe-
ickart, P. P., eds. *Gender and Reading:
Essays on Readers, Texts, and Contexts.*
London and Baltimore: Johns Hopkins
University Press, 1986.

Crew, H. S. "Not So Brave a World: The Representation of Human Cloning in Science
Fiction for Young Adults." *The Lion and
the Unicorn,* 28. 203–221, 2004.

Dodman, F. E. *The New Observer's Book of
Ships.* Harmondsworth, Middlesex: Frederick Warne, 1986.

Doonan, J. *Looking at Pictures in Picture
Books.* Lockwood, Gloucester: The Thimble Press, 1993.

Dowling, T. "'Johnnie! Put the Knife Down!'"
The Guardian. London, July 21, 2007.

Dunbar, K., and J. Fugelsang. "Scientific
Thinking and Reasoning." In Holyoak, K.
J. and Morrison, R. G., eds. *The Cambridge
Handbook of Thinking and Reasoning.*
Cambridge: Cambridge University Press,
2005.

Dunn, T., and K. Hiller. "Growing Home:
The Triumph of Youth in the Novels of H.
M. Hoover." In Sullivan III, C. W., ed. *Sci-
ence Fiction for Young Readers.* Westport,
CT: Greenwood Press, 1993.

Dunstan, A. E. *An Organic Chemistry for
Schools and Technical Institutes.* London:
Methuen, 1908.

Dyasi, H. M. "Celebrating Diverse Minds:
Using Different Pedagogical Approaches."
In Rhoton, J. and Shane, P., eds. *Teaching
Science in the 21st Century.* Arlington, VA:
National Science Teachers Association
Press, 2006.

Egoff, S., and J. Saltman. *The New Republic of
Childhood: A Critical Guide to Canadian
Children's Literature in English.* Toronto:
Oxford University Press, 1990.

Erisman, F. *Boys' Books, Boys' Dreams and the*

Mystique of Flight. Fort Worth: Texas Christian University, 2006.

_____. "Robert Heinlein, the Scribner Juveniles, and Cultural Literacy." *Extrapolation*, 32. 45–53, 1991.

Fenwick, L. "Periodicals and Adolescent Girls." *Studies in Education*, 1. 27–45, 1954.

Fisher, M. *The Bright Face of Danger*. London, Sydney, Auckland, Toronto: Hodder and Stoughton, 1986.

_____. *Intent Upon Reading*. London: Hodder and Stoughton, 1961.

Flavell, J. H., P. H. Miller, and S. H. Miller. *Cognitive Development*. Upper Saddle River, NJ: Prentice Hall, 2002.

Flynn, E. A., and P. P. Schweikart, eds. *Gender and Reading: Essays on Readers, Texts, and Contexts*. Baltimore and London: The Johns Hopkins University Press, 1986.

Follos, A. M. *Reviving Reading: School Library Programming, Author Visits and Books That Rock!* Westport, CT; London: Libraries Unlimited, Greenwood Press, 2006.

Ford, R. M. "Thinking and Cognitive Development in Young Children." In Maynard, T. and Thomas, N., eds. *An Introduction to Early Childhood Studies*. London: Sage, 2004.

Foster, J. "Australian Science Fiction for Children and Adolescents: 1940–1990." In Sullivan III, C. W., ed. *Young Adult Science Fiction*. Westport, CT: Greenwood Press, 1999.

Frank, M. A. "Women in Heinlein's Juveniles." In Sullivan III, C. W., ed. *Young Adult Science Fiction*. Westport, CT: Greenwood Press, 1999.

Fywell, T. (dir.) *Ice Princess*. Walt Disney, Home Entertainment, 2005.

Galbraith, G. T. *Reading Lives: Reconstructing Childhood, Books, and Schools in Britain, 1870–1920*. London: Macmillan, 1997.

Garner, A. *The Voice That Thunders*. London: Harvill, 1997.

Gillespie, J. T., and C. J. Naden. *Teenplots: A Booktalk Guide to Use with Readers Aged 12–18*. Westport, CT: London, Libraries Unlimited, Greenwood Press, 2003.

Goldberg, L. *Teaching Science to Children*. Mineola, NY: Dover, 1970.

Goldsmith, D. M. *Dead Famous: Inventors and Their Bright Ideas*. London: Scholastic, 2002.

Good, R. G. *How Children Learn Science: conceptual development and implications for teaching*. New York and London: Macmillan and Collier, 1977.

Gopnik, A., A. Meltzof, and P. Kuhl. *How Babies Think: The Science of Childhood*. London: Orion, 1999.

_____, _____, and _____. *The Scientist in the Crib: What Early Learning Tells Us About the Mind*. New York: HarperCollins, 2001.

Greenberg, B. S. "Saturday Morning Science." In Hays, K., ed. *TV, Science and Kids: Teaching Out Children to Question*. Reading, MA: Addison-Wesley, 1984.

Greenberg, N. *It's True! Squids Suck*. Crows Nest, NSW, Australia: Allen and Unwin, 2005.

Greenburg, J. C. *Andrew Lost: On the Dog*. New York: Random House, 2002.

Gunn, J. *The Science of Science-Fiction Writing*. Lanham, MD; London: Scarecrow, 2000.

Hall, C., M. Coles, V. Fraser, M. Youngman, J. Restorick, P. Bryant, and G. White. *The Children's Reading Choices Project at the University of Nottingham, sponsored by W H Smith plc*. Notttingham: University of Nottingham, 1995.

Hall, S. *Using Picture Storybooks to Teach Character Education*. Phoenix, AZ: Oryx Press, 2000.

Hartwell, D. *Age of Wonders: Exploring the World of Science Fiction*. New York: Walker, 1984.

Hays, K. "An Interview with Mr Wizard." In Hays, K., ed. *TV, Science, and Kids: Teaching Our Children to Question*. Reading, MA: Addison-Wesley, 1984.

_____, ed. *TV, Science, and Kids: Teaching Our Children to Question*. Reading, MA: Addison-Wesley, 1984.

Hebron, M. E. "The Mental and Scholastic Status of Pupils in the Various Streams of Secondary Modern Schools." *Studies in Education*, 5. 400–419, 1954.

Hendrix, H. V. "The Things of a Child: Coming Full Circle with Alan E. Nourse's *Raiders from the Rings*." In Sullivan III, C. W., ed. *Science Fiction for Young Readers*. Westport, CT: Greenwood Press, 1993.

Herald, D. T. *Teen Genreflecting: A Guide to Reading Interests*. Westport, CT; London: Libraries Unlimited, Greenwood Press, 2003.

_____, and B. Kunzel. *Strictly Science Fiction*. Greenwood Village, CO: Libraries Unlimited, Greenwood Publishing Group, 2002.

Hickam, Homer, Jr. *Rocket Boys*. New York: Delacorte Press, 1998.

Hintz, Carrie, and Elaine Ostry, eds. *Utopian*

and Dystopian Writing for Children and Young Adults. New York and London: Routledge, 2003.

Hodson, D. "Towards a Personalised Science." In Amos, S. and Boohan, R., eds. Teaching Science in Secondary Schools: A Reader. London and New York: Routledge/Falmer/Open University Press, 2002.

Hollindale, P. Signs of Childness in Children's Books. Woodchester, UK: Thimble Press, 1997.

Holton, G. "The Struggle for Scientific Maturity." In Hays, K., ed. TV, Science, and Kids: Teaching Our Children to Question. Reading, MA: Addison-Wesley, 1984.

Honeyman, S. "Mutiny by Mutation: Uses of Neoteny in Science Fiction." Children's Literature in Education, 35. 347–366, 2004.

Hubler, A. E. "Can Anne Shirley Help 'Revive Ophelia'? Listening to Girl Readers." In Inness, S. A., ed. Delinquents and Debutantes: Twentieth Century Girls' Cultures. New York and London: New York University Press, 1998.

Huck, C. S., Hepler, S. and Hickman, J. Children's Literature in the Elementary School. New York: Holt, Reinhart and Winston, 1987.

Hughes, M. "The Struggle Between Utopia and Dystopia in Writing for Young Children and Young Adults." In Ostry, Carrie Hintz and Elaine Ostry, ed. Utopian and Dystopian Writing for Children and Young Adults. New York and London: Routledge, 2003.

Hughes, T. Tom Brown's School Days. Cambridge: Macmillan, 1857.

Iggulden, C., and Iggulden, H. The Dangerous Book for Boys. London, HarperCollins, 2006.

James, E. "Yellow, Black, Metal and Tentacled: The Race Question in American Science Fiction." In Davies, J. P., ed. Science Fiction, Social Conflict and War. Manchester: Manchester University Press, 1990.

_____, and F. Mendlesohn, eds. The Cambridge Companion to Science Fiction. Cambridge: Cambridge University Press, 2003.

James, S. "Language Development in the Young Child." In David, T. A. N. T., ed. An Introduction to Early Childhood Studies. London: Sage, 2004.

Jones, D. W. "Interview with Diana Wynne Jones, conducted by Charles Butler, 22 March 2001." In Rosenberg, T., Hixon, M. P., Scapple, S. M. and White, D. R.,

eds. Diana Wynne Jones, An Exciting and Exacting Wisdom. New York: Peter Lang, 2002.

_____. Witch Week. Basingstoke: Macmillan, 1982.

Jones, G. Deconstructing the Starships: Science Fiction and Reality. Liverpool: Liverpool University Press, 1999.

Jones, P., P. Taylor, and K. Edwards. A Core Collection for Young Adults. New York: Neal-Schuman, 2003.

Jones, R. E. "'True Myth': Female Archetypes in Monica Hughes's The Keeper of the Isis Light." In Sullivan III, C. W., ed. Science Fiction for Young Readers. Westport, CT: Greenwood Press, 1993.

Jovanovic, J. "Individual-Contextual Relationships and Mathematics Performance; Comparing American and Serbian Young Adolescents." Journal of Early Adolescence, 14. 449–47, 1994.

Kerrod, R., and S.A. Holgate. The Way Science Works. London: Dorling Kindersley and the Science Museum, London, 2002.

Kincaid, P. What It Is We Do When We Read Science Fiction. Harold Wood, Essex: Beccon Publications, 2008.

Kramer, S. P. How to Think Like a Scientist: Answering Questions by the Scientific Method. New York: Thomas Y. Cromwell, 1979.

Kroll, J. "Gillian Rubenstein's Beyond the Labyrinth." Paradoxa: Studies in World Literary Genres, 2. 332–346, 1996.

Kunzel, B., and S. Manczuk. First Contact: A Reader's Selection of Science Fiction and Fantasy. Lanham, MD and London: Scarecrow, 2001.

Kuslan, Louise, and A. Harris Stone. Teaching Children Science: An Inquiry Approach. Belmont, CA: Wadsworth, 1968.

Lacy, L. E. Art and Design in Children's Picture Books: An Analysis of Caldecott Award-Winning Illustrations. Chicago and London: American Library Association, 1986.

Lanclos, D. M. At Play in Belfast: Children's Folklore and Identities in Northern Ireland. New Brunswick, NJ and London: Rutgers University Press, 2003.

Larbalastier, J. The Battle of the Sexes in Science Fiction. Middletown, CT: Wesleyan University Press, 2002.

Laybourn, K., and C. H. Bailey. Practical Science for Secondary Schools. London: University of London Press, 1962.

_____ and _____. Teaching Science to the Ordinary Pupil. London: The English Language Book Society and University of London Press, 1957.

Leffler, Y. *Horror as Pleasure: The Aesthetics of Horror Fiction.* Stockholm: Almqvist and Wiksell, 2000.

Le Guin, U. K. *The Word for World Is Forest,* New York: Berkeley/Putnam, 1972.

Lesnik-Oberstein, K. *Children's Literature: Criticism and the Fictional Child.* Oxford: Clarendon Press, 1994.

Levenson, E. *Teaching Children About Physical Science; Ideas and Activities Every Teacher and Parent Can Use.* New York: TAB Books, McGraw-Hill, 1994.

Levy, M. M. "Science Fiction for Children and Young Adults: Criticism and Other Secondary Materials." In Sullivan III, C. W., ed. *Young Adult Science Fiction.* Westport, CT: Greenwood Press, 1999.

_____. "Selected Bibliography." In Sullivan III, C. W., ed. *Science Fiction for Young Readers.* Westport, CT: Greenwood Press, 1993.

_____. "The Young Adult Science Fiction Novel as *Bildungsroman.*" In Sullivan III, C. W., ed. *Young Adult Science Fiction.* Westport, CT: Greenwood Press, 1999.

Lewis, D. "The Constructedness of Text: Picture Books and the Metafictive." *Signal,* 62. 131–46, 1990.

_____. *Reading Contemporary Picturebooks: Picturing Text.* London and New York: Routledge, 2001.

Lieberman, M. "The 'fiction gap': empathy, prestige, or what?" *The Language Log.* 2007.

Luckhurst, R. *Science Fiction (Cultural History of Literature).* London: Polity Press, 2005.

Lynch, S. "The Son of Skywalker Must Not Become a Jackass, or Finding the Ethical Core of the *Star Wars* films by Ignoring the Ghosts and Muppets." In Brin, D. and Stover, M. W., eds. *Star Wars On Trial; Science Fiction and Fantasy Writers Debate the Most Popular Science Fiction Films of All Time.* Dallas: Benbella Books, 2006.

Mallet, M. *Making Facts Matter: Non-Fiction 5–11.* London: Paul Chapman, 1992.

Manning, S. A., FLS. *A Ladybird Book of Butterflies, Moths and Other Insects.* Wills and Hepworth: Loughborough, 1965.

Martaus, A. "Reading Choices Among the Student Population of ASMA." *International Conference of the Fantastic in the Arts, 28.* Ft. Lauderdale, FL, 2007.

Marusek, D. *Counting Heads.* New York: Tor, 2007.

Mayer, R. E. "Should There Be a Three-Strikes Rule Against Pure Discovery Learning? The Case for Guided Methods of Instruction." *American Psychologist,* 59. 14–19, 2004.

Maynard, C. *Bugs: A Close-up View of the Insect World.* London: Dorling Kindersley, 2001.

Maynard, Tricia, and Nigel Thomas, ed. *An Introduction to Early Childhood Studies.* London: Sage, 2004.

Meek, M. *Information and Book Learning.* Woodchester: The Thimble Press, 1996.

Mendlesohn, F. "Crowning the King: Harry Potter and the Construction of Authority." In Whited, L. A., ed. *The Ivory Tower and Harry Potter: Perspectives on a Literary Phenomenon.* Columbia: University of Missouri Press, 2002.

_____. *Diana Wynne Jones: Children's Literature and the Fantastic Tradition.* New York: Routledge, 2005.

_____. *Rhetorics of Fantasy.* Middletown, CT: Wesleyan University Press, 2008.

_____. *Wherever I Lay My Cat, http://fjm. LiveJournal.com/333457.html,* 2006.

Mercer, J. B. "The Loss of Innocence." In Meet, M., Warlow, A. and Barton, G., eds. *The Cool Web.* London, Sydney, Toronto: The Bodley Head, 1974.

Millar, R., and J. Osbourne, ed. *Beyond 2000: Science Education for the Future.* London: King's College London School of Education, 1998.

Miller, W. M., Jr. *A Canticle for Leibowitz.* Philadelphia, PA: J. B. Lippincott, 1960.

Mills, R. "Perspectives of childhood." In Mills, J. and Mills, R., eds. *Childhood Studies: A Reader in Perspectives of Childhood.* London and New York: Routledge, 2000.

Mintz, S. *Huck's Raft: A History of American Childhood.* Cambridge, MA: Harvard University Press, 2004.

Mitchell, J. N. "Neo-Gnostic Elements in Louise Lawrence's *Moonwind.*" In Sullivan III, C. W., ed. *Science Fiction for Young Readers.* Westport, CT: Greenwood Press, 1993.

Molson, F. J. "American Technological Fiction for Youth: 1900–1940." In Sullivan, C. W., III, ed. *Young Adult Science Fiction.* Westport, CT: Greenwood Press, 1999.

_____. "The Tom Swift Books." In Sullivan, C. W., III, ed. *Science Fiction for Young Readers.* Westport, CT: Greenwood Press, 1993.

Moreno, Nancy, and Barbara Z. Tharp. "How Do Students Learn Science?" In Rhoton, J. and Shane, P., eds. *Teaching Science in the*

21st Century. Arlington, VA: National Science Teachers Association Press, 2006.

Morgan, N. *Blame My Brain: The Amazing Teenage Brain Revealed.* London: Walker Books, 2005.

Morgan, R. Bookshop Observation, 2007.

Morrisey, T. J. "Pamela Sargent's Science Fiction for Young Adults: Celebration of Change." *Science Fiction Studies,* 16. 184–190, 1989.

Mycio, M. *Wormwood Forest: A Natural History of Chernobyl.* Washington D.C.: Joseph Henry Press, 2005.

Nel, P. *Dr. Seuss: An American Icon.* New York: Continuum, 2004.

Nelson, K. *Language in Cognitive Development: Emergence of the Mediated Mind.* Cambridge: Cambridge University Press, 1996.

Nicholson, V. *Singled Out: How Two Million Women Survived Without Men After the First World War.* London: Viking Penguin, 2007.

Nikolajeva, M. *Children's Literature Comes of Age: Toward a New Aesthetic.* London and New York: Garland, 1996.

_____. and Scott, C. *How Picturebooks Work.* New York: Routledge, 2006.

Nodelman, P. "Children's Science Fiction as Retreaded Romance (review essay)." *Science Fiction Studies,* 13. 216–218, 1986.

_____. "Out There in Children's Science Fiction: Forward Into the Past." *Science Fiction Studies,* 12. 285–296, 1985.

_____. *Words Without Pictures: The Narrative Art of Children's Picture Books.* Athens and London: University of Georgia Press, 1988.

Norton, J. "Transchildren and the Discipline of Children's Literature." *The Lion and the Unicorn,* 23. 415–436, 1999.

Nuffield. *Nuffield Primary Science: Science and Literacy, A Guide for Primary Teachers.* London: Collins Educational, 1998.

_____. *Nuffield Primary Science: Understanding Science Ideas, A Guide for Primary Teachers.* London: Collins Educational, 1997.

Nugent, B. "Who's a Nerd Anyway?" *The New York Times.* August 12, 2007.

Nunn, G. *Handbook for Science Teachers in Secondary Modern Schools.* London: John Murray, 1951.

Ogborn, J., G. Kress, I. Martins, and K. McGillicudy. *Explaining Science in the Classroom.* Buckingham and Philadelphia: Open University Press, 1996.

Ormerod, M. B., and D. Duckworth. *Pupils' Attitudes to Science: A Review of Major Research.* Windsor: NFRER, 1975.

Osten, R. Vonder. "Four Generations of Tom Swift: Ideology in Juvenile Science Fiction." *The Lion and the Unicorn,* 28. 268–283, 2004.

Ostry, E. "'Is He Still Human? Are You?': Young Adult Science Fiction in the Posthuman Age." *The Lion and the Unicorn,* 28. 222–246, 2004.

Paolini, C. *Eragon.* New York: Laurel Leaf, 2001.

Pearce, R. P. *The Observer's Book of Weather.* London: Warne, 1980.

Petty, Kate, and Jennie Mazels. *Global Garden.* London: Eden Project Books (Transworld), 2005.

Phillips, D. C. "The Good, the Bad and the Ugly: The Many Faces of Constructivism." In Curren, R., ed. *Philosophy of Education.* Oxford: Blackwell, 2007.

Platt, R. *Forensics.* London: Kingfisher, 2005.

Pugh, S. *The Democratic Genre: Fan Fiction in a Literary Context.* New York: Seren, 2006.

Purves, L. "Boys, the Floor Is Yours." *The Times* (London), November 4, 2005.

Radway, J. *Reading the Romance,* Chapel Hill: University of North Carolina Press, 1984.

Rensberger, B. "Science on the Children's Shelves." In Hays, K., ed. *TV, Science and Kids: Teaching Out Children to Question.* Reading, MA: Addison-Wesley, 1984.

Rhoton, J., and P. Shane, eds. *Teaching Science in the 21st Century.* Arlington, VA: National Science Teachers Association Press, 2006.

Rice, F. P., and K. G. Dolgin. *The Adolescent: Development, Relationships, and Culture.* Boston and London: Allyn and Bacon, 2001.

Robinson, K. S. *The Years of Rice and Salt.* London: HarperCollins, 2002.

Rogers, R. S., and W. S. Rogers. *Stories of Childhood: Shifting Agendas of Child Concern.* New York: Harvester Wheatsheaf, 1992.

Rohmann, E. *Time Flies.* New York: Crown, 1994.

Rose, J. *Peter Pan and the Impossibility of Children's Literature.* Basingstoke: Macmillan, 1984.

Rothstein, E. "Reading Kids' Books Without the Kids." *The New York Times,* May 12, 2005.

Rottensteiner, F. "German Science Fiction for Young Adults." In Sullivan III, C. W., ed. *Young Adult Science Fiction.* Westport, CT: Greenwood Press, 1999.

Rowe, D. "Not Mad or Bad, Just Scared." *New Scientist.* London, July 16, 2007.

Rusch, K. K. "2 Barbarian Confessions." In

Brin, D. and Stover, M. W., eds. *Star Wars on Trial; Science Fiction and Fantasy Writers Debate the Most Popular Science Fiction Films of All Time*. Dallas: Benbella, 2006.

Sambell, K. "Carnivalizing the Future: A New Approach to Theorizing Childhood and Adulthood in Science Fiction for Young Adults." *The Lion and the Unicorn, 28*. 247–267, 2004.

_____. "Perspectives on the Meanings of Childhood in Near-Future Fantasies Produced for Young People." *Foundation: The International Review of Science Fiction*. 88. 33–45, 2003.

_____. "Presenting the Case for Social Change: The Creative Dilemma of Dystopian Writing for Children." In Ostry, Carrie Hintz and Elaine Ostry, eds. *Utopian and Dystopian Writing for Children and Young Adults*. New York and London: Routledge, 2003.

Sampson, F. "Childhood and Twentieth-Century Children's Literature." In Mills, J. and Mills, R., eds. *Childhood Studies: A Reader in Perspectives of Childhood*. London and New York: Routledge, 2000.

Sands, K., and M. A. Frank. *Back in the Spaceship Again: Juvenile Science Fiction Series Since 1945*. Westport, CT: Greenwood Press, 1999.

Schall, L. *Teen Genre Conections: From Booktalking to Booklearning*. Westport, CT; London: Libraries Unlimited, Greenwood Press, 2005.

Schwarcz, J. H., and C. Schwarcz. *The Picture Book Comes of Age: Looking at Childhood Through the Art of Illustration*. Chicago and London: American Library Association, 1991.

Segal, E. "'As the Twig is Bent...': Gender and Childhood Reading." In Flynn, E. A. and Schweickart, P. P., eds. *Gender and Reading: Essays on Readers, Texts, and Contexts*. London and Baltimore, 1986.

Sharpe, J. *Remember, Remember the Fifth of November*. London: Profile Books, 2005.

Shayer, M. *GCSE 1999: Added-value from Schools Adopting the CASE Intervention*. London: The Centre for the Advancement of Thinking, 1999.

Silverberg, R. "There Was an Old Woman." *Infinity*, 79. 81–93, 1958.

Simpson, A. "Fictions and Facts: An Investigation of the Reading Practices of Girls and Boys." *English Education*, 28. 268–279, 1996.

Skidmore, J. W. "The Romance of Posi and Nega." *Amazing Stories*, 7, 1932.

Sleight, G. "Visions of Delaware." Review of Jutta Weldes, ed. *To Seek Out New Worlds: Exploring Links Between Science Fiction and World Politics* (Palgrave, 2003). *Science Fiction Studies*, 32. 196–200, 2005.

Slusser, G. "The Forever Child: *Ender's Game* and the Mythic Universe of Science Fiction." In Westfahl, G. and Slusser, G., eds. *Nursery Realms: Children in the Worlds of Science Fiction. Fantasy, and Horror*. Athens: University of Georgia Press, 1999.

Spitz, E. H. *Inside Picture Books,* New Haven and London, Yale University Press, 1999.

Stanel, L. W. "The Maturation of the Junior Novel: From Gestation to the Pill." In Gerhardt, L., ed. *Issues in Children's Book Selection: A School Library Journal/Library Journal Anthology*. New York and London: R. R. Bowker, 1973.

Stephens, J. *Language and Ideology in Children's Fiction*. London: Longman, 1992.

Sterling, B. (dir.) *Lemony Snicket: A Series of Unfortunate Events*. Dreamworks and Paramount, 2005.

Stoneley, P. *Consumerism and American Girls' Literature, 1860–1940*. Cambridge: Cambridge University Press, 2003.

Styles, M. "Inside the Tunnel: A Radical Kind of Reading — Picture Books, Pupils and Postmodernism." In Watson, V. and Styles, M., eds. *Talking Pictures: Pictorial Texts and Young Readers*. London: Hodder and Stoughton, 1996.

Sullivan, C. W., III. "American Young Adult Science Fiction Since 1947." In Sullivan III, C. W., ed. *Young Adult Science Fiction*. Westport, CT: Greenwood Press, 1999.

_____. "Heinlein's Juveniles: Growing Up in Outer Space." *Science Fiction for Young Readers*. Westport, CT: Greenwood Press, 1993.

_____. "Preface." In III, C. W. S., ed. *Science Fiction for Young Readers*. Westport, CT: Greenwood Press, 1993.

_____. "Robert A. Heinlein: Reinventing Series SF in the 1950s." *Extrapolation*, 47. 66–76, 2006.

_____, ed. *Science Fiction for Young Readers*. Westport, CT: Greenwood Press, 1993.

_____, ed. *Young Adult Science Fiction*. Westport, CT: Greenwood Press, 1999.

Suvin, D. *Metamorphoses of Science Fiction: On the Poetics and History of a Literary Genre*. New Haven: Yale University Press, 1979.

Townsend, J. R. "Standards of Criticism for Children's Literature." *Signal*, 14. 93–105, 1974.

Traviss, K. "Comment to: 'Where have all the Juveniles gone? To Galaxies, far, far away.'" http://farah-sf.blogspot.com/2006/07/where-have-all-juveniles-gone-to.html# comments, July 27, 2006.

_____. "Driving GFFA 1; Or How *Star Wars* Loosened My Corsets." In Brin, D. and Stover, M. W., eds. *Star Wars On Trial; Science Fiction and Fantasy Writers Debate the Most Popular Science Fiction Films of All Time*. Dallas, Benbella, 2006.

Trease, G. *Tales Out of School: A Survey of Children's Fiction*. London: The New Education Book Club, 1948.

Trites, R. S. *Disturbing the Universe: Power and Repression in Adolescent Literature*. Iowa City: University of Iowa Press, 2002.

Turnill, R. *The Observer's Book of Unmanned Spaceflight*. London: Frederick Warne, 1974.

Vitale, Michael Ray, and Nancy R. Romance. "Research in Science Education: An Interdisciplinary Perspective." In Rhoton, J. and Shane, P., eds. *Teaching Science in the 21st Century*. Arlington, VA: National Science Teachers Association Press, 2006.

Volz, B. D., C. P. Scheer, and L. B. Welborn, eds. *Junior Genreflecting*. Englewood, CO: Libraries Unlimited, 2000.

Voort, Tom, et al. "Young People's Ownership and Uses of New and Old Forms of Media in Britain and the Netherlands." *European Journal of Communication*, 13. 457–477, 1998.

Ward, B. *Epidemics*. London: Dorling Kindersley, 2000.

Watson, G. "Young Adult Science Fiction in Canada." In Sullivan III, C. W., ed. *Young Adult Science Fiction*. Westport, CT: Greenwood Press, 1999.

Webb, J., and A. Enstice. *Aliens and Savages: Fiction, Politics and Prejudice in Australia*. Sydney: HarperCollins, 1998.

Weber, S., and S. Dixon. *Growing Up Online: Young People and Digital Technologies*. London: Palgrave Macmillan, 2007.

Wellington, J. "Practical Work in Science: Time for a Re-Appraisal." In Amos, S. and Boohan, R., eds. *Teaching Science in Secondary Schools: A Reader*. London and New York: Routledge/Falmer/Open University Press, 2002.

Westfahl, G. *Science Fiction, Children's Literature, and Popular Culture: Coming of Age in Fantasy Land*. Westport, CT: Greenwood, 2000.

White, A. *The Story of Our Rocks and Minerals*. Loughborough: Ladybird, Wills and Hepworth, 2000 (1966).

Wicks, J. "Patterns of reading among teenage boys: the reading habits and book preferences of 13–15 year old boys." *New Library World*, 96. 10–16, 1995.

Wilson-Max, K. *Big Silver Space Shuttle*. New York: Scholastic, 2000.

Wolf, M. *Proust and the Squid: The Story and Science of the Reading Brain*. New York: HarperCollins, 2007.

Wolfe, G. K. "Evaporating Genre: Srategies of Dissolutionion in the Postmodern Fantastic." In Hollinger, V. and Gordon, J., eds. *Edging into the Future: Science Fiction and Contemporary Cultural Transformation*. Philadelphia, PA: University of Philadelphia Press, 2002.

_____. *The Known and the Unknown: The Iconography of Science Fiction*. Kent, OH; Kent State University Press, 1979.

_____. "The Limits of Science Fiction." *Extrapolation*, 14. 30–38, 1972.

_____. *Soundings*, Harold Wood, Essex: Beccon Publications, 2005.

Wood, D. *How Children Think and Learn*. Oxford: Blackwell, 1998.

Wyndham, L. *Writing for Children and Teenagers*. Cincinnati, OH: Writer's Digest, 1968.

Wytenbrook, J. R. "The Debate Continues: Technology or Nature — A Study of Monica Hughes's Science Fiction Novels." In Sullivan III, C. W., ed. *Science Fiction for Young Readers*. Westport, CT: Greenwood Press, 1993.

Xanthoudaki, M., ed. *A Place to Discover: Teaching Science and Technology with Museums*. Milan: TandT Studio, 2002.

Yates, J. "Science Fiction." In Hunt, P., ed. *International Encyclopedia of Children's Literature*. London and New York: Routledge, 1996.

Index